THE COMPLETE
BOOK OF
PLEASURE
BOAT
ENGINES

ERNEST A. ZADIG

CONTRIBUTING EDITOR: *Motorboating & Sailing* MAGAZINE

CONTRIBUTOR: *Motorboat* MAGAZINE
          Boating MAGAZINE
          Rudder MAGAZINE
          Popular Science MAGAZINE
          Yachting MAGAZINE

AUTHOR: *Handbook of Modern Marine Materials*
     Inventor's Handbook
     The Complete Book of Boating (1st and 2nd Editions)

ADJUNCT PROFESSOR: Florida Institute of Technology

THE COMPLETE
BOOK OF
PLEASURE
BOAT
ENGINES

Ernest A. ZADIG

PRENTICE-HALL, INC.

Englewood Cliffs, N.J.

The Complete Book of Pleasure Boat Engines by Ernest A. Zadig
Copyright © 1980 by Ernest A. Zadig

Printed in the United States of America

Prentice-Hall International, Inc., London
Prentice-Hall of Australia, Pty. Ltd., Sydney
Prentice-Hall of Canada, Ltd., Toronto
Prentice-Hall of India Private Ltd., New Delhi
Prentice-Hall of Japan, Inc., Tokyo
Prentice-Hall of Southeast Asia Pte. Ltd., Singapore
Whitehall Books Limited, Wellington, New Zealand

10 9 8 7 6 5 4 3 2 1
Library of Congress Cataloging in Publication Data
Zadig, Ernest A
   The complete book of pleasure boat engines.
   Includes index.
   1. Motor-boat engines. I. Title.
VM771.Z32   1980   623.87'23   79-24306
ISBN 0-13-157636-4

To
AUDREY
mate, wife, and above all else sweetheart
and to
JANE

Contents

Foreword

I have written this book for the skipper to whom an engine is a complete mystery, and I have written it equally for the boat owner who is mechanically familiar with his powerplant but who would like to zero in on a complete technical understanding. Both will find every feature of boat engines explained clearly, concisely and without cabalistic jargon.

The chapter arrangement is based on my experience teaching the subject, lecturing about it, and enjoying a lifetime love affair with engines. My years of engine engineering have served me as an overall check. The sequence of the text is logical—from a general introduction to a final close inspection of every component part of the machine.

Part One is a broad view of all boat engines. The pros and cons of engines using gasoline and diesel fuels are discussed, and the two fundamental principles of operation are compared. Outboard motors are given a thorough examination with suggestions for their proper use. Engines hooked to electric generating plants are also given their share of attention.

Part Two concerns the systems that perform supporting functions for the engine during operation. The systems that supply ignition, fuel, cooling, lubrication and electrical current—all are studied in close detail. Examples are given of how engines are controlled from the skipper's station. Propellers, which form the eventual load for all marine engines, are discussed fully.

The many engine accessories found in the engine room and on the helmsman's console are the subject of Part Three. Even galvanic action and protection against it, normally arcane subjects, are unraveled in this part.

The care and feeding that produce happy engines are the subject of Part Four. The engine sounds and sights that can warn the skipper of imminent trouble are examined so he may be forewarned and take preventive action.

Part Five dissects the engine down to its basic parts. How each does its bit to keep the machine running is studied in detail. Pointers are given for keeping everything in good order.

Finally, Part Six devotes itself to engine husbandry. Putting the powerplant in mothballs for the winter and revitalizing it in the spring are explained from a commonsense viewpoint. Some of the related devices that share the engine room also are discussed.

The arrangement of the book permits it to be read in sequence if one is so inclined—and I hope such reading will give pleasure in addition to knowledge. If, however, your engine has just talked back to you or behaved badly, you can go directly to the section that will arm you with the facts for successful combat. Voluminous illustrations let the eye aid the mind.

As I said, I have had a lifelong love affair with engines. Perhaps this book will start you on your own love affair with your boat's powerplant.

Ernest A. Zadig

Florida Institute of Technology
Melbourne, Florida

PART ONE
ENGINES

1. Boat Engines in General

At the turn of the century, yachts in the 100-foot class were achieving their full theoretical hull speed with engines of less than 100 horsepower. Today, a fast runabout only 18 feet long frequently has more horses than that hung on its transom. This lavish use of force has been fostered by the ready availability of compact marine engines of very high power.

The zooming development of marine engines into the marvelous machines of today can be explained by their heritage. They are offshoots of the automobile. As automotive power increased in might, so did they. Now more than 200 horsepower can be had within the confines of an outboard motor!

Engines went to sea because the wind, which had been the universal motive power for ships, was not dependable and was beyond man's control, even though he could outfox nature to some extent by clever manipulation of his sails. So wind in turn was displaced as a prime mover, just as it earlier had evicted human muscle.

Large pleasure vessels of that era were propelled by steam engines. Steam had moved in as the wind was being phased out. In the beginning the two often worked together. Luxury yachts had sails above and boilers below to make the best of both worlds during the transition.

Steam also propelled small tenders and launches which serviced the yachts, but even scaled-down versions

Figure 1-1. The yachts of early century days did not entirely trust their new motive power and were also rigged for sail "just in case." (Motorboating & Sailing magazine)

of boiler and firebox and engine usurped too much interior space. Changing from coal bunkers to compact tanks of liquid naphtha for fuel eliminated some of the mess but did little else to help. Grotesque funnels to provide firebox draft became the hallmark of these little vessels that were known as "naphtha launches." (See Figure 1-1.)

Strangely, human muscle was the first "engine" to be hooked up to the propeller of a small pleasure boat—and this happened no further back than 1866. A human "engine" pushed a treadmill, which in turn rotated a screw surprisingly like the propellers of today. The cruising radius of this embryonic "motorboat" depended directly upon the stamina of its sweating captain. (See Figure 1-2.)

FOOT POWERED
PROPELLER

Figure 1-2. One of the earliest "power" boats made use of the skipper for its "power." Ironically, small, foot-power boats are becoming popular on quiet inland lakes.

Although we have yet only begun to explore the possibilities of electric propulsion for small boats, the first bona fide power installed in a small craft was electric. The rudimentary electric motor received its power from a boatload of wet-cell batteries. It worked, but it was not practical because the limited source of current allowed only short periods of operation. These were primary batteries which wasted away with use and could not be recharged as modern secondary storage batteries can.

A striking feature of this early drive machine was its resemblance in concept to the outboards of today. The motor was positioned like our present power units. The drive shaft was vertical, and right-angle gearing transmitted power to the propeller, just as this is done routinely now. It took only a small step forward to hang this contraption on the transom with swivels so that it could be swung from side to side to steer the boat in place of the usual rudder. (See Figure 1-3.)

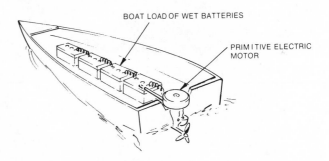

BOAT LOAD OF WET BATTERIES

PRIMITIVE ELECTRIC
MOTOR

Figure 1-3. The many wet batteries required to operate the first primitive electric outboard motor just about filled the boat and left little space for passengers.

The simplicity of the system attracted followers, and a more sophisticated electric fishing motor appeared in 1895. Despite its technical improvements, its drawback was the limited power available from a battery—the same drawback that still blocks the progress of electric propulsion for small pleasure boats. A battery that packs an amount of power competitive with a tank of fuel has not been developed, and this is why electric boats and electric automobiles are always in the future.

Meanwhile the internal combustion engine has been moving up. In 1896 it became an honest-to-goodness outboard, easily recognizable as the granddaddy of the millions we see buzzing around on our waters. Its cruising radius now attracted serious attention because of the many potential miles that could be stored in a compact fuel tank.

The idea of hanging a boat's motive power on its transom proved so eminently practical that several entrepreneurs jumped into the business of building outboard

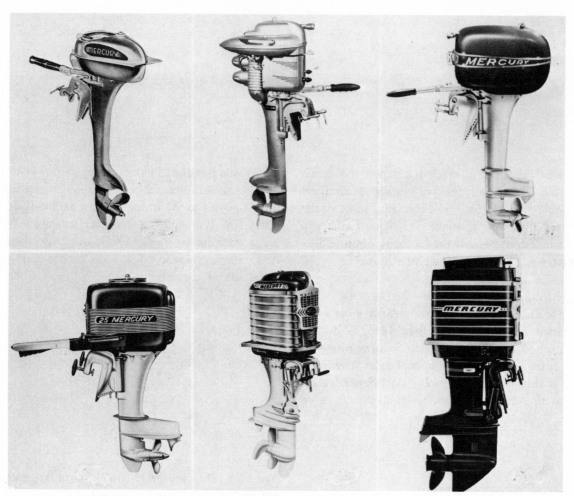

Figure 1-4. The development over the years of a popular outboard motor from a six-horsepower baby to the present giants is shown in these progressive photographs. (Mercury Marine)

motors. By 1908 thousands of units had been produced. But the mortality rate for the outboard builders was high in those early days of the marine business, and of the original group only Evinrude remains. Figure 1-4 depicts the early machines.

Some fuel tanks of this early period contained not petroleum but gas! This gas was produced on board in small ovens that burned and roasted coke in a manner currently employed by plants manufacturing illuminating gas. Eventually petroleum derivatives proved a cleaner, safer and simpler fuel and soon crowded out both oven and coke.

Throughout this period Dr. Rudolf Diesel was successfully developing his variation of the internal combustion engine. Instead of igniting the fuel with a spark, the common practice, he compressed air until it became hot enough to cause ignition without added help. By 1902 one of his engines was propelling a boat around Paris. Diesel's idea of compression ignition had eliminated the

troublesome electrical components required by competitive spark ignition engines.

Now the race was on between spark ignition and compression ignition, a race that has not been decided to this day. The choice is still open because of the many pros and cons. Spark ignition allows greater flexibility in speed and power, but the fuel must be highly volatile and therefore is dangerously flammable. Compression ignition tolerates fuel of considerably less flammability, but the engines must be built more sturdily and cost more. Dr. Diesel's original engine is shown in Figure 1-5.

If the terms "internal combustion" and "external combustion" need more clarification, consider that these designations mean exactly what they say. The internal combustion engine burns all its fuel inside the cylinder. The automobile is powered by an internal combustion engine. The external combustion engine burns its fuel outside the actual machine, as, for instance, under the boiler of a steam engine.

Figure 1-5. Diesel's first success was this one-cylinder oil-fueled engine, which in 1897 achieved a compression of about 30 atmospheres and had a thermal efficiency of 26 percent.

(A)

(C)

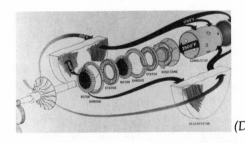

(D)

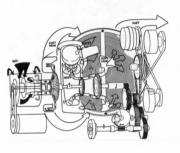

(B)

Figure 1-6. The gas turbine engine comprises only rotating components and hence does not exhibit the vibration indigenous to a reciprocating piston engine. Shown at (A) is an automotive gas turbine that has not yet been adapted to marine use but may one day find itself on the water; at (B) is a schematic of its operation (Chrysler Corp.); at (C) is another design of a gas turbine (General Motors Corp.); (D) explains the operation of a radically different design of gas turbine (Ford Motor Co.).

For the present, internal combustion is the sole preference in the world of pleasure boats. External combustion in the form of steam power was once king but was toppled. Nevertheless, steam still lurks in the background waiting for an opportunity to stage a comeback. Technological improvements could provide that opportunity; steam powerboats and steam motorcars may yet be in your future.

The advent of internal combustion engines on small powerboats brought bonuses. One was more space for passengers because this new power was far more compact than the steam plant. Another was greater safety resulting from the elimination of the open flames under a firebox. Operation also was simpler and did not require the trained supervision demanded by high-pressure steam.

The take-over by the internal combustion engine had one drawback which is still with us today—its exhaust pollutes the atmosphere. Whereas the exhaust of the steam engine is merely water, the internal combustor spews carbon monoxide and various nitrous oxides into the air in addition to an objectionable odor. The continuous flame in the firebox has a much milder polluting effect and is easier to clean up than the noxious waste from a series of explosions.

Gasoline and diesel engines have been emphasized because they are predominant, but other forms of power could be installed in small pleasure boats. The gas turbine is one. There have been tentative installations, and from time to time various manufacturers have announced available units, but the gas turbine is not yet a factor in pleasure boating. A gas turbine is shown in Figure 1-6.

The gas turbine could score because of its simplicity. Essentially, a flame causes pressurized gas and air to impinge on the buckets of a wheel, turning it much as you would a child's pinwheel by blowing on its cavities. But the turbine is practical only if it turns at very high speed, and this introduces problems in gearing down to a low-speed propeller. The turbine has no reciprocating motion, everything is rotational, and this permits a significant reduction in vibration and noise level.

Another possible source of power for motorboats is

almost unknown, even though it was invented nearly a century ago and holds great engineering promise. This is the Stirling engine, which uses air alternately heated and cooled as its power medium. The underlying principle is that hot air expands and cold air contracts. A piston is moved up and down by this expansion-contraction cycle to turn a crank.

Despite its unusual operating mode, the Stirling is a high-efficiency low-noise machine. Since it has a constantly burning flame (external combustion) instead of a series of explosions, its polluting effect is lower and its exhaust easier to cleanse. The original Stirlings were ultra-slow speed and very bulky. Recent experimental modernized designs have achieved speeds and bulks comparable with present commercial powerplants. Helium and hydrogen have been substituted for the original air, and this change shows promise. Add to this the absence of electrical ignition components, as in the diesel, and the Stirling may have a lot going for it. Incidentally, Stirling is not the name of a manufacturer but of the inventor.

Basically, all engines are devices for changing one form of energy into another form. Some do this directly, others through a series of steps. The gasoline engine unlocks the energy in gasoline and quickly transforms it into rotational power. The steam engine starts with coal and takes this energy through successive steps as heat and steam before it, too, becomes a source of rotational power. Since each transformation entails some loss, a worldwide search is on for more efficient methods. The fuel cell may be one answer.

The fuel cell changes the energy stored in any suitable fuel into electric energy in one self-contained reaction. This means that a tank of gasoline would run an electric motor without the presently intervening engine and generator. Since well-built electric motors are the most efficient energy converters, such a power source in a pleasure boat would yield fantastic advantages. The only cloud in this rosy sky is the immature development of the fuel cell itself.

Present fuel cells are laboratory creations, a far cry

from practical machines with which the boatowner would feel comfortable. Their power output is below the magnitude commonly accepted for small-craft propulsion. They employ exotic and hazardous materials and require close scientific control. Despite these difficulties, much research work is being done, and some inventor or laboratory could provide the breakthrough at any time. A fuel cell is shown in Figure 1-7.

(A)

(B)

CUTAWAY VIEW OF GENERAL MOTORS ELECTROVAN

Figure 1-7. The fuel cell transforms primary sources of energy, such as oxygen, hydrogen and hydrocarbons, into electrical energy chemically without the intervention of machinery. At (A) is an experimental fuel cell installation to power a van and at (B) a diagrammatic layout of the components explains the action. Design target is 125 horsepower. (General Motors Corp.)

All this discussion of power quite naturally brings up the questions of how a small pleasure boat uses all this energy and why it needs so much. The broad answer, of course, is to move from place to place. The details of that answer are interesting to examine.

Water is a dense medium, and any object moving through it encounters resistance in several forms, each of which requires energy to overcome. The amount of energy that needs to be expended varies with the size, shape, type and speed of the boat.

Wave making is the major form of resistance and gulps the greatest proportion of energy. The bow of a forward-moving boat pushes the water to both sides and produces the so-called bow wave. The size of this bow wave bears a direct mathematical relation to the speed of the boat. Its length from crest to crest is short at low speeds and increases as the boat goes faster until it becomes as long as the hull causing it. When this happens, the theoretical top speed for that vessel has been reached. This is true for all displacement hulls but does not hold true for planing hulls. (See Figure 1-8.)

The reason for this apparent discrepancy is that planing hulls raise themselves partially out of the water as speed is increased and thereby reduce their immersion and their resistance to forward motion. Displacement hulls, by contrast, maintain the same immersion whether stationary or moving. The shape of the hull, especially the underside, makes the difference between planing boats and displacement boats. Planing hulls also require greatly increased engine power. The photo in Figure 1-9 shows how a boat lifts itself out of the water when in the planing mode.

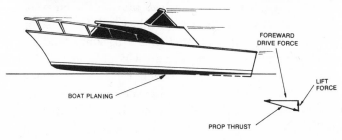

Figure 1-9. (A) shows a speeding cruiser up on plane. Note that only the after portion of the hull is now in the water (Stamas Boats). At (B) a boat in planing attitude has raised a portion of its hull out of the water and no longer displaces sufficient volume for complete buoyancy. The missing "lift" is restored as a result of propeller thrust, as shown by the force diagram.

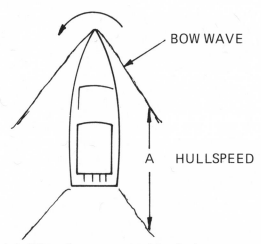

Figure 1-8. When the wave created by the bow crests at the stern, then that displacement vessel has reached its theoretical hull speed. Additional power applied in an attempt to gain speed will only cause the stern to squat. This does not apply to planing hulls.

The bow wave effectively locks the displacement boat into its usable top speed. Any attempt to go faster requires a great deal of additional power with very little result. Trying to solve this situation with more horsepower causes the transcom to squat, the bow to rise, and the fuel to flow as though it were free. Only with planing hulls will piling on extra power achieve more speed.

After wave making consumes its huge bite of the power supplied by the engine, skin resistance eats into some of what remains. The frictional effect of the outside of the hull (the skin) constantly drags a quantity of water along. Obviously a smooth skin will exert less friction than a rough one and therefore will pull less water and rob less power. It is not uncommon to find the hulls of racing boats waxed and polished until they glisten. But no matter what is done, skin resistance cannot be eliminated totally.

The portion of engine power left after these gluttons get through is diminished by various mechanical frictions and by the inefficiency of the propeller. An inboard engine can turn its propeller only through the medium of shaft, stuffing box and strut bearings, each of which contributes to a loss of power. Outboard motors are connected closer to their props and consequently are less affected by these ancillary losses.

The stuffing box must allow the shaft to turn and yet must encircle it tightly enough to prevent the entry of water. This creates friction despite the graphite, grease or other lubricants incorporated in the packing. Modern strut bearings are of rubber and are self-lubricated by the water; nevertheless, some friction remains. All these frictions turn their respective shares of the total energy into useless heat. Eventually, only a few cents of the fuel dollar arrive at the propeller to push the boat.

When the discussion of engines gets down to specifics, certain technical descriptions are used commercially and the knowledgeable boatman should understand them. Horsepower, to the initiated, is not merely horsepower but is split up into brake horsepower, indicated horsepower, shaft horsepower, propeller horsepower and effective horsepower. This breakdown permits the designer to check his selection of a particular engine by tracing the flow of power and deciding on its adequacy.

The engine itself is rated in *brake horsepower*. The original instrument for measurement was the prony brake, hence the origin of the term. The prony brake is a simple frictional device that measures the rotational effect (the torque) of the engine in pounds-feet, which, by the addition of speed into a formula, translates into horsepower. The prony brake has been superseded by more sophisticated forms of dynamometers, but the name remains. (See Figure 1-10.)

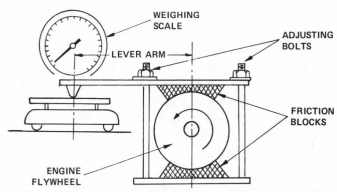

Figure 1-10. The earliest dynamometer was the Prony brake whose principle of operation is shown here. The lever arm, measured in feet, multiplied by the scale reading, in pounds, gives the torque in pound-feet.

The pound-foot is a common unit in engineering but must not be confused with foot-pound. If you took a wheel with a radius of 1 foot and hung a weight of 1 pound on its rim, the shaft would exhibit a torque of 1 pound-foot whether or not it were allowed to turn. In other words, multiplying the radius of effort with the actuating weight gives the answer. (See Figure 1-11.)

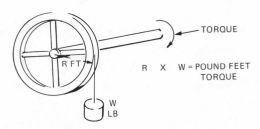

Figure 1-11. The force in pounds, multiplied by the radius in feet at which it is applied, gives the torque in pound-feet.

The foot-pound also is an engineering unit in wide use. If a weight of 1 pound is lifted 1 foot, 1 foot-pound of energy will have been expended; when the time taken to do this is introduced into the equation, the answer becomes power. One horsepower is equivalent to 33,000 foot-pounds per minute. As seen in Figure 1-12, 1 horse-

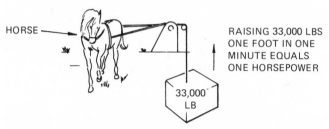

HORSE ⟶

RAISING 33,000 LBS
ONE FOOT IN ONE
MINUTE EQUALS
ONE HORSEPOWER

33,000 LB

Figure 1-12. Work is defined as force times distance. In the illustration, lifting 33,000 pounds one foot in one minute is equivalent to one horsepower. Lifting 3,300 pounds ten feet in one minute also would equal one horsepower, as would any other multiple of 33,000.

power has resulted when the weight of 33,000 pounds is lifted 1 foot in 1 minute. Of course, 330 pounds could be lifted 100 feet in 1 minute, and the result would still be 1 horsepower because the product remains 33,000. It is said that James Watt, an early developer of steam engines, actually measured the ability of horses in order to arrive at this figure.

The power of an engine can also be determined by calculation without an actual run on a prony brake or a dynamometer; the figure obtained in this manner is *indicated horsepower.* A pressure-sensitive instrument (an indicator) measures the pressures within the cylinder at every instance of a revolution while the engine is running. The average of these pressures is combined in a formula with piston area, length of stroke, and number of cylinders to obtain indicated horsepower.

In a way, indicated horsepower is a theoretical consideration. It represents the total force exerted by the burning fuel, a total that can never appear at the output of the engine because of mechanical and thermal losses. Only brake horsepower can be abstracted.

Nor can the brake horsepower listed in the catalog for an engine appear at the propeller because of the many interim losses already mentioned. Furthermore, tradi-

tionally the brake horsepower is measured under the most favorable circumstances, and the manufacturer's optimism is sometimes included. Usually, the measured engine is bare of the auxiliary pumps, generators, and other service equipment, all of which drain power. Hence, when this engine finally goes to work on a boat, it does not supply the full number of horses supposedly in the corral.

Shaft horsepower, as the name implies, is the power actually transmitted by the shaft. Equally logically, *propeller horsepower* is the power truly put into the prop. And *effective horsepower* is the real goodie at the end of the line that reacts with the water to push the boat. The run from indicated horsepower to effective horsepower is always in a descending scale because of the losses enumerated. (See Figure 1-13.)

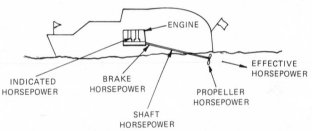

ENGINE

EFFECTIVE
HORSEPOWER

INDICATED
HORSEPOWER

BRAKE
HORSEPOWER

PROPELLER
HORSEPOWER

SHAFT
HORSEPOWER

Figure 1-13. The designation "horsepower" of an engine can mean many things as illustrated here. To be meaningful, the term horsepower must be precisely defined.

Compression ratio is still another of the descriptive terms usually found in the catalogs issued by engine manufacturers. It is expressed as a ratio such as 8 to 1 or 16 to 1, the former being about average for gasoline engines and the latter for diesels. This is a measure of how much the fuel charge in the cylinder is compressed before it is ignited. It is important because, generally speaking, the more a fuel charge can be compressed, the greater the power that can be derived from it—within limits, of course. Calculation of this parameter is easy: The volume of the cylinder with the piston at its lowest point is divided by the volume with the piston at its highest. (See Figure 1-14.)

"Bore," "stroke" and "displacement" are additional terms that a boatman should understand clearly. *Bore* is the diameter of the cylinder in which the piston moves,

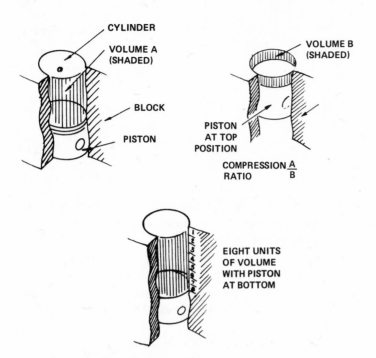

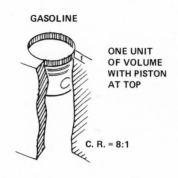

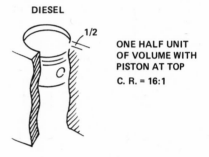

CYLINDER
VOLUME A (SHADED)
BLOCK
PISTON

VOLUME B (SHADED)
PISTON AT TOP POSITION
COMPRESSION RATIO $\frac{A}{B}$

GASOLINE
ONE UNIT OF VOLUME WITH PISTON AT TOP
C. R. = 8:1

EIGHT UNITS OF VOLUME WITH PISTON AT BOTTOM

DIESEL
ONE HALF UNIT OF VOLUME WITH PISTON AT TOP
C. R. = 16:1

Figure 1-14. The compression ratio of a cylinder is found by dividing volume A with piston at bottom, by volume B, with piston at top. Assume a gasoline engine and a diesel engine, both with volume A equal to 8 units. If volume B of the gas engine were one unit, its compression ratio would be 8 to 1. The diesel engine with volume B equal to ½ unit would have a compression ration of 16 to 1.

and the distance the piston travels from uppermost to lowest positions is the *stroke*. The volume of the cylinder between these two positions is the *displacement* of the cylinder. Multiplying this by the number of cylinders gives the displacement of the engine, stated either in cubic inches or in liters. (See Figure 1-15.)

Engineers study an engine's internal behavior with a form of pictorial shorthand called an engine diagram. An instrument attached to the running engine draws a closed graph that portrays the instantaneous relationships be-

tween piston position and pressure within the cylinder for a complete cycle. Each kind of engine creates its own distinctive shape diagram, which represents its cycle and is named for it. Thus we have the Otto cycle for the gasoline engine, the Diesel cycle for the diesel, the Rankine cycle for the steam engine and the Brayton cycle for the gas turbine. Often these diagrams are found in the more complete engine catalogs, and a sample is shown in Figure 1-16.

How does a designer determine the horsepower a

Figure 1-15. These illustrations graphically explain the meanings of the terms "bore," "stroke" and "displacement." The total displacement of an engine is the displacement of one cylinder multiplied by the number of cylinders.

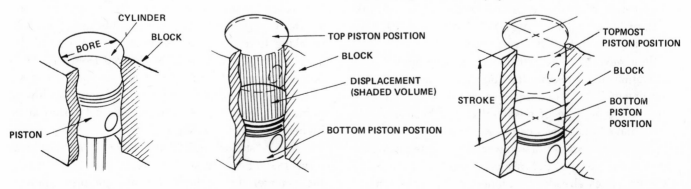

CYLINDER
BORE
BLOCK
PISTON

TOP PISTON POSITION
BLOCK
DISPLACEMENT (SHADED VOLUME)
BOTTOM PISTON POSTION

TOPMOST PISTON POSITION
BLOCK
STROKE
BOTTOM PISTON POSITION

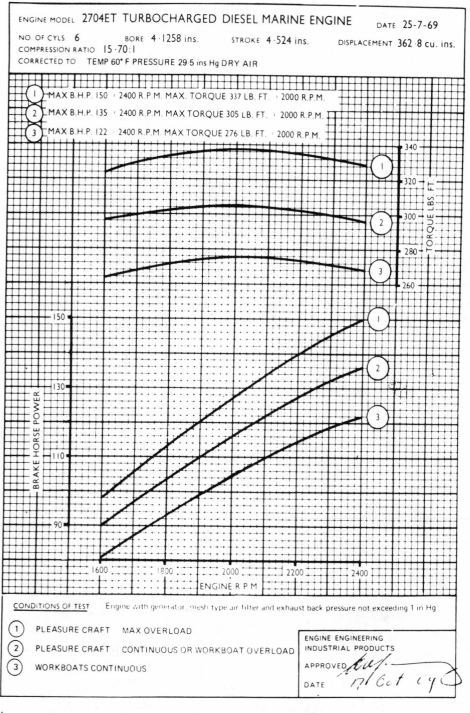

ENGINE MODEL **2704ET TURBOCHARGED DIESEL MARINE ENGINE**   DATE 25-7-69

NO. OF CYLS. **6**   BORE **4·1258 ins.**   STROKE **4·524 ins.**   DISPLACEMENT **362·8 cu. ins.**
COMPRESSION RATIO **15·70:1**
CORRECTED TO   TEMP 60° F PRESSURE 29·5 ins Hg DRY AIR

① MAX B.H.P. 150 / 2400 R.P.M. MAX. TORQUE 337 LB. FT. / 2000 R.P.M.
② MAX B.H.P. 135 / 2400 R.P.M. MAX TORQUE 305 LB. FT. / 2000 R.P.M.
③ MAX B.H.P. 122 / 2400 R.P.M. MAX TORQUE 276 LB. FT. / 2000 R.P.M.

TORQUE LBS. FT.

BRAKE HORSE POWER

ENGINE R P M

CONDITIONS OF TEST   Engine with generator, mesh type air filter and exhaust back pressure not exceeding 1 in Hg

① PLEASURE CRAFT   MAX OVERLOAD
② PLEASURE CRAFT   CONTINUOUS OR WORKBOAT OVERLOAD
③ WORKBOATS CONTINUOUS

ENGINE ENGINEERING
INDUSTRIAL PRODUCTS

APPROVED

DATE

(A)

(B)

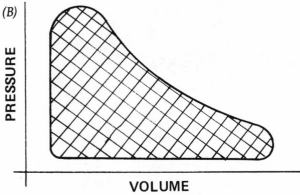

PRESSURE

VOLUME

Figure 1-16. (A) The parameters of an engine that are measured during a dynamometer test are graphed as shown. These curves give considerable information to a technician. (B) The pressure-volume relationships of a working engine are graphed into what is known as a "pv diagram." The shaded area represents the capability of the machine.

contemplated boat will require in order to perform as expected? One method is to make a carefully scaled model of the proposed vessel, place it in a testing tank and tow it at a simulated speed. The power absorbed to accomplish this is measured accurately by the tank instrumentation; this is the effective power. Calculating backward from this figure by inserting and adding the various known losses brings him to the required brake horsepower. From this point on, it becomes a matter of looking through the engine catalogs and selecting an appropriate unit. (See Figure 1-17.)

This is the academic procedure, but it is rarely followed except in totally new concepts of boat design or in high-priced custom vessels. In everyday practice the designer will rely on his own experience and on the empirical knowledge widely available in the technical literature. Nor is it too unusual for engines to be changed after shakedown runs prove disappointing.

Today's boatman has become so blasé by the everyday, routine use of his automobile that he often fails to appreciate the excellence of his modern boat engine. The car engine has a far easier life. It spends a great deal of its working time just loafing along, coasting downhill or just idling at a traffic light. No such ease for the boat engine!

From the moment the clutch is set in forward, it continually climbs a figurative hill. There is no coasting, and full power for each throttle setting must be delivered smoothly and without fail.

As stated earlier, the marine engine is an offshoot of the automotive engine, and it has become heir to all the improvements time and research have achieved. Exotic alloys have reduced weight while still increasing strength. Thermostatic controls maintain the best operating temperature. Seawater and its corroding effects are isolated from the internals of the engine in many installations to assure longer life. Profiles have been lowered to reduce objectionable covers that lessened passenger space.

Mathematical and empirical calculations are only one part of the procedure for selecting the most suitable engine for a particular boat. An assessment of the owner's intended use is the other part. Is he the cruising type who will make long, steady runs? Or the zip-zip Sunday morning skipper who makes a quick run out and soon returns to the pier for a lazy day? Perhaps he is a skiing buff who wants the spray to fly at full bore. Each of these types of service has a bearing on some facet of engine performance. Often the total decision must be a compromise.

Today's skipper turns the ignition key and is off on a

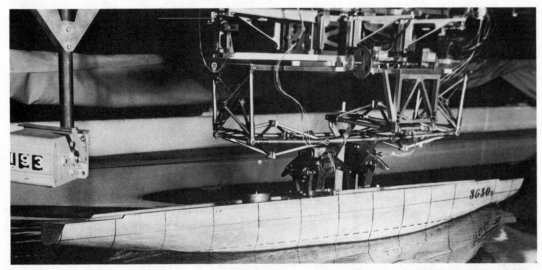

Figure 1-17. The power required to drive a hull at a desired speed can be determined accurately in a test tank such as the one shown. A scale model is attached to a trolley whose sensors record the various forces involved. The values of these forces then become the factors in a mathematical calculation. (Stevens Institute of Technology)

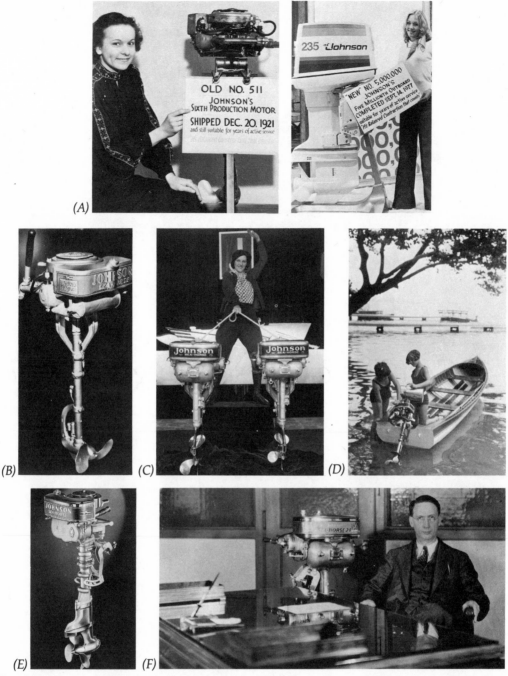

Figure 1-18. How has pleasure boating grown? One maker alone has produced 5,000,000 outboards in little more than 50 years! The photos above show the technical evolution of the outboard motor. At (A) is the comparison of old and new. Photos (B) to (F) depict the various stages. (Johnson Motors)

cruise with no more thought about the reliability of his engine than he gives to the honesty of the teller at his bank. He expects the engine to keep going, just as he expects the teller to keep his accounts inviolate. But back in 1902 it required a great deal of faith to put that much reliance on your motive power. Yet one skipper did.

In 1902 Abiel Abbot Low skippered a 38-foot motorboat across the Atlantic Ocean in thirty-eight days. His power plant was an internal combustion engine burning kerosene. He made it without incident, but nowhere in the record does it reveal how he managed to carry enough fuel.

The outboard scene, a microcosm of the boating world, vividly illustrates the great technical progress made in the comparatively few years since pleasure boating became a way of life. Photos (A) in Figure 1-18 show, in one leap, what has happened in little more than half a century. Photos (B) to (F) fill in the gap with details.

2. Gasoline or Diesel, Single or Twin?

Gasoline or diesel? That choice is open to purchasers of new boats and also to skippers who intend to repower their present craft. The correct decision can affect every facet of boat operation from pleasure to performance to economics. Like marriage, the right combination leads to happiness, the wrong one to thoughts of divorce.

In comparing diesel engines and gasoline engines, there is no implication that either is inferior. Both classes of powerplants have reached a high degree of perfection and reliability; both can provide excellent propulsion when installed in the right boat for the right type of use. That word "right" is the heart of the question and also the heart of the answer.

A broad distinction between the two kinds of power can be a helpful factor when making the choice. Gasoline engines are generally thought of as high-speed, easily controllable over wide ranges, comparatively light in weight, and moderate in cost. Diesel engines, by contrast, are considered to be more sluggish, heavier in weight, and more expensive. Moreover, diesels are available in higher powers than gasoline. These are very broad classifications, and an absolute demarcation between the two cannot be drawn; some very spry, lighter-weight diesels are on the market and could change places with some gasoline engines.

Many specifications cover the same features in both gasoline and diesel engines, as for instance, the number of cylinders and their cubic-inch displacement, whether these cylinders are inline, canted or vee, and whether the fuel is naturally aspirated or forced into the cylinders under pressure. Direction of rotation, whether clockwise or counterclockwise and the rated speed are other common specifications. Perhaps the most basic is the statement that the engine is either two cycle or four cycle. All of these terms will be discussed fully in later chapters.

Figure 2-1. This scaled drawing of a husky, turbocharged pleasure boat diesel engine gives dimensions of the space in the hull required for its installation. (Cummins Engine Co.)

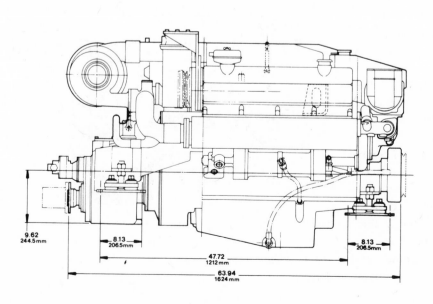
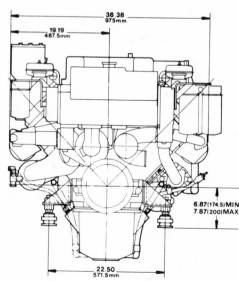

Safety is usually first on the list of advantages cited by diesel advocates. This is a valid claim; gasoline is exceedingly more volatile and hence more flammable than diesel fuel. Gasoline vapors are heavier than air and settle in the bilges and other low enclosed spaces and easily reach explosive concentrations. Diesel fuel spilled into the bilge certainly makes a mess but hardly an explosion hazard.

In days gone by, the diesel user had another potent advantage: price! Diesel fuel cost less than half the price of gasoline. Alas, the changing times have wiped out this boon; only a few cents now separate the prices of the two fuels at most marinas. Yet diesel retains a built-in bonus which the marketplace cannot eliminate, and that is its superior miles-per-gallon performance.

The better miles-per-gallon ability of the diesel is not merely a kindness to the pocketbook. It means greater cruising range than gasoline for a given size of tank or weight of fuel. This could be a deciding factor, for example, for an offshore fisherman because it could assure a run to a distant fishing ground and a safe return.

The great inherent advantage of the diesel engine is its independence from all electrical ignition equipment. (As mentioned earlier, the diesel ignites its fuel by compressing air to a searing temperature.) Most service interruptions of gasoline engines are traceable to the ignition system. The high voltages required at the spark plugs are acutely vulnerable to the damp marine environment because the current can leak away before it jumps the internal gap to make a spark. The dampness and its tendency to corrode also raise havoc with the breaker points that control the spark. These are obvious weak points in the gasoline engine scheme and the diesel profits by their absence.

But the higher compression ratio of the diesel engine makes it harder to turn over, and thus more electric power is required for cranking. This means larger and heavier storage batteries with greater maximum current-supplying ability—and in turn more generator or alternator output to keep these batteries charged. Naturally, the expenditure for batteries is greater at the outset and greater at renewal time.

The diesel can also be instrumental in saving money. The economy arises in boat insurance. Many insurance companies allow a premium discount for diesel-powered craft because of the lessened fire risk.

Despite all the foregoing advantages of its competitor, the gasoline engine still powers the vast majority of pleasure boats. One statistical reason for this is that vessels too small for currently available diesels constitute all but a small percentage of the pleasure fleet. Most of this power consists of outboard motors, a field in which the diesel has hardly made an impact.

Figure 2-2. This high-speed, turbocharged diesel engine develops 125 horsepower at 3,600 revolutions per minute and weighs approximately 1,000 pounds. (Volvo Penta)

Figure 2-3. This twelve cylinder, vee, turbocharged diesel is the ultimate in pleasure boat power. Note the oil and fuel filters and the large heat exchanger for fresh water cooling. (Detroit Diesel)

Figure 2-4. *This twin engine installation under the salon deck leaves space in the center for a generating plant.* (Detroit Diesel)

Figure 2-5. *Some of the many components that function inside a vee type diesel engine are shown in this cutaway photo.* (Detroit Diesel)

The gasoline engine is more complex than the diesel, and yet in the mind of the average boatman it is simpler. The explanation of this anomaly lies in the automobile. The universal use of the motorcar has made everyone familiar to some extent with the engine under the hood—and thus, by similarity, with the gasoline boat engine. Even professional gasoline engine mechanics are often loath to delve into a diesel.

A generation ago, the gasoline engine was frequently chosen because a comparable diesel was too heavy for the boat. In those days 80 pounds per horsepower was an accepted figure for replicas of Dr. Diesel's creation. Weight has been reduced consistently since then until today a figure of 6 pounds per horsepower is achieved by many diesel engines.

The odor and composition of the exhaust is another point of contention in the tug-of-war between gasoline and diesel. The nose knows when a diesel-powered boat goes by, and this has kept some boatmen alienated. As if to atone for its proclivity to smell, diesel exhaust is almost devoid of carbon monoxide, the deadly agent in gasoline engine exhaust. Why this is so is explained in later chapters. Another indictment is that a hardworking diesel has a tendency to smoke, whereas a gasoline engine will commit this crime only under the stress of mechanical defect.

The carburetor is another often troublesome fixture of the gasoline engine that the diesel has eliminated. However, this cannot be counted an unmitigated blessing. The injector system, which is the diesel's counterpart, is highly precise, vulnerable to foreign matter in the fuel and requires exact adjustment by highly trained personnel. The boatman seldom wins when he tangles with his injector.

Both gasoline and diesel engines can be operated as naturally aspirated, supercharged or turbocharged. These terms refer to the manner in which the fuel charge is placed into the cylinder. The *naturally aspirated* engine draws or sucks its charge by creating a partial vacuum in the cylinder. This is the simplest method but not the most efficient, because the cylinder could hold more explosive charge if it were forced in rather than merely sucked in.

Supercharging and turbocharging both accomplish this forced feeding by packing the fuel charge into the cylinder under pressure. In essence, both systems are similar in their final result of compressing the initial cylinder charge and thereby increasing the engine's power output. The difference lies in the manner of driving the turbine or fan that does the compressing.

The *supercharger* is driven by a belt or by gearing from an engine shaft. The required driving force can reach several horsepower, and this is subtracted from the engine output, although this output, to be sure, is greater than it would be without supercharging. This power loss is the drawback in supercharging and also the reason why turbocharging is the general rule.

The *turbocharger* is driven by the engine exhaust, which is normally wasted. A turbine wheel placed in the exhaust stream is turned at extremely high speed by the gases rushing by. This would seem to be getting something for nothing, but nature never permits that; there is a small penalty on engine power for obstructing the free passage of the exhaust to the atmosphere. This penalty is much less than that imposed by the direct drive of the supercharger, hence the greater efficiency and popularity of the turbocharger.

Many high-horsepower engines are turbocharged as standard equipment, and their output is rated with that device in operation. Often, supercharging or turbocharging is optional on smaller engines. Kits are on the market that bring this method of beefing up engine power into the realm of the do-it-yourselfer.

It is said that the automobile engine is often denied its fair share of attention because it is under a hood, out of sight and out of mind. The marine engine is generally hidden away even more effectively, except in the smallest boats, and so the tendency to neglect is greater. Access is gained only by lifting hatches, and this can seldom be accomplished without removing carpets, furniture and other impediments. The human reaction in such a situation is to avoid it, and detrimental effects are more likely to fester without the boatman's knowledge.

A tiny leak can go unnoticed until the drops become a puddle. A corroding wire connection is less and less

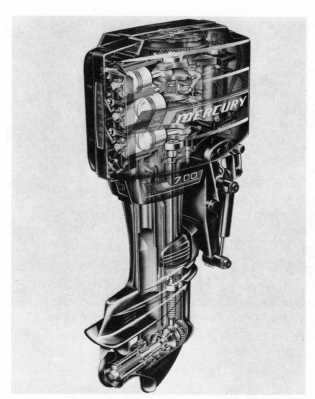

Figure 2-6. How a modern outboard motor looks inside is shown in this X-ray view. (Mercury Marine)

Figure 2-7. This high-speed, V-8 gasoline engine has a full throttle operating range of 3,800 to 4,200 revolutions per minute. Its four barrel carburetor makes it highly responsive. (Mercury Marine)

effective until it falls off and finally breaks the circuit. A hose that shows its age continues on to a cataclysmic demise. Perhaps the most detrimental effect would be the hidden spread of a fire hazard. All these happenings can be the lot of the engine so placed that it is unavailable for easy inspection.

Safety is not the only factor to be considered in these compartmented engine installations. Free access to the atmosphere is a feature of paramount importance because a running engine "breathes" huge quantities of air. The major constituent of the fuel charge from which the engine derives its power is air. Any restriction on in-coming air is paid for by a decrease in power and an increase in fuel consumption.

The diesel engine is rather tolerant in its fuel tastes, but the gasoline engine is finicky. The grade of gasoline on which it will perform properly is fixed by certain characteristics of its design, and only a small leeway is obtained by subsequent adjustment. The engine shows its displeasure with incorrect fuel by knocking, thereby announcing that the gasoline's octane number is too low. Names such as "regular," "high test," "special" and "super" are the trade's manner of listing octane numbers in an ascending order.

Figure 2-8. This single outboard motor easily keeps this boat on plane. (Evinrude)

By contrast, the diesel seems able to run on almost anything, although manufacturers issue certain specifications for its fuel. Chief among these are cetane number (comparable to gasoline's octane number), sulfur content and residual ash. Various additives touted by the petroleum industry are more or less effective in their ability to keep an engine's disposition sweet. Strange as it may seem, a bacteriacide is often added to prevent bacterial growth in diesel fuel tanks!

In the early days, boatmen found diesel fuel sparsely available; today the marina without diesel is a rarity. Gasoline in the various grades is found at every fuel dock. So the choice between gasoline and diesel propulsion is never dependent upon the availability of either fuel.

The familiar fan and radiator of the automobile are absent from marine engines. Whereas the car motor transfers its excess heat to the ambient atmosphere, the marine powerplant uses the surrounding water as its heat sink. This it does directly or indirectly, as later chapters will explain. Water has a much greater ability than air to absorb heat, and the marine engine makes full use of this and thereby gains in efficiency.

An ancilliary question pops up once the gasoline-versus-diesel matter is settled. Should the power be single or twin? Is it better to confine all the horses to one unit or to divide them into two? Neither choice can be

Figure 2-9. "Return insurance" is on the transom of this sailboat. This 4-horsepower outboard motor has a special long shaft to accommodate the high transom of small sailboats. (Johnson Motors)

labeled correct (and its opposite called wrong) because either system could be installed in most boats. Here, again, the type and size of boat and the use to which it is to be put determine whether single or twin would yield the greater benefit.

There is great comfort in knowing you can always limp home on the remaining engine if one of the two decides to quit. This feature is probably the greatest incentive to dual engine installations. But there are others. Most twin-engine boats will turn in their own length, a great boon in a crowded situation. The twins will maneuver a boat and dock it precisely by throttle manipulation alone without use of the rudder. It may be easier in some hulls to install the total required power in two smaller units rather than in one large one. Sometimes the total desired power calls for a larger engine than the market provides or the space allows and two units are the only answer. Then there are boatmen who like twin engines simply because they like them.

In this real world, an advantage often carries with it some penalty. In the case of twin engines, the penalty is added cost and added complication. A given number of horses is more expensive if purchased in two machines because fixed costs in manufacturing engines do not decrease proportionately if power output is cut. Dual engines mean duplicate controls, a double set of instruments and twice the price.

The question of fuel consumption is another part of the single-versus-twin decision. The identical horsepower developed in two engines consumes more fuel than if it were generated in one. Some boatmen overcome this by using only one power unit when cruising at low speed. But this requires considerable rudder correction in order to maintain a straight course, and the added hull resistance this causes turns the idea into a doubtful economy.

A single engine normally drives through a shaft log which places the propeller directly behind the keel. The

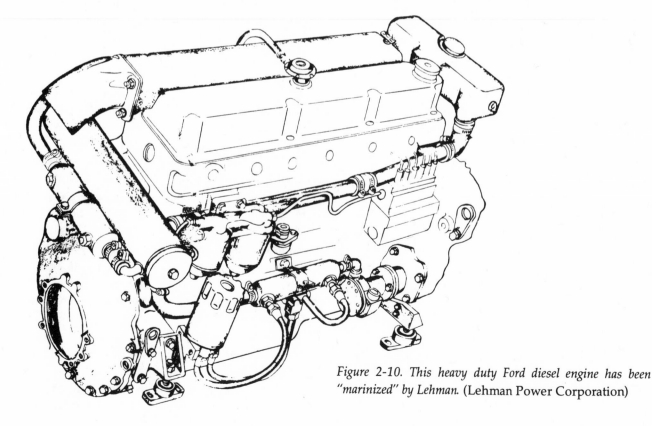

Figure 2-10. This heavy duty Ford diesel engine has been "marinized" by Lehman. (Lehman Power Corporation)

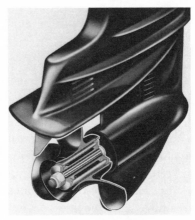

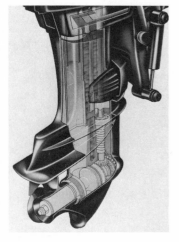

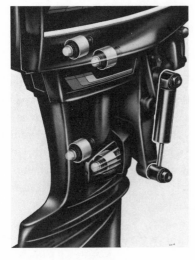

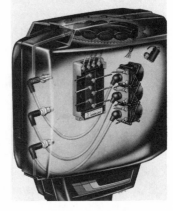

Figure 2-11. The relative locations of the various major components of a modern outboard motor are shown in these X-ray photos. (Mercury Marine)

keel then shields the prop in the event of a light grounding. Twin engines drive propellers that protrude on each side of the keel where they and their shafts are exposed and open to damage. Although this may not prove to be a primary factor in the power decision, it is something to bear in mind.

The outboard-powered boat is at the top of the list in ease of engine installation. Here the question of single versus twin is decided on purely monetary considerations, except in the rare instances when extreme power is desired. It is almost as easy to hang two motors on the transom as to install one.

Many outboard boatmen make use of an idea that is a derivative of the twin installation. They have two motors, a large one and a small one. The large unit is the propulsion engine, which is centrally located and used for cruising speed. The small one, to one side, is the trolling engine for slow-speed fishing. This one is also the get-you-home engine when the big machine becomes recalcitrant. The bonus to security in this case is the ability to run economically at very slow speed.

Often the market offers a choice of a desired cubic-inch displacement in more or fewer cylinders. Here the guiding rule is that the more cylinders, the smoother the flow of power and the less the vibration. The number of cylinders for a given displacement will have only a marginal effect on the rate of fuel consumption, provided compression ratios and horsepowers are identical.

Finally, the idiosyncrasies in the handling of a single-screw vessel should be considered when deciding upon one engine or two. Many boats with one engine back erratically when the power is put in reverse. The rudder has little effect on the direction the stern goes until considerable backward speed is reached; meanwhile the propeller rotation, whether right or left, is the determining factor. The cause of this aberration is the nature of the reactive force on a working propeller (see Chapter 14).

The peculiarities in behavior of a single-screw vessel are felt to some extent even when going ahead at slow speed. Response to the rudder is mushy and subject to the same effects of reactive forces already mentioned. Such boats have a favorite side for docking, and the wise skipper will humor his charge and bring her alongside whenever possible either to port or to starboard, whichever she favors.

Twin-screw craft do not exhibit these whims because the two propellers turn in opposite directions. Thus, the reactive forces on one are canceled by the converse forces on the other. In fact, by operating one engine at a time, these forces can be made to assist in a desired maneuver.

3. *Two-Stroke Cycle or Four-Stroke Cycle?*

All internal combustion engines must perform a series of fixed actions in each cylinder in order to produce power; this series is called a *cycle*. A running engine endlessly repeats this cycle. How this cycle is accomplished is the basis for dividing internal combustion engines into two broad groups known as "two-stroke cycle" and "four-stroke cycle." Colloquially, this nomenclature is shortened to "two-cycle" and "four-cycle."

The series of actions begins with the ingestion of fuel. Next the fuel is compressed. Then the combustion of the fuel causes expansion and results in power. Finally, the burned fuel must be expelled to clear the way for a repetition of the cycle. These four events are basic and universal. However, these actions are not always taken as four distinct steps, one after the other; some engines combine them, as later discussion will show.

In all conventional engines a piston moves up and down in a cylinder to achieve the necessary results. One complete travel of the piston, either up or down, is called a *stroke*. If it takes four such strokes to complete a cycle, the engine is a four-cycle machine. If the actions are combined into two strokes, the engine is two-cycle. Whether an engine operates in the two-cycle or the four-cycle mode is determined by its design and cannot be changed.

Two-cycle operation in gasoline engines is generally reserved for outboard motors, and even some large horsepower units are in this category. (A four-cycle outboard engine was available on the market until a few years ago; another has recently arrived.) All larger multicylinder gasoline powerplants operate on the four-stroke-cycle principle. The situation is different in the diesel world. There large-output two-cycle engines are found almost equally with the more conventional four-cycle type. This diversion is possible because the diesel ingests and compresses only air and not a fuel mixture, as the gasoline engine does.

Although the next chapter discusses in detail every action that takes place inside a marine engine, it is helpful at this time to have a quick preview of how a cycle is actually accomplished. In Figure 3-1 a cylinder and its

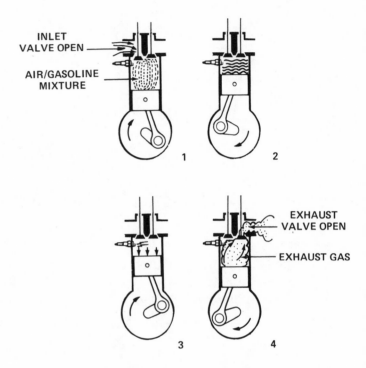

Figure 3-1. The first downward stroke of the four-stroke cycle gasoline engine draws in the fuel-air mixture. The next upward stroke compresses the mixture and readies it for ignition. The high pressure gases resulting from combustion force the piston down in its power stroke. The following upward stroke forces the burnt gases out of the cylinder. These four strokes form a cycle and are repeated endlessly while the engine is running.

piston are shown diagrammatically for a four-stroke-cycle engine. At (A) the piston is beginning its downward stroke, and the partial vacuum created will draw in the fuel mixture. At (B) the piston has reached its lowest position, has filled the cylinder with an explosive mixture and is about to return to the top, thereby compressing the charge. At (C) the spark has just ignited the fuel, and the resulting expansion will drive the piston to the bottom and crate the power stroke. The residue of burned gases will be pushed out of the exhaust valve when the piston returns to the top from its position at (D). Since four distinct strokes, the equivalent of two revolutions, have

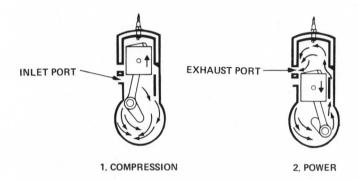

1. COMPRESSION   2. POWER

Figure 3-2. The two-stroke cycle engine accomplishes its cycle in half the number of strokes required by the four-stroke cycle engine because the piston uses both its top and its bottom and does double duty. On the first downward stroke, resulting from the previous ignition, the piston compresses the fuel mixture in the crankcase, forcing it into the cylinder and thereby scavenging the burnt gases. The next upward stroke compresses the mixture, readying it for ignition, and draws new fuel into the crankcase. Thus the four operations necessary for power output from a gasoline engine are completed in only two strokes.

been taken to complete one cycle, this is obviously a four-stroke-cycle engine. The steps from (A) to (D) are repeated continuously when the engine is running.

Figure 3-2 contrasts the simplicity of the two-stroke-cycle engine with what has just been shown. The secret lies in the fact that the piston does double duty on each stroke; both its top and its bottom are put to work. At (A) the piston is at the top, having compressed the fuel mixture from the previous cycle while its undersurface has created a vacuum in the crankcase and pulled in fuel for the next cycle. A spark ignites the charge and sends the piston to the bottom on its power stroke; this also compresses the fuel in the crankcase forcing it through the transfer port. The deflector on the piston top causes the incoming fuel to push the burned gases ahead and out of the exhaust port. Although the four necessary steps have taken place, they have done so in only two strokes, or one revolution.

The salient point to note from the foregoing descriptions is that the four-cycle engine has only one power stroke during two revolutions while the two-cycle machine has a power stroke in every revolution. Obviously, this is an advantage in total power output. If one of two otherwise similar engines has twice as many power impulses as the other, naturally it will develop more power—not twice as much (because the two-cycle engine is not an efficient fuel user), but certainly considerably more.

This is another way of saying that the two-cycle engine can be smaller and lighter than a four-cycle unit for the same horsepower. Furthermore, the two-stroke-cycle engine is minus the valves and the valve-operating mechanism, which add to the weight, bulk and complexity of the four-cycle. All these features are the reason why the outboard manufacturers have zeroed in on the two-cycle.

The reason for the lower efficiency of the two-cycle engine can be found in its method of ingesting its fuel. The burned gases in the cylinder at the end of the power stroke are literally "chased out" by the incoming fuel mixture. Some of this fuel always follows its quarry out the exhaust without doing its share of work.

The two-cycle/four-cycle debate will never be won decisively because each side has legitimate pros and cons. The four-cycle engine is accused of wasting two of its strokes while being simply an air pump. This is true. During its intake stroke and on its compression stroke, the machine is only pumping and getting things ready for the power stroke. As already noted, the two-cycle engine eliminates this weakness by constantly doubling up on its chores, doing two things at once.

The four-cycle advocates then point to the need for mixing oil with the gasoline, often a nuisance, but a lubricating necessity for the two-cycle engine. The four-cycle engine has an oil sump and a lubrication system, which make such babying unnecessary.

It follows that the two-cycle engine constantly burns up its lubricating oil while the four-cycle constantly recirculates it. This has an effect not only on the cost of operation but also on the environment. To the burned gases that are spewed into the atmosphere is added the residue of the burned oil, although the latest developments by the outboard manufacturers have reduced this source of pollution.

It is well to emphasize at this point that these strictures do not apply to the two-cycle diesel engine because it ingests only air and not a fuel mixture. (The fuel is sprayed in separately.) Thus, a separate blower can fill the cylinder with air at the required times and leave the crankcase free to become the usual oil sump. The air also scavenges the cylinder, and there is no loss if some of it goes out through the exhaust valve.

How can you tell a two-cycle engine from a four-cycle one? The absence of cylinder-head valves is a positive mark of the gasoline two-cycle. Another method is to check for the location of the exhaust pipe connection to the cylinder. Since the exhaust is through ports or holes cut into the cylinder near the bottom, the pipe would naturally be attached at that location. The sketch in Figure 3-3 shows this. The simplest way of all: If the manufacturer's instructions are to mix oil with the gasoline, then it is a two-cycle machine for sure.

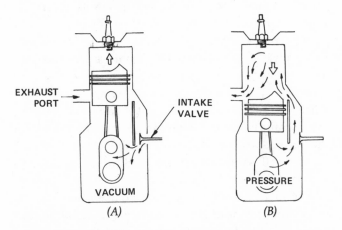

Figure 3-3. The paths that fuel takes before and after combustion in a two-stroke cycle engine are shown. The upstroke of the piston causes crankcase vacuum and the induction of raw fuel (A). The downstroke creates pressure that drives the fuel into the combustion chamber and forces burnt gases out (B). Fuel and exhaust are represented by the small arrows.

The four-cycle engines used for inboard power are installed with their crankshafts horizontal or nearly so. The crankcase can then serve its usual purpose of acting as a sump for the lubricating oil. The two-cycle engine does not have an oil sump, and thus it can be installed with its crankshaft vertical. This is the position it occupies in outboard "motors." The advantage is the straight line for power transmission down to the lower unit that carries the propeller. In addition, the flywheel is at the top, readily accessible for starting with a rope in the smaller horsepowers. (One manufacturer provides a groove in the rim of the flywheel of a 50-horse electrically started outboard for emergency starting with a rope if the battery is dead.)

With the crankshaft vertical, the cylinders of course are horizontal, and the pistons slide back and forth on the lower cylinder wall. This would seem to create the conditions for excessive wear, but actual practice does not bear out this fear. The same hesitancy was felt when automobile engines first assumed the vee style, for there, too, the piston weight is mostly on the lower cylinder wall.

The onus of mixing oil and gasoline can be avoided at many marinas, thanks to the petroleum companies. They have installed pumps that do the mixing automatically as the fuel is delivered. The desired ratio, be it from 25 to 1 to 50 to 1, is dialed in and the mixing then proceeds, as the saying goes, "untouched by human hands"—no more frantic shaking of heavy six-gallon portable fuel tanks!

The greatest operating benefit for the skipper with a two-cycle gasoline engine comes not because the machine is two-cycle, but because it is an outboard. The boon is in steering agility. The outboard swings on the transom and directs its thrust in any direction the skipper wants to turn. The four-cycle inboard engine's propeller always thrusts directly aft, and the rudder alone must do the total job of steering. The rudder is far less effective than the directionally oriented propeller of the outboard.

An exception to the foregoing limitation of the inboard engine is the stern drive, originally called an inboard/outboard. Although this is a four-cycle engine installed inside the boat, the driving unit is attached to the transom outside the boat and swings from side to side for steering exactly like an outboard. Both it and the outboard can be tilted up to avoid damage in shoal water. The ability to raise the propeller above the keel is a great advantage for the skipper who likes to beach his boat. In this instance the two-cycle engine and the four-cycle engine serve about equally, although the latter is always more efficient with its fuel consumption.

The two-cycle engine is much easier to maintain than the four-cycle because of its simpler construction. It does not have the valve assembly, the camshaft and the gearing that the four-cycle needs in order to operate. Of course both engines are equal in their electrical requirements, both need spark plugs, coils, distributors and more or less complex wiring. (Again, the two-cycle diesel engine is an exception.)

The foregoing unbiased discussion of two-cycle versus four-cycle power buttresses the earlier statement that both types of engines have been developed into excellent motive power for pleasure boats. The ingredients of the final choice should be the kind of boat, the intended use and, of course, the proclivities of the skipper.

The correctly timed opening and closing of valves in relation to piston travel and position is basic to the four-stroke-cycle mode of operation. Figure 3-4 illustrates this theoretically. In actual commercial engines, slight variations on the theoretical ideal occur as a result of modern engine design.

For example, the intake valve and the exhaust valve in a cylinder may be open simultaneously for a small part of piston travel. This is necessitated by the finite time required for the fuel to enter the cylinder and for the spent gases to leave. Although this arrangement would seem to cause a drop in output power, actually only a negligible amount is lost. The saving grace is the inertial effect of the fast-moving streams of fuel and exhaust. Both have already attained high velocity when the simultaneous valve opening takes place.

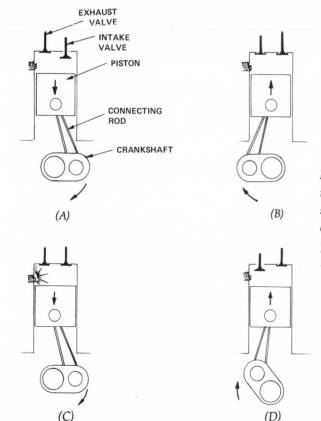

Figure 3-4. The relationship of valve openings to piston travel in a four-stroke cycle engine is shown systematically. The suction stroke (A) finds the intake valve open. Both valves are closed on the compression stroke (B), and remain closed on the power stroke (C). The exhaust valve is open during the exhaust stroke (D).

4. *The Basic Engine and Its Functioning*

The modern, sleek, compact, powerful marine engine is a formidable machine that can easily overawe the nontechnical skipper. Nevertheless, breaking the demon down into its component parts, and examining each part closely, enables almost anyone to acquire a useful comprehension. This knowledge brings confidence and familiarity. Soon minor adjustments become routine, and intelligent diagnosis of major problems becomes possible.

The entire power-generating system depends upon the combustion of fuel. A valid question, therefore, is What is a fuel and why does it burn? Why is one liquid, like gasoline, highly flammable, whereas another, carbon tetrachloride, for instance, is a powerful extinguisher?

An early stage in combustion, oxidation, may give a clue. To oxidate (or oxidize) is to combine with oxygen—and a fuel is a substance with which oxygen can combine rapidly enough to raise the temperature to flame and cause combustion. Oxygen cannot do this with carbon tetrachloride.

Combustion is a complex chemical process with many undesired but unavoidable end products (in addition to the heat and expansion that make the internal combustion engine go.) These unwanted substances are recombinations of the elements in the fuel and in the air and include carbon monoxide, carbon dioxide, nitrous oxides and water, which itself is an oxide. All go out the exhaust pipe. Note that in nature nothing is ever destroyed; for example, the oxygen needed for the reaction is still there but in various new forms.

Hydrocarbons are the universal fuel for pleasure boat engines. In this classification are gasoline, kerosene and diesel oil. The most volatile is gasoline, and hence it can easily be ignited by a spark. Kerosene and diesel are less flammable and therefore more difficult to ignite.

Hydrocarbons are so-called because each molecule of the substance is composed of atoms of carbon and atoms of hydrogen, a combination that contains tremendous latent energy. This energy is released during combustion to become the useful power of the engine plus the end products already mentioned. The hydrogen reappears in

the water vapor seen in the exhaust. (Do not confuse this with the cooling water emanating from many boat exhaust pipes.) (See Figure 4-1.)

The energy locked in a fuel can be expressed in British thermal units (abbreviated Btu's) and this is a convenient manner in which to compare the efficacy of one combustible with another. The higher the Btu's, the more power an engine can derive from any suitable fuel. (A Btu is the amount of heat energy required to raise the temperature of 1 pound of water 1 degree Fahrenheit.)

Btu content also helps explain the statement made in an earlier chapter that the diesel can extract more power from a gallon of fuel than can the gasoline engine. Diesel fuel will average 137,000 Btu's per gallon; gasoline will average 123,000 Btu's per gallon. Of course the higher compression ratio of the diesel then widens this fuel advantage in its favor.

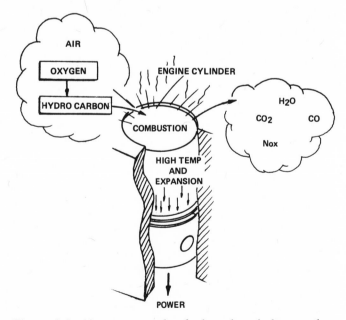

Figure 4-1. Air, oxygen and a hydrocarbon fuel enter the combustion chamber and are burned. The result is useful power and the release into the atmosphere of water, carbon dioxide, carbon monoxide and various nitrous oxides.

The oxygen needed for combustion is taken from the atmosphere, of which approximately 20 percent is this element. An internal combustion engine consumes huge quantities of air, which is why enclosed engine spaces must have generous ventilation openings. The proportionate mixture of air and fuel for the gasoline engine is critical within narrow limits because the mix must be sufficiently explosive to be ignitable by a spark. The diesel engine does not have this requirement because it breathes only air and not a fuel mixture. The harder-to-burn diesel fuel is sprayed into the highly compressed, intensely hot air and ignites spontaneously.

The concept that all matter is composed of atoms and molecules is helpful in understanding why the pressure of an enclosed gas rises when its temperature is increased. All molecules and atoms in all substances are constantly in motion, although you could not see this even with the most powerful microscope. As energy is added by the heat of combustion, the motion becomes ever faster and the molecules hit the cylinder walls harder and harder. (This is just another way of saying that the pressure has increased.)

The excited, fast-moving molecules also hit the top of the piston with such force that it is moved downward on its stroke, thus turning the effect of the combustion in the cylinder into useful work. It is hard to imagine how all this action can take place in the tiny portion of one second which a speeding engine allots to it.

With the basic function of combustion and its resulting pressure increase clearly in mind, each action inside an internal combustion engine becomes logical and easy to understand. Remember that every internal combustion engine must perform the same fixed series of operations in order to derive power from its fuel. It must ingest fuel, compress it, ignite and expand it and then exhaust it. These four functions carried out in sequence become a cycle. They are shown diagrammatically in Chapter 3 but now will be scrutinized more closely to reveal the innermost secrets of the machine that propels the boat.

Despite its greater mechanical complexity, the four-cycle engine is more suitable than the two-cycle as an explanatory model because each of its strokes performs

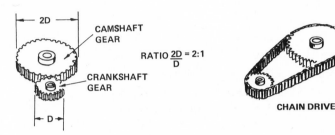

Figure 4-2. The camshaft of a four-stroke cycle engine must run at half the speed of the crankshaft. This is accomplished by having the camshaft gear twice the diameter and twice the teeth of the crankshaft gear. Direct drive or chain, the same ratio holds.

only a single function. So four-cycle motive power will be dissected first.

The piston is the part that draws fuel into the cylinder and pushes it out again after the fuel's energy has been released by combustion. The intake and exhaust valves act as traffic directors that determine whether the movement is in or out, and they set the exact time at which each shall occur. (The valves themselves are studied in Chapter 26.)

Each cylinder of a four-stroke-cycle engine has at least two valves, one intake and one exhaust. The term "at least" is used because some high-performance engines double the number of valves in order to provide quicker ingress and egress of fuel. However, the action is the same except that two valves would open for intake and two for exhaust. Two smaller valves result in better engineering construction than one large one.

Since the four-stroke cycle extends over two revolutions of the engine, the opening and closing of the valves must be timed accordingly. The intake valve operates during the first of these two turns and the exhaust valve during the second. This synchronization is accomplished by driving the camshaft that controls valve motion at half the speed of the engine. Such a transition is made easily by having the gear on the camshaft twice the diameter of the gear on the crankshaft that drives it. Figure 4-2 shows the principle, with both gears and chain.

The designer has a choice of several locations for the valves required in each cylinder. The position finally chosen determines the configuration of the engine and gives it its name. Thus we have T head engines, L head engines, I head engines and even F head engines. The sketch in Figure 4-3 should clear this up a bit.

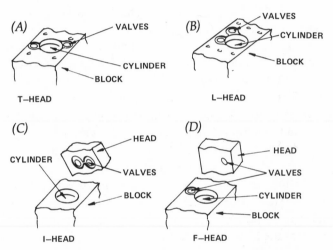

Figure 4-3. The arrangement of the valves determines the classification of the engine. Shown are the T-head with a valve on each side of the cylinder, the L-head with both valves to one side of the cylinder, the I-head with both valves in the cylinder head and the F-head with one valve in the block and the other in the head.

At (A) in this drawing the valves are located one on each side of the cylinder. The similarity to a T is not hard to see, and hence this is the T head engine. At (B), both valves are on one side of the cylinder, and this conforms to an inverted letter L to make it an L head engine. At (C), both valves are above the cylinder, and this is the I head engine, although it takes a bit of imagination to see the letter I. Finally, with one valve above and the other to one side, half L and half I, the F head engine evolves at (D). The L head and the I head are commercially favored; the T head is obsolete, and the F head is in the minority.

As long as the valves permit efficient flows of the fuel mixture and of the exhaust, their location is not critical to engine performance if other contributing factors are

taken into account. Yet each engine type has an optimum position and size for its valves, and the designer calculates this while the unit is still on the drawing board. The I head engine, more commonly called the overhead valves type, makes its valves more accessible for service and adjustment and is a favorite for marine use and for automobiles as well. The relative position of the intake valve and the spark plug is important in gasoline engines because this affects flame propagation and efficient combustion.

The layman often thinks of combustion in an engine as being a sudden explosion. Actually, in a properly operating machine, combustion is an orderly progression of the flame from the spark plug in the gasoline engine and from the injector in the diesel. However, "orderly" does not mean slow; the action takes place in a minute fraction of a second. When the flame propagation is not orderly and the fuel really does explode, the result is the detonation or "knock" that robs power and ruins engines.

The kind of combustion that takes place in an engine is affected greatly by the size and shape of the combustion chamber, the space left at the top of the cylinder when the piston is at the end of its upward stroke. Early on, it was found that merely compressing the fuel mixture was not enough to accomplish maximum power. Turbulence was necessary to make certain that every particle of fuel was consumed. Figure 4-4 explains one method of creating turbulence.

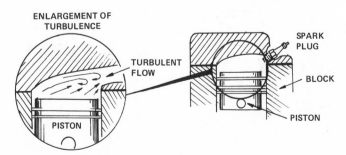

Figure 4-4. Turbulence in the combustion chamber is essential to efficient burning of the fuel. One method of attaining turbulence, a wedge-shaped combustion chamber, is shown here.

In this drawing a portion of the cylinder head overhangs the opening containing the piston. As the piston reaches the top, it violently squeezes out the fuel mixture between it and the overhang and squirts this into the rest of the combustion chamber to cause extreme turbulence. Flaming particles are hurled everywhere, and the entire charge burns up completely.

The overhead valve design allows the greatest range in combustion chamber configuration and therefore in compression ratio and in turbulence. Often the tops of pistons are formed into protrusions or other shapes to enhance the turbulent effect. One reason for the demise of the T head engine is the inherent inflexibility of its combustion chamber and its poor turbulence.

Regardless of the valve's position, the method of opening and closing it is almost always standard and is dependent upon the camshaft mentioned earlier. This camshaft has a number of off-centered disks called cams, one for each valve. Since the camshaft is driven at one-half crankshaft speed (see Figure 4-2), each valve functions only once during every two revolutions of the engine in response to its cam. Cams push their valves open either by direct contact or else through intermediate push rods, as shown in Figure 4-5. The closing of valves is always accomplished by strong springs. The exact point in each revolution when valves open and close—in other words, "valve timing"—is fixed at manufacture. Marks on the engine assure that this will not be changed during subsequent maintenance. Short adjustable rodlike parts called lifters are located between cams and valves and allow for clearance adjustments necessitated by the expansion of metal at operating temperatures.

Chapter 3 has described how the two-stroke-cycle engine completes in one revolution what the four-stroke-cycle engine needs two revolutions to do. Part of what makes this possible is doubling the work of the piston, making it combine intake and compression in one stroke and then power and exhaust in the next. But the major explanation lies in substituting ports for valves.

The beauty of a port lies in its simplicity. Camshafts and all the other accouterments of valves are eliminated when ports are used to control the inflow and outflow of a cylinder. A port is simply a hole or slot in the cylinder wall which is covered and uncovered by the piston in its travel. The time at which a port "opens" or "closes" is governed entirely by its position in the cylinder and is fixed at the time of manufacture.

In a standard porting of a two-cycle gasoline engine, the exhaust port is located so as to be uncovered at the bottom of the piston stroke. Directly opposite, and also uncovered, is the intake port whose passage leads to the enclosed crankcase. In the position shown, the fuel mixture in the crankcase, which was compressed by the downward travel of the piston, has rushed into the cylinder and has pushed the remains of the previous combustion into the exhaust. The suction from the pre-

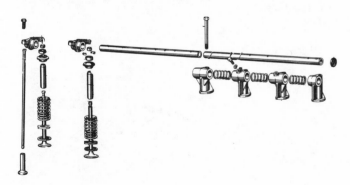

Figure 4-5. *A valve system on a marine engine comprises many components, some of which are shown here. (Lehman Power Corporation)*

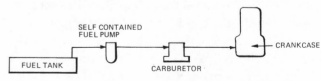

Figure 4-6. *The path of fuel from tank to outboard motor is shown in this diagram. A selfcontained pump on the engine forces fuel from the tank to the carburetor whence engine suction draws the fuel into the crankcase.*

vious upstroke of the piston had pulled the fuel mixture through the reed valve and into the crankcase.

An alternate method of porting does away with the reed valve in the crankcase. An extra port called the intake port is provided at a level below the usual exhaust port. This is uncovered by the piston skirt only at the very topmost position of the upward stroke. During the up travel of the piston, a strong suction is created in the enclosed crankcase, and this draws in fuel mixture when the intake port is "opened."

Still another method can eliminate the reed valve. A solid circular disk on the one side of the crank throw is flush against a flat surface in the crankcase. Both disk and surface have a hole or open segment. When these holes line up during the turning of the crank, fuel mixture can go through to the crankcase; at other times during each revolution the passage is closed. As before, crankcase vacuum is the "pulling" force on the fuel mixture.

In every one of these two-cycle engines the crankcase was needed as a container for the incoming fuel mixture, and therefore it had to be tightly enclosed. Obviously, it could not serve simultaneously as a sump for lubricating oil, as is the case with all four-cycle engines. The only way remaining to get the necessary lubrication into the engine is to mix the oil with the gasoline. Hence this is standard procedure on all commercial two-stroke-cycle gasoline engines.

The two-stroke-cycle diesel engine is different. It makes use of its crankcase as a lubricating oil sump in the normal manner. How is this possible in view of what has just been said? Since the diesel ingests only plain air, a separate pump can supply this and thus relieve the engine of using its crankcase for this purpose.

Figure 4-7 shows diagrammatically how this is done. The pump or blower is driven from an engine shaft and keeps an air box supplied with air under pressure. When the port connecting the air box with the cylinder is uncovered by the piston, the air rushes in. From that point on, the action is the same as in the two-cycle gasoline engine with the exception that exhausting is taken care of by a valve instead of by another port. Just a reminder in

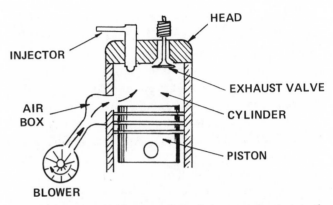

Figure 4-7. An air blower and an air box supply air into the cylinder of a two-stroke cycle diesel engine. The incoming blast of air also scavenges the fumes from the previous combustion.

case there is a bit of puzzlement because fuel has not been mentioned: The diesel fuel is sprayed into the cylinder by the injector near the top of the piston stroke when the air has become intensely hot. Note that now both port and valve are closed, and no fuel can escape into the exhaust and be wasted as in the gasoline two-cycle.

Two-cycle diesels are a popular installation in large pleasure boats. They start easily without the help of glow plugs (see Chapter 7) or similar aids, they are uncomplicated and they provide twice as many power strokes for a given number of revolutions.

The combustion process within the cylinder, which generates the actual power of the engine, could not continue without the support of a number of ancillary systems. These are the ignition system, the fuel system, the lubricating system, the cooling system and the electrical system. Each of these has a later chapter devoted exclusively to it.

Nature's laws of thermodynamics are part of the reason for an earlier statement that only a few cents of the fuel dollar end up doing useful work. The laws state that an engine can reject its heat only to a cooler body and that the process is not reversible. As a consequence, energy in the form of heat is wasted, and it will always be impossible to harness every single Btu in the fuel molecule.

Nevertheless, marine engines are constantly being improved, and they are fast approaching the limit of efficiency that nature imposes.

One avenue of approach that engineers are using to increase efficiency and catch up on nature is the reduction of piston lineal speed. (This should not be confused with reducing engine speed because revolutions per minute may actually increase.) A piston is stationary at the top and at the bottom of its stroke. Between these two positions it must cover the distance of its stroke in the time determined by the speed of the engine. If the stroke is shortened but the engine speed held constant, then the piston covers less distance in the same time; its lineal speed has been reduced. Lower piston lineal speed causes less wear, wastes less energy in the form of friction and is therefore more efficient.

Higher-speed, short-stroke engines are on the market and are setting a trend. Higher speed makes it possible to draw the same power from a smaller engine, while the shorter stroke keeps the pistons from paying the penalty. The advantage to the boatowner is obvious.

Other, more esoteric methods are also being employed in this never-ending striving for efficiency. One of these is exhaust tuning in vogue on outboards, some larger engines and even in automobiles. The theory is that exhaust pipes act upon the fast-traveling gases like organ pipes act upon sound; there is a known relationship between the length of the exhaust pipe and the length of the wave within it at a given engine speed. Tailoring the exhaust pipe to that critical dimension facilitates exhaust and ekes out just a little more power from the same combustion.

The great annoyance on a powerboat is noise, and in this regard all reciprocating engines are almost equally guilty. Vibration is often a concomitant offender but multi-cylinders and careful manufacture can reduce this. This area of noise and vibration is what the turbine will eventually conquer.

5. *Outboard Motors: Gasoline, Electric, Diesel*

The outboard motor made the boating boom possible. Where before only the very rich could afford to go yachting, now Middle America, with a vastly slimmer pocketbook, enjoys the pleasure of being on the water. "Yachting" became boating, thanks to the motive power you can hang on the transom, and millions are doing it.

The outboard motor has been around since the turn of the century (see Chapter 1), but only since the era of World War II has it achieved wide popularity. Today, outboards outnumber inboards by approximately ten to one. The portability of the motor and the trailerability of its boat made skippers out of landlocked people living far from navigable water. Automobiles sprouted trailer hitches on their back bumpers, and powerboats became common sights on the highways.

Several important improvements accelerated the acceptance of the outboard motor. Increased power permitted the use of larger boats, even driving them faster. Greater reliability permitted serious cruising. Electric starting eliminated the sometimes backbreaking yanking of a starting rope. An integral gearbox capable of selecting forward, neutral and reverse with a single lever made operation more nearly like the driving of a car, with which nearly everyone is familiar.

Additional significant improvements helped the outboard attain its present popularity. Underwater exhaust reduced noise and, at the same time, objectionable smoke and odor. With some motors the exhaust passes through the hollow hub of the propeller with the claim that efficiency is improved. Alternate firing of cylinders opened the way to smoother running. Vee construction, long standard in the automobile world, permitted outboard motor power heads to be compact despite more cylinders. Loop charging and scavenging, explained in Figure 5-1, lets the incoming fuel mixture do a more effective job of cleaning out the residue of the previous explosion and adds to power. Providing an additional intake port, as shown in Figure 5-2, is another move to greater efficiency. All the while the outboard motor has

Figure 5-1. This drawing has been exaggerated in order to clarify what happens in a loop-charged cylinder of an outboard motor. Piston slots and additional ports cause the incoming charge to sweep the combustion chamber in a loop, effectively clearing out burnt gases. (Evinrude Motors)

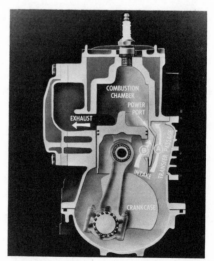

Figure 5-2. Adding second intake port is another move to attain greater efficiency in charging and scavenging. The regular intake passage A is aided by the additional passage B uncovered by the piston. (Mercury Marine)

gotten lighter in weight for its horsepower—although calling a 150-horsepower motor "portable" is somewhat of an optimistic misnomer.

This same motor is too heavy to tilt up and out of the water comfortably, even by a husky person, and so electric and hydraulic tilting mechanisms appeared. A touch of a finger on a console switch now raises or lowers this brute gently as a lamb. An adjacent knob takes control of the shift lever and selects forward or reverse—again at the touch of a finger. Solid-state technology has removed the troublesome breaker points from ignition systems in many motors and assures hotter sparks.

As stated earlier, all popular outboard motors now on the market operate on the two-stroke-cycle principle. The manufacturers adopted this style in preference to the four-stroke cycle because of the advantages accruing from the simpler construction and the greater power output for a given size. In addition, the absence of an oil sump allowed the cylinders to be set horizontally, a basic requirement for a compact design.

Because outboard motors take more punishment from the elements than inboard engines, design and construction must anticipate this hazard. Many outboards are operated in salt water, which places the immersed portions in jeopardy because of the saline attack on aluminum components. New resistant alloys and especially new improved paint coatings have met this challenge to a great extent. Salt water is a powerful electrolyte (as explained in Chapter 17) and subjects dissimilar metals in electrical contact with each other to strong galvanic deterioration. Hence, raising outboard motors out of the water when they are not in use is still the best procedure.

Theoretically, each type of service that an outboard motor performs should mandate a propeller with specifications tailored to such use. An outboard motor pushing a slow, heavy boat needs a different propeller for optimum efficiency from a motor on a ski boat going fast enough to skim the water. Yet, in actual practice, most skippers seem to get satisfactory service from an outboard motor fitted with a propeller whose specifications are an average compromise.

The propeller determines the load on the boat engine—and therefore its top speed—and a correctly chosen prop effectively prevents the outboard motor from overspeeding. This factor, together with a tachometer, can be used as a rule-of-thumb check on propeller selection. If at full throttle the engine revolutions per minute exceed the manufacturer's rating, the propeller is not providing sufficient load. Conversely, if the rpm will not reach the manufacturer's rating at full throttle, the propeller load is too great. In the first case, a propeller with greater pitch will have to be selected; in the second case, the pitch must be reduced. Of course, these tests are made with the boat carrying its normal complement of passengers and gear.

The propeller of an outboard motor operating in its correct position on the transom is sensitive to features in the hull immediately surrounding it. A deep, wide keel whose after end has not been rounded off (faired) can interfere with the smooth flow of water to the prop, and, what is worse, it can introduce air bubbles into the stream. The result is cavitation, a condition in which the prop loses its hold on the water with resultant loss of thrust and waste of power. Similar ill effects can be caused by hull protuberances, such as speedometer tubes and depth-sounder transducers, and this possibility must be sorted out when making a determination.

The outboard motor and its boat are strongly interdependent, and top performance requires that both be at optimum efficiency. The motor, naturally, must be mechanically in tune. The rest then depends on the condition of the boat's bottom. Barnacles and grass increase friction and reduce speed. A bottom that is slightly concave (hooked) or slightly convex (rockered) also reduces speed and adds undesirable riding characteristics and uncertain steering control. The drawings in Figure 5-3 visually explain the terms "hooked" and "rockered."

The proper choice of horsepower of the outboard motor for a selected boat falls between two limits. The

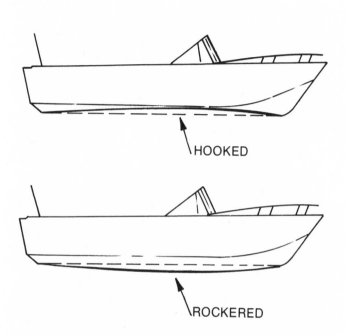

Figure 5-3. Hull bottoms may become hooked or rockered from careless support on trailers or chocks. These deformities rob the hull of its ability to perform at top efficiency.

Figure 5-4. All small boats are required to carry a horsepower plate, such as shown above, installed by the manufacturer. With this information directly at hand, a skipper can find no excuse for overpowering and overloading.

lower limit is the least horsepower that will move the boat in an acceptable and safe manner; this is based on experienced opinion. The upper limit, the greatest safe horsepower, is determined by the boat builder, and it should never be exceeded. By law, every boat in the outboard class carries a plate stamped with this figure. Figure 5-4 is a photograph of such a plate.

Standard outboard motors are offered with a choice of two lengths of lower unit to match boats with similar transom dimensions. The lengths are 15 inches and 20 inches, and the sketches in Figure 5-5 show how the measurements are taken. Mismatching should not be done. A "short" motor on a "long" transom places the propeller too near the surface and invites cavitation and useless water churning. Mismatch in the other direction immerses too much of the outboard motor's lower unit, causing drag, power waste and loss of speed. Larger boats and motors are almost universally fitted at 20 inches.

The angle of the outboard motor with respect to the horizontal is another important factor in obtaining efficient and comfortable boat operation. The goal is to have

the anticavitation plate of the motor (located directly above the propeller) just below and parallel to the surface of the water. This condition is realized when the motor itself is exactly vertical, as in Figure 5-6.

Boat transoms are rarely vertical, and therefore, to obtain the condition shown in Figure 5-6, a tilting mechanism is incorporated in the motor mount. The range of tilting adjustment is so wide in most motors that an incorrect amount can be chosen, and this will degrade boat performance. Figure 5-7 depicts boat attitudes resulting from too much and too little tilt.

Too much tilt of the motor in the aft direction causes the boat to ride bow up. The stern squats, causing excessive drag, which is paid for in loss of speed and obscured forward vision for the skipper. This is a very common error, and hardly a boating area is without an example.

Too much tilt in the forward direction has the opposite effect. Now the bow points down as if contemplating a dive. Often the propeller rises close enough to the surface to suck air and cavitate, causing the engine to overspeed.

The correct position of the outboard motor on the

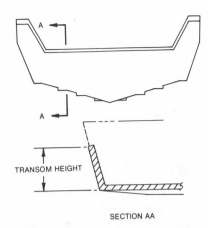

Figure 5-5. The height of the transom determines the selection of the correct outboard motor.

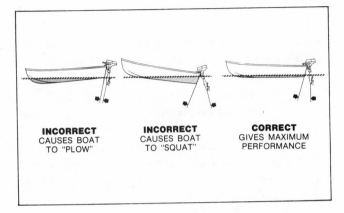

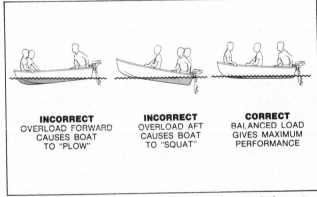

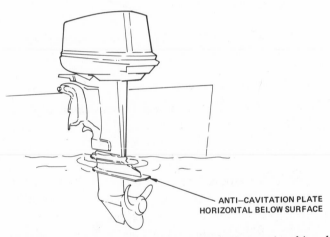

Figure 5-6. The optimum tilt of the outboard motor is achieved when the cavitation plate is horizontal just below the surface of the water.

Figure 5-7. The correct tilt of the outboard motor is important for seaworthiness and for fuel economy. Correct load distribution is equally important, as these sketches show. (Evinrude Motors)

transom is the one shown in Figure 5-6, and, by way of repetition, this occurs when the cavitation plate is horizontal and just below the surface. A well-built and -balanced boat will run level and on plane with maximum comfort and greatest fuel economy when its motor tilt is right. Water will be thrown low to each side, and the wake will be minimal. This is the ideal manner in which to operate an outboard boat, and skippers should strive to attain it.

The beauty of the power-tilting mechanism described earlier is that the tilt adjustments to obtain perfect boat stance can be made while running and from the comfort of the steering position. Changes in boat load and the effects of unbalance created by passengers moving about can be compensated for by the same control.

The recoil starter appeared on outboard motors before

the electric starter did and had a great influence on the early popularity of outboarding. Its predecessor was the rope starter, which many found exasperating; the rope had to be coiled manually about the flywheel for each attempt at starting—and with uncertain starts this often could mean many rewindings. The recoil starter improved on this by retracting the rope with a spring and making it immediately ready for the next pull.

The idea of cooling an internal combustion engine by air without the complication of water passages has always appealed to designers. From automobiles to lawn mowers, air cooling has its adherents. In the realm of outboard motors, air cooling remains in use only on units of very low horsepower. Larger motors take advantage of the medium in which they work and employ water cooling.

The difference in construction between the two systems of cooling is readily apparent on inspection. The air-cooled cylinder has a number of integral external fins to increase its area of contact with the atmosphere and thus facilitate the transfer of heat. The water-cooled engine is minus these fins. It has internal passages around the cylinder through which the cooling water flows.

The modern, and best, method of circulating the cooling water is with a mechanical pump driven by the engine. The pickup scoop is in the area of the propeller and usually gets a boost from the prop discharge current. The outflow of water is often used to cool the exhaust before it is dumped overboard.

Some early outboard motors attempted to achieve greater simplicity by eliminating the mechanical pump. One such design placed a pickup scoop directly aft of the propeller tips and took maximum advantage of the high-velocity current to force water up into the engine. The outflow was placed just ahead of the prop and counted on the lower pressure in this area to draw the cooling water out again.

The outboard motor is devoid of conventional valves, and this is the main reason for its simplicity. However, the taking of fuel mixture into the crankcase requires directional control, and this job is taken over either by a simplified device called a "reed valve" or else by a "rotary valve" (described in the previous chapter), which is not a true valve at all but rather a rotating opening. The purpose of both is to act as a one-way gate into the crankcase.

A representative reed valve is shown in Figure 5-8. It consists essentially of a base with holes that are covered by a thin springy leaf or reed of metal. Passage in the direction of arrow A is unobstructed because the reed lifts and uncovers the holes. Any attempt at passage in the direction of arrow B forces the reed to a tight closure. The actual shape of the reed varies in different engines, but the principle is the same.

Despite their simplicity, reed valves perform complex functions. They keep the carburetor effectively isolated from reverse surges of fuel. They equalize the distribution of fuel in multi-cylinder engines and make for smoother running. They automatically vary their degree of opening in accordance with the fuel demands of the

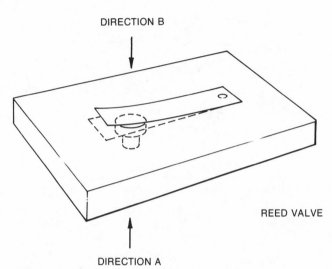

DIRECTION B

REED VALVE

DIRECTION A

Figure 5-8. The principle of the popular reed valve is shown in this schematic drawing. A fuel mixture can pass easily in direction A but flow is prevented in direction B.

engine under various loads. The tendency of the reed to whip excessively at high engine speed is dampened by the stop plate shown in the illustration.

Although the traditional position for the reed valve is in the crankcase, ingenious designers have gone beyond this. One example is a multiple reed valve whose support block also serves as the main crankshaft bearing. This is a money-saving improvement in multi-cylinder two-cycle engines, whose individual crankcases must be isolated from each other. (See Figure 5-9.)

Ignition for outboard motors can be divided roughly. into two systems. One is entirely self-contained and generates its own necessary electric current with a flywheel magneto or a flywheel alternator. The other is dependent upon an accessory battery and in many models cannot function without it. (The mysteries of electric current and of magnetos and alternators are dispelled in Chapter 8.)

A further subdivision of the two systems would differentiate between motors using the time-honored breaker points to control the spark and the much more modern

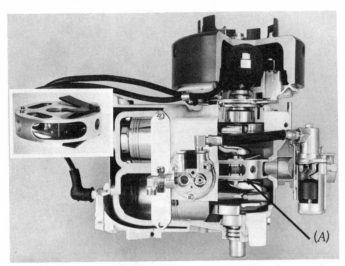

Figure 5-9. An innovation in outboard motors is a main bearing that also acts as a fuel intake valve. The insert explains the valve/bearing itself, while (A) shows its position in the engine. (Mercury Motors)

designs that eliminate these common sources of ignition trouble. Breaker points need frequent adjustment and even periodic replacement. The breakerless systems are set at the factory and remain in perfect operating condition "forever." The reason for their longevity is that no component makes mechanical contact with any other and consequently there is no wear. Would that we could make that statement about the rest of the engine!

Optimum relationship between the amount of throttle opening and the exact instant when the ignition spark occurs (the timing) is of extreme importance in efficient, economical outboard motor performance. Various types of linkages between ignition and carburetor accomplish this. As the throttle is opened wider, spark timing is advanced accordingly, until, at full throttle, timing is maximum. One design permits the throttle to be pulled back slightly when the boat reaches its top speed without at the same time reducing the degree of advance. Experience has proved that this modification increases the miles per gallon.

The total thrust developed by the outboard motor is transmitted to the boat transom through the motor support brackets. Obviously, both transom and brackets must be able to take the load. In addition, the brackets must permit the motor to swing from side to side easily enough to allow effortless steering. The sudden jolts that can arise during actual boat operation are subdued and ironed out by shock absorbers.

Two-stroke-cycle engines, with their mandated mixture of gasoline and oil, have a common failing. Although the oil and gas are in a homogeneous suspension when the mixture comes from the carburetor, the heavier oil droplets tend to condense out in the passage from crankcase to cylinder. This condensate eventually collects in the crankcase and would hinder operation unless disposed of. One system passes this oil-rich fluid through the bearings for additional lubrication before mixing it with incoming fuel and burning it.

As Chapter 14 points out, propellers develop an undesired twisting reaction in addition to the fore-and-aft thrust, which is the reason for their installation on a vessel. This leads to uneven steering on an outboard boat because the motor swings more easily to one side than to the other. An ingenious little gizmo called a trim tab overcomes this. This trim tab is attached underneath the anticavitation plate and looks like a little rudder—in fact, acts like one. It is adjusted to provide the amount of counter torque required to correct the steering. On many motors this tab is made of an anodic alloy and serves the additional purpose of counteracting galvanic deterioration of the immersed portion of the motor.

The Honda outboard brings a four-stroke-cycle gasoline engine back to the American market. This motor eliminates the messy chore incumbent on all owners of standard two-stroke-cycle engines: mixing lubricating oil with the fuel. The Honda has its own oil sump in the crankcase, and lubrication is accomplished just as it is with automobiles, namely, by maintaining oil at a dipstick level. (See Chapter 3.)

An excellent feature for assuring motor longevity is an indicator on lubrication while the engine is running. A small green pilot light glows when the pressurized lubricating system is functioning normally. This would be the equivalent of the warning light on the instrument panels of many automobiles, except that the auto light comes on only to indicate trouble while the Honda light is a constant reassurance under way.

Other advantages of the Honda are an overhead camshaft for its two-cylinder engine and easily accessible breaker points. In contrast with most outboard motors that require flywheel removal for breaker point access, the Honda points are in a separately located housing; lifting the cover puts breaker points in full view for adjustment.

An outlet receptacle on the Honda outboard makes direct current available for battery charging or for navigational lights. Up to 5 amperes at 12 volts may be drawn. An ingenious fuel tank arrangement provides space for all tools that might be needed for underway emergency.

Although rated at only 7½ horsepower, the motor develops great thrust. In one instance, an 85-foot yacht, caught in a maneuvering difficulty, pushed its bow around with its Honda-equipped dinghy. Figure 5-10 shows the Honda.

Outboard advertising stresses the pleasure of beaching the boat on an island shore and of gunkholing in shallow waters. Such navigation invites sudden and unwelcome contact between the whirring propeller and a submerged rock or debris, with a high probability of damage. Early designs minimized injury to the propeller by interposing a breakable shear pin. The sudden shock of hitting something broke the pin and not the propeller. Of course, the pin had to be replaced, not necessarily a difficult job. (See Figure 5-11.)

Later designs eliminated the pin and substituted a simple clutch or a shock absorber, thus doing away with the need to stop and make repairs. The clutch slips harmlessly at the instant of impact and resumes normal operation when the trouble is over. The shock absorber dissipates the destructive energy of impact by distorting itself temporarily. Figure 5-12 illustrates both methods of protecting propellers on outboard motors.

Whether the protection is by shear pin, clutch or shock

Figure 5-10. The Honda is a four-stroke cycle gasoline outboard motor that eliminates the chore of mixing fuel and oil. Its pressure lubrication system includes a telltale pilot light. Its fuel tank carries the tools needed for adjustments. (American Honda)

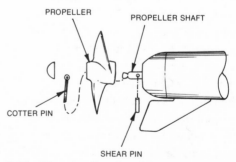

Figure 5-11. The propeller shear pin serves the same purpose in the outboard motor drive train as does a fuse in an electric circuit—it lets go when an overload develops. Thus, hitting an obstruction will result in a broken pin rather than a ruined prop. The cotter pin is a safety lock.

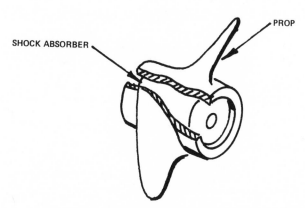

Figure 5-12. A rubber insert in the hub is one method of providing a shock absorber for a propeller and averting damage when the blade accidentally hits debris.

absorber, obviously the best procedure is to avoid striking obstacles with the propeller. Some damage to propeller blade tips can result despite the countermeasures. The shear pin, by its very nature, introduces a weakness into the system. It is designed purposely to be the weak link, and it could even reach the limit of its strength under abnormal sea conditions. The boat could be endangered by thrust failure at such a time.

Designers of outboard motors have achieved significant success in noise reduction. Many modern motors are whisper quiet and let their presence be known only when they are at full throttle. The problem was attacked on several fronts and has been licked by the combination of improvements. The motor shroud (the cover) has been insulated generously with sound-absorbent material. Water is combined with the exhaust gases to eliminate the roar. Rubber cushions separate the various parts of the motor so that vibration and noise cannot be amplified and transmitted to the boat. (See Figure 5-13.)

It was inevitable that the success of diesel engines for inboard power should make itself felt in the outboard world—and a diesel outboard motor has finally arrived on the market. It is available so far only in two sizes, 6 horsepower and 16 horsepower, although the manufacturer claims that the boat-pushing ability of each ex-

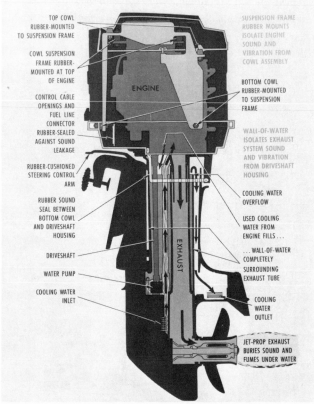

Figure 5-13. Noise reduction has become an important phase of outboard motor design. This skeleton photo shows how one manufacturer has quieted its powerful outboards. (Mercury Marine)

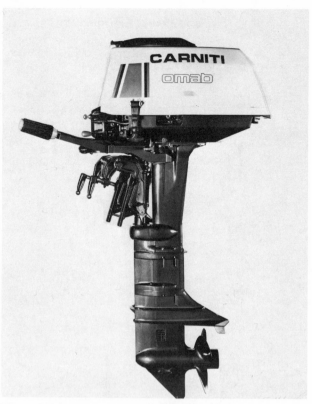

Figure 5-14. *It was inevitable that the influx of diesel engines into pleasure boating should bring a diesel outboard motor. This four-stroke cycle machine is available in 6 and in 16 horsepower. (Carniti)*

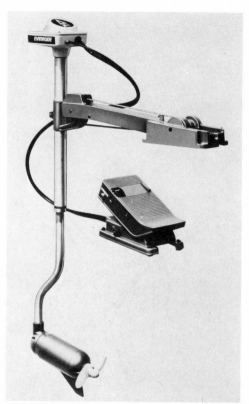

Figure 5-15. *History repeats itself, but this modern electric outboard motor bears little resemblance to its earliest forebear. Speed and direction are under the control of the pedal under the fisherman's foot, and the silent drive, it is hoped, will not spook the fish. Energy is supplied by a storage battery. (Evinrude)*

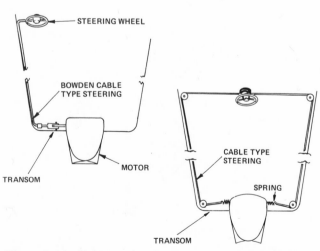

Figure 5-16. *The Bowden cable steering system eliminates the need for pulleys and cables. By contrast, the cable system requires a pulley or sheave at every change in direction of the cable; springs also must be included to take up shock and slack.*

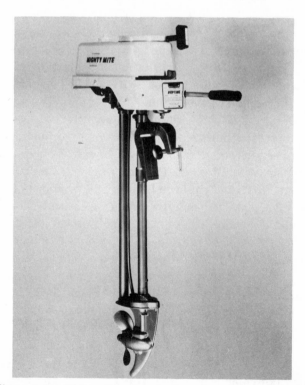

Figure 5-17. *This outboard motor is truly portable, in the full sense of the word because it weighs only 17 pounds, but it is a midget in output with only 1.7 horsepower. (Mighty Mite)*

ceeds that of gasoline engines of equal ratings. The reason for this apparent anomaly lies in the greater torque output of diesel machines.

These diesel outboards operate on the four-stroke-cycle principle (see Chapter 3) instead of on the two-stroke, which is standard in the industry. This is understandable because it eliminates the air blower found on two-cycle diesel engines and thus makes for compactness. Of course, it also brings greater complexity because camshafts and valves must be added, components which the two-cycle gasoline outboard does not have. However, these diesel outboards gain a point by being air-cooled, having no ignition and doing without water passages and a pump. (See Figure 5-14.)

The appearance of electric outboard motors brings the matter full circle because historically the first outboard was an electric, as noted in Chapter 1. Of course, there is no other similarity. Modern electric outboards are superbly engineered little machines that squeeze maximum thrust out of every watt of electric energy. Their weakness, and this too is historical, is the limited power that can be drawn from a reasonably portable storage battery.

The usual design of electric outboard motors is to have the motor itself in a watertight housing at the bottom of a vertical tube that has the steering arm and control at the top. A foot-operated speed control, actually a rheostat (see Chapter 8), is connected by an electric cable. Foot-operated steering is also an option.

The electric outboard motor probably owes its existence to the fact that fish are spooked easily and are caught most effectively from a silent, slow-moving boat. This method of fishing is called "trolling," and electric outboards are usually known as "trolling motors." Figure 5-15 shows a representative unit.

Outboard steering can be as simple as an extended arm on the motor or as elaborate as a posh steering wheel on a fancy console. The low-horsepower units come under the first description, and the more powerful units qualify under the second. In the latter case the connection between wheel and motor can be a push-pull flexible cable or a plain taut cable running over sheaves. The push-pull cable has the preference because it can be installed easily to follow the contour of the boat. The push-pull cable is able to absorb the shocks indigenous to steering; the cable and sheave combination needs springs in the steering system to absorb them. The illustrations in Figure 5-16 show both methods.

The preachings of the Coast Guard, plus perhaps the general public's increased awareness of danger, have borne fruit in outboarding. The possibility of an outboard boat whizzing merrily on after its operator has fallen overboard is made much less likely by an ingenious switch. The switch key is tied to the operator by a cord. Large outboard cannot be started unless their gears are in neutral, an arrangement familiar on automobiles.

Consideration is even given to the motor's own "safety." Strong clamps and brackets reduce the chance of its falling overboard, but if it does, safety chains keep it from going to the bottom. The motor can be retrieved to repent and run another day.

The trend in outboard motors is to make them larger, heavier and more powerful—and consequently less portable. One firm has gone in the other direction and has made easy portability its aim with a motor that weighs only seventeen pounds. Of course, at the present state of our technology, when weight goes down so drastically, then output power must follow; this motor produces 1.7 horsepower. It is shown in Figure 5-17.

6. *Engines for Sailboats*

T he wind is free, the wind is fun—but the wind is also undependable. Often the spanking breeze that started the day's cruise has disappeared when it is time to go home. The solution then rests with "petroleum wind," either gasoline or diesel. Even when the wind holds up, it is the rare skipper who makes his slip under sail. Again, the answer lies in the auxiliary engine.

Sailboat hulls are streamlined and far easier to push through the water than the standard powerboat. Further, sailboats are displacement vessels not designed to plane with great expenditure of energy. Thus, foot for foot of length, the engine power necessary for adequate propulsion is far less for sailboats than for modern powerboats. This is fortunate on many counts, one of which is the limited space available on sailboats for engine installation.

The outboard motor is the most common auxiliary power for small sailboats. The smaller vessels hang the outboard on the stern, often with retractible brackets such as shown in Figure 6-1. The advantage of retraction is

the reduction of drag when the outboard is not in use and sails have taken over. Additional bonuses from retraction are the ability to keep the motor attached but yet out of the water when moored or at the pier, and being able to raise the motor high enough to avoid interference with trailering.

An alternate outboard installation method is with a motor well. The well is located in the fantail and is fitted with a hatch cover that continues the fair line of the deck when it is closed. The outboard, of course, projects down far enough to get its cavitation plate a few inches below the water surface. Figure 6-2 depicts a sailboat with a motor well.

Although the sailboat motor well has cosmetic advantages, it also has some shortcomings that cause many sailors to avoid it. For one thing, the motor is constantly immersed and this results in unwanted drag when under sail. In turn, the immersion requires some form of protection against barnacles and corrosion. Of course, these

(A)

(B)

Figure 6-1. An outboard motor on the transom of a small sailboat (A) aids maneuverability and assures getting home, wind or no wind. The retractable bracket (B) lifts the motor out of the water when not in use and eliminates its drag. (Johnson Outboards)

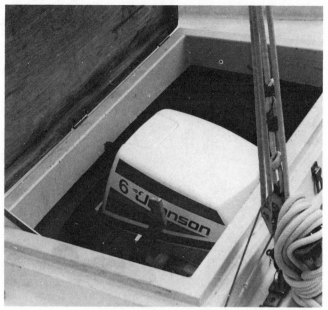

Figure 6-2. *The outboard motor in the well of this sailboat is out of sight when the cover is down. Not all sailors are happy with motors in wells. See text.*

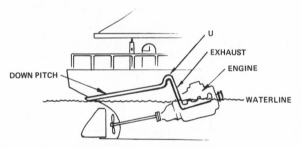

Figure 6-3. *Auxiliary engines on sailboats are often installed wholly or partially below the waterline and provision must be made to prevent water getting into the exhaust line.*

drawbacks disappear if there is enough room in the well for the installation of retractible brackets that allow the motor to be pulled up when not in use.

Some sailors steer the vessel with the outboard motor while it is providing propulsion. Others continue steering with the regular tiller and the outboard is fixed in the dead-ahead position. The large rudder area common to sailboats easily overcomes any directional tendency caused by an off-center motor.

The permanently installed auxiliary engine of a sailboat functions as does any other inboard engine; the information in this book directed at powerboats pertains as well to it. The major difference between it and the powerplants of the stinkpotters is that the sailboat auxiliary is generally located below the waterline. This requires protection against water influx through the exhaust pipe and necessitates specialized exhaust line techniques. (See Figure 6-3.)

An elbow or U in the exhaust pipe, so located that it remains above the waterline at all angles of heel of the hull, is the distinguishing feature of the sailboat engine installation. Of course, all the cautions having to do with safe installation, mentioned elsewhere in this book, are applicable to sailboats as well. Principal among these safety measures is the avoidance of fire hazards by proper location of exhaust and fuel lines and the use of correct materials.

Small diesel engines are exceeding their gasoline counterparts in popularity with sailors as auxiliary powerplants. The diesel is uniquely well adapted to the rigors of sailboat service. The absence of a vulnerable ignition system is a strong point in the diesel's favor on a vessel that often takes seas aboard. The ruggedness of the machine is another. And the fact that designers have brought the weight of the small diesel engine down to manageable levels is perhaps the clinching argument.

The auxiliary engine market for sailboats has become large enough to motivate manufacturers to produce special models designed specifically for this service. One ingenious design might be called an adaptation of the familiar stern drive. It is pictured in Figure 6-4. The engine is a two-stroke-cycle, two-cylinder gasoline machine of 15 horsepower. The lower unit conforms itself to the dead rise of the average sailboat hull and projects a three-bladed propeller into the slipstream. The prop freewheels when not engine-driven in order to reduce drag. The engine may be remotely controlled from an after cockpit, a center cockpit or any other location convenient to the skipper.

The sequence of steps that are taken to install this unique sailboat driving unit is shown in Figure 6-5. At (A) the shape of the necessary cutout is marked out at the specified location by means of the template applied by the manufacturer. The hole is cut out, and the surrounding area is sanded at (B) to assure proper adhesion of the subsequent fiberglassing. The engine mount itself is shown at (C), and at (D) it has been glassed to the hull. How this looks from outside the hull is depicted at (E). The engine portion of the unit is installed at (F) with a gasket for watertightness. At (G) the installation has been completed, and the propeller now extends into the slipstream as at (H).

Figure 6-4. This sailboat driving unit is a new and novel auxiliary power that can take over when the wind dies. Most components are identical with outboard motor parts and easily replaceable if need to do so arises. (Outboard Marine Corp.)

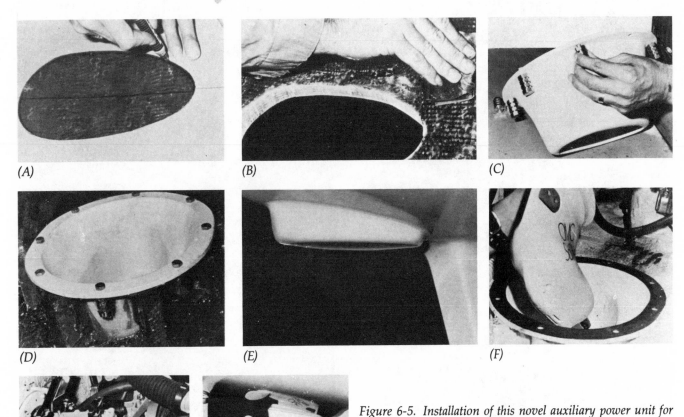

Figure 6-5. Installation of this novel auxiliary power unit for sailboats is a simple matter: (A) mark the cutout with the supplied template, (B), and, rough the surrounding surface for resin application. (C) shows the motor mount itself, (D), in position, and (E) the mount protruding beneath the hull. The gasket at (F) provides watertightness for the complete installation (G). The propeller projects into the slip stream at (H). (Outboard Marine Corp.)

51

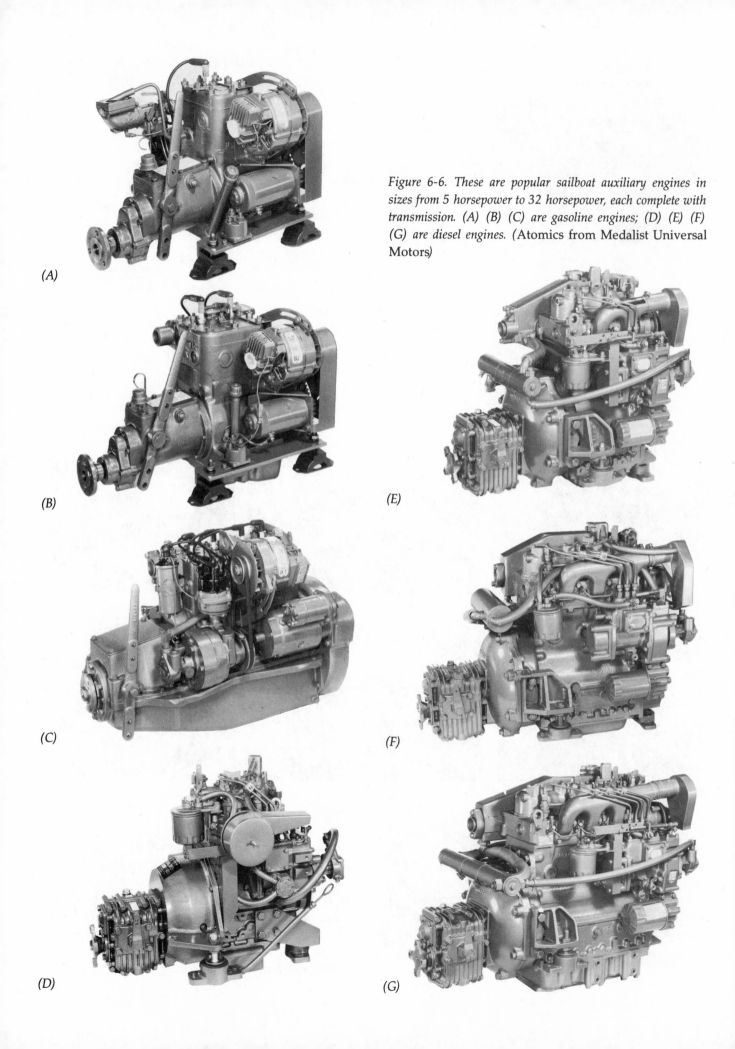

(A)

(B)

(C)

(D)

(E)

(F)

(G)

*Figure 6-6. These are popular sailboat auxiliary engines in sizes from 5 horsepower to 32 horsepower, each complete with transmission. (A) (B) (C) are gasoline engines; (D) (E) (F) (G) are diesel engines. (*Atomics from Medalist Universal Motors*)*

The makers of this compact auxiliary power unit for sailboats claim that its initial cost is lower than the price of a comparable engine and that the installation also presents a saving. A point of interest to skippers is that the component parts are almost totally identical with the same manufacturers' outboard motor parts and therefore are available worldwide. Approximately 250 pounds of static thrust is directed at the hull at full output. Rope starting is possible in the event of battery failure.

Pictured in Figure 6-6 is a series of engines designed to function as permanently installed auxiliary power for sailboats. The models constitute single-cylinder, two-cylinder and four-cylinder units, each with an integral transmission containing the reversing gear. The drive to the propeller may be had as direct, reduction or even a vee for situations where lack of space requires that the drive line fold back upon itself. The fact that the designers had sailboats in mind has resulted in ultra-compactness and such a unique feature as a hand sump pump for removing crankcase oil.

One aspect of auxiliary power that appeals to skippers of small sailboats is provision for hand starting the engine. The nature of sailboat service, where engines do not run continuously but often only at random periods, may make the charge level of storage batteries a chancy thing. When the electric starter does not respond to the switch, a hand crank becomes an important piece of equipment. Knowing that the iron horse can be started with a few yanks on a crank is great moral insurance. Of course, hand starting is available only on the smaller powerplants.

The higher compression ratio of the diesel engine makes it more difficult to turn over than a gasoline engine of the same output. Thus the advantage of hand cranking is reserved for the mini-diesels. However, as mentioned earlier, sailboat hulls make sparse demands for power, and therefore this situation balances itself out.

The noise level of an auxiliary engine is generally not viewed as critically as is the noise made by the powerplant of a standard powerboat. The reason is the intermittent periods of operation; true sailors use their engines grudgingly and only when the wind truly has forsaken them. Thus the noise is considered a temporary nuisance, soon shut down. (Noise-reducing covers may be installed if desired. See Chapter 22.)

The auxiliary engines on sailboats benefit from fresh-water cooling just as much as do the engines in any other craft. (See Chapter 11.) The usual advantages of better temperature control, reduced corrosion problems and the ability to use cooling-system additives are enjoyed equally on sailboats. Locating the through-hull fitting for picking up cooling water is more difficult because it must remain immersed regardless of heel. The discharge fitting is placed above the waterline at any convenient point.

Two-blade propellers are favored for sailboat hulls designed with full keels. These props can be lined up vertically with the keel when the boat is under sail; in this position they present no projected area to the slipstream and cause no drag. A brake on the shaft holds them in this alignment. Some transmissions may be damaged by free-wheeling propellers because there is no provision for maintaining oil pressure on the gearing when the engine is stopped.

The quest for reducing the drag of idle propellers while the boat is on the wind has also led to the use of folding props that automatically take their blades out of the slipstream when the engine is not driving them. The action in many of these devices is centrifugal. Centrifugal force acts on the mass of the blades when the propeller is spun by the engine and forces them out to their designed hydrodynamic position; the reactive force of the water helps keep them that way. (See Figure 6-7.) (Propellers are discussed in Chapter 14.)

Electricity is a boon on sailboats for lighting and amenities, although many wind sailors prefer not to think so. With a small engine, small alternator and small battery, this source of current cannot be counted on for more than meager help. The answer is a generating plant, even as it is on powerboats. (See Chapter 7.) The commercial market offers these electricity producers as small as 400 watts, a size easily adaptable to a small sailboat. This amount of power permits judicious use of lighting, radio and a small appliance like a fan. More important, it permits keeping the starting storage battery in a charged condition. More elaborate use of electric current, as for

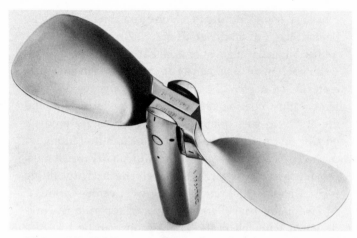

Figure 6-7. Folding propellers reduce drag for auxiliary sailboats when they are proceeding under sail alone. When not revolving, the blades fold together into a shape that creates little resistance. Makers claim that these folding props are as efficient thrusters as standard propellers, both forward and astern. (Martec Engineering Co.)

instance for air conditioning while away from the pier, requires a larger generating plant and rules out this convenience for the small boat.

While on the subject of electricity, it must be emphasized that safe and proper electric wiring is as important on a sailboat as it is on any other vessel, large or small. (See Chapter 8.) Keeping all wires out of the reach of bilge water is more difficult on a sailboat because of heeling. Even a small amount of water in the bilges can climb high up on the hull when the lee rail is awash.

Engine instrumentation (see Chapter 15) is usually minimal on a sailboat. Often the instrument console endemic to a powerboat is replaced on a sailboat by a gauge or two in the bulkhead forward of the tiller. The oil-pressure gauge assumes major importance when the number of instruments must be cut down. The next most necessary indicator is the temperature gauge. Careful attention to these two gauges can forestall trouble and will keep the engine acting like a good shipmate.

7. Electric Generating Plants

Electric stoves, air-conditioners and many other electrical appliances are common on pleasure boats, but without an onboard generating plant these amenities are available only at dockside. Once away from the power outlet on the pier, all these niceties become mere ballast unless an adequate source of current supply can feed them. That "adequate source" must never be the boat storage battery; only an electric generating plant can do the job.

The normal electrical system aboard an average pleasure boat centers about the boat battery, which, in turn, depends upon the small alternator or generator on the propulsion engine for its charge. This is a low-voltage, direct-current system, sufficient for a bilge pump, a few low-candlepower lights, the navigational instruments—but totally unable to deliver meaningful power for standard appliances. True, the battery handles the real man-size task of cranking the propulsion engine, but it can do this for only an extremely short period of time.

The word "watts" explains the need for an onboard electric generating plant. The watt is a unit of electric power. All major electric appliances consume many watts, and some even gulp thousands of watts or kilowatts. When you realize that 746 watts are equivalent to a theoretical horsepower, it becomes obvious that these gargantuan appetites require heavy generating machinery to appease. (Chapter 8 demystifies all electrical terms that may follow.)

It is possible to purchase some of the less current-hungry appliances designed especially for use on battery voltage. These could include small refrigerators, compact television receivers, light-duty fans and perhaps some others. However, this is not the way to go except under dire necessity. The cost per unit is high and its operation not so satisfactory as that of its counterpart, which functions on house current.

"House current" is the name of the game, and it permits standard household appliances to go to sea. The onboard plant generates current identical to that supplied by the power company for the home; only the

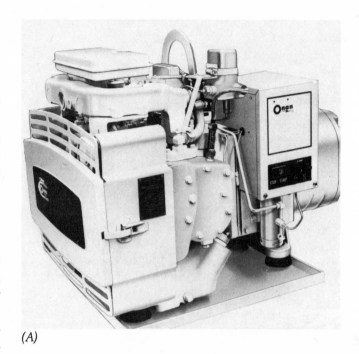

(A)

(B)

Figure 7-1. A representative gasoline powered electric generating plant at (A) and a diesel powered plant at (B). (Onan Corp.)

quantity is limited. Just as smaller homes are wired for 110-volt service and larger ones for 220 supply, so also, with boats. The small cruiser will find a 110-volt generating plant with a few kilowatts capacity adequate; the gold plater will choose a 220-volt unit with many times the kilowatt ability.

The electric generating plant essentially comprises an engine, either gasoline or diesel, connected to an alternator or generator. A representative unit is shown in Figure 7-1. Strictly speaking, a generator puts out direct current while an alternator supplies alternating current. Appliances almost universally work on alternating current.

As already stated, watts can translate into horsepower—but unfortunately not at the theoretical rate of 746 to 1. Stated differently, it requires an engine of more than 1 horsepower to make 746 watts available at the output. The reason is the relative inefficiency of the conversion. By way of illustration, one popular electric generating plant rated at 15 kilowatts output contains an engine capable of 40 horsepower.

Although the average boatman uses the term "kilowatts" to label the output of all generating plants, this designation is correct only for direct-current machines. Technically speaking, an alternating-current generating plant is rated in "kilovolt-amperes." Under some conditions, 1 kilowatt and 1 kilovolt-ampere are equivalent in power. Familiarity with both terms helps in understanding manufacturers' catalogs.

Proper selection of an electric generating plant for a pleasure boat considers two facets of the problem. The first decision is whether the engine shall be gasoline or diesel. The recommended practice is to select one that uses the same fuel as the propulsion engines do. This eliminates the bother and danger of having two kinds of fuel aboard. Except for units of very large output, which are mostly diesel, the market allows a choice in each similar size.

Once the matter of fuel is decided, the next obvious choice has to do with required power output. The answer is found by listing all the electrical appliances wanted on board together with their power appetites, then adding these to arrive at a total sum. The table in Figure 7-2 gives the pertinent facts. For this rough assumption, the final number of kilowatts can be considered equivalent to the kilovolt-amperes of a potential alternating-current generating plant.

The law of averages will say that hardly ever will all appliances aboard be running simultaneously. This means that some cutting can be done in the computed size of the desired plant. Further, appliances that contain motors take greater than listed power to start but simmer down to normal within a fraction of a minute. Perhaps the foregoing can be condensed into stating that it necessitates a bit of experience to know how far the tentative requirement should be cut in the interest of economy.

On the more modern, vee-hulled pleasure boats, the propulsion engines are set far enough apart to permit the

Air Conditioner	See Motors
Battery Chargers (Rectifiers)	up to 800 watts
Blankets (Electric)	50 to 200 watts
Coffee Makers	550 to 700 watts
Electric Drill	See Motors
Electric Range (Per element)	550 to 1500 watts
Fans	25 to 75 watts
Fry Pan	1000 to 1350 watts
Heater (Space)	1000 to 1500 watts
Hot Plate (Per element)	350 to 1000 watts
Iron (Electric)	500 to 1200 watts
Lights (AC)	As marked
Refrigerator	See Motors
Television	200 to 300 watts
Toaster	800 to 1150 watts
Vacuum Cleaner	See Motors
Waffle Iron	650 to 1200 watts
Water Heater	1000 to 1500 watts

Figure 7-2. The wattage requirements of the various appliances listed above will help determine the size of the onboard generating plant needed. (Onan Corp.)

installation of the generating plant between them. On round-bottom hulls this separation may not be sufficient to allow this, and other locations must be found, locations that will not interfere with the operation and servicing of other engine room equipment. This often relegates the electric generating plant off to one side, smack against the hull, making one side of the plant difficult to get at. It may also interfere with the athwartship (side to side) trim of the boat because of the heavy weight involved. Figure 7-3 depicts a representative generating plant in a moderate-sized cruiser.

Regardless of location, one caution to bear in mind is that fuel lines for engines and plant should be entirely separate right from the tank. The differing appetites of the two fuel users make it bad practice to attempt to feed them from a common pipe. Needless to say, the filtering in the fuel line to the generating plant should be at least as thorough as that for the engines. The carburetors and especially the injectors of electric generating plants are just as vulnerable to foreign matter as any others.

The ideal onboard electric generating plant is automatic in operation. This means that it starts up of its own

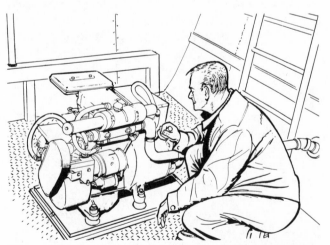

Figure 7-3. The ideal generating set installation provides easy access to all components for adequate maintenance and possible service—but, alas, the ideal seldom is achieved because space is at a premium in the engine room of the average yacht. (Onan Corp.)

accord whenever there is a demand for electric power from any outlet or appliance. The circuitry for doing this apparently difficult task is simple enough and is self-contained: A sensitive relay monitors the lines and switches on the starting motor. This happens so quickly that hardly a blink is noticed when a lamp is lit.

Slightly less deluxe is the manually started plant. The routine for the gasoline-fueled unit is no more complex than turning the switch key in an automobile. The diesel plant may be equally simple with some engines, but with others it may entail two steps. These are the engines with glow plugs. A switch must be held until the glow plugs become red hot as shown on an indicator; another switch then starts the engine. The delay is usually less than one minute and is soon taken in stride.

The electric generating plant quickly becomes such a comfort of living aboard that its presence is taken for granted, and the attention paid to its maintenance approaches nil. For this reason the machine should be equipped with automatic safeguards. Pressure failure in the lubrication system and unnatural rise in temperature should trigger immediate shutdown.

Voltages higher or lower than that specified on the nameplate of an appliance are detrimental to it, and therefore it is essential for a plant to maintain a constant correct output. Voltage at the terminals is determined by the internal electrical excitation of the generator or alternator and by the speed at which the engine is turning. The former is controlled by regulating circuits, the latter by an engine governor. Between the regulator and the governor, the output voltage of a good electric generating plant is surprisingly steady despite changes in load.

Most television receivers will function well onboard when powered by generating plants, although an occasional roll-over may mar the picture temporarily. But electric clocks will not keep accurate time. Clocks at home are kept on the second by the unvarying frequency (60 cycles per second) of the current supplied by the power company. Such accuracy is too much to expect onboard.

Generating plants of very low output can be had air-cooled; all larger units are water-cooled. Here, too, as mentioned earlier in relation to propulsion engines, the cooling method can be by freshwater or by raw water. Again, freshwater cooling prolongs the life of the engine and results in more efficient temperature control. But whether by fresh or by raw, water cooling is the way to go.

Some of the older, plush yachts carried generating plants that produced direct current at voltages ranging from 32 to 110. A bank of storage batteries was connected in tandem with the plant and worked with it as a unit. The system was a high-power version of the usual 12-volt battery on a car or in a boat. The advantage gained was the ability to operate appliances even though the plant itself was not running. This is not possible with an alternating-current generating plant of the type popular today.

The alternating-current producer must keep running because alternating current cannot be stored in storage batteries. This is the one shortcoming of this form of electric power generation aboard. It is a shortcoming because operation entails some noise—and noise can be disturbing to people trying to rest or to sleep. Some manufacturers offer so-called soundproof enclosures for their units; these markedly reduce the annoyance, but the sound transmission through the structural members of the boat is still something to be reckoned with. (See Figure 7-4.)

A generously sized electric generating plant can provide a bonus on a single-screw boat. It can take over the chore of turning the propeller in an emergency and thus provide a means of reaching home. This is accomplished by installing a pulley or sheave on the propeller shaft and a similar one on the engine side of the plant. The plant is then located so that the two sheaves can be connected by a belt. If the main engine decides to quit, the belt is put in place and the plant engine takes over the job of propulsion. Of course, speed control will leave a lot to be desired—but the boat can be brought to safety.

Most pleasure boats larger than open runabouts have an outside receptacle into which the shore power line is plugged at the pier. When the boat carries an electric generating plant, the internal wiring from this receptacle leads to a husky switch with three positions marked "Shore," "Off" and "Ship." With the switch in the "Shore" position, the boat takes its power from the pier. In the "Ship" position the plant supplies the power. This arrangement makes it impossible to connect pier and plant together—a connection that would be disastrous. Figure 7-5 shows such a switch.

Figure 7-5. A turn of this switch makes the changeover from shore power to onboard generating plant power. Both cannot be connected at the same time. (Onan Corp.)

Figure 7-4. This sound shield (shown with access door partly open) quiets the electric generating plant. (Onan Corp.)

The regulating circuits mentioned earlier, which maintain a constant voltage at the output of the generating plant, have been refined from originally complicated electromechanical devices into compact solid-state circuit boards. These operate on a feedback principle. They constantly sample the output of the machine and make the appropriate electrical correction when the voltage is high or low. They require no attention; the function is automatic. Light bulbs too bright or too dull are the telltale that something has gone awry.

The admonition to install a separate fuel line for the electric generating plant should have a companion bit of advice: Install a separate storage battery also. If propulsion engine batteries go dead while anchoring out and refuse to turn the big brutes over, the separate generator battery can save the day. Once electric power is available, batteries can be charged in short order. Plugging in the battery charger that all boats should carry is all that would be required. (Some smaller plants can be started with a rope, a la outboard motors.)

The generator of a direct-current electric plant has a commutator and brushes riding upon it. (See Chapter 8.) The brushes, usually made of carbon, wear and track the commutator to cause sparking due to the high current drawn. This presents a maintenance problem that the alternating-current electric plant does not have. The alternator delivers its current through fixed windings and thus avoids the commutator and the high-current-carrying brushes. The only brushes it does have are small, ride on collector rings, transmit only minimal exciting current and rarely need attention.

The engines of electric generating plants are started in either of two ways, depending upon their design. They may have small electric starting motors, similar to propulsion engines and automobiles. The more common method is to use the large generator or alternator itself as the starting motor. This is done by incorporating a special internal winding. Often this same winding is put to subsequent use for charging the plant's starting storage battery.

The 110-volt plants have two output terminals from which the power is taken; a third may be added for grounding. The 220-volt units have three output terminals with a possible additional one for grounding. Two wires, one from either outward terminal and the other from the center one, will supply 110-volt current. Two wires, each attached to an outward terminal, will provide 220-volt current. Thus the larger generating plants allow great flexibility aboard in the use of electricity. Two separate branches can run 110-volt lights and small appliances, and the 220-volt main line can take care of large loads such as air-conditioning motors. (See Figure 7-6.)

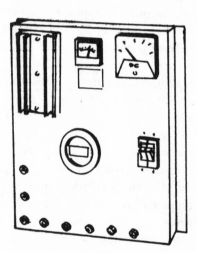

Figure 7-6. The control panel of a typical small electric generating plant will have volt and ampere meters, circuit breakers and the necessary terminals.

Often the electric generating plant will get harder usage than the propulsion engines. Many skippers turn it on when leaving the pier. It will then run continuously, even through overnight anchorings, until the boat returns to the dock, perhaps days later. Fortunately, these machines are built to take it—and do.

A small portable generator, on a boat without a fixed generating plant, can be the fabled "last chance" if everything aboard goes dead while anchored. A quick pull on a starting rope then becomes the beginning of resurrection for the run-down main battery and finally the starting of the propulsion engine.

Honda has introduced to the American market a portable electric generator that fits this role admirably. It is shown in the photo of Figure 7-7. It occupies almost exactly one cubic foot of space and weighs less than forty pounds.

The heart of the Honda unit is a four-stroke-cycle gasoline engine of one cylinder. As explained in Chapter 3, this type of engine eliminates the need for mixing oil and gasoline. An oil sump with a dipstick permits the use of standard lubricating oil as in an automobile. The generator output is regulated automatically, and a separate winding in the machine supplies the ignition voltage.

The Honda portable generator supplies direct current and alternating current, but not the two concurrently. The alternating current output is 300 watts continuously and 400 watts for short intervals. (As noted elsewhere, AC power is stated more correctly as volt-amperes.) The direct-current output is approximately 8 amperes for charging 12-volt batteries.

The unit has a self-contained tank that holds enough fuel for four hours' operation. Starting is by pull-rope. A green pilot light glows during operation to indicate that everything is in order. Emergency tools are located within the case.

The dearth of space available on a sailboat often mandates that the electric generating plant be installed below the waterline. The overboard disposal of the cooling water then presents a problem because it must be discharged above the waterline. A simple device devoid of moving parts and utilizing hydraulic lift is the solution. (See Figure 7-8.) The unit not only lifts the cooling water but also acts as an effective muffler of the exhaust. The maker claims the device requires no service, even though it does the work of a pump.

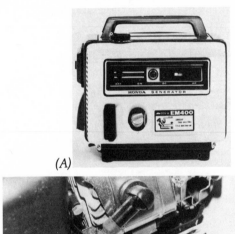

(A)

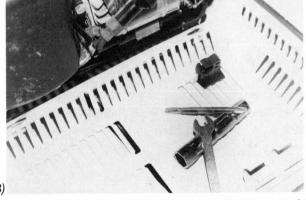

(B)

Figure 7-7. This compact, lightweight portable generator (A) can supply up to 400 watts of electric power at the pull of a starting handle. It is a four-stroke cycle machine and eliminates the mixing of oil with the gasoline. Terminals are provided for battery charging and a pilot light keeps tab on lubrication. (Honda) The back cover of this portable generator (B) carries the tools needed for emergency service. (Honda)

Figure 7-8. Generating plants on sailboats often are installed below the waterline, presenting the problem of cooling-water disposal. This unit lifts the cooling water automatically and also acts as muffler. (Onan Corp.)

Figure 7-9. This alternator with its constant speed drive is a substitute for a small complete electric generating plant. It attaches to the propulsion engine with brackets and supplies more than three kilovolt-amperes of electric power for the operation of onboard appliances. (Mercantile Manufacturing Co.)

A substitute for the installation of a complete electric generating plant may be had in the form of the add-on unit shown in Figure 7-9. This is a constant speed alternator that attaches to the propulsion engine and is capable of more than 3 kilovolt-amperes at 120 volts and a frequency of 60 cycles per second.

The constant speed is achieved, despite changes in speed of the engine, by a system of variable pulleys and clutches. (The constant speed is necessary to maintain constancy of frequency.) The unit is attached to the engine by means of suitable brackets, which the manufacturer supplies for standard powerplants.

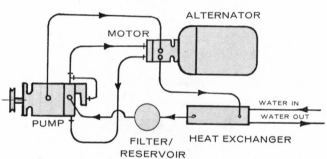

Figure 7-10. This alternator is driven by a propulsion engine but is located remote from it. Tubing or hose connects the alternator with the high pressure hydraulic pump on the engine. The claimed output is 6,000 watts at 60 cycles per second. (Onan Corp.)

An "add-on" alternator that is not really added on to the engine may solve some problems of available space. The alternator unit itself may be located remotely; it is pictured in Figure 7-10. The device actually placed on the propulsion engine is a small high-pressure hydraulic pump. The connection between pump and alternator is made with hose or tubing in the manner depicted in the diagram. The maker claims an output of 6 kilowatts.

PART TWO
ENGINE SYSTEMS

8. Electrical Systems

A n electrical system in some form, whether rudimentary or complicated, exists on almost every pleasure boat as part of the powerplant, and a skipper must be able to cope with it to ensure not only his enjoyment but also his safety. Electricity, to the extent it is encountered on a boat, does not warrant the mystery attributed to it. Actually, the knowledge gained from a study of this chapter can make a skipper comfortable with his volts and amperes.

Only a few of the terms in the electrician's vocabulary need be understood to enable intelligent handling of the ship's electric power. Foremost among these terms are direct current, alternating current, cycle per second (now called hertz), volt, ampere, watt, ohm, farad and henry. The definitions that follow will make each term familiar when it is encountered in later explanations of simple electric theory. Two terms that apply to the character of electric circuits, "series" and "parallel," should also be understood because they will be found in common usage.

As everyone who has attended a science class knows, an electric current is a movement of electrons. Electrons are the negative component of an atom whose other parts are positive protons and neutral neutrons. Some materials hold their electrons so tightly that movement is prevented, and therefore an electric current cannot flow in them. These are insulators such as the rubber, plastic or impregnated cotton insulation around electric wires.

The electrons in some other substances can move about freely, and obviously these materials would be conductors of electricity. Copper is one such material, hence its wide use as the central conductor in electric wires. Only silver exceeds copper's ability to conduct an electric current. This precious metal is therefore used where the resistance to the passage of electricity is required to be minimum, as, for instance, in contacts. (See Figure 8-1.)

Earlier theory considered electricity to flow out from the positive terminal of a battery and into the negative terminal, but we now know this to be incorrect. The negative terminal has the excess of electrons whose movement constitutes the electric current. It follows,

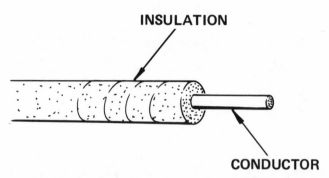

INSULATION

CONDUCTOR

Figure 8-1. The central metal conductor of wire used for electrical installations is covered by insulating material of various grades for various purposes. See Figure 8-18.

therefore, that electricity must flow from the negative to the positive, and this is corroborated by modern science.

In order to initiate a flow of electric current, there must be an excess of electrons in one part of the circuit and a deficiency of electrons in another part. Current will then flow until the excess and the deficiency have balanced each other out. This is exactly like water flowing from a higher level to a lower one until both levels are the same. The comparison with water flow holds throughout the study of electricity and aids its understanding.

Of the two wires from the boat battery, one is always negative, the other always positive. This is a *direct current,* and it is so named because the polarities are constant and do not change. By contrast, the two wires from an *alternating current* source, such as shore power on the pier, change their polarities constantly, and neither can be called either positive or negative. With the standard 60 cycles per second (60 hertz) supply, each wire alternates between positive and negative continuously at this rate.

Direct current is usually referred to simply as DC, and alternating current as AC. Generators and batteries produce direct current, alternators supply alternating current. The fact that the AC alternator on the propulsion engine charges a DC battery may be confusing without an explanation in light of the foregoing statement: The alternating current developed by the alternator is changed to direct current by elements within the machine called rectifier diodes. Since batteries supply direct current, they can be recharged only with direct current.

We speak of the 12-volt direct-current system from the battery and of the 120-volt alternating-current system from the pier. What are these "volts" that apply equally to DC and to AC?

The *volt* is the unit of electrical "pressure." The 120-volt circuit has ten times the pressure of the 12-volt circuit, ten times the ability to force an electric current to flow. The small flashlight cell produces 1½ volts; even if it were made very much larger, its voltage would remain the same. One cell of the lead-acid storage battery commonly found on boats registers 2 volts; increase its size by any amount and it would still be only 2 volts. In both batteries the terminal voltage is dependent upon chemical action and is independent of size. However, in both cases the enlarged size would increase the ampere capacity of the battery, its ability to do work.

An *ampere* is a unit indicating the strength of an electric current. By way of perspective, the small light bulbs illuminating the instrument console draw perhaps 1 ampere, the starting motor turning over a big engine could easily require 300 amperes. Amperes govern the size of the wire needed in a circuit; the greater the number of amperes, the thicker the required wire. This is the reason for the comparatively thin wire to the console lights and for the very heavy cable to the starting motor.

The *watt* is the unit of power. Multiply volts by amperes and the answer is in watts. In the examples above, assuming a 12-volt battery, the light bulbs consume 12 watts while the starting motor gulps 3,600 watts. (The latter is a theoretical figure because in actuality the battery voltage would drop below 12 volts because of the heavy load.)

Note that the watt is a unit of power and *not* of work. Power does not become work until it is expended over a period of time. Thus 1 watt, doing work for 1 hour, becomes a watt-hour. If the starting motor were kept cranking for ten seconds, the work done would be 36,000 watt-*seconds*, which, dividing by 3,600 to change seconds to hours, would be the equivalent of 10 watt-hours.

Just as water flowing through a pipe meets resistance caused by the pipe diameter, so also does an electric current encounter resistance determined by the nature of its path through the circuit. The less the wire diameter, the greater the resistance, just as with the pipe. However, reducing the diameter of the wire is not the only way that resistance to electric-current flow can be created. A change in the material of the wire turns the trick; Nichrome, for instance, offers many times the resistance of copper.

The unit of electrical resistance is the *ohm*. When the volt, the ampere and the ohm are taken together, simple calculations may easily be made to solve many electrical problems aboard. The basic interrelation of these three units is called Ohm's law and is illustrated in Figure 8-2. How much current will a device require whose voltage and resistance are known? The answer is available by ordinary arithmetic.

$$I = \text{CURRENT} \qquad E = I \times R$$
$$R = \text{RESISTANCE} \qquad I = \frac{E}{R} \qquad \left.\vphantom{\begin{matrix}1\\1\\1\end{matrix}}\right\} \text{OHM'S LAW}$$
$$E = \text{VOLTAGE} \qquad R = \frac{E}{I}$$

Figure 8-2. The simplicity of Ohm's Law is apparent from these three arithmetic relationships. When any two quantities are known, the third is found easily. Example: When 12 volts are applied, a certain device takes 1/2 ampere. Its resistance must be 24 ohms (12 divided by 1/2 equals 24).

Perhaps the most important phenomenon for the skipper to understand is how electricity is generated by mechanical means. Once this is understood, generators, starting motors, bilge pumps and a host of other motor-driven gadgets lose their mystery.

It is all based on magnetism and motion. A permanent magnet has an invisible magnetic field around it. A wire carrying an electric current has a similar field. If this wire is wound around an iron core, the field will be intensified both by the number of turns and by the iron. The wire-wound iron is an electromagnet and in its many possible forms becomes the heart of many electrical devices ranging from meters to motors. (See Figure 8-3.)

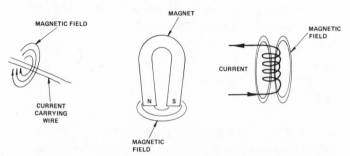

Figure 8-3. The passage of electric current always creates a magnetic field. This field encircles a wire, emanates from a coil. A similar field exudes from the poles of a magnet.

If now a wire is moved through any of these magnetic fields, an electric voltage will be generated, and if the circuit is completed, an electric current will flow. The reason is the influence of the magnetic field upon the electrons in the wire, causing them to move in one direction. As already stated, an electron flow is an electric current. Figure 8-4 illustrates how this happens.

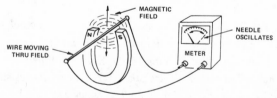

Figure 8-4. This simple experiment proves that moving a conductor through a magnetic field generates electric current.

In the terminology of the science, a wire moving through a magnetic field is said to "cut the lines of force." It is immaterial whether the magnetic field moves, the wire moves or both move; the important thing is that there be relative motion so that the lines of force are cut. The voltage developed will depend on the number of wires cutting the field, the speed of the cutting and the strength of the field.

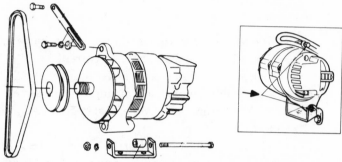

Figure 8-5. Details of generator or alternator mounting and drive are shown. The arrow in the insert points to the two bolts with which the drive is tightened. (Lehman Power Corporation)

The inside story of an electric generator is shown schematically in Figure 8-5. The electromagnets on each side of the rotor are the *poles* and constitute the *field*. (Some small generators substitute permanent magnets for the wound electromagnets.) The rotor is the *armature*, and the cylindrical contact plates at its end are the *commutator*. In the demonstration model illustrated there are only two commutator segments; an actual machine would have many. The *brushes* permit electrical contact with the rotating commutator.

Spinning the armature causes its wires to cut the lines of magnetic force, and this, by prior explanation, results in the generation of an electric current. The faster the spin, the higher the voltage. A stronger field or more wires on the armature would also boost the voltage. Connecting a load between the two terminals, as shown in the drawing, completes the circuit, and current will flow as long as mechanical work is being expended to turn the armature.

The commutator is always found on direct-current machines and serves to identify them. The commutator fulfills a very special purpose in a generator; without it direct current could not be delivered. The segments continually allow the brushes to make contact only with those wires in which current is flowing in the direction needed to maintain a direct current. If the commutator were replaced by two *slip rings*, as shown in the added drawing, the output would be alternating current. The reason for all this is that the wires cut the magnetic field downward during half a turn and upward during the other half with consequent changes in polarity.

A transformer makes use of the principle of a conductor cutting a magnetic field, yet it has no moving parts. Only the magnetic field moves. One winding, the primary, is energized by an electric current, and this establishes a magnetic field. The current is cut off, and the field collapses. As the field collapses, it cuts through the wires of the other winding, the secondary, and induces a voltage. This alternate expansion and contraction of the magnetic field can be induced by switching the current on and off, as by the breaker points in the ignition system, or by an alternating current, which itself is constantly pulsating. A transformer cannot function on uninterrupted direct current.

The transformer is employed both to raise the voltage from primary to secondary and also, in some cases, to lower it. The output voltage is determined by the ratio of primary turns of winding to secondary turns. Three times as many turns in the secondary, for instance, as in the primary, produces an output voltage three times that applied to the primary. In the case of the ignition coil, which is a form of transformer, the ratio of secondary to primary is so great that the initial pressure of 12 volts is multiplied as much as several thousand times. (See Figure 8-6.)

In electrical parlance, the device upon which current is expended is referred to as the *load*. The load can be almost anything electrical. On a boat the load would include light bulbs, small pumps, radios, depth sounders, horns and perhaps other things on the battery circuit and air-conditioners and stoves on the alternating-current line. Small refrigerators and small television receivers are often built and connected to operate on both low-voltage direct current and high-voltage alternating current.

Loads can be connected to the source of power either in *series* or in *parallel*. The drawing in Figure 8-7 explains this. Associating series with a chain and parallel with a ladder will fix the scheme in the memory. A series string of electric bulbs would be like the links of a chain with the current going through each unit to the next one. The same lamps connected in parallel would assume the configuration of the rungs of a ladder, each bulb being a rung and all connected to the two side rails or wires.

Both series and parallel connections have their reasons and their advantages. In the series connection, the required final voltage is the sum of all the individual voltage ratings of the bulbs, but the current in amperes needed is that of only one bulb. The parallel hookup keeps the voltage down to the rating for one bulb but raises the total current drawn to the sum of all the individual currents. One disadvantage of the series connection is that if one bulb fails, all bulbs go out. This follows naturally, since the current must traverse each bulb as it goes down the line.

The series/parallel options present many possibilities. Two 6-volt bulbs, for example, may be placed in series and be powered by a 12-volt battery. The same battery can operate a number of bilge pumps, lights or whatever, each rated at 12 volts, if all are connected in parallel. It is even possible to combine the series and the parallel into the series-parallel, as shown in Figure 8-7.

Open the switch controlling a light bulb and the spark is minimal, often imperceptible. Open the switch to a

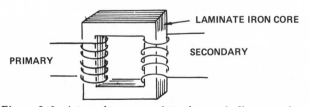

Figure 8-6. *A transformer consists of two windings, a primary and a secondary, on an iron core. The core may take any of several forms.*

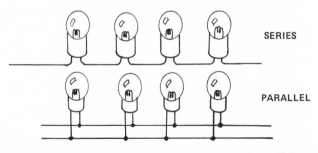

Figure 8-7. *The difference between series and parallel connections is shown here. One lamp failing in the series connection extinguishes them all; in the parallel mode, it does not.*

transformer or a motor and the spark is strong. Why? The lamp is a docile, resistive load, but the transformer and motor are inductive loads, meaning wire wound, with a kick. It's those collapsing lines of magnetic force again, boosting the voltage, and the resultant spark, as they cut the windings when the switch is opened. An *inductor* is an electrical coil, and the unit of inductance is the *henry*.

The *farad* (the unit of electrostatic capacity) is a more familiar term aboard because the capacitors that squelch the radio noise from alternators, generators and voltage regulators are rated in microfarads, or millionths of one farad. An additional important rating of capacitors and condensers is the highest voltage to which they may be exposed without breakdown. This voltage rating should never be exceeded; it is even wiser to restrict capacitors to circuits operating at well below this voltage.

Electricity in knowledgeable hands is a willing slave; used carelessly or ignorantly, it can be a destructive demon. Safeguards are a necessary part of every circuit, especially on a boat, which, in many ways, is more vulnerable to electrical trouble than a home on land. Fuses and circuit breakers are the common protective devices. Properly installed, both will open the circuit before shorted wires or failed appliances can cause damage or fire.

The fuse is the purposely chosen weak link in the circuit. The fusible link in the fuse can take the form of wire or strip, and it is designed to conduct no more than the number of amperes for which it is marked. Current in excess of this melts the link. Once "blown," the fuse must be replaced after the circuit difficulty has been corrected. Fuses are manufactured in screw-in type (plug) and clip-in type (cartridge). The latter is preferred for marine use and is shown in Figure 8-8.

Circuit breakers provide continuous protection because they may be reset after a "blow" and need not be replaced as fuses must be. Circuit breakers function either thermally or magnetically. If the rated current is exceeded in a thermal breaker, an internal sensor becomes hot and releases the internal switch. Excess current through the magnetic type increases the strength of an internal electromagnet which opens the internal

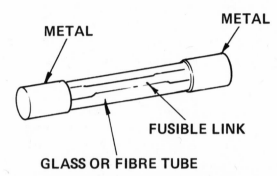

Figure 8-8. A fuse acts as a "safety valve" in an electric circuit. An overload current melts the fusible link.

switch. Both are preferred in the so-called trip free construction, which prevents forcible maintenance of the circuit when the breaker has opened it. See the cross-sectional drawing of a circuit breaker in Figure 8-9.

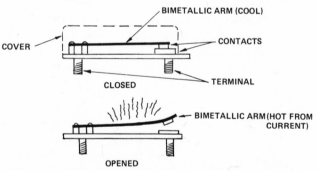

Figure 8-9. How a thermal circuit breaker functions is explained by these two sketches. Passage of abnormal current heats the bimetallic strip sufficiently to bend it away from the contact and open the circuit.

Of course, the actual alternator or generator provided on the propulsion engine for keeping the battery charged is more complicated than the skeletal illustration in Figure 8-5. Modern marine engines have standardized on the alternator in preference to the generator. There are two main reasons for this. One is the greater simplicity of the alternator because it eliminates the commutator, which has often been a source of trouble because the

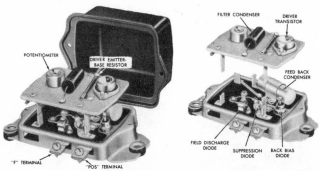

Figure 8-10. The voltage regulator maintains the output of the generator or alternator at a level sufficient to meet the needs of battery and load. Shown is a modern electronic transistorized type. (Detroit Diesel)

vulnerable brushes must carry the heavy output current. The second is that the alternator can supply charging current to the battery at a much lower engine speed than the generator requires. Not unimportant is the fact that alternators are more compact and less expensive to build.

The output voltage of both generator and alternator would climb to dangerous levels when engine speed is increased unless some automatic regulation were provided. Hence a voltage regulator is a necessary part of every battery-charging installation.

As noted earlier, the output voltage is determined by the speed of rotation, by the number of turns on the windings and by the strength of the magnetic field. Of these, the easiest to control is the magnetic field, and this is what the voltage regulator does. As the engine speeds up, the field is weakened by reducing the current feeding it; when the engine slows down, the field is strengthened by increasing the current. The voltage regulator does this automatically at all engine speeds, and thus the output voltage to the battery is kept to the designed value.

The voltage regulator continually samples the output voltage of the alternator or generator. It does this by means of an electromagnet wound with very fine wire which remains connected across the output circuit. Changes in magnetic strength caused by variations in voltage have the effect of switching in or out several resistors contained in the regulator case. These resistors affect the current through the field winding.

Although the nominal value of the battery circuit is 12 volts, the charging voltage must be higher in order to force current back into the battery. (See Chapter 16.) The usual setting of the voltage regulator is 14.3 volts, and when the charging circuit reaches this point, the charging stops because the battery is full. A schematic drawing of a voltage regulator is shown in Figure 8-10.

Older installations that depend on generators instead of the more modern alternators include a "cutout." This is a magnetic switch, usually contained in the voltage regulator case, that disconnects the battery when the engine stops. Without this, the battery would discharge itself into the stationary generator, to the detriment of both. Alternator installations do not require cutouts be-

cause the self-contained rectified diodes prevent reverse flow of battery current.

Problems arise whenever heavy current must be drawn through brushes riding on a revolving surface, as is the case with the direct-current generator. The alternator can be constructed so that the output current is a solid wire connection *without* brushes. The brushes in the modern alternator carry only the minimal current needed to excite the rotating field. Incidentally, the heavy current output winding is stationary and is called the *stator*, and the rotating field winding is the *rotor*.

The stator winding in present marine engine alternators consists of three coils connected together at one end. The three coil terminals and the common terminal feed into the integral bank of diodes that rectify the alternating current to direct current. The rotor is the source of the magnetic field that cuts the stator when the machine is turned. The rotor receives its current via the two brushes and the collector rings. All this is shown in Figure 8-11.

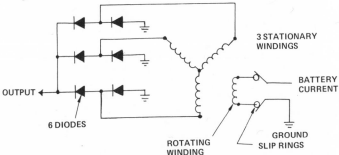

Figure 8-11. The voltage in an alternator is generated in three stationary windings, connected together in a Y configuration as shown, and located around a central rotating winding that supplies the magnetic field. The voltage generated is alternating; self-contained diodes rectify it to direct current for battery charging.

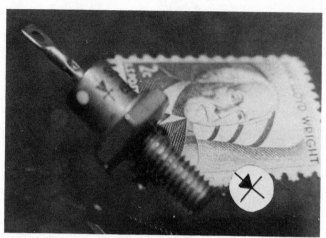

Figure 8-12. *The small, semi-conductor power diode shown above is able to carry a current of 20 amperes. The symbol used on wiring diagrams to denote a diode is shown in the insert. The arrow is the anode, the line below the cathode.*

Figure 8-13. *The basic starting motor circuit consists of two branches, one of smaller gauge wire carrying light current and the other of larger diameter cable carrying heavy current. These are shown by light and dark lines respectively. The groundings indicated take place through the metal of the engine. (Lehman Power Corporation)*

Diodes may be considered to be electrical one-way valves. They permit current to flow in one direction and cut it off when polarity reverses. Consequently, alternating current passed through diodes becomes a pulsating direct current suitable for battery charging. A diode is a semiconductor device devoid of moving parts; it is an important component of solid-state electronics. (See Figure 8-12.)

Direct-current machines can function either as generators or as motors. If current is fed into them, they will develop a turning force and do work. If they are driven by an outside force, current can be taken from their terminals. Theoretically, the same is true of alternators; they can function as motors, but the scheme is more complicated.

The generator or alternator on the propulsion engine is not running for free but is consuming power in proportion to the current being generated. As an arithmetical example: Assume that the battery is receiving all the current generated at the rate of 30 amperes at 14 volts.

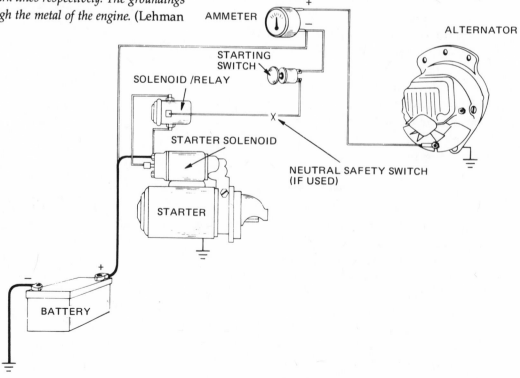

Multiplying these two figures equals 420 watts. Since 746 watts is equivalent to 1 horsepower, in this case 0.563 horsepower is being drawn from the engine.

The cranking system of an internal combustion engine depends upon a compact starting motor designed to deliver tremendous amounts of power for very short periods of time. Under most conditions the starting motor is energized for only two or three seconds, and this is enough to start the engine. A cranking period of fifteen seconds, for instance, would be considered extremely long, would probably heat the motor unduly and would indicate a malfunction in the engine.

The current of several hundred amperes drawn by the starting motor requires heavy contacts and could not possibly be handled by the usual ignition switch. The problem is solved by the solenoid switch located atop the starting motor; it is a form of relay. Now the ignition switch need handle only the nominal current that actuates the solenoid. The solenoid, in turn, completes the circuit through the heavy cables to the starting motor. The drawing in Figure 8-13 shows the connections.

The starting motor must engage the flywheel of the engine only until the engine fires and starts and then must immediately disengage itself. Failure to disengage itself would subject the starting motor to dangerously high speeds that would ruin it. The engaging and disengaging are accomplished in a variety of ways on different engines.

The rim of the engine flywheel has gear teeth; the small pinion at the end of the starting motor shaft has similar gear teeth. These two gears mesh to start the engine. The fact that the motor gear is small and the engine gear is large gives the starting motor great mechanical advantage. This relationship is also the reason why the starting motor would be spun at extremely high speed if there were no disengagement.

In one method of engagement/disengagement, the starter pinion is pushed into meshing with the flywheel by the same solenoid that makes the electrical contact. When the ignition switch is released, the pinion is returned by a spring. Another method makes use of a spiral track cut into the starter shaft to move the pinion forward and back. An overrunning clutch protects the motor from excessive speed after its work is done. There are also variations of these methods. The illustration in Figure 8-14 clarifies the action.

Figure 8-14. Some starter solenoids, (A) common on outboard motors, do not shift the starting motor pinion but simply make contact between starter and battery. (Johnson Motors)

The various components of a typical starting motor are shown in this exploded view (B). The solenoid responds to the starting switch and not only connects the motor to the battery but also brings the starter pinion to mesh with the flywheel. (Lehman Power Corporation)

(A)

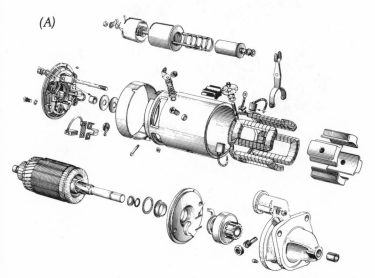

(B)

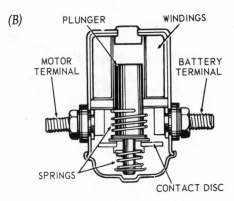

With motors as with generators, functioning depends upon the interaction of magnetic fields. In the motor the magnetic fields act upon the rotor to turn it; in the generator the rotor is turned by outside forces and reacts upon the field to produce electricity.

The foregoing discussion has concerned itself with the boat's direct-current system, which usually operates at 12 volts. All but the smallest vessels have an additional electrical system that functions on alternating current at 110 and 220 volts. This system is fed either from the shore power receptacles on the pier or from an onboard generating set when under way. The home-style electrical appliances aboard would derive their power from the alternating-current system.

It is customary to have a special receptacle on the outside deck for the complementary cable that leads to the pier and connects to the shore power. This receptacle is male, and the matching cable end is female. Receptacles intended for various maximum currents have different prong arrangements that prevent all but the correct cable from being plugged in. Figure 8-15 illustrates receptacle and cable.

Wires from the outside shore cable receptacle supply power to the main alternating-current distribution panel. This contains the fuses and circuit breakers for the various high-voltage circuits radiating from it. The output of an onboard alternating-current generating plant would also be brought to this panel. It is not permissible to combine the low-voltage direct-current circuits and the alternating-current circuits in the same panel box; it is mandatory that they be separate.

One conductor in the shore cable is purposely maintained at ground potential, although it carries current; it is usually referred to as the "neutral" conductor. A separate grounding wire, usually green, which is *not* permitted to carry current, is also often included in the cable. Its purpose is to ground metal panel boxes and metal enclosures of appliances. Controversy surrounds the desirability of this latter wire on boats, and this is explained in Chapter 8.

The 12-volt system is incapable of inflicting a shock on anyone touching an open terminal carelessly. By contrast, the 120/240-volt alternating-current system can cause a lethal shock under the right accidental conditions.

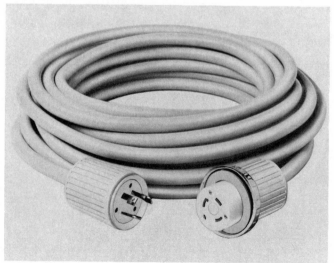
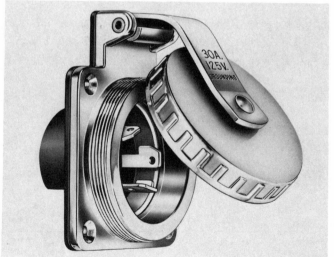

Figure 8-15. The power inlet receptacle, mounted conveniently on the hull, accepts the shore power cable and connects the boat with the electricity on the pier. The twisting locking arrangement assures a positive connection. (Hubbell)

Obviously, great care must be exercised both in installing and in handling the high-voltage circuits.

It is even more important to keep the high-voltage lines clear of any possible contact with bilge water than to follow the same precaution with the low-voltage direct-current lines. All receptacles and plugs that are exposed to the weather should be the waterproof type. High- and low-voltage wires should not be intermingled in the same harness nor run together in any conduit.

Common sense and remembering that larger currents need larger wires will go a long way toward ensuring a good electrical installation. Electric wires are rated by the Brown & Sharpe (B&S) gauge, and this can be confusing because gauge numbers and wire diameters run con-

versely. A #60 wire is finer than a human hair while a #0000 (pronounced four-oh) is a pretty sturdy piece of metal. The wire tables in Figure 8-16 should provide enlightenment on this.

Each branch of the alternating-current system should be assessed at the maximum current it will require to operate the devices attached to it; the totals determine the wire sizes needed. Lamp bulbs are marked with their wattage, and, by the earlier-mentioned Ohm's law, watts divided by volts equals amperes. Heating appliances and motorized devices carry nameplates with wattage and often with amperes as well. Bear in mind that motor-starting current is always greater than the running current. Additional information on current requirements is

CHARACTERISTICS OF CONDUCTORS

WIRE SIZE	AREA CIRCULAR MILLS	OHMS PER 1000 FT. 25° C or 77° F.	BARE COPPER POUNDS PER 1000 FT.	ALLOWABLE AMPACITIES OF INSULATED COPPER CONDUCTORS - Based on Ambient Temperature of 30° C (86° F). For additional details, refer to the National Electrical Code (NEC) Tables 3 10-16 through 3 10-19.		
				3 Conductors or less in raceway or cable Type T, TW, ot UF.	Copper conductor in free air Type T, ot TW	4 through 6 in raceway or cable Type T, TW, ot UF
14	4,109	2.575	12.43	15	20	12
12	6,520	1.6 19	19.77	20	25	16
10	10,380	1.018	31.43	30	40	24
8	16,510	.641	49.98	40	55	32
6	26,240	.410	79.46	55	80	44
4	41,740	.259	126.4	70	105	56
2	66,360	.162	205.0	95	140	76
1	83,690	.129	258.0	110	165	88
0	105,560	.102	326.0	125	195	100
00	133,080	.0811	411.0	145	225	116
000	167,770	.0642	518.0	165	260	132
0000	211,600	.0509	640.5	195	300	156

Figure 8-16. Each size of electrical conductor has a limit to the number of amperes of current it may carry safely. This limit is necessary because the passage of current creates heat. The table above shows the ratings for copper wire in sizes from No. 14 to No. 0000 gauge. (Onan Corp.)

H.P.	115 V 1 PHASE AC		230 V 1 PHASE AC		120 VDC		240 VDC	
	A	W	A	W	A	W	A	W
1/6	4.4	14	2.2	14				
1/4	5.8	14	2.9	14	3.1	14	1.6	14
1/3	7.2	14	3.6	14	4.1	14	2.0	14
1/2	9.8	14	4.9	14	5.4	14	2.7	14
3/4	13.8	12	6.9	14	7.6	14	3.8	14
1	16.0	12	8.0	14	9.5	14	4.7	14
1-1/2	20.0	10	10.0	14	13.2	12	6.6	14
2	24	10	12.0	14	17.0	10	8.5	14
3	34	6	17.0	10	25.0	8	12.2	12
5	56	4	28.0	8	40.0	6	20.0	10
7-1/2	80	1	40.0	6	58.0	3	29.0	8
10	100	0	50.0	4	76.0	2	38.0	6

(A)

Motor Size	Starting	Running
1/6 horsepower..........	900 watts	200 watts
1/4 horsepower...........	1300 watts	300 watts
1/3 horsepower...........	1500 watts	360 watts
1/2 horsepower...........	2200 watts	520 watts
3/4 horsepower...........	3400 watts	775 watts
1 horsepower...........	4000 watts	1000 watts

(B)

Figure 8-17. The table above (A) shows the number of amperes of current that motors of various horsepowers will draw from the pier (or from an onboard generator). These are the running currents; starting currents could be almost twice as much. Recommended wire sizes are given. The power requirements depicted at (B) are for capacitor-start motors. Repulsion-induction motors require less power than split phase motors. (Onan Corp.)

given in Figure 8-17. Not only wires but fuses and circuit breakers must also be matched to current. Careful attention to current, wire size and fuse and breaker ratings is equally important for the 12-volt system.

Electric wires are supplied with various types of insulation, and each is intended for a specific use. The tables in Figure 8-18 list the insulations and the American Boat and Yacht Council recommended respective services. The limiting temperatures to which the insulations may be exposed are well above any that should be found on a safe boat.

The wiring on most marina piers will follow the scheme shown in Figure 8-19. It will consist of two "hot" wires, a "neutral" wire and possibly also a "ground" wire.

How the shore power cable from a boat can abstract either 120-volt current or 240-volt current is explained by the diagram. Often the pier terminal box will not have a receptacle from which 240-volt current can be taken directly, but the higher voltage can be had nevertheless by a "siamese" connection to A and B. This is also shown.

Nonpolarized plugs on the 120-volt shore cable make it possible to get a reversed connection with consequent reversed polarity to the boat. This could mean that the supposed neutral wire becomes a hot wire, and in some installations this could be undesirable. Polarity indicators are available that automatically warn of such a condition by light or sound or both. The connecting plug should be reversed when this warning occurs. Some polarity indi-

COLOR	ITEM	USE
Yellow w/Red Stripe (YR)	Starting Circuit	Starting Switch to Solenoid
Yellow (Y)	Generator or Alternator Field	Generator or Alternator Field to Regulator Field Terminal
	Bilge Blowers	Fuse or Switch to Blowers
Dark Gray (Gy)	Navigation Lights	Fuse or Switch to Lights
	Tachometer	Tachometer Sender to Gauge
Brown (Br)	Generator Armature	Generator Armature to Regulator
	Alternator Charge Light	Generator Terminal/Alternator Auxiliary Terminal to Light to Regulator
	Pumps	Fuse or Switch to Pumps
Orange (O)	Accessory Feed	Ammeter to Alternator or Generator Output and Accessory Fuses or Switches
	Accessory Common Feed	Distribution Panel to Accesory Switch
Purple (Pu)	Ignition	Ignition Switch to Coil and Electrical Instruments
	Instrument Feed	Distribution Panel to Electric Instruments
Dark Blue	Cabin and Instrument Lights	Fuse or Switch to Lights
Light Blue (Lt Bl)	Oil Pressure	Oil Pressure Sender to Gauge
Tan	Water Temperature	Water Temperature Sender to Gauge
Pink (Pk)	Fuel Gauge	Fuel Gauge Sender to Gauge

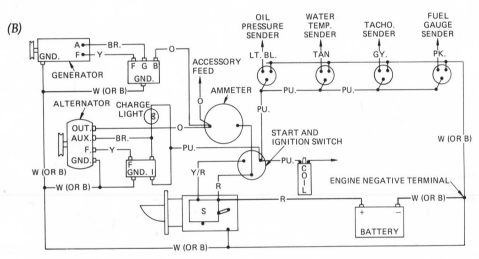

Figure 8-18. The color coding for low voltage direct current wiring aboard recommended by the American Boat & Yacht Council is shown in this table at (A). How these colors apply to a typical boat wiring system is explained at (B). Note that both alternator and generator are included in the diagram for explanatory purposes; only one would be used in an actual installation.

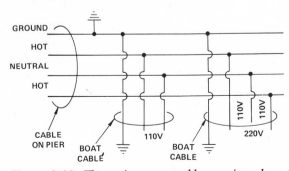

Figure 8-19. The main power cable running along the pier contains four wires and is polarized as shown. Boat shore cables contain either three or four wires and all have a green ground. The three-wire boat lines deliver 110 volts; the four-wire boat cables supply both 110 volts and 220 volts.

cators are installed as a permanent part of the system; others, like the one shown in Figure 8-20, are merely plugged into an outlet.

A simple changeover switch connects the boat alternating-current system either to the pier or to an onboard generator. This makes it impossible to have both power sources on line at the same time. It would be disastrous if both attempted to work together. (See Chapter 6.)

It is recommended practice to have all switches aboard in the "off" position before the shore cable is either connected or disconnected. This prevents ruinous arcing at the plug. The same practice is recommended for the

onboard generator to prevent sudden acquiring or dumping of the total load, a bad procedure for the machine.

The early days of boating saw many nondescript electric power outlets on marina piers. Getting hooked up often turned into a game of chance. Today's outlets are fairly well standardized and so coded that a wrong connection possibility is rare. Figure 8-21 shows modern standard forms of outlet receptacles.

Electricity is a slave that responds to intelligent treatment and willingly becomes the skipper's strong helper. The principles discussed in this chapter provide the means for command.

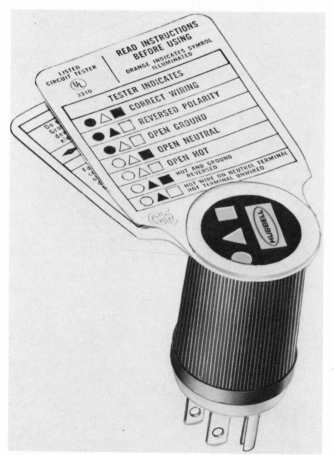

Figure 8-20. *Plugging this device into any receptacle gives an immediate reading of the condition of the power line and indicates the nature of any trouble.* (Hubbell)

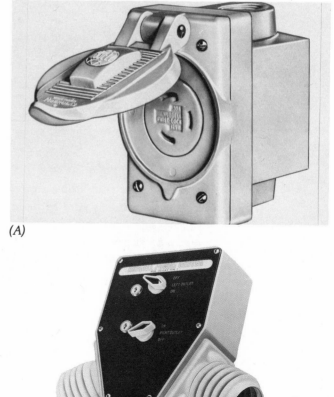

(A)

(B)

Figure 8-21. *(A) & (B) These modern power outlet fittings may be encountered on marina piers. Both are weatherproof and convenient for a quick hookup.* (Hubbell)

9. Fuel Systems

The joy of boating, the thrill of listening to the humming song of a powerful engine, can be dulled somewhat by the necessary evil of purchasing the fuel and storing it safely. Purchasing becomes less and less a pleasure as the prices on the fuel pumps grow larger. Storage itself does not cause inroads on the pocketbook, but it does create the responsibility of preventing fire and pollution.

Obviously, safety is the main consideration when dealing with a system containing a highly flammable liquid, and the need for safeguards is emphasized by the potentially harmful conditions that exist in the marine environment. The goal is achieved by careful design in two directions. One is correct selection of the materials for each component of the fuel system. The other is a solid installation that permits accessibility for inspection and preventive maintenance and resists the inertial forces generated by the rolling of the ship in a seaway.

The fuel system extends from a filling opening on an outside deck to the intake manifold of the engine. The system comprises deck fixtures, piping, tanks, valve filters and finally the carburetor on a gasoline engine or the injector pump on a diesel engine. Working within this system may be electrical or mechanical devices such as fuel capacity gauges, remotely operated shutoff valves and perhaps even gadgets that keep tabs on the gallons-per-mile appetite of the engine. Figure 9-1 is a diagrammatic representation of an average fuel system as installed.

Except for outboard motors with their own portable containers, fuel aboard is stored in tanks. These tanks may be independent vessels securely fastened to the hull, or else they may be built integrally with the hull. The latter are not considered the best practice and are permitted only with diesel fuel—and are frowned upon even then. The materials of which fuel tanks are constructed include aluminum, monel, iron, variously coated steels and also fiberglass. The last lends itself well to integral construction into fiberglass hulls, but it is acceptable only for diesel fuel, not for gasoline.

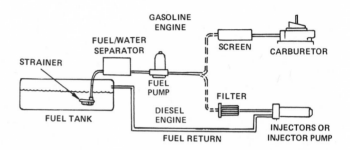

Figure 9-1. The basic components of the fuel systems for gasoline engines and for diesel engines are shown diagrammatically. Note the fuel return line which is unique to diesel systems.

Tanks made of fiberglass require special consideration to the manner in which pipe fittings are attached. The drawing in Figure 9-2 illustrates some of the special provisions that must be made in deference to the nature of the basic material. Bosses (extra thicknesses) of fiberglass are placed wherever a fitting is to be attached. The screws, bolts or rivets that hold these plumbing pieces in place must then be covered over with fiberglass. The purpose of this extra precaution is to prevent leakage of fuel or seepage of vapors through the fastening holes.

Filled fuel tanks are a concentrated weight, usually the

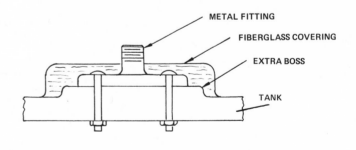

Figure 9-2. The recommended method of attaching fittings to fiberglass tanks is illustrated above. The overall covering of fiberglass prevents leaks through the bolt holes.

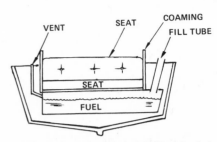

Figure 9-3. Fuel is prevented from spilling back into the boat because fill tube and vent are both outside the coaming.

heaviest single mass aboard except for the engines. As such, fuel tanks have a strong effect upon the trim of the ship. From a purely theoretical standpoint of their effect on trim, fuel tanks would ideally be located just above the keel and along it, but this is impossible in a practical commercial boat design. Alternate locations vary with the designer's choice of interior space use.

A favorite solution places one tank against the port side of the hull and another against the starboard side, both approximately amidship. Often, each such tank feeds only its neighboring engine in a twin installation. It is assumed that the two engines will drink equally and that therefore trim will be maintained. Frequently an equalizing pipe will connect the two tanks to prevent unequal fuel content, which could cause a list.

Preferably, the sides of tanks installed in this manner should not be flush against the hull. An air space should exist so that good air circulation can take place at all times. The bonus will be a reduction in the tendency to corrode through otherwise trapped moisture and the ability to inspect a large area of the tank with minimal difficulty.

Some larger boats fill the space between two adjacent transverse bulkheads from side to side with fuel tanks.

This tank assemblage then forms the forward or after end of the engine room and shields the adjoining space from noise and heat. Such tanks are also equalized, commonly with multiple valves that allow the skipper to adjust the contents of the various sections and thus control his trim. Installations of this kind are almost always diesel and not gasoline.

Small boats with permanent fuel tank installations can often make use of the athwartship configuration. One method is shown in Figure 9-3. In this case the tank is fitted under the two forward seats; its low contour makes this possible without interference. The fill pipe extends to the outer deck on one side, and the vent pipe runs to the opposite outside deck. The provisions that spilled fuel go overboard and vapors not reenter the boat are thus met.

Safety codes specify the required thickness of the various tank materials for given capacities and the types of welding that may be used in manufacture. Figure 9-4 lists this information and shows that alloys of copper are held in high regard as tank material. This does not exclude other materials but puts the burden of proving

FUEL TANK CORROSION RESISTANCE REQUIREMENTS

MATERIAL	SPECIFICATION	MINIMUM NOMINAL SHEET THICKNESS	GAUGE	WELDING PROCESSES (1)
Nickel-Copper	ASTM – B127 Class A	.031 in.	22 U.S. std.	Resistance Seam Inert Gas Shielded Arc, Oxy-acetylene
Copper-Nickel	ASTM – B122	.045 in.	17 A.W.G.	Inert Gas Shielded Arc, Oxy-acetylene Resistance
Copper (2)	ASTM – B152 Type E.T.P.	.057 in.	15 A.W.G.	Inert Gas Shielded Arc, Carbon Arc, Oxy-acetylene
Copper-Silicon	ASTM – B97 Types A, B & G	.050 in.	16 A.W.G.	Inert Gas Shielded Arc, Carbon Arc, Oxy-acetylene Metal-arc
Steel Sheet (3)	ASTM – A93	.0747 in.	14 Mfrs.	Metal-arc, Oxy-acetylene, Inert Gas Shielded Arc, Resistance
Aluminized Steel (6)	ASTM – A463	.0478 in.	18 Mfrs.	Metal-arc, Oxy-acetylene, Inert Gas Shielded Arc, Resistance
Terneplate Steel (5) (6)	ASTM – A308	.0478 in.	18 Mfrs.	Resistance
Aluminum (4)	Alloy 5052 or 5083 or 5086	.090 in.	—	Inert Gas Shielded Arc, Resistance

NOTES:

(1)   Tank seams produced by the welding processes listed shall be ductile and non-porous.

(2)   Copper tanks shall be internally tin coated.

(3)   Steel Sheet tanks, when constructed for gasoline, shall be galvanized inside and outside by the "hot-dip" process. Tanks intended for use with fuel oil shall not be internally galvanized.

(4)   Aluminum tank fittings are recommended to be made of 6061–T6 Aluminum or 300 series Stainless Steel.

(5)   Terneplate Steel tanks shall have a 12 lb. coating – minimum of 0.35 ounces lead per square foot by triple spot test.

(6)   Terneplate Steel tanks and Aluminized Steel tanks shall have a corrosion inhibiting baked paint or equivalent coating not less than .0015 in. thickness applied to the total tank exterior.

Figure 9-4. The materials for the construction of fuel tanks recommended by the American Boat & Yacht Council are listed above. Welding instructions also are given, together with permitted usage of the tanks.

their fitness up to the maker. Tanks for diesel fuel are always considered separately because of the possible chemical effect of the fuel's sulfur content; iron, steel and nickel-copper are recommended materials.

Tanks are normally made of several sections of sheet metal cut to the correct shape and fastened together to produce the desired configuration. The joints must be tight, even to liquids under pressures higher than those encountered in normal service. Merely crimping and soft soldering to achieve this tightness is an unacceptable technique, although it is common in other fields. Seam welding and hard soldering are approved. The hard solder easily meets the specification that the seam-filling material must resist melting up to a temperature of 1800° F.

Liquid in tanks of large capacity can slosh badly when the boat is under way, and the resultant pounding on the tank ends can have the effect of hammer blows. Baffles are built into the tank to mitigate this source of possible damage. Accepted practice is to have these baffles no further than 30 inches from each other or from tank ends. The openings in the baffles are restricted to less than 30 percent of the tank's cross-sectional area. Of course, these baffles must be rigid; usually they serve a second purpose—that of strengthening the tank. Figure 9-5 illustrates this construction. An added safety rule is that the baffles may not trap fuel at the bottom and thus prevent complete emptying of the tank, nor should they trap fuel vapors at the top.

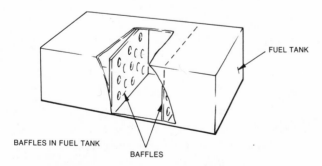

FUEL TANK

BAFFLES IN FUEL TANK

BAFFLES

Figure 9-5. Baffles located in a fuel tank are shown above. The baffles keep the liquid in the tank from sloshing heavily against the tank ends when the boat is in a seaway.

An object as apparently simple as a tank is nevertheless hedged about by strict specifications in the interest of safety. All other parts of the fuel system should be guarded with equal scrutiny. The universal adherence by builders to such extreme caution may be the reason why boat fires are rare. When the occasional fire does occur, investigation almost always points to operator negligence.

The rule that fuel tanks may not have any fittings in their bottoms eliminates the possibility that human forgetfulness could leave a drain cock open. All piping connections to or from the tank must be from the top with pickup and fill pipes extending internally almost to the bottom. The ends of these pipes are supported so that it is impossible for them to touch the bottom and close themselves off. Gauges and sensors, when used, are also introduced from the top of the tank.

Equally dangerous as an open drain cock would be a fuel line so installed that it would be subject to siphoning in the event of a break. Siphoning means that gravity would keep the open end spurting fuel until the tank went dry. Since gravity is the force that activates siphoning, the preventive lies in the manner in which the piping is laid out with reference to relative heights. No run of pipe may be lower than the bottom of the tank.

The fill pipe to the tank should originate in a tightly fitted metal deck plate. The location of the plate should be such that under no circumstances could spilled fuel flow into the boat; spillage must run overboard. A gasketed screw cover is desirable. If the connecting piping is nonmetallic, then an electric wire must ground the fill plate to the tank and eventually to the boat ground. The latter is a precaution against static electricity. Figure 9-6 shows the deck plate grounding connection, which could be of copper strip instead of wire.

Static electricity is often generated by the rapid flow of the fuel through the delivery hose. Without grounding, a spark at the nozzle could cause a fire. Proper fueling procedure requires that the nozzle be in contact with the deck plate before the dock pump is started. All static charges are carried harmlessly to ground if this is done.

Nonmetallic sections are perfectly acceptable in the fuel line if the electrical connections for grounding mentioned above are provided. Of course, the tubing ma-

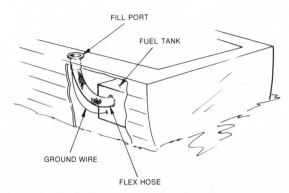

Figure 9-6. Gasoline flowing through a hose may create static electricity which could cause a spark. A preventive is to bridge the flexible hose connecting fill plate and tank with a grounding wire. The fuel pump nozzle is held in contact with the grounded fill plate while fueling to kill the static.

terial must be impervious to the fuel and in no way reactive with it. The diameter of hose on the filling side of the tank must be ample to allow reasonable speed in taking fuel aboard; one authority places the figure at 1½ inches. Most hose used for this purpose is internally reinforced with a metal spiral to prevent collapse, but heavy wall thickness alone could accomplish this safeguard. Hose sections between tank and engine can be of much smaller diameter.

The standard method of securing hose to metal fittings is with metal clamps, and this is acceptable in the fuel system. Well-established yachting practice holds that a single clamp can never be trusted; clamps should always be installed side by side in pairs. Clamps that tighten with positive screws should be used; clamps that rely solely on spring tension should not. Clamp width should be such that the comparatively soft material of the hose is not cut during tightening. A good point to remember is to align the clamp screws in a direction that permits easy retightening whenever needed.

The fuel path from the tank to the fuel filter and the engine should be through metal tubing, with cupronickel, nickel-copper and copper preferred for gasoline; steel is preferred for diesel. Fuel hose cannot be used exclusively for the entire line from tank to engine except in open boats where the entire installation is accessible and visible. Short lengths of reinforced nonmetallic hose are permitted to help the fuel line get around difficult locations in the hull.

Only flared fittings are allowed for making connections between metal tubing sections. The so-called pres-sure fittings that do not require the tubing to be flared are not acceptable. Only high-temperature hard solder may be employed in situations where permanent homogeneous connections need to be formed. While all these restrictions sound stringent, they are no more than a knowledgeable mechanic would follow instinctively. How flared fittings do their job is shown in Figure 9-7.

The fuel line should be attached solidly to the hull at a height well above any possible bilge water level. The connection to the engine becomes a transition to a vibrating mass, and this requires an approved flexible section. Old practice was to make a loop in the metal tubing to absorb the movement of the engine, but the flexible hose is far better. Metal in constant vibration can fail through a condition known as fatigue.

The flammable vapors that exist in a tank filled with volatile fuel must be disposed of safely. This chore is taken over by the vent line mentioned earlier. In addition to preventing reentry of the fumes into the boat, the vent outlet must be proof against seawater and rain.

It is recommended practice for valves to be installed in the fuel line at points where quick emergency shutoff is possible. The valves can be manual, with clear indications of the open and shut positions, or they may be electric and remotely operated. The latter are hooked into the ignition line and are open only during the time the ignition switch is on. Provision for manual operation of these electric valves is desirable in the event of current failure.

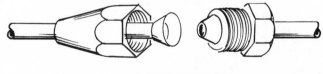

FLARED FITTINGS

Figure 9-7. The principle of flared tube fittings is shown in this illustration. The end of the tubing is flared to the same angle as the male portion of the fitting. Subsequent tightening of the two halves results in a leakproof joint.

None of the permanent fuel tanks aboard is permitted to be pressurized. In all installations the fuel is withdrawn by the suction either of a pump located on the engine or of a separate electric pump. The only pressurized fuel tanks in pleasure boat service are those in use with outboard motors, and these are portable.

Many skippers find it hard to believe that atmospheric pressure can collapse their fuel tanks if air cannot get in to replace the contents that are removed. If the vent pipe accidentally becomes clogged, the fuel pump will create a vacuum in the tank. This means that the natural atmospheric pressure on the outside is no longer balanced by the same pressure internally. Except for tanks with extremely heavy walls, the result is collapse or, at least, deformation.

In addition to the fuel line from tank to engine, diesel installations have a return line from the engine back to the tank. Such a return line is never used with gasoline engines. The unique method of feeding fuel to a diesel makes the return line necessary. Whereas the gasoline engine burns all the fuel fed to it, the diesel is fed an excess over what it needs to do the work in hand. This excess helps to cool the injectors and the injector pump before it is sent back to the tank via the return line. Figure 9-8 diagrams this.

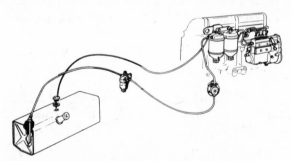

Figure 9-8. A typical fuel system for a diesel engine begins at the fuel tank, leads through primary filter, fuel pump and secondary filters to the injector pump. Note return fuel line, typical of diesel fuel systems. (Lehman Power Corporation)

The return line explains why it is more difficult to measure the fuel consumption of a diesel engine than to get the equivalent reading of a gasoline engine. The metering system designed for diesel use must be able to account for the unused fuel returned to the tank. This makes for a more complicated instrument and consequently a more expensive one.

Condensation is an enemy of all fuel systems that derive their power from liquid in a tank, but it becomes especially worrisome in the damp marine environment. The moisture in the air that enters the tank to replace the withdrawn fuel condenses on the colder metal walls and produces water. The water sinks to the bottom because it is heavier than the fuel and coalesces there into puddles. Theoretically, these puddles will do no harm if they stay out of the intake pipe. Actually, however, they are bound to be picked up to cause damage and stoppage as the boat rolls. Various additives are on the market that combine with the water and allow it to be expelled through the engine without harm. One way to fight condensation is to keep fuel tanks topped at all times.

Fuel gauges are common on the instrument panels of automobiles, yet such useful indicators are rare on the consoles of boats. One reason may be that the simple, inexpensive float device used on cars is not suited to marine use. The constant surging of the fuel in the tank would make the readings erratic. A more sophisticated method of monitoring fuel level is needed for boats, and again the marine version is more expensive. Many skippers depend on the old reliable yardstick marked off in gallons, but this basic "tool" can be used only where there are no bends in the fill pipe between deck plate and tank.

Despite the care taken by makers and vendors of fuel to keep it uncontaminated, minute debris of some kind inevitably enters. The first barrier to these contaminants is at the input of the pickup tube in the tank. It is a small metal screen such as shown in Figure 9-9. The opening in the tank top is large enough for withdrawing this screen

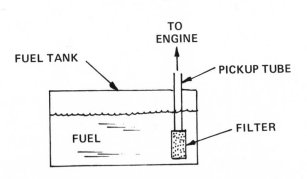

Figure 9-9. *A filter in the pickup tube in the fuel tank is the first barrier to foreign matter entering the fuel system.*

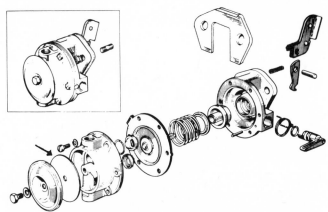

Figure 9-10. *The many parts that make up a heavy duty, diaphragm-type fuel pump are shown in this exploded view. The actual diaphragm is marked by an arrow.* (Lehman Power Corporation)

for inspection and cleaning. This tank screen serves as a preliminary check; the final word lies with the fuel filter just ahead of the engine.

The importance of the fuel filter in protecting the system from foreign matter cannot be overemphasized. Tiny particles of dirt loom large when compared with the minute jets in carburetors and injectors. Many a cruise has been saved by the little removable bowl at the bottom of a filter that collected debris before it could stop the engine.

Fuel pumps for gasoline engines are generally of the diaphragm type actuated by a cam. The pressure of delivered fuel is governed by the strength of the spring at

the diaphragm, and this is low enough to be shut off by the needle valve in the carburetor. In contrast, diesel engine fuel pumps are generally of the positive displacement type. Any attempt to shut off the output of such a pump with a valve would create damaging conditions, hence the return line mentioned above. (See Figure 9-10).

Injector pumps are one of the finest examples of extremely close tolerance manufacturing. Pistons and their cylinders are fitted to each other by a process of honing that keeps dimensions within a few *ten*-thousandths of one inch. These microscopic clearances are the reason for the constant caution about filters and cleanliness. (See Figure 9-11.)

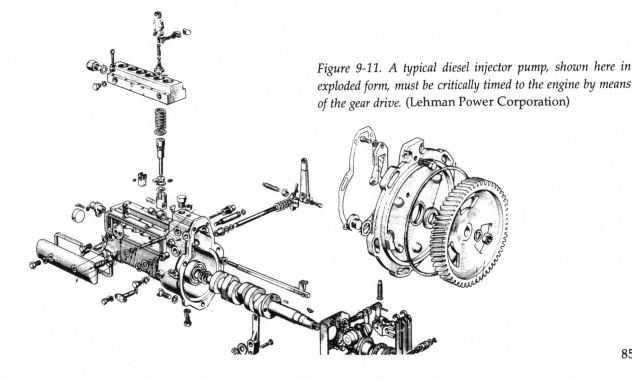

Figure 9-11. *A typical diesel injector pump, shown here in exploded form, must be critically timed to the engine by means of the gear drive.* (Lehman Power Corporation)

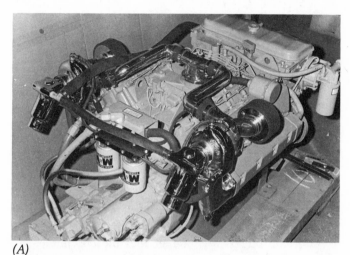

(A)

(B)

As explained elsewhere in the text, supercharging and turbocharging pack more fuel into the cylinder and thereby make it possible to draw more power from an engine. Turbocharging is the preferred method because the turbocharger is driven entirely by exhaust gases without the need for belts or gears. The exhaust gas drive has an inbuilt "regulating" feature that automatically adjusts the turbocharge to the load on the engine. Figure 9-12 shows a turbocharger.

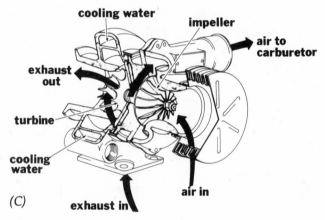

(C)

Figure 9-12. A turbocharger packs more charge into a cylinder than is possible by natural aspiration alone and thus increases the maximum horsepower. Turbochargers are driven by exhaust gas. At (A) two turbochargers are installed in a vee engine. The cutaway view at (B) shows internal construction and (C) names the parts. (M & W Gear Co.)

10. *Lubricating Systems and Lubricants*

A film of lubricant, not half so thick as the wing of a fly, separates high-speed surfaces and prevents an engine from running itself to quick destruction from the heat of friction. This critical function of oil and grease is seldom appreciated because it takes place deep within the machine. That lubricants can perform this difficult feat is one of the wonders of nature and of petroleum technology.

Millions of years ago, nature began the processing of the marine, plant and animal life that comes from oil wells today in the form of petroleum. During that long period, geologic heat and pressure made the transformation. The chemist then stepped in and by various ingenious processes extracted gasoline, diesel fuel and lubricating oil from the viscous mass. The reactions he worked out in the laboratory now take place routinely on a gigantic scale in hundreds of refineries.

As an outgrowth of its organic origin, petroleum is an organic mineral, composed of endless repetitions of molecules of carbon and hydrogen, hence the family name "hydrocarbons." The products obtained from petroleum range from water-white benzine to black and gummy asphalt, yet all are built around the carbon-hydrogen combination. The basic "building block" of this entire fabulous chain is a molecule composed of one carbon atom and four hydrogen atoms and called methane or marsh gas.

It is generally believed that nature's alchemy took place at the bottom of seas that disappeared eons ago. As the petroleum and its accompanying gas were formed, they rose through the water by gravity and permeated porous stones. Impervious rocks formed dams that outlined huge underground lakes of petroleum; these are the sources that oil wells tap.

The composition of petroleum varies slightly with the region from which it is pumped. Three distinct variations exist. They are crude petroleum that contains paraffin, crude that is high in asphalt, and also crude that contains a mixture of both paraffin and asphalt. Processors claim great exclusive merits for each of these as a base for superior lubricating oils—and advertise accordingly.

The petroleum industry has come an unbelievably long way since the first commercial well started gushing oil in 1859. Of course, mineral oil had been known and used before, but not as a refined product tailored to specific uses. Indians had scooped it up from geolithic faults that seeped oil, and they used it medicinally. The Chinese are believed to have drilled for oil more than a thousand years ago; they used it as unguents and lamp fuel.

The boatman's interest in petroleum centers only on two classes of refined products made from it: fuels and lubricating oils. The transformation is achieved through chemical processes called extraction, adsorption, crystalization and fractional distillation. The most important of these methods, fractional distillation, heats the crude to a temperature high enough to vaporize it. The vapor of each of the desired components of the crude rises to a known height, and at this point it is withdrawn and condensed.

Fractional distillation did not yield enough gasoline per barrel of crude to satisfy our engine-oriented world, so thermal cracking, catalytic cracking and polymerization were introduced. These sophisticated tricks from the chemist's bag rearrange the molecules beyond what nature intended. The results are fuels that burn cleaner with more Btu's and lubricants that can withstand the grueling demands modern marine engines make. The greases so necessary on a boat are combinations of lubricating oils and chemical soaps. (See Figure 10-1.)

Additives are the final magic touch. Additives in gasoline improve its antiknock quality (its octane number), protect the fuel system against corrosion, reduce the tendency toward icing in the carburetor and also exert a detergent action. Quite a role for this apparently simple fuel to play! Additives in diesel fuel raise the cetane number (similar to octane number in gasoline) and also do an all-around job in maintaining clean combustion. But in the doctoring of lubricants is where additives really shine.

Straight lubricating oil, as it comes from the distiller, would be almost worthless in high-speed, high-power internal combustion engines. Not until additives do their

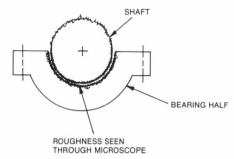

Figure 10-2. The polished shaft and bearing that appear so smooth to the eye look like mountains and valleys when examined through a microscope. Lubricating oil under pressure keeps these rough surfaces separated and prevents their interlocking, which can cause friction.

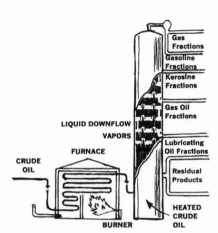

Figure 10-1. The heated crude oil enters the fractionating tower and is distilled. The vapors rise and are collected and condensed at various levels to yield many petroleum products. (American Petroleum Institute)

stuff can it measure up to the work in hand. Additives enable oils to hold their viscosity within ranges of temperature. They prevent the formation of deleterious by-products such as excessive carbon, varnish, gum and acids. Amazingly, additives give lubricating oils a detergent ability that has a cleansing effect on the lubricated surfaces and holds debris in suspension.

Granted that lubricating oil has these diverse abilities, just how does it prevent the high-speed rubbing surfaces of a marine engine from destroying themselves by friction? Exactly how does a lubricant perform its job?

A logical explanation starts with a microscopic look at the surfaces of the bearing and of the shaft that runs within it. What appears glass-smooth to the naked eye becomes a scene of mountains and valleys under the great magnification of the microscope. The impression is of two rough files attempting to slide over each other. Relative motion of these two objects seems impossible without disastrous consequences. Figure 10-2 shows this.

Lubricating oil makes smooth motion of these "rough" surfaces possible with a minimum of friction. The oil fills all the valleys, and the film stretching above the peaks "floats" the shaft in the bearing. If the correct oil with

adequate film strength and proper viscosity has been chosen, the metal of the shaft and the metal of the bearing will not actually touch despite high speed and load.

Admittedly, the foregoing is an introductory simplification. An engineer would tell you that there are two categories of lubrication: hydrodynamic and hydrostatic. Hydrodynamic is the lubrication between moving surfaces. Hydrostatic, often called boundary lubrication, takes place between stationary surfaces. Obviously, hydrodynamic is the more important of the two when considering the hardworking marine engine.

A multi-cylinder engine has several main bearings in which the crankshaft turns, and a detailed examination of one of these will explain how lubrication does its job. In Figure 10-3A a cross-sectional view shows the crankshaft

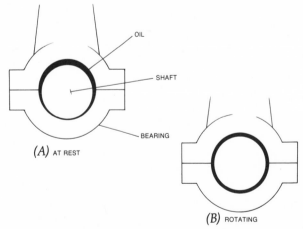

Figure 10-3. At rest, the weight of the shaft squeezes the lubricating oil out from under. The rotating shaft "pumps" the oil to fill the entire annular cavity; the shaft now floats "friction free."

at rest. Gravity has forced the shaft to touch the bottom of the bearing, hopefully separated from metal to metal contact by whatever minute oil film remains from previous operation.

In Figure 10-3B the shaft has begun to rotate. Because of the adhesion of the oil, the surface of the shaft is acting like a pump to pull the lubricant down, under and around in the form of a spiral wedge. The shaft has been lifted from actual contact with the bearing, and hydrodynamic lubrication has taken over the important task of maintaining a supporting film of oil within which the shaft can turn with a minimum of friction. Of course, the space between shaft and bearing has been exaggerated in the sketches for the purpose of illustration; in actuality, the difference between the two diameters is only a few thousandths of an inch.

The viscosity (thickness) of the oil is the determining factor in its ability to form the required film under all operating conditions. The refiners achieve the desired viscosity by blending light and heavy stock in proper proportion and by including additives. The familiar grades 10W-20, 30, 40 and 60 at the service station are the standard markings for viscosity, with thickness increasing as the numbers become greater. The "W" signifies that the viscosity was measured at zero temperature, and hence the oil will maintain its character in cold climates. The specifications for each designation are the result of cooperation between the American Petroleum Institute and the Society of Automotive Engineers.

Viscosity is measured by several methods, the simplest being the Saybold test. A given quantity of oil at a fixed temperature is placed in a container whose outlet is a restricted tube of carefully standardized diameter. The number of seconds of time required to empty the container becomes the Saybold reading.

A more complicated but faster viscosity test comprises a motor-driven rotating paddle in a container. When this container is filled with the oil under test, the speed of the paddle decreases and motor current increases because of the drag. The viscosity is computed from these factors. There is provision for heating or cooling the oil under test so that viscosity may be determined at any temperature.

The two standard temperatures for viscosity measurement are 0°F. and 210°F. Certain additives to oil tend to restrict the natural changes in viscosity that take place with changes in temperature.

Modern refining techniques are able to produce lubricating oils able to carry a double designation for viscosity; these include the letter "W" in their marking. For example, an oil labeled 10W-30 has met the specifications required for a 0°F. test and also has been able to pass the test at 210° F. This means that it acts like a 10 oil at 0° F. and like a 30 oil at 210° F. and will remain reasonably constant from cold to hot.

In addition to the numbers that designate viscosity, lubricating oil is classified according to the severity of the work it is designed to do. These markings originally had the prefix "M," but a recent revision has changed this to the letter "S." Thus SA marks a straight mineral oil able to perform only the very lightest service and unsuited for marine engines. The progression toward heavy-duty is alphabetical and ends with SE, a lubricant that can handle the toughest lubricating jobs. The table in Figure 10-4 explains the entire list.

The more stringent demands that diesel engines make upon their lubricants calls for a separate set of classifications. These have the prefix "C" and run from CA to CE, with toughness again increasing in alphabetical order. Incidentally, the "C" oils may be used in gasoline engines, but the "S" types are not necessarily suitable for diesel engines.

Technically, oil does not "wear out." However, its efficacy in the engine is reduced by many factors, and repeated replacement therefore becomes necessary. Exposure to high temperature and to air causes oxidation with resultant formation of varnish, sludge and carbon deposits. Although the oil may not wear out, the additives do. The oil loses its ability to hold debris in suspension. Blow-by from the combustion chamber combines with moisture and contaminates the oil with acids. Some oil inevitably gets by the piston rings and is consumed. The net result of all these degrading forces is the necessity to comply with that oft-heard slogan: Change your oil! The frequency of change is spelled out in the owner's manual.

API/SAE/ASTM DESIGNATIONS		SERVICE AND OIL DESCRIPTIONS
NEW	**OLD**	
SA	ML	*Utility Gasoline Engine Service*—Mildest operating conditions. No performance requirements. No additives except perhaps pour and/or foam depressants.
SB	MM	*Minimum Duty Gasoline Engine Service*—Conditions so mild that only minimum compounding is required. Oil has some resistance to oil oxidation and bearing corrosion—also some antiscuff qualities.
SC	1964-1967 MS	*1964 Gasoline Engine Warranty Service*—1964 through 1967 automobile manufacturer gasoline engine operating conditions. Oil designed to control high and low temperature deposits, wear, and corrosion.
SD	1968-1971 MS	*1968 Gasoline Engine Warranty Service*—1968 automobile manufacturers gasoline engine operating conditions. Performance better than that of SC oils and may be used in their stead.
SE	—	*ASTM Engine Test Sequence*—Oil designed to meet the 1972 requirements of the automobile manufacturers and to stand up under high operating temperatures caused by today's high speeds and heavy loads. Contains greater quantities of anti-oxidants which keep oil from turning into molasses-like sludge. Safeguards against bearing failure and total engine breakdown.
CA	DG	*Light Duty Diesel Engine Service*—Oils intended for service in light to moderate duty normally aspirated diesel engines using high quality low sulfur fuel. Meets MIL-L-2104 (1954).
CB	DG	*Moderate Duty Diesel Engine Service*—These oils are similar to CA oils except that they are capable of providing the protection when high sulfur fuels are used.
CC	DM	*Moderate Duty Diesel and Gasoline Engine Service*—Oils meeting requirements of MIL-L-2104 (1964). Provides low temperature anti-sludge and anti-rust performance in lightly supercharged diesel engines.
CD	DS (Series 3)	*Severe Duty Diesel Engine Service*—These oils are for service typical of supercharged diesel engines in high speed, high output duty requiring very effective wear/deposit control. Provide protection versus bearing corrosion and high temperature deposit formation in supercharged diesel units using wide quality range fuels. CD oils meet the Caterpillar Tractor Co. Series 3 Specification.

Figure 10-4. Lubricating oils are classified by a two-letter code that designates the service for which the oil is intended. A number following the code subdivides each type into a range of viscosities. (Onan Corp.)

Oil must often be added between changes, and this entails a caution. The additives used by the lubricating oil industry are so varied that one refiner's additive may well be another refiner's poison. In other words, additives are not necessarily compatible; one could neutralize another. Thus it is best to stay with the same brand when replenishing the oil in the crankcase.

Another feature of additives often emphasized by engine makers is that well-known commercial lubricating oils contain everything that modern chemistry considers essential—and therefore there is no point in adding various advertised nostrums. These canned and bottled secret formulas promise miracles, but no proof exists that they deliver.

Regardless of how excellent an oil may be, it can do its work only if it is delivered to the various engine friction areas in adequate volume and with sufficient pressure. Such delivery is the function of the lubrication system. Figure 10-5 is a schematic diagram of a typical system in a four-stroke-cycle engine. (Remember that two-stroke-cycle engines, except certain diesels, are lubricated by a mixture of oil with the gasoline and do not have a pressure system.)

The crankcase sump of the engine is the oil reservoir. Here the oil is picked up for circulation, and, after performing its duty, it is returned here to dissipate its heat. A positive pressure pump, driven by an accessory shaft and sometimes submerged, does the circulating. This is the pressure that registers on the console indicator.

The entrance to the pump pickup pipe in the sump is protected by a screen that serves to prevent large debris from entering. The output pressure of the pump is held to a predetermined maximum by a check valve. These are positive displacement pumps, and a blockage in the output could raise pressures to a dangerous level. The check valve is the safety relief. Operating pressures of the lubricating oil vary with different makes of engines, so there is no standard, but the usual range is between 30 and 60 pounds per square inch on the gauge.

Figure 10-5.

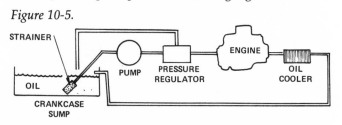

91

The pressured oil circulates through the engine via an ingenious network of tubing, drilled holes and distribution passages called galleries. External tubing connects points that cannot be joined conveniently by internal drilling. Holes are drilled from two directions with such accuracy that they meet at a precise point inside the casting. Bearings requiring pressured lubrication are made with oil holes and grooves that mate with oil holes drilled in their shafts. Figure 10-6 shows the complicated drilling needed to carry oil through a crankshaft to its bearings; also shown is the mating bearing with its grooves.

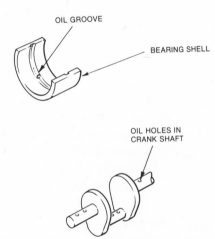

OIL GROOVE

BEARING SHELL

OIL HOLES IN
CRANK SHAFT

Figure 10-6. Grooves in bearing shells and drilled holes in journals and shafts are all parts of the oil circuit in an engine's pressure lubricating system.

Much of the internal lubrication of an engine is done by spray and mist. Strategically placed holes squirt oil that has already been around the pressure circuit. These streams lubricate cylinder walls and other surfaces. Early engines did this with small scoops on the lower ends of piston rods that splashed through the sump.

All the oil eventually drains back into the crankcase. It brings with it heat collected at many critical internal points that must be kept from overheating. One of the little-realized functions of lubricating oil is this cooling. Some engines have a separate oil cooler to remove this heat; in most engines the heat is simply distributed over the large-volume sump and the crankcase itself.

Internal gears and chains are lubricated by spray or mist; so also are those portions of the valve mechanisms not reached by flowing or pressured oil. In this insistence that the flow reach every nook and cranny of a complicated machine, the engine lubrication system bears a resemblance to the heart, veins and arteries of an animal body.

Bearing surfaces must be lubricated over their entire width, so it is to be expected that some oil will leak out at the edges. Inside the engine this is of no consequence; the oil simply drains back into the sump. However, at both ends of the crankshaft this leakage would be outside the machine and into the boat—something that cannot be permitted. The cure is in the form of oil seals that effectively dam the flow and that are described in Chapter 17.

Since the clearances between the surfaces that must be lubricated are minute (of the order of thousandths or even ten-thousandths of an inch), the oil that enters must be absolutely clean and devoid of foreign matter. The cleansing and monitoring of the oil necessary to accomplish this purity is done by filters in the lubricating system. The various types of filters in use are described in Chapter 17. Filters have a limited useful life and must be replaced periodically to assure engine longevity.

Good brands of modern lubricating oil are sold sealed in cans of almost antiseptic purity, and one may wonder how the "foreign matter" gets in for the filter to take out. These contaminants are the result of the heat and chemical changes entailed in engine operation. Minute particles of carbon are often the offshoots of combustion. Tiny bits of metal are worn off highly stressed surfaces. Humidity in the atmosphere changes to water in the sump. Dirt inadvertently may get in through the filling spout. Like a great river, the lubricating oil washes all these impurities away—and later would carry them into forbidden areas if the filter did not stand guard.

Under normal operating conditions the pressure in the lubricating system will be below that for which the relief valve is set. Its fluctuating value on the gauge will be determined by the clearances between moving parts. When these clearances are small, as in a new engine, the resistance to flow is great and the pressure is high. As the engine wears and clearances become larger, the pressure drops markedly when the operating temperature is reached. This drop could be great enough in an old, badly worn engine to make the remaining pressure too low for good lubrication.

Often this final stage of decrepitude can be warded off temporarily by switching to an oil of greater viscosity, that is, with a higher number. This is chancy medicine at best. The thicker oil results in more internal friction. It means a heavier drain on the battery when the starter turns over a cold engine. However, heavy lubricating oil can sometimes mask piston slaps and bearing knocks and make the engine sound more contented than it actually is.

With so many points of oil delivery, the lubrication system must be balanced to assure that every part receives its share. A bearing that, because of looseness, takes more than its intended supply, can starve bearings further down the line and cause failure. Similarly, a bearing so tight that oil has difficulty entering will remain starved until its demise.

Oil sprayed on the cylinder walls must lubricate pistons in their travel and yet not get into the combustion chamber—although, as mentioned earlier, some inevitably does. The so-called oil ring in the bottom groove of the piston has the ticklish job of scraping the excess oil off the wall and returning it to the sump. Incidentally, oil helps the "compression rings" in the other grooves of the piston seal off the high pressures developed by combustion and prevent their blow-by. This combustion gas blown by the piston is the major cause of acidic contaminants in the sump.

Ideally, the lubrication system is completely sealed within the engine and no oil can leak outside. In practice, there is always a little leak here or there. Because of this, it is wise to install drain pans under marine engines, both for cleanliness and for fire safety. Nothing is nastier than a mixture of bilge water and oil that has been churned into a gooey emulsion.

A word should be said about lubricating oils for outboard motors because these powerplants are the vast majority. Great care is taken in a four-stroke-cycle engine to keep the oil from creeping into the combustion chamber and being burned. Contrarily, the oil is mixed with the gasoline and purposely burned in the two-stroke-cycle engine. Thus the specifications for two-cycle lubricating oil are different.

Outboard manufacturers warn against the use of multigrade and high-detergent oils in their engines. Oils that contain metallic additives likewise are under the ban. The added chemicals break down during combustion and form harmful deposits that are known to have caused severe piston and other damage.

The outboard people are equally adamant on the subject of oil/fuel proportion. The optimum ratio of oil to gasoline can vary with different brands of lubricant. Too little oil will obviously be damaging because of insufficient lubrication and resultant wear. An oversupply of oil in the combustion chamber causes spark-plug fouling, erratic running and hard starting. The carburetor is also shortchanged because the designed amount of actual fuel is not passing through its jets.

Recommended outboard lubricating oils carry the designation "TC-W." While each outboard manufacturer naturally wants his own oil used in his engines, it seems to be acceptable to substitute the TC-W when the name brand is not available.

Adequate lubrication is the number-one requisite for every marine engine. Even a few minutes' operation without sufficient oil pressure registering on the gauge can be disastrous. Good engine installations include a warning horn or bell that sounds immediately when oil pressure drops. The only thing to do on hearing that warning is to shut down immediately.

In addition to its task of reducing friction, the lubricating oil also takes on the job of helping the cooling

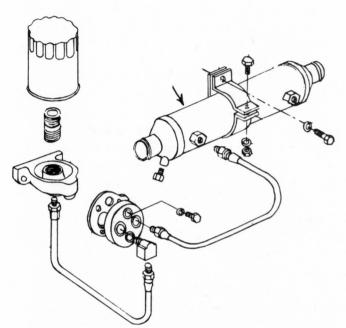

Figure 10-7. Lubricating oil plays an important part in carrying off the waste heat of an engine. On low power engines, the oil transfers the heat to the crankcase. High power marine engines make use of oil coolers (arrow) that transfer the heat from the oil to the cooling water. The line from the filter also is shown. (Lehman Power Corporation)

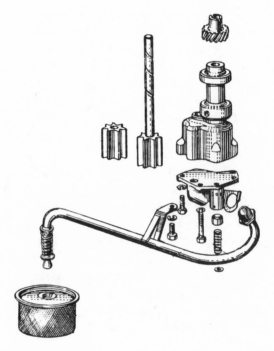

Figure 10-8.   Lubricating oil pumps must be able to generate pressure high enough to force oil to all engine lubrication points. A preferred pump type is the interlocking lobe design shown above. (Lehman Power Corporation)

water take away waste heat. The oil must therefore have some means of shedding this acquired heat to prevent its temperature from rising to dangerous heights. The oil cooler provides this means; it is illustrated in Figure 10-7.

The oil cooler is a heat exchanger. Hot oil and cooler water flow through it in contiguous passages. In accordance with the laws of thermodynamics, heat flows to the water, and the oil is cooled before its return trip through the engine.

The lubricating oil follows its course through the engine and through the oil cooler under the impetus of the lubricant pump shown in Figure 10-8. This pump is generally inside the engine.

The diesel engine is stopped by cutting off its fuel. One method of doing this from a remote point is with the small solenoid shown in Figure 10-9. This solenoid is activated by a push button on the console; its plunger moves the fuel rack to the closed position.

Figure 10-9. One method of making certain that lubrication is adequate before the engine starts running is shown above. The arrow points to a solenoid that opens the throttle only after lubricant pressure has been created by sufficient cranking.

11. Cooling Systems

T he immutable, natural laws of thermodynamics govern the operation of all heat engines everywhere, and of course this includes pleasure boat powerplants. These laws, in effect, state that no matter how perfectly designed our power generating system may be, only a regrettably small portion of the energy locked in the fuel can ever be reclaimed to turn the propeller. Just as with the law of gravity, the thermodynamic laws cannot be appealed or repealed.

The energy in the fuel that is beyond our reach for propulsion issues forth as useless heat. Not only is this heat of no value to us, but we must spend money, equipment and maintenance to get rid of it before it destroys the engine. Disposing of this heat is the job of the cooling system.

Heat can flow only from a warmer substance to a colder one, never the other way. In a pleasure boat, the warmer "substance" is the engine, and the colder, or "heat sink," is the surrounding water or the surrounding atmosphere. Some small outboard motors use the atmosphere as their heat sink; all larger boat engines use the water. Since water absorbs heat more readily than air, a greater overall efficiency results from choosing the water.

An air-cooled outboard motor has a number of integral fins to increase its contact with the atmosphere. (An automobile engine makes use of a radiator for the same purpose.) The water-cooled marine engine employs some form of heat exchanger or else makes direct contact with the water around the boat by pumping it through its internal heated areas.

In every case the law is adhered to strictly: Heat flows from the hot engine to the cool heat sink. Mathematically, the difference in temperature between source (the hot engine) and sink sets the theoretical maximum that the efficiency of the system can reach. Note the word "theoretical"; the actual result will be below that figure.

Modern marine engines, unlike their forebears, are finicky about their operating temperatures. When temperature is too low, efficiency dwindles, and fuel is wasted. The moisture, which is a by-product of combustion, condenses, and the resulting water eventually gets down into the pan to contaminate the lubricating oil. Incomplete combustion leaves soot, which combines with other noxious elements present to form a grimy sludge. Then the engine does not respond to the throttle as it should, and it is unable to deliver its rated power.

If the cooling system permits engine temperatures to rise too high, conditions can become catastrophic. Oil thinned beyond its required viscosity fails to lubricate and allows wear; since extreme expansion is taking place simultaneously, the wear may even cause total seizure. Elevated temperatures accelerate the oxidation of the oil with resulting carbon and varnish. Piston rings that should slide easily in their grooves are stuck fast by this goo and are unable to do their assigned job of maintaining compression and wiping cylinder walls. Most likely, before all this happens, the overheated condition will have caused detonation and consequent piston damage.

In the terminology of cooling, there are "raw-water systems" and "freshwater systems." Raw water is that in which the boat is floating, and often it is called seawater, even though it may be a river or a lake. Freshwater is what the name implies; it is contained in a closed circuit and recirculates, just as in an automobile. The raw water is pumped through and does not recirculate. Figure 11-1 shows schematic diagrams of both systems, and these will be discussed in greater detail.

Water has the greatest ability of all solids and liquids to absorb heat; only hydrogen can beat it. Luckily, therefore, the ever-present water is the most satisfactory means of carrying off the excess heat of a running engine. The volume of liquid needed to keep an engine cooled to its correct operating temperature is a minimum when water is used.

The raw-water system of cooling is the simpler. A forward pointing scoop on the immersed portion of the hull directs water into a through-hull fitting. A screen or strainer prevents grass and other debris from entering. A

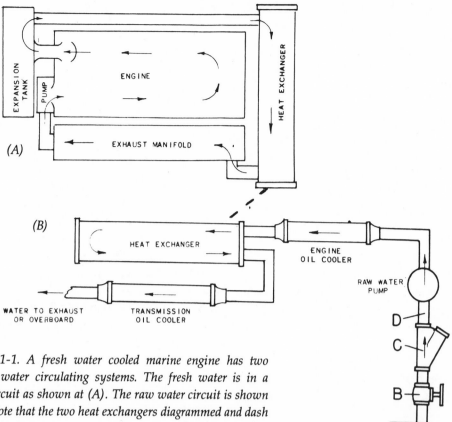

Figure 11-1. A fresh water cooled marine engine has two separate water circulating systems. The fresh water is in a closed circuit as shown at (A). The raw water circuit is shown at (B). Note that the two heat exchangers diagrammed and dash connected are two parts of one unit. "A" is the scoop, "B" the valve, "C" the strainer/cleanout and "D" the needed hose for connections. (Lehman Power Corporation)

valve, preferably of the type known as a seacock, guards the internal opening of the through-hull fitting and permits total shutoff during engine repair or for other reasons. From this point, a pump, known as the raw-water pump, forces the water through the engine and eventually to a discharge port above the waterline. Figure 11-2 shows the scoop, strainer and valve.

From the pump, the water generally travels to the cylinder block and flows through all the internal passages

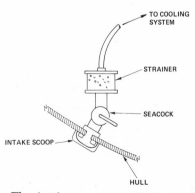

Figure 11-2. The intake scoop outside the hull is pointed forward so that the motion of the boat aids pickup of water. A seacock for shutting off and a strainer to eliminate debris are essential.

that encircle the cylinders and takes heat from them. Next on the circuit are the areas around the valves and the cylinder head with its combustion chambers. Finally, the route is to the exhaust manifold and then to overboard discharge. This is the water seen spurting out of the exhaust pipes in the transoms of many powerboats.

The exhaust manifold is a very important port of call for the cooling water. The tongues of flame from the exhaust valves would soon bring the manifold to red heat without this coolant. In addition to the problems of expansion and cracking that such heat would cause, a red-hot manifold would be an obvious fire hazard. A bonus here is that the waste water flowing through the exhaust pipe acts as a muffler and deadens what otherwise would be an unacceptable exhaust noise.

The basic system just described would not meet today's state of the art nor a sophisticated boatman's approval. The reason would be the lack of control over the actual engine temperature which would be governed entirely by the ambient water. In most cases, the engine would run too cool.

The thermostat corrects this situation and holds the engine to a preset temperature regardless of the ambient water. This device is a gate in the water flow that opens and closes in response to a "brain" that senses coolant

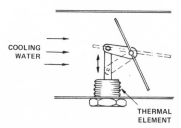

Figure 11-3. The underlying principle of engine thermostats is shown in this schematic drawing. The valve is opened and closed as the thermal element expands and contracts in response to water temperature. Actual thermostat construction, of course, is much more complicated.

temperature. When the engine is cold, the gate closes either partially or entirely to the influx of new water. The trapped water on the other side of the gate keeps recirculating through the engine until the temperature rises sufficiently for the gate to open to normal flow. A schematic of a thermostat is shown in Figure 11-3.

The brain or sensing element is either a small bellows containing a volatile substance or else a pellet of wax. Both expand when heated and contract when cooled. This expansion and contraction is harnessed to the gate to open and close it. (The pellet is simpler, cheaper and more modern than the bellows.) Thermostats are sold for various temperature ranges, and these usually are marked on the device. The owner's manual is the source of the required range for any engine; this is a critical parameter and should be obeyed.

The raw-water system works, vast numbers of engines are cooled in that manner, but it is not the best way to go. A boatman choosing a new craft, other than a very small one, is wise to avoid raw-water cooling. The great indictment of this system is the rust and corrosion that it causes inside the engine. Since the water is constantly expelled, it is impossible to add any preventive chemicals. When salt water is used for cooling, the situation is even worse. At operating temperatures salt water forms a coating of scale on the walls of the engine passages. This scale acts as an insulator, an effective barrier to the transfer of heat from the engine to the water. As this scale thickens, the engine becomes more and more difficult to cool. A

further disadvantage is the minute debris that manages to get through the strainer and over a period of time can clog water passages.

The freshwater system is the modern and best way to cool a marine powerplant. It largely keeps the problems of scale and corrosion out of the engine and makes possible the addition of chemicals to ensure this. It permits exact engine temperature control. Best of all, freshwater cooling is not that much more complicated nor that much more costly.

Actually, only two additions transform the raw-water system to the freshwater type. These are a heat exchanger and a pump (in addition to the pump already on the engine). Then with a slightly more extensive run of piping, the job is done. The additional pump circulates the seawater. The heat exchanger is the only new item that may prove to be unfamiliar.

The heat exchanger is a simple device through which two separate streams of water can flow without commingling. They are separated by the walls of the internal piping through which heat can exchange (transfer) from one stream to the other. In marine use, one stream would be the fresh engine-cooling water and the other the raw water pumped from the sea. Engine heat is thus brought out by one stream and dumped into the water surrounding the boat by the other. Think of the radiator of an automobile as a heat exchanger; the engine-cooling water is one stream, and a stream of air substitutes for the second stream of water. A representative marine heat exchanger is shown in Figure 11-4 A.

Since the freshwater system is a completely closed circuit, provision must be made for the expansion of the water when it becomes heated. A surge tank takes care of this; it can be either a space in the top of the heat exchanger or a separate tank.

A final advantage of freshwater cooling is that the engine side of the system may be pressurized. The boiling point of water rises when under pressure, and this means that the modern high-speed engine's need for a higher, more efficient operating temperature can be satisfied. Automobiles routinely have pressurized cooling systems, and the marine method is similar.

The flow of water through the engine in the freshwater

(A)

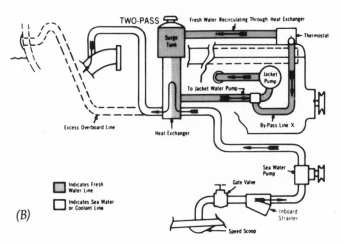

(B)

Figure 11-4. The heat exchanger (A) is the junction point of two separate circuits of cooling water. One is the closed circuit of fresh water in the engine; the other is the raw water that is circulated and discharged overboard. The diagram (B) explains this. Fresh water cooling prolongs engine life. (Sen-Dure Products Inc.)

system is much like that described for raw water except that, as already noted, the coolant is entirely retained and recirculated. A thermostat sets the operating temperature by diverting internal coolant flow when necessary. Antifreeze solutions are added for their rust and corrosion-inhibiting ability and for protection where extreme cold weather may be encountered.

The heat and noise of exhaust are present in the freshwater system and must be neutralized, just as with raw water. This is no problem because seawater is being circulated continuously through the heat exchanger and can be dumped overboard through the exhaust pipe. The schematic diagram in Figure 11-5 shows this clearly.

A well-engineered powerplant installation on a pleasure boat may have two heat exchangers in addition to the main one, which cools the engine. These would be an oil cooler and a transmission cooler, and the raw-water circuit would include both. The oil cooler transfers the

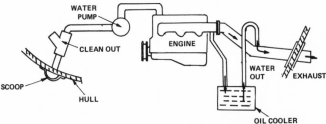

Figure 11-5. The path the raw water takes in cooling the engine, the oil cooler and the exhaust manifold is shown above. The cleanout fitting contains the essential screen.

heat from the lubricant and aids in keeping the engine at its correct temperature. The fluid in the transmission is cooled by being circulated through the second heat exchanger. All three heat exchangers are in series on their raw-water sides, and thus the total waste heat of engine and transmission is dumped into the sea.

One very special form of heat exchanger has not yet been mentioned: the keel cooler. (The name could mislead a novice into thinking that the keel of a boat must be cooled.) The keel cooler is a more or less streamlined array of piping fastened to the underside of the hull with inlet and outflow pipes connecting into the boat. The keel cooler is in series with the freshwater system of the engine and transfers the heat of the coolant to the surrounding water. A photo of the device is shown in Figure 11-6.

The advantage of the keel cooler is the elimination of the raw-water intake and the raw-water pump, which otherwise are necessary with the freshwater system. The main disadvantage is the increased resistance of the hull to forward motion. Often the raw-water pump, which the keel cooler supposedly makes unnecessary, must be installed anyway in order to supply cooling and silencing water to the exhaust pipe.

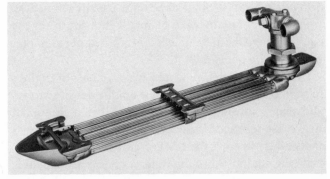

Figure 11-6. This keel cooler fastens to the bottom of the hull and transfers engine heat to the surrounding water. The ingenious combination inlet/outlet fitting makes it possible to drill only one hole to handle both feed and return. The streamline design reduces drag. (Walter Machine Co.)

A sort of internal "keel cooler" can be employed on metal-hulled boats. What amounts to a narrow integral tank is built along the inside of a submerged hull plate. This tank is in the circuit of the freshwater cooling system. The heat of the coolant that is pumped through the tank is transferred to the surrounding water through the metal skin of the ship. The advantage of this construction is that no resistance is added to the forward motion of the vessel.

The pumps that circulate the coolant in both fresh- and raw-water systems are of several types: gear, impeller, vane and centrifugal. The first three are positive displacement and have a certain amount of self-priming ability. Their operating principle is the changing internal volume as the rotating element turns and the consequent vacuum-pressure relationship that sucks in water and then pushes it on. The centrifugal pump derives its pressure (and its suction once it is primed) from centrifugal force. Engine pumps are usually of the centrifugal type because the enclosed system keeps them totally filled at all times and, therefore, primed. Figure 11-7 illustrates several types of pumps.

A pump with flexible impeller often begins operation as a positive displacement device and then, when speed and pressure increase, automatically changes to a centrifugal mode. This happens because the impeller blades become folded back and lose contact with the pump housing. This phenomenon is common in outboard motors and actually aids in regulating the flow of water to the needs of the engine at various speeds.

How and why each pump does its job can be inferred from the drawings—with the possible exception of the

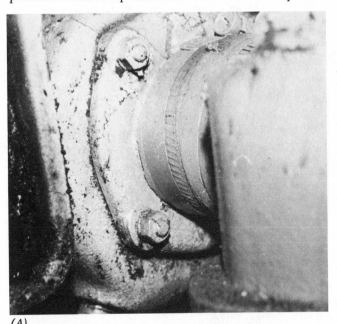

(A)

(B)

Figure 11-7. At (A) the fresh water pump and at (B) the raw water pump of a representative marine diesel engine. Note the tell-tale salt encrustation on the salt water pump.

centrifugal unit, which, because of its large space between impeller and housing, may prove confusing. Water enters the impeller at the center and is thrown outward into the housing by centrifugal force when the impeller turns fast. The housing is spiral in shape (a volute), and its gradually increasing volume changes the velocity of the thrown water into pressure. The centrifugal pump is more forgiving of small debris in the water than are other types.

Corrosion is an ever-present factor when water, especially salt water, is circulated through a metallic system. When dissimilar metals are present, galvanic disintegration may be added to the problem. Rust is the main worry on the engine side of a freshwater cooling arrangement, and this can be counteracted by adding an antifreeze containing a rust inhibitor. Not changing the freshwater any more often than absolutely necessary also helps because the old water will have lost much of its contained oxygen, the real culprit doing the damage.

Some provision must be made to counter galvanic deterioration (electrolysis) whenever salt water flows in metal passages. Protection is created by installing zinc anodes, which are less noble than the iron and bronze of the engine. (See Chapter 18.) With this scheme, the zinc wears away and protects the other metals. The zinc is available as a screw-in plug and must be replaced when galvanic disintegration has proceeded to a degree that impairs its ability to protect. (See Figure 11-8.)

The pump and piping on the engine side of a fresh-water cooling system are almost always integral with the engine. Heavy wall rubber hose is satisfactory for the raw-water side provided that double clamps be used at all connections and that a suitable seacock, or other valve, guard the through-hull intake. The reason for the "double insurance" is that a hose slipping off its fitting could flood the boat and sink it. Where long runs must be made in the raw-water line, polyvinyl chloride (PVC) pipe is suitable because temperatures are moderate and because such plastic pipe is installed easily.

Driving the second pump required by the freshwater cooling system could be a mechanical problem. A preferred location is to have the pump sheave in line with an engine pulley so that belt drive can be employed. Often this can be achieved by fastening the pump directly to the engine block with a suitable bracket. Another solution, but a less desirable one, is an electrically driven pump wired into the ignition circuit. Both electric current drain and the complication of additional wiring become negative factors here. Figure 11-9 is a photograph of a pump installation.

All pumps are sensitive to air leaks in their intake lines, and therefore absolutely tight joints are imperative. When air leaks are present, the pumps will suck air and will fail to pick up water. The higher the lift to the pump intake, the more pronounced will be the bad effects of air leaks. Packings and seals also are a source of leaks in pumps.

Figure 11-8. Zinc anodes are placed in the cooling system for galvanic protection. The zinc withdrawn above has been in service for several months and shows deterioration.

Figure 11-9. The raw water pump on a fresh water-cooled engine often is belt driven and an add-on installation as shown.

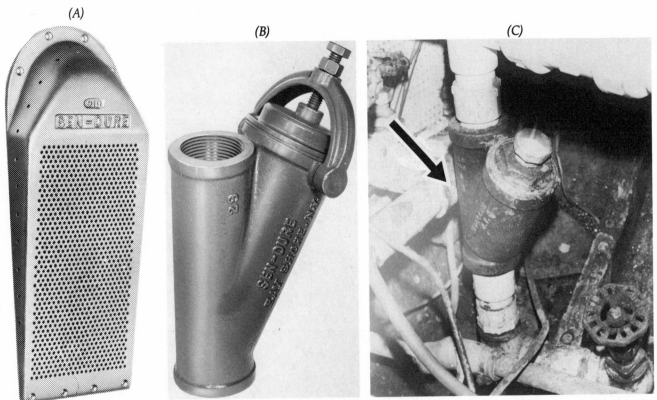

(A)   *(B)*   *(C)*

Figure 11-10. Grasses and debris in the water make strainers necessary on intake pipes of the cooling system. The primary strainer (A) is outside the hull at the intake opening. The secondary strainer/cleanout (B) precedes the pump in the internal piping; its screen is easily accessible for cleaning. The Y cleanout fitting is shown installed at (C). (Sen-Dure Products Inc.)

Turbochargers and superchargers, on engines so equipped, bring additional work for the cooling system. The air which these devices supply to the engine intake is at high temperature, and hot air reduces the efficiency of the engine. The answer is an intercooler, a form of heat exchanger, through which the air passes before it reaches the intake and that takes some of the heat away. Like all waste engine heat, this heat abstracted from the intake air also goes overboard eventually.

Whatever system of cooling is employed, it is standard to have an engine temperature indicator on the console. The simplest of these devices is electric. (See Chapter 15.) A sensing unit is installed in the water manifold of the engine and transmits its findings to the indicator. Only the temperature of the fresh water is monitored in the fresh-water cooling system.

Often a skipper makes a mental comparison with his automobile and wonders why so much more fuss is made about cooling the marine engine. The reason already has been stated, although perhaps not in cooling terms. The marine engine works continuously and so much harder; rarely does it idle without a load. The higher horsepower output means a greater amount of waste heat for the cooling system to take away. To top it all, the marine engine does not have a nice cool stream of air blown over it continuously by a fan to help in the cooling process.

The temperatures which occur in various parts of the engine can be fantastically high, and the wonder is that the cooling system can tame them. Ignition of the fuel for the power stroke can reach thousands of degrees Fahrenheit, and at high speed this condition is practically continuous. Turbochargers are in the direct line of the searing engine exhaust. Manifolds, as already stated, have flames licking at their insides. Yet the cooling system keeps all engine parts within a safe operating range.

The alpha and the omega of the cooling system is water, and so the water that is dumped overboard with the exhaust can be a quick telltale in checking whether all is in order. It should be a habit to look and make certain that this water is flowing from the exhaust pipe as soon as the engine is started. The automatic reflex on failure to see a flow of water should be to shut the engine down.

The plumbing industry people knew what they were doing when they devised the Y clean-out fitting shown in Figure 11-10. The open branch of the Y contains a cylindrical wire mesh screen easily accessible under the removable plug when cleaning is necessary. All cooling water drawn by the pump must pass through the screen, and debris is prevented from entering the cooling system.

Every fluid expands when it is heated, and water is no exception. The expansion tank shown in Figure 11-11 provides room for this expansion and prevents loss by overflow of the fresh water in a dual cooling system. Since this water usually contains antifreeze and other additives, saving it makes sense.

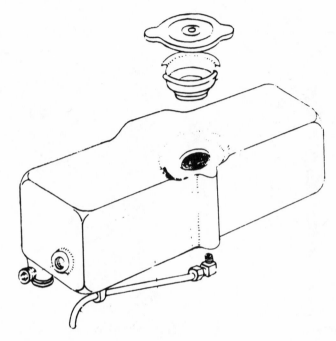

Figure 11-11. An expansion tank, shown above, forms part of the fresh water cooling system. Its purpose is to prevent loss of coolant due to expansion of the hot liquid and consequent overflow. Anti-freeze and cooling water additives thus are saved. (Lehman Power Corporation)

12. *Ignition Systems*

An electric spark is the magic key that unlocks the energy in gasoline. Until that spark arrives, chemical bonds hold quiescently captive the tremendous dormant power in the fuel. When the fuel-air mixture in the combustion chamber of a gasoline engine is properly compressed, a spark triggers the explosion that pushes the piston down and creates horsepower. But maximum power will result only if the spark is precisely timed and occurs at exactly specified intervals. Not only does the ignition system generate the spark, it delivers it continuously to the right point at the correct time.

The ignition system is the one thing about which the skipper of a diesel-powered boat need not concern himself. All the other pleasures and worries of boating he shares equally with the skipper who relies on gasoline, but in the matter of ignition he is completely in the clear. He is grateful that the diesel engine ignites its fuel spontaneously, entirely by the heat of compression, and that therefore his powerplant has no "ignition system."

The ignition systems of today are skillfully engineered combinations of components that are based on the latest technologies. Even transistors, only lately arrived on the electronic scene, now are firmly ensconced as important parts of gasoline engine ignition equipment. It was not always so.

The earliest ignition system created its sparks by striking two current-carrying wires together as one would strike a match. In effect, the electrical circuit was made and the spark occurred when it was broken. Quite logically, this system was called "make-and-break" ignition. The earliest gasoline engines for boats were fired in this manner, and one of these is shown in Figure 12-1 for its historical interest. Actually, the interest is more than historical because the identical unit is still being manufactured today for North Coast fishermen who want the utmost in simplicity.

A few dry cells in series supplied the current for the make-and-break system, and an iron-cored coil with a single winding boosted the voltage to supply a fat spark. This was a low-voltage system and almost immune to stoppage by rain or spray. If worse came to worst, the part

that did the making and breaking, the igniter, could be replaced in a few minutes with nothing more than a wrench.

In contrast, modern ignition systems are high voltage, so-called high tension. The original single winding coil has been superseded by a two winding coil that boosts voltages hundreds of times higher than in make and break and able to jump spontaneously between two electrodes without the striking action.

When the voltage, that is to say, the electric tension between two points, becomes sufficiently high to ionize the space separating them, a current in the form of a spark will jump across. This is as true of the electrodes of a spark plug as it is true of the clouds and the earth during a lightning storm. While the lightning stroke may be many miles in length, the spark at the plug of a gasoline engine need be only thirty one-thousandths of an inch long in order to do its job adequately.

Figure 12-1. This early engine still is manufactured in its original form. Ignition is "make and break." The spark is created by two electrodes that strike together, much like striking a match.

A spark plug is surely familiar to every driver of an automobile. A tubular holder that screws into the combustion chamber holds a ceramic insulator extending above and below it. Through the center of this insulator runs a metal rod that becomes one of the two electrodes when it protrudes at the lower end. A corresponding second electrode juts out from the bottom of the metal holder to form the gap. The entire construction is sealed to prevent the loss of any of the compressed fuel to which it is subjected in service. The cross-sectional view in Figure 12-2 shows how the unit is put together.

The bottom end of the ceramic insulator is exposed to the searing heat of the combustion chamber. Unless it can pass most of this heat on to the engine cooling system, it will be destroyed. The necessary transfer of heat is accomplished through the spark-plug shell and into the metal of the engine. The length of the exposed ceramic tip determines how well the heat transfer takes place.

A short tip passes heat faster; a long tip takes more time, and thus more of the heat remains. This has led to classifying spark plugs as "hot" or "cold" and thereby fitting them to the needs of various engines. A combustion chamber that operates with relative coolness (bear in mind that this is only *relative* coolness) requires a hot plug with a long ceramic tip. A hardworking, high-speed hot racing engine will be fitted with a cool, short ceramic tip plug that can divest itself of the extreme heat and thereby survive. Figure 12-3 shows how the heat travels from the spark plug to the engine.

A new spark plug has made its appearance to keep pace with modern ignition systems. It is called the "surface gap plug," and its firing end does not have the usual protruding insulator. Instead, the end is flat and looks like a ceramic washer with a metal center. Sparks jump across the surface of this washer to the metal rim, hence the designation "surface." The manufacturer claims extra-

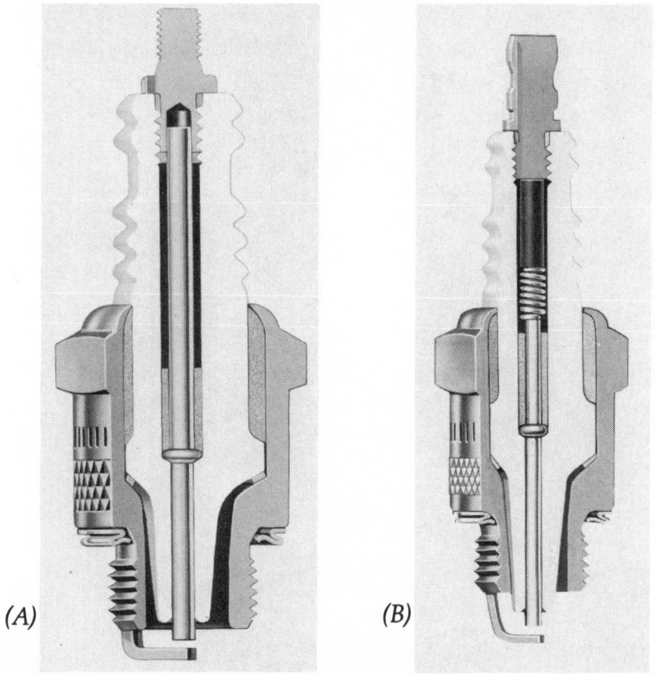

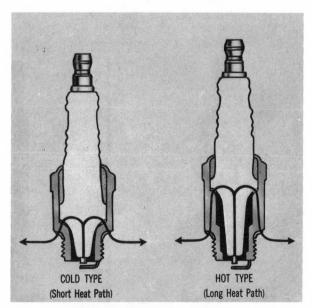

Figure 12-3. The porcelain core of a spark plug is subjected to intense heat. It is able to survive because it transfers this heat to the surrounding engine as shown and eventually to the cooling system. The length of the protruding porcelain determines whether a plug is "hot" or "cold"; the longer the hotter.

(A)   *(B)*

Figure 12-2. A standard spark plug is shown in cross-section at (A) and a resistor spark plug at (B). (Champion Spark Plug Co.)

107

ordinary resistance to fouling but states that this plug should be used only in engines that have capacitor discharge ignition, which will be described in detail later.

The appearance of the working end of a spark plug can tell a trained eye a great deal about the condition of an engine. What happens in the combustion chamber, good or bad, leaves its telltale mark on the spark plug. Is the firing end gooey with a damp, black carbon deposit? In an outboard motor this could mean too much oil in the fuel mix or even a wrong plug choice; in an inboard engine the message could be that the piston rings and the valve guides are worn. A spark plug with a clean, dry insulator that has changed from its original white to a light tan or gray is good news; engine purring along as it should. Between these two extremes is a gamut of conditions, as depicted in the actual photographs of Figure 12-4.

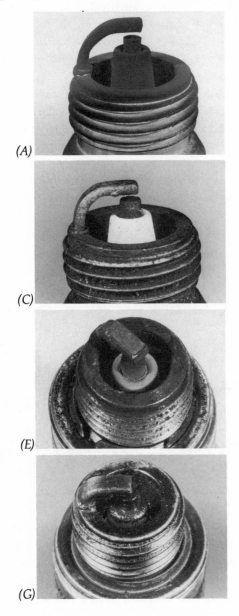

(A)

(C)

(E)

(G)

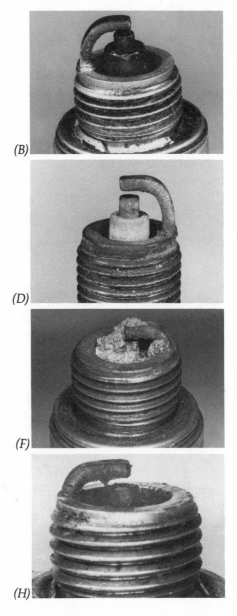

(B)

(D)

(F)

(H)

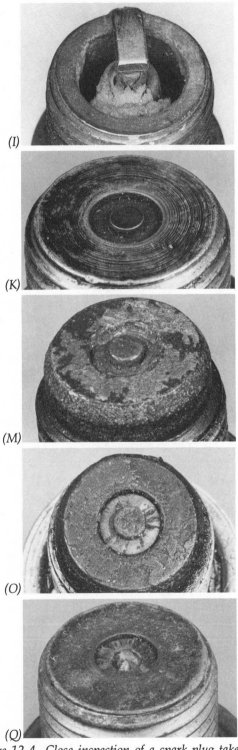

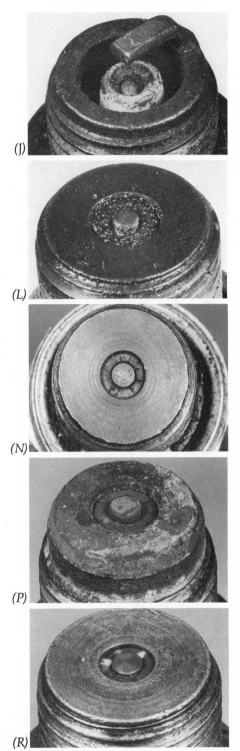

Figure 12-4. *Close inspection of a spark plug taken from an engine that has been in service can tell a great deal about what is happening inside the machine and is an important step in trouble shooting. Compare plugs with these photographs. (A) inboard engine, carbon fouled, too cold; (B) inboard engine, fouled by oil, wet; (C) inboard, over heated; (D) inboard, normal; (E) outboard, normal; (F) outboard, aluminum throw-off; (G) outboard, wet, fouled by oil; (H) outboard, inboard, gap bridged and shorted; (I) outboard, core bridged; (J) outboard, overheated; (K) surface gap, carbon fouled, too cold; (L) surface gap, oil fouled, too cold; (M) surface gap, aluminum throwoff; (N) surface gap, channelling; (O) surface gap, carbon tracking; (P) surface gap, normal; (Q) surface gap, worn out (R) surface gap, concentrated arc. (Champion Spark Plug Co.)*

The ignition coil is the immediate source of the high voltage that arcs across the gap of the spark plug. The coil is a simple transformer (see Chapter 7); a schematic diagram of the coil and its internals are shown in Figure 12-5. No service can be given the coil other than keeping it clean. If it succumbs to an internal short circuit or to a break of the wiring inside the shell, the only remedy is replacement.

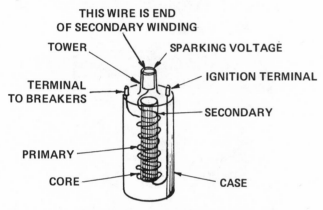

Figure 12-5. *The ignition coil consists of two windings over an iron core, the whole encased in insulating plastic. This X-ray drawing shows the internal arrangement.*

As the diagram makes clear, the ignition coil consists of two independent windings over an iron core. One winding, called the primary, has few turns of comparatively coarse wire and is traversed by the 12-volt battery current. The other winding, the secondary, consists of many turns of fine wire, and generates the current that often attains 24,000 volts and is able easily to jump the gap in the spark plug. The ignition coil is an inert device with no moving parts.

Intermediate between the high-voltage connection tower of the ignition coil and the spark plugs is the "distributor," which does exactly what its name implies: It distributes the sparking voltage to the correct plug at the proper time. The sequence of distribution is determined by the "firing order" of the engine and is fixed at manufacture. A typical engine might fire its six cylinders by starting with #1 and continuing to #5, #3, #6, #2, and

ending with #4 for the complete cycle. This explains the single wire from coil to distributor and the multiple wiring from distributor to the spark plugs in the various cylinders. The distributor and its attendant breaker are driven by a shaft geared to the engine.

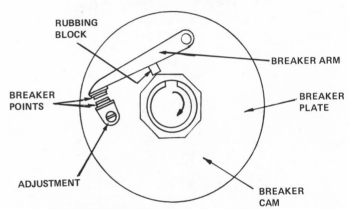

Figure 12-6. *The rotation of the breaker cam moves the breaker arm through the rubbing block and thereby opens and closes the breaker points. The breaker plate is moveable also, as shown in Figure 12-14.*

The firing order shows that the power strokes of a multi-cylinder engine do not proceed in sequence along the engine block but are skipped back and forth deliberately. This is done in the interest of smooth operation and a minimizing of torsional stresses on the crankshaft. Most engines have the numbers that signify their firing order cast into their blocks.

The distributor and the breaker point mechanism directly below it are an inseparable combination because one is dependent upon the other. The breaker points determine the exact instant during each revolution when the spark should take place; the distributor takes the sparking voltage to the designated cylinder. This synchronization of the ignition system is called timing and is discussed later.

The breaker points make and break electrical contact in accordance with the force exerted by a central cam mounted on the engine-driven shaft, which also carries the rotor of the distributor. The cam has one lobe or high spot for each cylinder of the engine that it controls. The high spots open the breaker point contact; the valleys between allow intermediate resumption of the circuit. The plan view in Figure 12-6 shows the arrangement.

Why all this should generate an accurately controlled spark is easily explained with the pictorial help of Figure 12-7 and the knowledge gained from Chapter 7.

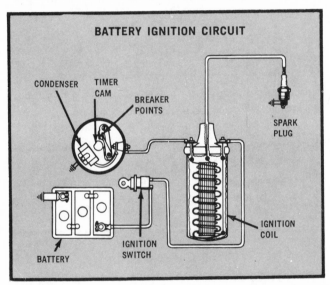

Figure 12-7. *The battery ignition system consists of a primary and a secondary circuit. Battery, switch, primary winding of the cell, breaker points and condenser constitute the primary circuit. The secondary winding, the distributor and the spark coil form the secondary circuit.* (Champion Spark Plug Co.)

When the breaker points are making contact because of a valley in the cam, battery current flows through the primary winding. An invisible magnetic field is created around the coils and through the iron core. When the points are opened by a cam lobe, the current ceases and the field collapses through the windings. This induces a voltage in the secondary winding which, because of the great many turns of wire, is very high—in the thousands of volts. On being delivered to the spark plug, this high voltage ionizes the space between the plug electrodes and jumps the gap to become the ignition spark.

One important ingredient has been omitted from this electrical discussion: the *condenser* (or "capacitor," as it is often known). Without the condenser, the same collapse of the magnetic field that induces the high voltage would also cause a damaging condition at the breaker points. Constant arcing would occur there and would soon pit and burn the points in addition to preventing the desired secondary high voltage from reaching its peak. In the properly connected and adjusted system the damaging arcing voltage is stored by the condenser and then returned automatically to boost the secondary voltage.

The condenser is a very uncomplicated device despite the complexity of its function. As Figure 12-8 shows, two long strips of foil are rolled up tightly with an intervening strip of insulating film. The whole is sealed in a metal can for protection and for ease of attachment. One foil strip is electrically connected to the can, the other to a wire terminal. The condenser works because of the unseen stresses of its electrons, and nature takes care of this without any worry or attention by the skipper.

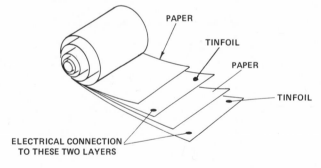

Figure 12-8. *A condenser, or capacitor, is the only device that actually stores electricity. Two long strips of tinfoil are separated by paper or other insulation; there are no moving parts.*

The only additions needed to make the foregoing a viable ignition system are an ignition switch and often a ballast resistor plus a connection to actuate the starting motor. The ballast resistor maintains a constant voltage to the ignition coil despite variations in battery voltage. Usually, the ballast resistor is short-circuited automatically during cranking to compensate for the low voltage the battery assumes under the starter load.

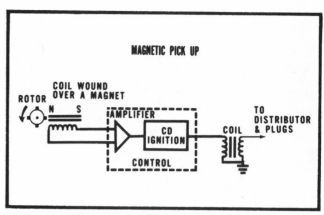

Figure 12-9. The most advanced ignition systems have abandoned breaker points in favor of magnetic pickups that are not subject to wear. A rotor and a small coil supply the ignition impulses formerly derived from the breaker. (Champion Spark Plug Co.)

What has been described is the standard ignition for gasoline engines, and it has not changed since almost the turn of the century. Vastly newer methods are available today, and they have been adopted for most modern pleasure boat engines. These improved ignition systems rely on electronics—the so-called solid-state electronics that employs transistors in place of short-lived vacuum tubes—and theoretically could last "forever."

The transistor can be considered an electronic switch that does its switching through the medium of unseen electrons without any mechanical action. A very small current can actuate a transistor to control a large current. Thus, in one electronic system, a minimal current through the breaker points causes the transistor to handle the comparatively heavy current needed by the ignition coil. The points now do not burn and pit, and the transistor, by its nature, shows no wear. However, this is a primitive method because technology has advanced to a complete elimination of the breaker points and the attendant condenser.

Of course, the correctly timed impulses that the cam supplies are still needed, but the new system generates them without any mechanical contact or wear. One method is to substitute a toothed trigger wheel for the cam and a small sensing coil for the points. As each tooth passes the sensor, pulses equivalent to the opening and closing of breaker points are produced; nothing touches, nothing deteriorates. How trigger wheel and sensing coil are positioned can be seen from Figure 12-9.

One shortcoming that has always plagued ignition systems, whether operated by breaker points or transistors, is the comparatively long time required for the secondary sparking voltage to reach its maximum value. Even though this delay time is measured only in *milli*-seconds, it allows the current to leak around the gap of a partially fouled plug instead of leaping across as a spark. Consequently the fuel charge is not ignited and the power stroke is missed. The capacitor discharge ignition system was developed to correct this.

The name tells the story. A capacitor is charged and then discharged through the ignition coil at the right instant to produce an almost instantaneous peak in

secondary voltage. There is no time for leakage around the electrodes of a partially fouled spark plug, and it fires despite the hindrance. This fast action is made possible because of the characteristics of a capacitor. As a comparison between the two methods, one would be like emptying a jug of water in a stream while the other would dump the jug all at once. The comparison of rise times between standard and capacitor discharge ignition is shown graphically in Figure 12-10.

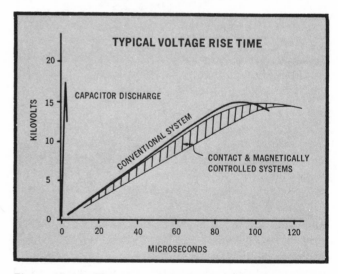

Figure 12-10. The great advantage that capacitor discharge ignition has over conventional systems is illustrated in the above curves. The voltage rise time of capacitor discharge is almost instantaneous (see near vertical curve at left). In contrast, the remaining curves show that standard ignition methods require as much as 100 times as long to reach sparking voltage. (Champion Spark Plug Co.)

Figure 12-11 A. This protective metal enclosure contains all the electronic components needed for converting a standard ignition system to a capacitive discharge system. Only a few simple connections between distributor and coil are required. (Eico Electronic Instrument Co.)

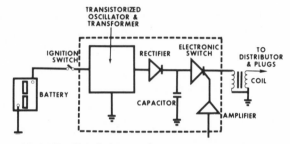

Figure 12-11 B. Simple instructions enable any skipper to add this capacitor discharge conversion unit to his ignition system. The bonus is better engine performance and freedom from breaker point replacement. The diagram gives the internal connections of the factory-supplied unit. (Eico Electronic Instrument Co.)

Add-on units are sold that convert any standard breaker point ignition system into capacitor discharge usually with an increase in engine efficiency. These can be installed by any novice following simple instructions. A capacitor discharge conversion unit is shown in Figure 12-11 together with its circuit. Factory-installed capacitor discharge ignition systems also do away with breaker points, and thus such engines bring a double bonus.

The discussion to this point has covered the ignition systems on conventional multi-cylinder inboard engines. Of course, outboard motors also need ignition systems. Do these differ?

Small outboard motors universally employ flywheel magnetos as their ignition source. These devices function without a battery, generate their own current and then raise the voltage to the high value needed for sparking. The magneto is built into the flywheel and has its own

breaker points for timing the resulting spark accurately. These are called high-tension magnetos to distinguish them from low-tension flywheel magnetos which supply only low voltage and are merely small alternators. Figure 12-12 shows a flywheel magneto diagrammatically.

An explanation of the internal action of a magneto reverts again to a magnetic field "cutting" a wire. In the ignition coil, the magnetic field caused by the current in the primary winding "cut" the secondary winding and induced a high voltage in it. In the magneto, the magnetic field from a permanent magnet cast into the flywheel "cuts" the windings of an adjacent special ignition coil when the wheel rotates. Naturally, voltages are induced, their value depending on the number of turns in the windings. Again, it falls to a cam and breaker points to initiate the spark at the desired piston position. Advancing and retarding the spark is accomplished by slight movement of the breaker points relative to the cam.

Why is advancing and retarding the spark necessary? To compensate for the finite time it takes the fuel charge to burn completely under various conditions of load and speed. The breaker point position and the throttle opening on small outboard motors are linked by an ingenious

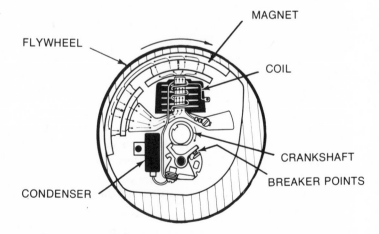

Figure 12-12. This diagrammatic representation of a flywheel magneto shows how the passing of the magnet in the flywheel generates current in the coil. The secondary winding in the coil raises the voltage to spark plug requirements. (Champion Spark Plug Co.)

113

Figure 12-13. *A critical relationship exists on many outboard motors between spark timing and throttle opening. One method of maintaining this relationship is the cam arrangement shown above. The cam and roller (arrow) open the carburetor butterfly valve as the magneto housing is rotated. (Champion Spark Plug Co.)*

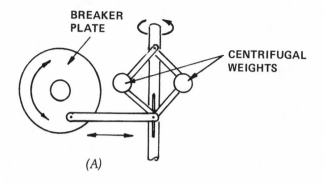

(A)

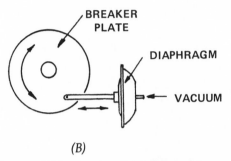

(B)

Figure 12-14. *Turning the breaker plate a small distance in either direction advances or retards the spark, and compensates for engine speed and load. Centrifugal weights sense speed (A), while a vacuum diaphragm senses load (B). Both sensors function simultaneously in a modern engine.*

system of levers, which makes spark timing quasi-automatic. (See Figure 12-13.) On inboard engines the spark timing is automatically controlled through the mediums of centrifugal force and vacuum. A spark occurring too soon causes piston knocking; a spark too late wastes fuel and unduly heats the engine.

The base plate upon which the breaker points are mounted in the distributor head of an inboard gasoline engine can be rotated about its central cam. Rotating it in the same direction as cam rotation causes the breaker points to open later in each revolution, and this is the equivalent of retarding the spark. Rotation of the plate in a direction opposite to the cam has the effect of advancing the spark. Since the cam turns at half crankshaft speed in a four-stroke-cycle engine, a 5° movement of the breaker points, for instance, has a 10° effect on the engine.

The amount of base plate rotation on modern engines is controlled automatically. A weight, attached to the plate by a lever mechanism, swings out in response to the centrifugal force of rotation and does the work. Additional control of the breaker point base plate is responsive to the vacuum in the engine manifold. A diaphragm, connected to the engine intake, adds its movement to the plate in accordance with engine vacuum, which in turn is a measure of speed and load. The illustrations in Figure 12-14 explain these mechanisms.

The use of both centrifugal and vacuum advance is strictly automotive practice and will not be found on true marine engines, although marine conversions may be so equipped. Ignition for marine engines confines itself to

only the centrifugal advance. The reason, of course, is that marine powerplants are not confronted with the constant changes of load that an automobile engine encounters. A propeller absorbs a fixed amount of power at any given speed, and the needed change in ignition advance for that speed is provided by the centrifugal weights. A distributor minus the vacuum diaphragm is shown in Figure 12-15.

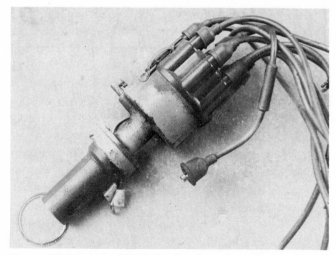

Figure 12-15. *This distributor is minus the vacuum advance that is standard on automotive engines. Marine engines do not encounter the constantly varying loads to which the vacuum advance responds.*

Because an electric current is a movement of electrons, polarity makes a difference in the high voltage fed to the spark plugs. The lead to the plug should be negative in a correctly functioning system. If this lead is positive through error, then about one-third higher voltage will be required for adequate sparking. The polarity of the high-voltage side of the ignition coil is reversed by interchanging the connections on the primary side.

Figure 12-16 shows how a common lead pencil may become a polarity detector at the spark plug. The wire is unhooked from the plug and held about ¼ inch away. The lead of the pencil is interposed, and a slightly orange arc will bloom when the engine is running. Correct polarity will place this arc on the plug side of the pencil. Care must be taken to avoid electric shock.

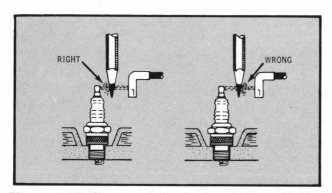

Figure 12-16. Correct polarity is important for the best operation of an ignition system. The illustration explains how a common lead pencil may be used to determine the right polarity of the sparking voltage. (Champion Spark Plug Co.)

The wide use of radio communications on the water has forced a change in the nature of spark-plug cables. The reason is the strong radio interference that an unprotected ignition system sends out as long as the engine is running. (Diesel engines do not create this interference because they have no ignition systems.) The disturbing effect of ignition interference is felt not only by the radio and electronic equipment onboard but also for a considerable distance away.

Radio interference can be cut down almost to the

vanishing point by adding resistance to the circuit. The necessary resistance is added to the spark-plug cables and sometimes to the plugs themselves by various means. One is to insert an actual small resistor. Another is to replace the wire at the center of the cable with a filling of carbon or metal dust. In most cases, 10,000 ohms is an accepted value for the required resistance.

A totally different method of eliminating interference, and from an engineering standpoint a much better one, is shielding. The entire ignition system—cables, plugs, distributor, everything—is enclosed in a continuous metal conduit, which in turn is grounded to the engine. Radio waves from the ignition cannot penetrate this shield to get out and cause interference. Unfortunately, shielding is expensive and on many engines become unhandy. A shielded spark plug is shown in Figure 12-17.

Before cost became such an important factor, the finest gasoline engines were fitted with high-tension magnetos as their ignition source. These fine self-contained ma-

Figure 12-17. The spurious radio frequency pulses emitted by the ignition system of gasoline engines often create interference with onboard radio reception. The perfect solution is shielded spark plugs, like the one shown here in cross-section, and shielded cables. This is standard aircraft practice. (Champion Spark Plug Co.)

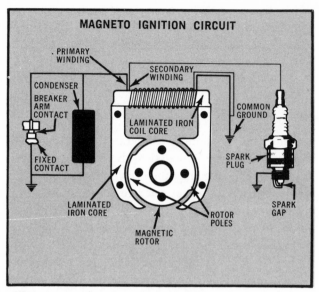

Figure 12-18. The selfcontained high tension magneto is accurately geared to the engine. This diagram shows how the internal components are connected to produce the high voltage for the spark plug. (Champion Spark Plug Co.)

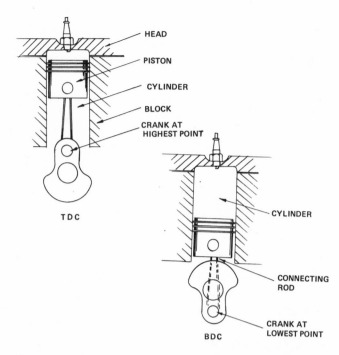

Figure 12-19. The meaning of "top dead center" (TDC) and "bottom dead center" (BDC) is illustrated by these drawings. Both positions are used in engine adjustments.

chines supplied ignition independently of the battery and contained their own breaker points and distributors. A diagram of one is shown in Figure 12-18. These magnetos should not be confused with the flywheel magnetos described earlier for outboard motors.

The length of time the breaker points are closed in any ignition system is called the *dwell.* Since the dwell determines how long battery current can flow in the primary winding of the ignition coil to energize it fully, it is desirable to have the maximum dwell an engine design permits. Dwell may be measured by simple meters properly calibrated for this service, and it can be shown on the face of the cathode-ray tube in modern engine testers. However, it may be impossible to get a correct dwell reading, or any reading at all, when a dwell meter is used on a breakerless system.

The inherent limitation on actual dwell time stems from geometry. The breaker cam must have a lobe for each cylinder, but it all must come out of the 360° that comprise the circumference. Thus an 8-cylinder engine can devote only 45° (360° ÷ 8) to the ignition of each cylinder—and only a portion of this travel can be allocated to dwell.

A good ignition system will develop a secondary voltage higher than the bare minimum needed to fire the spark plugs. The excess can be considered insurance

against the demands made by transient conditions such as changes in fuel mix, temperature and load. As pointed out earlier, the condenser across the breaker points has great influence on peak secondary voltage; it must be adequate and in good condition.

Two abbreviations are often seen when reference is made to ignition timing. They are "TDC" and "BDC." The meanings are top dead center and bottom dead center respectively, or the highest and lowest positions of the piston in any cylinder. (See Figure 12-19.)

TDC and BDC may be determined in several ways, but most easily they are found through marks placed on the engine flywheel by the manufacturer. For instance, the timing instruction for a certain engine might be to have the spark occur 10° before top dead center. In the shorthand of the industry, this would be written 10° BTDC, and, most likely, a convenient mark on the flywheel would establish this position without measurement or calculation.

The primitive method of determining when the breaker points open, and thus when the spark takes place, is with an ordinary incandescent bulb of the same voltage as the battery. This bulb is connected across the points as shown in Figure 12-20. The bulb lights up at the instant the breaker points open. Obviously, this test cannot be made with the engine running.

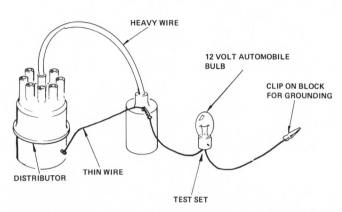

Figure 12-20. An ordinary 12-volt light bulb is the simplest timing indicator. Connected as shown, the bulb will light the instant the breaker points open; this is the instant the spark would take place.

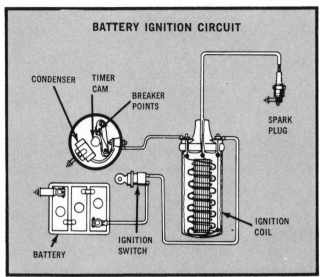

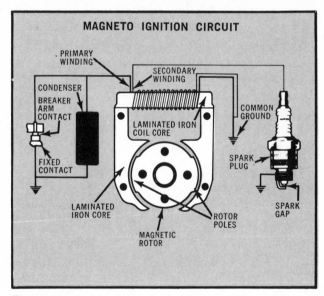

Figure 12-21. The basic similarities and differences that distinguish battery and magneto ignition are shown by these two diagrams. (Champion Spark Plug Co.)

A much more accurate and more useful timing check is made with a so-called timing light. This is a device that contains a high-intensity flash tube similar to the light source in an electronic photographic flash. In use, the light is connected to the ignition system and pointed at the flywheel markings of a running engine. The stroboscopic effect appears to hold the timing marks stationary and allows them to be read easily.

Today's ignition systems, even the older, breaker point types, are designed to make full use of the latest electrical engineering precepts. Coils, plugs, condensers—all are built for long efficient service life. A look back to the early days of single-cylinder putt-putts will confirm this.

These early pleasure boat "powerplants" were fired with low-tension make-and-break ignition incapable of jumping the gap in a spark plug. Two electrodes inside the cylinder were wiped against each other to make a spark. It was like brushing the bare ends of two wires from a battery together until they sparked. A booster coil helped things along. This was a simple single-winding coil, unlike the primary/secondary ignition coils in use now.

These early make-and-break ignition systems had remarkable success despite what we today consider their very primitive concept. Users became very adept. An experienced operator could reverse the engine by opening and closing the ignition switch at just the right instant during a revolution of the flywheel.

Although the ultimate purpose of magneto ignition and of battery ignition is identical, the means for achieving that result are quite different, as evidenced by the diagram in Figure 12-21.

13. Control Systems

A man sat in the engine room of olden-time yachts and manipulated throttles and transmissions in response to bong-bongs and ding-dings from the wheelhouse. Up above, near the helmsman, stood an imposing, waist-high, polished brass stand with projecting levers, the engine room telegraph. Moving these levers to appropriate positions set the bells to jangling down below and told the engineman what was wanted in the way of power. And these vessels were not of ocean liner size, but pleasure craft in the 60- to 100-foot class.

Today, equivalent yachts are controlled entirely from the wheelhouse or from the flying bridge. The engines and the transmissions respond to easy movement of the small levers at the helmsman's console. All powerplant performance data that the man at the wheel should know are displayed on instrument dials in front of him. Switches or buttons start and stop the engines. The ship, large or small, truly is under one-man command.

The art and science of controlling marine power has advanced tremendously to the great advantage of the skipper. Even on the smallest outboard, the twisting of a hand grip simultaneously sets the throttle and the correspondingly correct spark. Often, sliding this hand grip back and forth also puts drive into forward or reverse. From this minimal power source right up to the huskiest turbocharged diesel, the story is the same; one or two small levers at the steering station regulate speed and direct the engines to apply their power to forward, to reverse, or to remain in neutral.

On all boats but the very smallest, the steering position and the engines are some distance removed from each other. A system of remote control therefore becomes necessary, and this can be actuated mechanically, hydraulically or electrically. The simplest of these and the one in widest use is mechanical action.

A time-honored, basic component of many mechanical systems is the so-called Bowden wire, whose principle of operation is shown in Figure 13-1. A stiff wire is encased in a flexible tube. A knob or lever is attached to the wire at the control position, and the other end of the

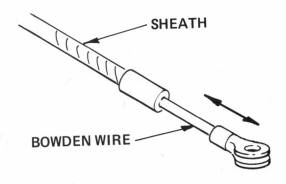

Figure 13-1. The Bowden wire cable consists of a stiff wire within a sheath. It can transmit pushes as well as pulls.

wire is affixed to the device to be controlled. Because the wire is constrained by the tube and can move only longitudinally, pushes and pulls may be transmitted without lost motion. Earliest automobiles used a Bowden wire from dashboard to carburetor to open and close the choke. (Lubricant in the tubing reduces friction.)

The Bowden wire type of control is extremely popular with builders as well as with skippers and is installed almost universally on outboard boats whose steering stations are remote from the motor. Either single-lever or double-lever controls command each engine. One lever of the double-lever design regulates engine speed; the second lever positions the gearshift for forward, reverse or neutral. Each lever has a Bowden cable connecting it with the engine. The single-lever control unit either combines throttle and shift into one cable or employs two Bowden cables operable from the one lever. A double cable steerer is shown in Figure 13-2.

It is recommended that the control units be installed at the steering station in such a manner that the levers swing parallel to the center line of the boat. This position orients the forward and aftward movement of the levers with the corresponding motion of the boat and avoids confusion. The shift lever has a clearly defined midposition which identifies neutral. The throttle lever increases speed when it is pushed forward.

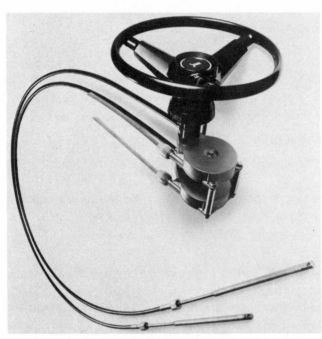

Figure 13-2. *The need for more "muscle" in steering systems to make them adequately and safely able to control today's higher horsepower outboard motors has brought the twin cable steerer shown above. The unit is suitable for single as well as twin installations. (Teleflex Marine)*

Figure 13-3. *The two motors of an outboard boat are controlled handily by these two levers that may be moved singly or together with one hand. (Evinrude Motors)*

For ease of recognition and to help prevent error under shipboard conditions, the throttle control knob of the double-lever unit is red and the shift knob is black. Further standardization for single-engine installations using the double-lever control puts the throttle to the right and the shift to the left.

Throttle and shift are independent of each other in the double-lever controls. Consequently, the shift may remain in neutral while the throttle is moved for starting and for revving the engine during warm-up. Many single-lever controls cannot do this because throttle and shift are interconnected. In these, engine speed in neutral is restricted to idling because any further movement of the lever shifts the transmission to forward travel. However, single-lever controls that employ two Bowden cables have provision for temporarily disconnecting the shift, usually by pressing a button.

Console control for twin engines may be had in several variations; one is shown in Figure 13-3. A favorite consists of a double housing with four levers. The two central levers are throttle controls, the two outside levers control the transmission. The far left lever and the adjacent central lever are for the port engine, and the far right lever and its adjacent lever are for the starboard engine. This arrangement makes command of power easy for the helmsman. After moving the outside levers to forward, he can change speed of both engines simultaneously by gripping both central levers in one hand moving them back and forth together. For maneuvering, all levers are manipulated separately as required.

On larger vessels, where the distance from wheelhouse to the engines is great, the Bowden wire is superseded by ordinary cables and pulleys. (See Figure 13-4.) Obviously, this is a more complicated system, harder to install and less amenable to circumventing obstacles in its path. Nevertheless, the cables can terminate at the console in control units similar to those already described and as easy to operate.

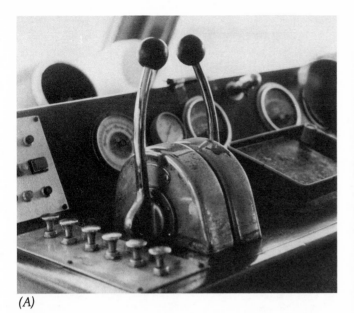

(A)

Figure 13-4. Shown here are the two terminals of a cable and pulley engine control system suitable for large boats where considerable distance separates console and engines. At (A) are the two single levers, each controlling one engine. A double steel cable leads from each, through pipes, to its engine, where the cable terminates in a chain that turns a sprocket (B) connected to throttle and transmission.

(B)

Fluid cannot be compressed, thus there is no backlash, and it is conducted through flexible tubing without regard for bends needed to get around obstacles. This makes fluid ideal for remote-control applications. Although most hydraulic control systems are used for steering, some are available for actuating throttle and transmission of propulsion engines. The principle of operation is simply that movement of the control lever creates a pressure that moves a piston at the far end. The piston is attached to whatever component one desires to regulate.

Modern automobile shift levers will not permit the engine to be started unless it is in neutral; this is an important safety feature. Many remote controls, especially those for outboard motors, incorporate this same safety device. Having the boat shoot ahead wildly when the engine is started because the shift inadvertently was left in gear thus becomes impossible.

The single-lever controls have a bonus safety aspect. Since the control lever passes through the idle speed position when shifting from forward to reverse, the change in the transmission takes place under correct idle speed conditions. With separate levers for throttle and for transmission, a forgetful skipper could make the shift with a speeding engine to the accompaniment of a ruinously clashing mechanism and perhaps an accident.

Control units should be installed sufficiently far from

the steering wheel to avoid interference. The helmsman must be able to turn the wheel freely without at any time having his hand come closer than 3 inches to the levers; this prevents banged knuckles. Proximity to the compass also must be considered if any part of the control is constructed of magnetic material.

Vibration is a factor on most boats, and this could cause the throttle lever to fail to hold a set speed unless a friction brake is incorporated in the control. Usually the amount of friction is adjustable to meet local conditions. Control units especially designed for flybridge use are available; these are without the slots that could allow rain to enter.

Older boats, with handles at the transmission for manual shifting, may be adapted to remote control. One such conversion is shown in Figure 13-5. A Bowden cable with the proper fittings attaches to the shift lever at a point that allows the needed travel and goes to the console. The limiting factor that determines whether or not this scheme can be used on a particular engine is the pounds of pull and push necessary to accomplish shifting. The strength of the Bowden cable sets the maximum figure.

The effort in pounds needed to make the manual shifts is measured with a spring scale hooked to the handle of the manual shift. The test is made with the engine running. The reading on the spring scale is correlated

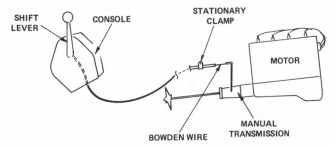

Figure13-5. A Bowden wire cable may be rigged to control a manual transmission from the console.

with the specifications given by the Bowden cable manufacturer.

The starting control on the console of a boat powered with a gasoline engine will be an ignition switch similar to those found on automobiles. The engine is stopped by turning this same switch off. Starting and stopping a diesel engine is slightly more complicated because of the absence of an electrical ignition system. A button, perhaps with a key for security, energizes the starting solenoid, which in turn powers the starter. Stopping is done either with another button and a solenoid fuel shutoff or else with a Bowden cable that shuts off the fuel.

One common form of such a shutoff is shown in Figure 13-6. A small solenoid, actuated by a push button on the console, moves the governor/throttle mechanism to a fully closed position and cuts off the fuel supply completely. The push button is held down only long enough for the engine to stop and is then released. The solenoid draws current only while the button is activated.

A properly installed propulsion engine will have automatic shutoffs that stop the machine in the event of excessive temperature or insufficient lubrication. These two conditions are rapid destroyers, and the engine could be ruined in the short time it takes the skipper to react to instrument readings. Again, the diesel installation is more complicated than the one for gasoline. The sensors for temperature and oil pressure need only break the ignition circuit to stop the gasoline engine while they must actuate some form of fuel cutoff in order to halt the diesel engine.

Figure 13-6. The stop solenoid on a diesel engine is activated by a button on the console. Application of current to the solenoid causes its armature to be drawn in, thereby closing the connected throttle or governor.

One ingrained fault often appears in the sensors that monitor excessive temperature. They must be in contact with the cooling water in order to function. Consequently, low water in the system, which leaves the sensor dry, may make it fail to respond in the emergency condition.

The two engines of a twin installation must run at identical speeds; in other words, they must be synchronized for best performance. It is possible but painstaking to synchronize engines manually; this chore is best left to electrical or mechanical synchronizers. One such device is shown in Figure 13-7.

One engine is chosen as the lead engine, and the other engine becomes the slave. Automatic engine synchronizers operate by taking speed information constantly from the lead engine and then manipulating the throttle

Figure 13-7. The skipper need control only the one throttle of the engine designated as "master" whereupon this device automatically brings the other engine, the "slave," into synchronism. (Glendinning Marine)

of the slave engine until it matches the leader's speed. The difference in speed, when such exists, is the "error signal" that activates the synchronizer. This error signal is amplified in various ways until a force strong enough to move the throttle is developed.

Unsynchronized engines in a twin installation can be an uncomfortable nuisance because the "beat" that is generated can be heard and even felt throughout the boat. The beat results from the difference in engine speeds. Thus with one engine turning at 2,600 rpm and the other at 2,500 rpm, a beat of 100 impulses per minute is produced. In minor cases, this will be merely a continuous low-pitched sound. The hull itself often amplifies this sound until it can be felt as a vibration and become uncomfortable.

Synchronizers also make it possible to control both engines by moving only one of the throttle levers, the one governing the lead engine. As explained, any change in the lead will be reproduced immediately in the slave. (Manual synchronization is aided by the electronic indicator described in Chapter 15.)

Some outboard motor remote controls include a so-called hot horn. The small, vibrator type horn can be mounted on the instrument panel or left integral with the control. A raucous noise is triggered by an overheated engine.

Figure 13-8. This is the device on the engine that divides the single lever motion from the console into two components—one to control the transmission and the other to move the throttle.

The pitching of the boat in a heavy sea often raises the propellers out of the water. This relieves the engine of its load and causes immediate overspeeding, a detrimental situation. It is almost impossible for a helmsman to react to this situation with a throttle adjustment quickly enough to be effective. By contrast, a mechanical governor does react instantly and prevents excessive speed. Hence, many propulsion engines are equipped with governors set for the maximum rpm specified by the manufacturer.

Many transmissions use a "servo" method of operation. This means that the actual work required to make the shift called for by the remote control is done by a force generated in the unit. In this instance the remote control merely controls and need supply no work; as a consequence, the Bowden cable can be of lighter construction.

The lineal motion of the cable from the single control at the console must be divided into two motions in order to govern both throttle and transmission. The mechanism that does this is shown in Figure 13-8. An ingenious system of gearing inside this device separates the initial movement of the console lever into forward-neutral-reverse control of the transmission. Subsequent movement opens the throttle from the idling position. When the console lever is returned to its initial position, the sequence of actions is reversed.

14. *Transmissions, Drives and Propellers*

The marine engine is essentially a high-speed machine; a propeller functions best at comparatively low speed. These divergencies are solved by the transmission that interfaces between them and connects them. In addition, the transmission allows power to be directed to forward or reverse and provides a neutral position wherein the propeller can be stationary while the engine is running.

The transmission may be only that housed in the lower unit of an outboard motor, or it may be a complicated, heavy housing containing gears and clutches at the flywheel end of a huge diesel engine. It may be operable manually by an integral lever or subject to remote control with responsive servo action. Whatever forms it takes, the transmission acts as the variable connection between engine and propeller. Figure 14-1 shows a representative marine transmission.

Actually, the transmission commonly found attached to inboard engines performs two distinct functions, even though the "works" may all be in one housing. It selects forward, neutral and reverse by means of clutches. It

Figure 14-1. The marine transmission is much sturdier than its automotive counterpart because it must be able to transmit full engine power continuously. The unit is controlled by the small lever shown with two adjustment holes. (Warner Gear)

reduces engine speed to the desired propeller speed by means of gearing. Overall, some form of control is utilized to shift the mechanism from one condition to another.

Clutches are devices that depend for their action on the friction between two surfaces. These surfaces can be flat plates, drums with encircling bands or mating cones. In each case, one drives the other when the two are pressed tightly together. In this condition the clutches are said to be "engaged." When the surfaces are separated, no torque or force is transmitted and the clutches are "disengaged." Engagement and disengagement are manual in the simplest units and hydraulic from a remote point in the more advanced.

Some friction surfaces are designed to function without lubrication, and these are called dry clutches. Others, wet clutches, are bathed in lubricant when running. Since the lube reduces the frictional ability of the surfaces, wet clutches carry less power than dry ones. The dry variety must really be kept dry because water or oil seriously affects their operation.

It is important that clutches be either fully engaged or completely disengaged. Partial engagement allows slippage between the friction surfaces, and this can quickly destroy them. This is the reason why stress is laid on the necessity for moving transmission controls to the limit of their travel when shifting.

Gears are wheels with teeth that have been machined to a standard size and shape so that gears of various diameters can "mesh" and drive each other. When two meshed gears are of equal diameter, equivalent to having equal numbers of teeth, their speeds of rotation will be identical. If the gear applying the driving force is twice the diameter or has twice the number of teeth of the driven gear, then the latter will rotate twice as fast as its driver and the ratio is said to be one to two (written 1:2). Were the smaller gear to do the driving, the larger would rotate at half the speed of the smaller, and the ratio would be 2:1. Figure 14-2 explains this graphically.

Gears are a convenient method of reversing rotation between two shafts, and this phenomenon is the basis of

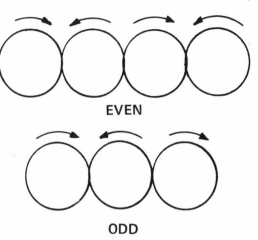

Figure 14-3. *The output direction of a system of gears or pulleys with an even number of components is the reverse of the input. An odd number of components allows the output to rotate in the same direction as the input.*

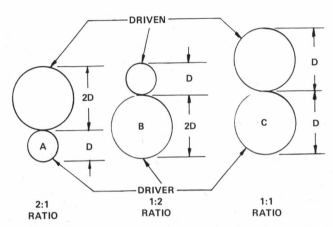

Figure 14-2. *The drive ratio of gears and pulleys is the ratio of their diameters. At (A) the driver is half the diameter of the driven and the ratio is 2 to 1. At (B) the situation is reversed and the ratio becomes 1 to 2. At (C) with both diameters equal, the ratio is 1 to 1.*

reversing gears in boats. When the drive is through an even number of gears, as for instance two or four, the driven shaft will be opposite in rotation to the driver. An odd number of gears in the drive will cause the final driven shaft to turn in the same direction as the driver. Figure 14-3 makes all this clear.

Combine the concepts of clutches and of gears, and the result is a complete marine transmission. The name "transmission" may imply a similarity with automobile transmissions, but this is not true.

The difference between the manual automobile transmission and the marine transmission lies in the manner of obtaining forward and reverse. The car unit actually shifts gears into mesh and then unmeshes them. The marine unit moves no gears because all gears are constantly in mesh; clutches pick power off the desired ones. Car automatic transmissions also keep their gears in constant mesh, hence a limited similarity.

The major difference between automobile and marine transmissions is in the heft of their construction. The marine version is the stronger. A car engine seldom transmits its full power through its transmission; usually only a small fraction of the rated horsepower is going through. A marine transmission carries the total output

of its engine most of the time it is under way. Nor does a boat require the one-two-three change in speed needed by a car.

A special form of gearing called planetary (because of a supposed similarity to the sun and its planets) forms an internal part of many marine transmissions. A small central gear called the sun meshes with a number of surrounding small planet gears on a carrier, and these in turn mesh with an outside ring having internal teeth. (See Figure 14-4.) Complex relationships exist between the relative rotations of the ring gear, the sun gear and the carrier of the planets, and this fact is used to achieve speed changes and reversals. The rotational variations are obtained by holding either the outside ring gear or the planet carrier stationary.

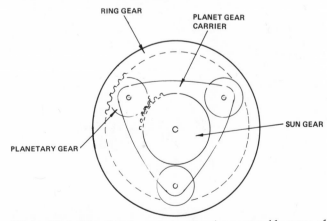

Figure 14-4. *The planetary gear system is so named because of its resemblance to the sun and its planets. Relative sizes of the gears determine the drive ratios. Reversal is accomplished by holding the carrier stationary.*

Some transmissions provide straight-through drive. In other words, the crankshaft of the driving engine and the propeller shaft exiting from the housing are in a straight line. Others, especially transmissions that include reduction gearing, have offset drives; driving shaft and driven shaft are at different levels. The offset makes it possible to keep the propeller shaft either lower or higher than the engine crankshaft, as conditions demand. How transmissions and engines are joined is shown in Figure 14-5.

The internal control system of a typical manual transmission comprises two clutches or else one clutch and a brake band around a planetary cluster, all responsive to an external lever. The lever has three distinct positions at which either a clutch or a brake band or neither would be activated, corresponding to forward, reverse and neutral. A Bowden cable from the engine control on the helmsman's console moves the lever. A certain force is required to do this, and the cable must be able to transmit it.

The more advanced, hydraulically operated transmissions relieve the Bowden cable of doing any actual work. The cable merely positions the lever, and oil under pressure actuates the clutches and brakes. The pump that supplies the pressured oil is self-contained in some transmissions and attached to the engine in others. A spring-loaded relief valve keeps the pressure within design limits regardless of speed. Some transmissions share their oil with the engine while other types keep their oil segregated in a sump. Heat exchangers to keep the oil cool are fairly common components.

It should be fairly clear by now that it is impossible to "clash gears" on a marine transmission. That, however, does not mean that a marine transmission cannot be abused. Going into forward or reverse with the engine at too high a speed gives a shock to the entire drive system, from engine to propeller. An instant change from forward to reverse while running at high speed

Figure 14-5. How transmissions and engines join into one solid unit is shown below. (Warner Gear)

does the same, only more so. Of course, emergency conditions may demand this latter maneuver regardless of consequences.

Often it is desirable to place the engine in the stern of the hull to segregate its odor and noise from the passenger portion of the vessel. A specialized transmission called a vee drive makes this possible.

The vee drive allows the drive train from the engine to

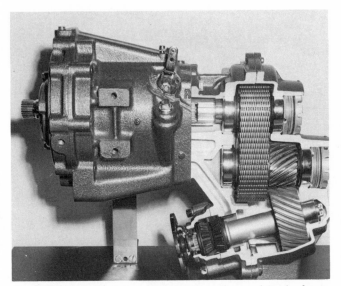

Figure 14-6A. The internal mechanism of a vee drive is shown above. The silent chain and the herringbone bevel gears accomplish the reversal in drive direction. (Warner Gear)

Figure 14-6B. The vee drive permits an engine to be set far back in the hull. This unit passes the propeller shaft back under the engine to the propeller. (Walter Machine Co.)

the propeller to be bent (see Figure 14-6B) back upon itself as shown; it also permits a more level engine installation with more space under the crankcase. The internals of a vee drive are shown in Figure 14-6A.

A transmission with gears and clutches is not the only manner in which power can be transmitted from the engine to the propeller. The drive medium can be entirely hydraulic, and the engine can be located anywhere in the hull without an intervening shaft to the propeller. The connection between power and prop is tubing carrying high-pressure oil.

The propulsion engine drives an oil pump. A hydraulic motor connected to the propeller runs on the pump output. Valves in the tubing joining the two provide forward, neutral, reverse and changes of speed. The system is a closed circuit so that the oil is recirculated continuously without waste. This method is not in general use, but it has been installed in some small boats. A schematic drawing of a hydraulic drive installation is shown in Figure 14-7.

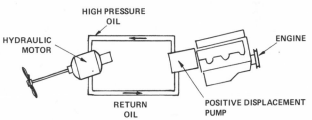

Figure 14-7. Hydraulic drive eliminates the propeller shaft between engine and prop. Oil under high pressure does the work. The engine drives the pump and the hydraulic motor turns the propeller. The oil circulates in a closed circuit.

Another transmissionless method of propelling a boat also utilizes a pump, but this time the device is pumping sea water. The pump ingests water from under the boat and forces it through a nozzle at high velocity. With the stream directed aft, the boat moves forward, and when the stream is turned to the forward direction, the boat goes into reverse. (See Figure 14-8.)

Why this scheme should work is puzzling until recourse is had to laws discovered by Isaac Newton nearly three centuries ago. He stated that every action has an equal and opposite reaction. In this case the "action" consists in hurling masses of water out toward the rear. The reactive force against the nozzle pushes the boat forward. The more water shot out, and the faster, the greater the push. It is important to realize that the jet of water does not push "against" anything; whether the jet is directed into the water or into the air makes very little difference.

The makers of jet drives emphasize simplicity and safety. The total installation consists of the pump driven by the engine plus intake port and outflow nozzle with a reversing scoop. The safety lies in the absence of a dangerous propeller. The lack of a prop extending down below the hull makes a jet-propelled boat ideal for shallow water and for beaching. Weed pickup is an only partially solved problem.

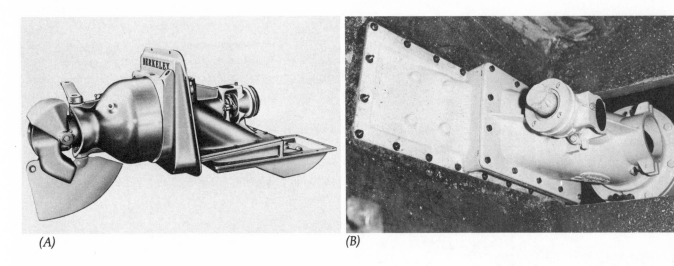

(A) (B)

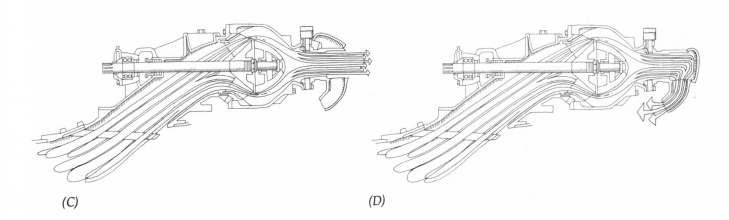

(C) (D)

Figure 14-8. These illustrations tell the complete jet-drive story. The jet-drive unit itself is shown at (A) without the driving engine. A view of this unit installed in a boat and ready for its engine is at (B). The water flow through the unit for forward propulsion is diagrammed at (C), and the action of the deflector for reverse is pictured at (D). (Berkeley Pump Co.)

A very specialized form of propulsion is employed by the "airboat" shown in Figure 14-9. This method combines boat and airplane technology to produce a craft that draws only inches of water and can skim over marshland and often even over wet grass. The engines used range from automotive to aircraft. The propeller is a standard type used on small planes. The need for the complete wire mesh enclosure is obvious.

The simple transmission contained in the lower unit of an outboard motor was mentioned earlier, and is now shown in detail in Figure 14-10. A central bevel gear driven by the motor meshes with two bevel gears riding free on a common shaft. Between these two gears, and splined to the same shaft so that it may be slid back and forth, is a "dog." Moving this dog into contact with one of the two gears with the shift lever results in forward thrust of the propeller; contact with the other gear brings reverse.

This is rather crude shifting, and unless done at very low motor speed, it can be uncomfortable for the passengers and unhealthy for the machine. The difficulty is that no provision for slip exists. An improvement that does allow for slip and adds remote control as a bonus is one form of the electric shift shown in Figure 14-11. Power to the drive shaft is transmitted through springs, which add resilience and smoothness. Electric solenoids or electromagnets anchor either spring when the shift is made. When no current is applied, the springs ride free and the outboard motor is in neutral.

The stern drive, also called inboard/outboard drive, is the latest form of propulsion to become popular with

Figure 14-9. The airboat derives its thrust from a large airplane propeller. The principle is the same as that which governs the marine propeller: A large mass of air is driven rearward at high velocity and the reaction provides forward thrust. (International Airboat Co.)

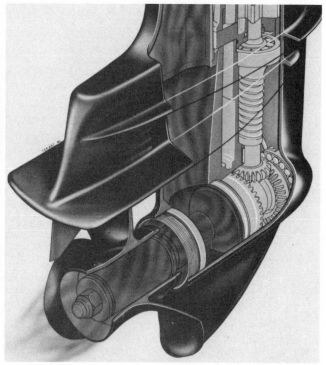

Figure 14-10. How the vertical drive shaft meshes with the horizontal propeller shaft in the lower unit of an outboard motor is shown in this cutaway photo. Note the gearing for forward and reverse. (Mercury Marine)

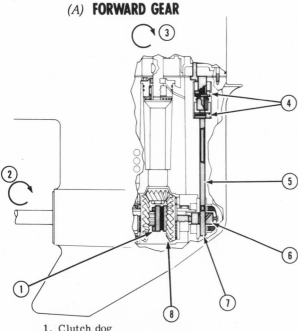

(A) **FORWARD GEAR**

1. Clutch dog
2. Propeller rotates clockwise
3. Driveshaft rotates clockwise
4. Piston down
5. Push rod down
6. Plunger forward
7. Shift rod
8. Forward gear

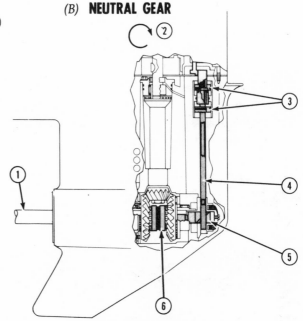

(B) **NEUTRAL GEAR**

1. No propeller rotation
2. Driveshaft rotates clockwise
3. Piston in neutral
4. Push rod
5. Plunger in neutral
6. Clutch dog in neutral

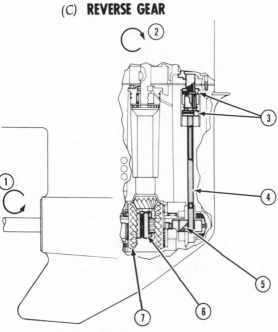

(C) **REVERSE GEAR**

1. Propeller rotates counterclockwise
2. Driveshaft rotates clockwise
3. Piston up
4. Push rod up
5. Plunger in reverse
6. Clutch dog
7. Reverse gear

Figure 14-11. On the larger outboard motors, shifting is done remotely, either with the aid of electric solenoids or of hydraulic pistons. These three drawings explain the piston actions that take place for forward, reverse or neutral conditions. At (A) the shift has been made into forward, at (B) into neutral and at (C) into reverse. (OMC Stern Drive)

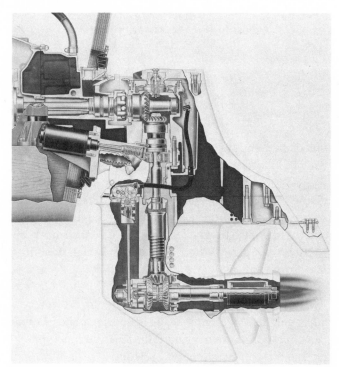

Figure 14-12. *The path power takes from the engine to the propeller in a stern drive unit is shown clearly in this cutaway photo. The right angled changes in direction are accomplished by bevel gears. The lowest bevel gears provide the forward/ reverse capability. (OMC Stern Drive)*

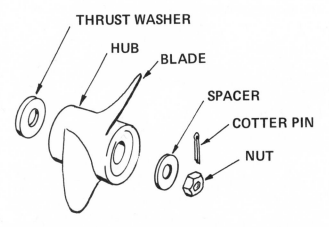

Figure 14-13. *The parts of a typical propeller are named. The "twist" of the blades relative to the hub determines the "pitch."*

pleasure boat skippers. The cutaway view in Figure 14-12 shows that the engine is inside the boat at the extreme stern, and that the drive unit is fastened to the outside of the transom. Thus the best features of inboard drive and outboard drive are combined, and the engine is moved away from its traditional inboard position at the center of the boat.

A strong advantage of the stern drive is that it employs a standard four-cycle engine and not the two-cycle type found in outboard motors. This relieves the skipper of the chore of mixing lubricating oil with the fuel (see Chapter 3) and gives him a more economical powerplant. Engines with greater horsepower output than those available as outboards may be selected for heavier or speedier boats.

Advantages also exist on the other side of the transom. The stern-drive unit swings for steering. This directs the propeller thrust in the desired direction and makes the boat much more responsive to the helm than it would be with a rudder. The stern-drive unit copies the outboard motor in its ability to be tilted up for boat trim, clearance of obstacles or trailering. With many stern drives it is even possible to tilt them sufficiently to change propellers while under way.

A stern-drive installation can bring problems to some hulls because the great weight of the engine is so far astern. This becomes more acute as larger engines are selected and imposes an automatic limit on the maximum power that can be installed in any given craft. Best success is had with stern drives when they are built into boats designed for them.

By far the vast majority of pleasure boats relies on standard propellers at the end of the drive train to generate the needed thrust. Propellers are made in diameters ranging from a few inches to many feet and with from two to six blades. The drawing in Figure 14-13 gives the nomenclature for the various parts.

Propellers are called screws colloquially, and this may give rise to a misconception of how they function. Many think that a prop screws its way through the water in the manner of a common screw driving into wood. This is incorrect. A propeller is an inertial device and follows the Newtonian law of action and reaction. It accelerates a mass of water and hurls it sternward, and the reaction from this action is forward thrust. (Note the similarity to the jet.) But this is only part of what the revolving propeller accomplishes.

The thrust just discussed is created by the face of the propeller blade, the surface away from the boat. This surface is shaped to throw water aftward at a high rate. The back of the blade, the surface toward the boat, has a totally different mission. Its shape in cross section is an airfoil similar to that of an airplane wing. When the propeller revolves, the water flows across this airfoil at increased velocity and becomes subject to a law expounded by another scientist two centuries ago, Bernoulli. The law states very simply that the greater the velocity, the lower the pressure. Thus the back of the blade is an area of low pressure or partial vacuum and the water is drawn to it. This pull is quite considerable (the airplane people call it lift), and, in fact, its force exceeds the pushing force developed by the face. The sum of the push and the pull makes up the total thrust exerted by the prop on the boat. (See Figure 14-14.)

Propellers are rated by three parameters in addition to the nature of their material, the number of blades and the

AREA OF HIGH PRESSURE (THRUST SIDE) **AREA OF LOW PRESSURE (SUCTION SIDE)**

Figure 14-14. The blades of a turning propeller are subject to the forces pictured above. The after side of the blade creates high pressure and thrust. The forward side reduces pressure and "draws" the water to it.

size of the shaft hole. These are: diameter, pitch and rotation. The diameter is the diameter of a circle that just includes the prop; it is specified in inches for pleasure boats. The pitch is the amount the propeller would advance in one revolution if it were moving through a solid like a screw through wood; this, too, is specified in inches. Rotation can be clockwise, or right-hand, and counterclockwise, or left-hand. Rotation is always de-

termined as though the viewer were standing behind the boat and looking forward.

It is generally assumed, though very loosely, that the diameter of the propeller bears a close relation to the power required to drive it (the larger, the more power) and that the pitch bears a relation to speed of the boat (the greater, the faster). When diameter and pitch are equal, the prop is called square and is considered to be at best efficiency.

The selection of the correct propeller for a given boat takes engine power, hull shape, displacement and other facts into consideration and then relies as much on experience as on mathematical science. A rule of thumb available to technician and layman alike makes use of a tachometer and the rated rpm of the engine. The right propeller will hold the engine to its rated top speed. If the engine will not come up to this speed, the pitch is too great. If the engine exceeds its rated speed, the pitch is too small.

Propellers often cause a rumble in the after part of the vessel. The noise is the result of pressure waves from each blade striking the hull. Many times the cure is to change to a prop with a different number of blades.

"Cavitation" is a common disease among high-speed propellers. Simply stated, in this condition the propeller blades lose full contact with the water either because of excessive speed or because the suction pressure on the blade back has become too high. Vapor and air bubbles in the cavitation zone collapse onto the blade with thunderclap intensity and, unbelievably, can erode the metal. One cure for cavitation is lower rpm. Outboard motors have a cavitation plate directly over the propeller, and this is an effective deterrent.

As emphasized earlier, the propeller is not a screw working in a solid. It can never advance in one revolution the distance its pitch rating calls for. The difference between the actual advance and the theoretical is called slip. The word "slip" has a pejorative connotation and may convey the impression of an inherent fault. This is not the case. There can be no thrust without slip, and every installation has a percentage of slip that is optimum. The end point would be a boat firmly tied to a pier but with its propellers revolving at maximum rpm. In such a purely illustrative situation, the slip would be 100 percent.

Propellers are available on which the blades can be turned to achieve different pitches. These are called variable pitch, and the more complicated can be varied from inside the boat while under way. The newest Coast Guard cutters use props of this kind and thereby are able to dispense with reverse gears. For going astern, the blades are turned to the opposite hand.

Sailboats with installed auxiliary engines may have trouble with their transmissions when the vessel is under sail alone because the propeller "freewheels." In this mode, the movement of the water turns the prop, even though the engine is stationary. Some transmissions do not have provision for adequate lubrication when this happens.

Although the propeller usually extends below the hull, but not necessarily below the keel, a type of design called a "tunnel stern" keeps the prop entirely within the confines of the hull. This is shown in Figure 14-15. One advantage is the reduction in draft, which makes the boat able to navigate in shallow water.

A further advantage of the tunnel-driving arrangement is an increase in propeller efficiency because the tunnel acts as a shroud that confines and directs the inflow of water and reduces eddying. Another bonus is that the propeller is positioned more nearly vertical than is possible with standard inboard drive and therefore directs its thrust more effectively along the direction of boat travel. Figure 14-16 illustrates this.

Another scheme places a close cylinder around the propeller to increase its efficiency. This is the equivalent of a pseudo-housing for a propeller that normally operates as a "pump" without a housing.

A single propeller pushing a boat often introduces an undesired sideward component which necessitates rudder correction in order to follow a straight course. Twin propellers turning in opposite directions neutralize this tendency. In addition the skipper is given the choice of using either or both props in forward or reverse as an aid in close maneuvering. The usual installation has a left-hand propeller to port and a right hand prop to starboard as shown in Figure 14-17. The opposite of this arrangement is also used, but is less desirable from a maneuvering standpoint.

Good propellers are balanced statically and dynami-

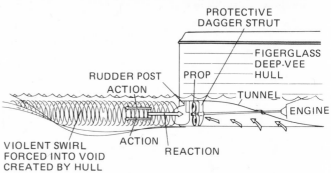

Figures 14-15 & 14-16. The photograph shows the actual construction of the tunnel stern in a fiberglass hull. The accompanying drawing explains propeller action. Note that the drive shaft is almost horizontal, permitting the prop to be vertical for maximum forward thrust. (Penn Yan Boat)

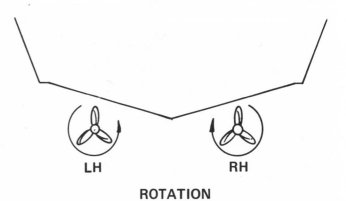

Figure 14-17. The rotation of propellers is specified when viewed from astern. Props turning counterclockwise are called "left hand," those turning clockwise are called "right hand."

cally by the maker and should run without vibration. If vibration suddenly ensues, it is a certain sign that the blades have been damaged by having been bent or nicked. The higher the speed at which the propeller rotates, the more likely that a small change in its mass will be felt aboard as vibration. Bad vibration not only is uncomfortable but has a damaging effect on shaft, bearings and even the engine.

When all is said and done, when the slide rules have been pushed and the electronic calculators punched, the question whether a propeller is fitted correctly to boat and engine may still be devoid of a definitive answer. Trial runs may be the only way to reach a final solution.

A standard propeller on an auxiliary sailboat may become a speed-reducing drag when the vessel is under sail alone. One solution for a hull with a large full keel is to employ a two-blade prop and clamp it vertically in the shadow of the keel, out of the way of the slipstream. A solution for other types of sailboat hulls is the folding propeller, two models of which are shown in Figure 14-18.

When the auxiliary engine is not in use, the blades of these propellers swing into a horizontal position and produce negligible drag. Centrifugal force brings the blades into operative position when the engine is turned on.

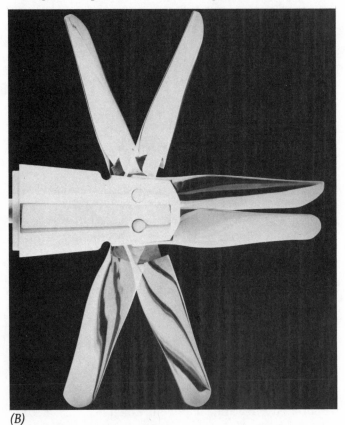

(B)

Figure 14-18. Folding propellers reduce the drag on the hull of an auxiliary sailboat when it is proceeding under sail and eliminate the need for a shaft brake. The photos show the various positions of the blades for slow, fast, and reverse. At (A) an American design by Martec Engineering; at (B) a Danish design by Gori Marine.

(A)

Figure 14-19 explains some transmission relationships. Figure 14-20 portrays a transmission designed with extra-short fore and aft length. This could prove to be a boon for boats where engine space is at a premium.

A boat must swing its stern in order to change the direction in which its bow points. This peculiarity makes maneuvering in tight places difficult. Big ships traditionally have alleviated this difficulty with bow thrusters, and now a bow thruster, scaled down for small yachts, is available on the market.

A bow thruster literally thrusts the bow, pushes it to one side or the other at the command of the helmsman. Large vessels accomplish this thrusting with a propeller at the bow that can be swung in any desired direction. Activating this propeller by means of a console control moves the bow independently of the stern. The power for this prop may be an electric motor, a hydraulic motor driven by a pump on the main engine, or even a separate local engine.

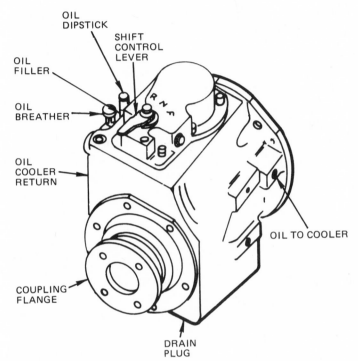

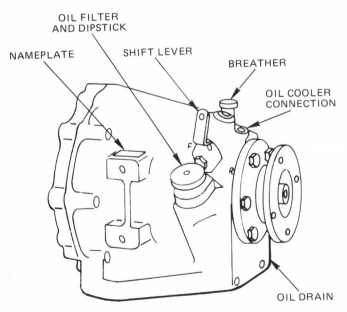

Figure 14-19. Named above are the important items on two popular marine transmissions.

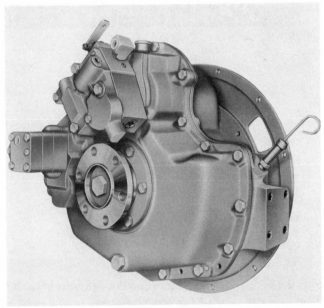

Figure 14-20. This transmission, designed with an extremely short case, permits compact power installations. The in-line style reduces overall height. (Twin Disc Co.)

(A)

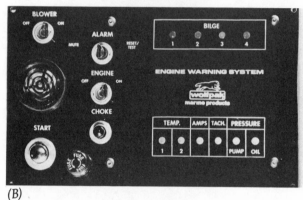

(B)

The separate engine type of bow thruster designed for a small yacht is shown in Figure 14-21. At (A) is the engine with its pump; this is a gasoline unit, note the flame arrestor. The control panel for the installation is pictured at (B) and it includes a horn for aural warning of any operational failures. An explanatory schematic diagram of the system is at (C).

The makers state that this bow thruster may be installed in a locker forward or even under a bunk. Since the Coast Guard has mandatory regulations governing enclosed engine spaces, such installations must strictly conform.

Bow thrusters of this type direct a high velocity stream of water either to port or starboard from the bow. Just as in the more familiar jet drive, the reaction provides the thrust. A stream to port pushes the bow to starboard; a stream to starboard pushes the bow to port. This is shown by the diagram in Figure 14-22.

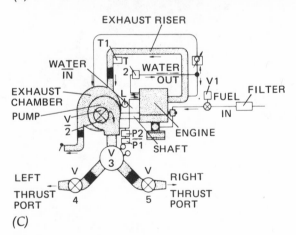

(C)

Figure 14-21. A gasoline-driven bow thruster for small yachts is at (A); note the flame arrestor. The remote control panel is shown at (B). The schematic drawing, (C), explains the action of the unit. (Wolfpak Marine)

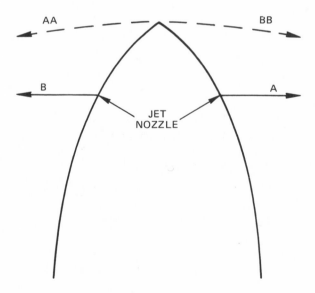

Figure 14-22. This diagram shows how a high velocity jet of water at (A) pushes the bow in direction (AA) because of reaction. Similarly, the jet (B) thrusts the bow in direction (BB). (Wolfpak Marine)

PART THREE
ENGINE ACCESSORIES

15. *Instruments, Gauges and Sensors*

T he modern high-speed marine engine needs closer supervision than the unaided senses of man can provide. Instruments have stepped into the breach. By letting his eyes roam casually over the console panel, a skipper is now able to keep accurate track of every phase of operation of his powerplant. Modern installations even have warnings of trouble that alert his ears if his eyes become careless.

Low-voltage electricity from the battery is the force that operates most of the instruments on the console panel. Other instruments function either mechanically or by means of pressure. Variations in these actuating forces caused by fluctuations within the running engine appear on the instruments as readings of the various parameters being monitored. The internal working of the powerplant is judged by measuring lubricating oil pressure, temperature, speed of rotation, battery charging ability and, on the more sophisticated panels, even the rate at which fuel is being gulped and the pressures in the engine manifolds.

The simplest instruments, and perhaps the most rugged, are those that measure pressure mechanically without electricity. They may be recognized because a tubing rather than a wire will connect them. When the pressures to be measured are above atmospheric, these instruments are called pressure gauges; below atmospheric pressures or vacuums the name changes to vacuum gauges. The internal structure of both gauges is the same except for the heft of the component parts.

Pressure gauges will be found universally in the lubricating oil circuits of engines as a means of checking for adequate flow. Some transmissions also have them. Vacuum gauges are often connected to the intake manifolds of gasoline engines, and a trained eye can learn much from the movements of the pointer under various conditions of engine load.

The heart of the mechanically operated pressure gauge is the Bourdon tube, shown in Figure 15-1. This is a metal tube of oval cross section which has been bent into circular shape. One end of the tube is anchored fast and is connected to the line to be measured. The other end is sealed, free to move, and linked to the dial pointer so that

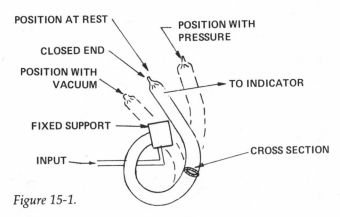

Figure 15-1.

any movement appears as a change in dial reading. The Bourdon tube for a pressure gauge would be heavier-walled and stiffer than a similar tube intended for a vacuum gauge.

It is the nature of a Bourdon tube that any pressure applied to its internal cavity will cause the tube to unbend; any vacuum will cause it to bend tighter. The linkage to the dial pointer magnifies the resultant travel of the tube's free end and allows clear readings on the calibrated dial.

The instruments that function electrically are really volt meters whose dials have been calibrated for each particular service, as, for instance, in pounds of pressure, gallons of fuel or whatever. The movements inside these meters range from the primitive, with approximate accuracy, to the complex, with extreme accuracy; the cost is in that same ascending scale.

The highly accurate meters are of the so-called d'Arsonval type illustrated in Figure 15-2. A light, carefully wound loop of fine wire carrying the pointer is free to turn between the pole pieces of a strong permanent magnet. The loop is pivoted between jewels much like those in a fine watch, and hairsprings maintain its zero position. Everything is so well balanced and friction-free that a light breath can swing the pointer to its far stop. Any current through the loop generates a magnetic field which interacts with the field of the magnet and deflects the pointer. Instruments of this caliber are expensive and therefore not often found on the panels of control consoles.

Figure 15-2. The so-called d'Arsonval meter movement is as finely constructed as a watch. Note the jewelled bearings that hold the moving coil in alignment between the magnet's poles.

Electrically operated instruments of lesser quality, those that make up the standard equipment of most boats, function either through the magnetic field created by an electric current through them or through the heat the current generates. The latter are the more common, and the general principle of their working is shown in Figure 15-3.

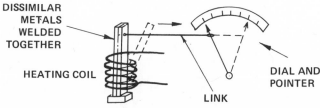

Figure 15-3. Thermal meters are among the simplest and least expensive indicators. A bimetallic strip bends in proportion to the heat generated by current flowing through the heating coil and moves the pointer across the calibrated scale.

A small strip of bimetallic material is wound with fine resistance wire that acts as a heating coil. The circuit to be measured is connected to this coil, and the resultant heat is proportional to the current flowing. The more heat, the more the strip bends, and the greater the movement of the dial pointer to which it is linked. This type of meter movement has taken over the field because it is cheap to manufacture and, at least in the opinion of its makers, sufficiently accurate for the job in hand.

The low-cost magnetic movement is a bit more complicated because it requires a wire coil, a pivoted pointer and a delicate spring or a magnet to maintain the zero position. The works are shown in Figure 15-4. The magnetic field resulting from current through the coil either pulls a link connected to the pointer or interacts with the magnet to move the pointer.

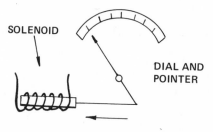

Figure 15-4. The solenoid pulls its armature in proportion to the current passing through the coil, thereby moving the pointer across the calibrated scale.

The ammeter is different in that the pointer must zero at the center of the scale and be able to swing to right or left. The actuating coil, or its equivalent, is composed of a few turns of very heavy wire, which offer minimal resistance to the current flowing through it. Ammeters are always in series with their circuits (see Chapter 8), hence the need for low resistance. An indication left of center by the pointer shows that current is being taken from the battery; a swing to the right means current is going into the battery.

The instruments so far described are sensitive to current and voltage fluctuations and cannot give correct readings unless their voltage is maintained at a steady value. But battery voltage is far from steady, swinging from 12 when the system is at rest to more than 14 when the generator or alternator is running fast enough to produce charging current. The answer is a simple voltage regulator, not to be confused with the large voltage regulator that monitors the generator or alternator.

The voltage regulator for the instruments is usually built into one of the meter cases. In its simplest form it is a

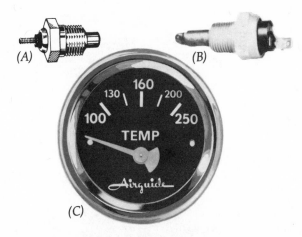

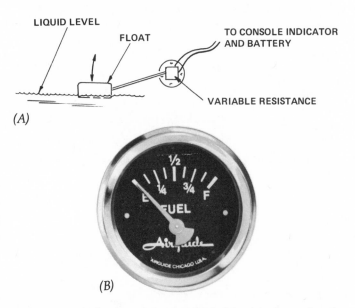

small buzzerlike device whose vibrating contacts keep the instrument voltage down to approximately 5 volts. Naturally, the instruments are calibrated at this value.

The instruments, of course, need sensors attached to the various parts of the engine to provide them with the information they register on their dials. The sensor for oil pressure is attached to a point of full pressure in the lubricating system. It is shown diagrammatically in Figure 15-5. A diaphragm bends in response to the pressure against it and moves a contact over a resistance element. The position of the contact determines the current flowing to the meter and thus the dial reading. In some sensors a compressible resistor takes the place of the movable contact.

*Figure 15-5. Engines provide a tapped hole in the lubricating circuit into which either sensor (A,B) is screwed. The changes in the sensor's electrical resistance in response to changes in oil pressure actuate the oil pressure meter (C) on the helmsman's console. (*Aqua Meter Instruments*)*

The temperature sensor also contains a variable resistance element, but this time the contact is moved by the bending of a bimetallic strip reacting to the water in the cooling system. (See Figure 15-6) Water does not actually touch the bimetal; heat is conducted through the sensor case, which extends into the cooling flow. Here, also, a

*Figure 15-6. Either sensor (A,B) is placed with its tip in the cooling water circuit. Its changes in electrical resistance govern the reading of the water temperature meter (C) on the console. (*Aqua Meter Instruments*)*

compressible resistor may be used to eliminate the movable contact.

The meter showing fuel tank content is dependent for its information on a sensor in the tank. Again the variable resistance plays its part by varying the current sent to the meter and thus the dial reading. The contact traverses the resistance in response to the rising and falling of a float that follows the fuel level. Figure 15-7 shows how this is done. This form of fuel indicator really is not adequate for marine service.

Figure 15-7. The float (A) rides the fuel level in the tank and thereby varies the electrical resistance of the sender. The console gauge (B) translates the variations in current into gallons in the tank.

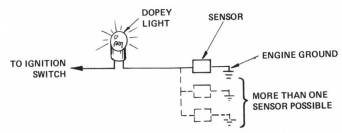

Figure 15-8. The exigencies of economics have caused many manufacturers to substitute dopey lights for the more meaningful meters. The simple circuit required is shown here.

Often, as is the custom in many automobiles, the panel is devoid of instruments, and blinking pilot lights keep the skipper apprised of what goes on in the engine room. These "dopey-lights" are the bane of the technically inclined person and a boon to those to whom a meter indication is "Greek." Manufacturers seem to love dopey-lights and with good reason; these visual indicators are the cheapest manner by which to impart information.

The dopey-light bulbs are standard, low-candlepower units of the correct voltage rating for the boat battery. The associated sensors do not contain the variable resistors already described but have only simple, make-and-break contacts. The temperature or the pressure, as the case may be, opens and closes the contact and illuminates or extinguishes its panel bulb. The colors used are usually red for any malfunction and green for "all's well." The dopey-light circuit is shown in Figure 15-8.

The tachometer for the skipper takes the place of the speedometer for the motorist. From a construction standpoint, the mechanical tachometer and the automobile speedometer are identical. A flexible cable transmits engine revolutions to the rotating element in the tach. This element is a round permanent magnet within a closely fitting rotatable metal cup. A pointer riding over the scale is attached to the cup and held at zero by a light spring.

This form of mechanical tachometer functions because of a phenomenon known as "magnetic induction." The rapidly rotating magnet induces an electric current in the surrounding metal cup. The resulting polarities are such that the cup moves against the spring, the pointer swings over the scale and the engine rpm is indicated. Figure 15-9 clarifies this. An even simpler system relies on the air drag between the two cups.

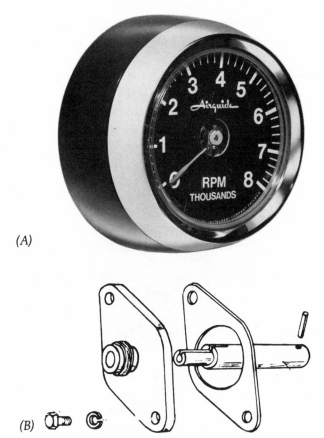

(A)

(B)

Figure 15-9. Mechanical engine tachometers (A) function on the same principle as automobile speedometers and are driven by flexible cable. (Airguide Instrument Co.) One form of cable attachment to the engine is shown at (B).

There are also other forms of tachometers. One is electronic. It is connected to the ignition system of a gasoline engine and actually counts the number of sparks taking place in a unit of time. This information is integrated by an electronic circuit whose output voltage is fed to a meter calibrated in rpm. The voltage varies in direct relationship to the speed of the engine, hence the reading. (See Figure 15-10.)

Obviously, the standard electronic tachometer will not work on a diesel engine, which, by nature, has no electric ignition. However, adapters that simulate the electric pulses and enable an electronic tach to be used are available for attachment to the diesel. The beauty of electronic tachometers is their independence of a long, bothersome, flexible cable. They can be installed at any reasonable distance from the engine because only a wire connects them. The meters supplied with the better

electronic tachometers are the d'Arsonval type and are quite accurate.

Electric tachometers (not to be confused with the electronic variety just described) are installed routinely with diesel engines. These are simple devices of high accuracy whose operation is understood easily. Figure 15-11 shows that the electric tachometer system consists of a miniature generator connected to a high-grade voltmeter calibrated in rpm.

(A)

(B)

(A)

(B)

Figure 15-10. Electronic engine tachometers (A) utilize a transistorized counting circuit that translates ignition pulses into revolutions per minute. (Airguide Instrument Co.) This electronic engine tachometer (B) actually is an electronic counter calibrated in revolutions per minute. (Aqua Meter Instruments)

Figure 15-11. The sending unit for an electric tachometer system is a small, highly accurate, engine-connected generator (A) whose output is read as revolutions per minute on a meter (B). Twin engines require two tachometers.

The generator is of instrument grade, perhaps less than 2 inches in diameter and 3 inches long, driven from a takeoff provided on the engine. The direct-current output voltage is linear with respect to speed; in other words, the voltage increases in direct proportion to the increments in revolutions per minute. Two wires lead the output voltage directly to the meter, which has been matched to the generator and calibrated with it. No battery is used.

The diesel engine has one idiosyncrasy for which a preventive control should be provided. Under certain adverse conditions, the engine could run away and divorce itself from throttle control even as a runaway horse ignores its bridle. It could continue to run, even at overspeed, after the fuel is shut off. Volatile flammable gases ingested by the air intake could cause this. An engine in bad repair that allows lubricating oil to get into the combustion chamber could be another offender; the machine will run on its own lubricant as fuel.

The runaway diesel can be stopped only by shutting off its air supply. This is accomplished by flaps that are dropped over the air intake, sealing it. The simplest flap control is a Bowden wire cable from the flaps to the console panel terminating in a knob within the helmsman's reach.

Synchronization of the two engines in a twin installation is important for passenger comfort because the recurring vibration and noise are irritating. Synchronizing is also important for the boat's longevity; the pulses of peak vibration are detrimental to boat and engine alike. Earlier, in Chapter 13, automatic synchronizing devices were discussed in which one engine leads and the other is slaved without operator attention.

Synchronization can be achieved manually by the helmsman's careful manipulation of the throttles of the two engines. Experienced skippers can "sync" by ear; they listen as the pulses become fewer and fewer and then disappear at the correct settings. But most operators need instrumentation to guide them and show them when the job is done. Tachometers are not sensitive enough to do this.

Synchronizers for gasoline engines take their inputs from the two ignition systems. They monitor and com-

*Figure 15-12. The synchronism indicator tells the skipper which engine throttle must be adjusted in order to bring both engines to exactly the same speed and thereby avoid annoying vibrations. (*Airguide Instrument Co.*)*

pare the frequencies of the sparks and indicate when both are identical; at this point both powerplants are exactly in step. A common form of indication is a blinking light that extinguishes at the critical point. Figure 15-12 shows a more sophisticated instrument with a pointer that swings right or left to indicate which engine must be speeded and rests at exactly midscale when the synchronization is achieved.

The recurring problem of having no electric ignition to which to attach is common with synchronizers for diesel engines. As with tachometers, adapters must be interfaced to send pulses indicative of the engine speed and thus give the synchronizers something to work on. This extra component, of course, increases the cost.

The universal tendency to digitalize, to have all indications appear in actual numbers, is being recognized in marine instruments as well. Pointers and scales are giving way to light-emitting diodes, nixie tubes and other means of creating lighted numbers. So far, tachometers have been the most noticeable advances into this field by engine monitoring instruments.

An instrument called a dwell meter is not yet a part of any gasoline engine cluster, but many do-it-yourself skippers have one aboard. The length of time during each revolution (the number of degrees) that the ignition breaker points remain in contact is called the dwell. This meter measures dwell while the engine is running. Correct dwell is important for best engine operation; the recommended degrees is found in the engine manual.

Switches for various electric circuits have their place

Figure 15-13. This digital battery condition meter displays battery terminal voltage to the nearest tenth of a volt in easy to read numerals. (Precision Digital Gauges)

Figure 15-14. The number of hours the engine has run is a more important gauge of engine condition than actual age. Meters such as this keep tabs on use. (Airguide Instrument Co.)

on the console panel, and in the marine environment they can become a bother. Moist air, especially salt moist air, has a corroding effect strong enough to impair the action of the switch. An insulating film forms on the contact surfaces that prevents the passage of current. A generally effective countermeasure is to move the switches from "off" to "on" to "off" rapidly and frequently. This often brings the unit back to operating condition through internal abrasion.

A voltmeter on the panel to check battery condition is an excellent addition, but this must be a type specially designed for the purpose. (See Chapter 16.) The terminal voltage of a storage battery varies only slightly between the fully charged and the partially charged conditions, and the difference is too small for an ordinary voltmeter to register meaningfully. These battery meters are called suppressed zero or expanded scale. They magnify the small voltage changes into telltales of battery condition. A digital battery monitor is shown in Figure 15-13.

For those skippers who want to monitor every heartbeat of their powerplants, engine instrumentation could include exhaust gas analyzers. A sensor in the exhaust manifold reports to the panel indicator to show the percentage of carbon monoxide in the exhaust. This is a reliable measure of how efficiently combustion is proceeding in the cylinders.

The engine hour meter is an instrument that relates more to maintenance than to the immediate running condition of the powerplant. It may also become an ally or a hindrance at the time of a future sale, depending upon whether its display of numbers is small or large.

The hour meter measures the total time that an engine has been running from the day of its installation. The simplest meters function merely as a clock that is turned on and off and runs concurrently with the engine. They do not reflect whether the engine was idling or racing during that period. More sophisticated hour meters integrate this information and give a reading that is more representative of probable engine wear.

Many skippers base their maintenance programs on engine hour meter readings. Many buyers form their opinions of the viability of powerplants by looking at these same meters. (See Figure 15-14.)

The engines of generating plants are governed automatically to maintain correct generator speed and hence proper output. Nevertheless, it is a good idea to supply instrumentation with which the skipper may keep an eye on what is going on.

The two meters shown are recommended. One is an alternating-current voltmeter. Output voltage is important because too high a value may burn out bulbs and cause other damage. The other is a frequency meter. In a way, this may also be considered a speed meter, because the frequency is directly dependent upon the revolutions per minute of the generator. The ideal reading for standard equipment is 60 cycles per second and 120 volts. (Frequency is now expressed in hertz.)

With his eye on the instrument panel and his ear alert to automatic warnings, skipper and engine can become happy shipmates.

16. *Storage Batteries and Chargers*

Despite their name and the common concept of them, storage batteries do not store electricity. They store a reversible chemical reaction, whose cause as well as effect is an electric current. Nevertheless, most skippers will probably continue to think of the storage battery as a container of electricity, and, strangely, this distortion of fact may even aid them in understanding the storage battery's function as the heart of the boat's low-voltage electrical system.

Batteries in general are of two types: primary and secondary. Primary batteries are those in use for flashlights and similar purposes and today are manufactured only in the "dry" form. Storage batteries make up the secondary class. Primary batteries will produce current until their internal active material is consumed; then they must be discarded. Secondary batteries may be discharged and recharged many times without substantial loss in their efficiency. Correctly speaking, a single unit of any of these two forms is a "cell," and a battery is composed of two or more cells together.

Storage batteries in commercial use are either lead-acid or alkaline, the former being almost universally the type installed in automobiles and boats. We owe the lead-acid storage battery to a scientist named Gaston Planté, who discovered the principle in the very early days of electrical knowledge. Much later, Thomas Edison found that a combination of nickel, iron and caustic potash could be made into an alkaline storage battery. Each of these two kinds of batteries has its niche, but the lead-acid unit is superior for the job of starting internal combustion engines.

The lead-acid storage battery will be understood more easily if comprehension of the internal reactions of a primary cell is acquired first. Two different metals immersed in a solution that attacks one of them constitutes a primary cell. The chemical attack causes a difference of potential between the two metals, and when this exists (as explained in Chapter 7), an electric current will flow. The two metals in the flashlight cell are a carbon rod and a zinc cup, and the "solution" that acts upon the zinc is a paste of ammonium chloride, zinc chloride and water.

The solution is known technically as an "electrolyte." A cross section of a "dry" primary cell is shown in Figure 16-1.

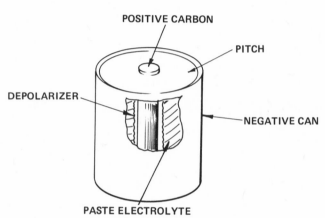

Figure 16-1. *This flashlight cell typifies the construction of primary batteries. The zinc container acts as the negative electrode and holds the electrolyte, the depolarizer and the positive carbon electrode. The depolarizer extends the useful life of the cell by neutralizing the polarizing or "choking" effect caused by normal use.*

Since an electric current is a flow of electrons, the chemical reactions within the cell must create a condition conducive to electron flow. The ammonium chloride does this by attacking the zinc. The result of this chemical reaction is an excess of negative electrons in the zinc, making it the negative terminal. The reaction also drains electrons from the mix around the carbon rod, which thus becomes the positive terminal. (An excess of electrons makes an object negative, a deficiency of electrons makes it positive.)

If the battery cell is not connected to any device requiring current—in other words if it is on "open circuit"—the foregoing reactions will take place until equilibrium is reached. In the case of carbon and zinc, this will be with a terminal voltage of 1.5 volts. Were copper to be substituted for the carbon, the terminal equilibrium would be at 1.1 volts. Each combination of metals has a preordained equilibrium voltage.

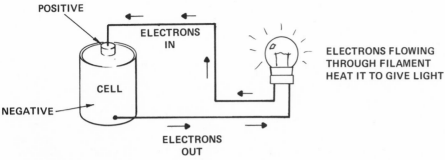

Figure 16-2. All electric current is a flow of electrons. When the circuit from cell to load is completed, electrons leave the negative pole and follow the wire back to the positive pole.

Connect the cell to a current requirement—for instance, a flashlight bulb, as shown in Figure 16-2—and the equilibrium is ended. Now the electrons have a path to follow from one terminal to the other. They will leave the negative terminal, light the flashlight bulb and return to the positive terminal to remedy the deficiency of electrons there. This will continue until either the zinc is consumed or the electrolyte is spent.

Apparently ignoring the fundamental requirement for dissimilar metals in an electrolyte, Planté constructed a cell by placing two lead plates into a jar of dilute sulfuric acid. Of course, no current was generated. Then came the stroke of genius. He connected his cell to a source of current. He had invented the lead-acid storage battery and he was charging it! (See Figure 16-3.)

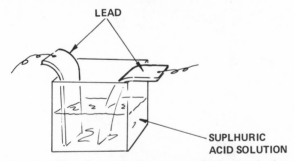

Figure 16-3. Planté's original storage cell consisted of two plain lead electrodes in a sulphuric acid solution. Forcing electric current into the cell (charging it) changed the composition of the electrodes and enabled them subsequently to produce current by chemical action.

The charging current changed the chemical nature of the two lead plates and vindicated the basic requirement for dissimilar metals to make a cell function. The surface of one lead plate became lead peroxide; the surface of the other became spongy lead. This set up an electron imbalance similar to the one mentioned earlier and met the conditions necessary for current generation.

Storage batteries are no longer manufactured by the Planté process because it is long and costly. The plates of modern batteries are intricate grids cast of a lead-antimony alloy. These grids are packed under great pressure with lead dioxide or peroxide for the positive plate and sponge lead for the negative plate. In effect, the Planté condition has been achieved artificially faster and cheaper.

What the container of a commercial storage battery holds is shown in the cutaway view of Figure 16-4. The terminal lugs of all the positive plates are welded together to form a positive group. Enough space is left between the parallel plates for subsequent interleaving. The negative plates are welded into a similar negative group. The two groups are then interleaved with insulating separators to keep plates of opposite polarity from touching; this is now the complete element for a single cell. The negative group always has one more plate than the positive group; this is done to make both outside plates in each element negative, because this helps prevent plate warpage.

Figure 16-4. This cutaway view of a three-cell/six-volt storage battery shows how the plates are connected into groups. Negative and positive groups are interleaved in each cell. (Surrette Storage Battery Co.)

The separators play an important part in the life-span and the current-supplying ability of a battery. Their primary object is to prevent short circuits, but their function goes beyond this. Of course, separators must be immune to attack by the acid. They also must allow free acid circulation because adequate current delivery depends on this; hence they are ribbed in addition to being porous. Many materials are used, among them cellulose, fiber glass, minutely porous rubber and combinations of these, even including wood. (See Figure 16-5.)

The chemical action within the storage cell involves changing the lead peroxide and the spongy lead to lead sulfate during discharge and reversing the procedure back to the original composition on charging. During discharge, the negative sulfate ion in sulfuric acid combines with the positive lead ion in the spongy lead and forms lead sulfate. At the same time, the hydrogen in the acid combines with the oxygen in the lead peroxide to form water while sulfate ions join the remaining lead and become lead sulfate. Thus, when the battery has been fully discharged, both plates will consist essentially of lead sulfate and the electrolyte will have become watery. (See Figure 16-6.)

This cycling of the electrolyte between stronger and

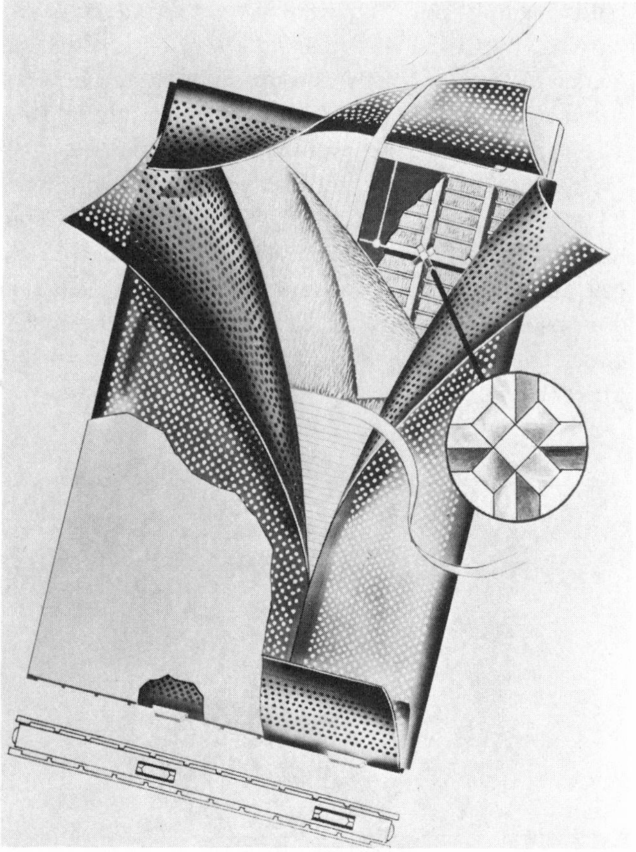

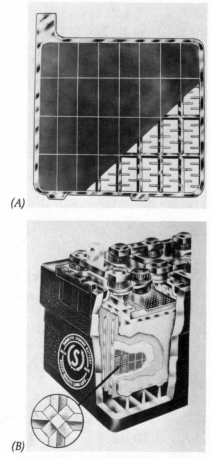

(A)

(B)

Figure 16-5. One form of separator that acts as insulation between plates of opposite polarity is shown in this closeup view of a positive storage battery plate. The enlarged portion shows a reinforced rib construction. (Surrette Storage Battery Co.)

Figure 16-6. The construction of a typical plate of a storage battery is shown at (A); how the plates fit into the assembly is illustrated at (B). (Surrette Storage Battery Co.)

weaker acid during charge and discharge is the reason why battery condition can be checked with a hydrometer. A hydrometer, shown in Figure 16-7, is a carefully weighted float used for measuring specific gravity. Sulfuric acid is heavier than water, has a greater specific gravity, and therefore the hydrometer will float higher. When the battery is discharged and the sulfuric acid is weakened by water, the hydrometer floats lower.

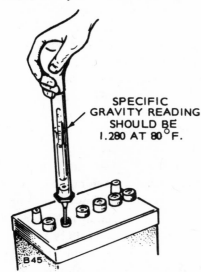

SPECIFIC GRAVITY READING SHOULD BE 1.280 AT 80°F.

Figure 16-7. The simplest and most accurate method for determining the state of charge of a lead storage battery is by using a hydrometer. A reading is taken of each cell. (Onan Corp.)

The hydrometer reading for pure water is 1.000 because the specific gravity of pure water is taken as unity. The reading for a fully charged storage battery cell is approximately 1.270 and for a fully discharged cell it is 1.130. These readings depend to some extent on the nature of manufacture and presuppose an electrolyte consisting of 25 percent sulfuric acid and 75 percent water at full charge. The readings are also influenced by the temperature of the electrolyte, and good hydrometers will include a thermometer. The standard electrolyte temperature for taking hydrometer readings if 80°F.; .004 is added to the indication for every 10°F. above this, and the same amount is subtracted for every 10°F. below.

Battery condition may also be gauged with a voltmeter especially designed for this purpose. (See Chapter 15.) The terminal voltage of a new, fully charged storage cell is approximately 2.2 volts on open circuit; a discharged cell on open circuit reads only slightly less. Note that this small difference is true only on open circuit. Contrarily, the voltage of a cell delivering current to a load changes markedly with its state of charge. A fully charged cell maintaining a light load has a terminal voltage of 2 volts; now grind the starter until the battery gives up, and this voltage may drop to little more than 1 volt.

This matter of cell voltage is confusing to some skippers who equate it with cell size—and there is no connection between the two. The terminal voltage of any electrochemical cell is determined entirely by the metals immersed in the electrolyte. The simple dry flashlight cell discussed earlier could be made with the identical materials to the size of a barrel, and the terminal voltage would still be only 1.5 volts. The lead-acid storage cell, regardless of its size, would never register more than the nominal 2 volts.

But size does have a great effect on the current-delivering ability of a cell. The larger the active elements and the greater the quantity of electrolyte, the more current the cell can supply to its load and for a longer time. In the storage cell this means more and larger plates so that a greater area is exposed to the acid, and chemical action is speeded.

The storage battery found on boats is a sealed plastic or rubber container holding several cells connected in series. As noted in Chapter 15, the voltages of the individual units are added in a series connection. Three cells make the so-called 6-volt battery; six cells are combined in the more popular 12-volt battery. The plate structure in these batteries is designed to provide the short-duration, heavy current required by the starting motor of an internal combustion engine.

Storage batteries are rated by their "ampere hour" capacity. By agreement among the manufacturers, this capacity is computed on the basis of a constant current discharge over a period of 20 hours, with the value of current to be 1/20 of the rating. By way of explanation, a

100-ampere-hour battery will provide 5 amperes for a period of 20 hours. Theoretically, this should also mean that the battery could supply 100 amperes for 1 hour, 25 amperes for 4 hours or any other combination resulting in 100, but this is not true. The higher the discharge current, the less linear the relationship will be. A final voltage of 1.8 per cell is permitted in the 20-hour rating.

Not all of the hydrogen available in the sulfuric acid goes into the formation of the water developed on discharge, and additional hydrogen is produced by electrolysis in the cells. This gas escapes through the vents in the top of the container provided for this purpose. Hydrogen is extremely flammable and can make the storage battery a fire and explosion hazard if sparks or flames are brought near the vents. Ventilation should always be provided and insulating covers should make it impossible for a dropped tool to cause a short circuit of the terminals.

The storage battery aboard should be installed in as cool and accessible a space as can be found reasonably near the engine. The reason for nearness is the heavy current drawn by the starter and the consequent voltage drop in the wires. The greater the distance between battery and engine, the greater should be the diameter of the starter cables. The battery hold-downs must secure it from motion in any direction in a seaway; a loose battery can cause tremendous damage with its weight and acid. (See Figure 16-8.)

Batteries are shipped by the manufacturer in either of two conditions: dry-charged or else fully charged, full of

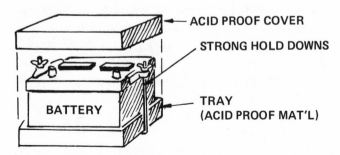

ACID PROOF COVER

STRONG HOLD DOWNS

BATTERY

TRAY (ACID PROOF MAT'L)

Figure 16-8. A storage battery is potentially dangerous because of its weight and because of its acid. Strong hold-downs and a proper cover neutralize the danger.

acid and ready for immediate service. The plates of the dry-charged storage battery are in a chemical state equivalent to full charge, but the cells contain no acid. Before being put in service, the dry-charged battery cells must be filled with an electrolyte of the correct specific gravity, and a booster charge is recommended. Dry charging makes it possible to ship batteries by common carriers without the former special safety packing. This, and the fact that the batteries are lighter in weight when minus their acid, reduces shipping costs.

In the early days, battery manufacturers insisted that the cells be filled with distilled water. This is no longer a requirement, and, in fact, distilled water is hard to come by should a skipper wish to use it anyway. The broad specification for battery water now is that it be potable and not of high mineral content. Iron in the water is especially harmful to battery life.

Ambient temperature affects battery performance. The rated capacity of the storage battery is not available in cold weather because the low temperature inhibits chemical activity. The reduction in extreme cold is drastic. Taking the capacity of the battery as 100 percent at 80°F., only 65 percent will be available at a temperature of 32°F. and only 40 percent at 0°F.! Although this aspect may not be of much value to boatmen, a fully charged storage battery will not freeze at any winter temperature normally encountered.

The storage battery has some natural ailments. Slight chemical impurities present in the plates or the grids have a tendency to self-discharge the battery. This takes place at a very slow rate but becomes noticeable after a battery has been left idle for a period of time; the speed of this action increases with increase of ambient temperature. The battery's ability to cycle from charge to discharge and back becomes less efficient with age, and after a few years, at best, even a well-treated battery will give up its ghost. The chemical conversion to lead sulfate within the cells finally becomes a one-way street, and the battery is said to be "sulfated" and dead. Occasionally, a sulfated dead battery can be brought back to this world by extra long periods of charging with minimal current, but the results are chancy.

Charging a storage battery takes advantage of the

reversible chemical reaction that is a characteristic of the lead-acid cell. Current is forced into the battery by connecting it to a source of direct current whose voltage is slightly higher than its own. The positive of the charging source is connected to the positive terminal of the battery, negative to negative. The standard voltage differential, and the one for which most voltage regulators on generators and alternators are set, is 14.3 volts for a 12-volt battery.

The current going into the battery (the number of amperes) is determined by the difference in voltage. Starting with a discharged battery whose terminal voltage is about 11 volts, the difference is about 3 volts, and the charging current will be high. As the battery becomes charged, the difference will fall, and the charging current will decrease accordingly. This is the theoretical aspect. Actually, manufacturers recommend that their storage batteries be charged at the rate of 1 ampere for each positive plate in one cell. For a 13-plate battery cell having 7 negative and 6 positive plates, the requested charging current would be 6 amperes.

On a weekend morning, a skipper boards his boat that has been idle for some time and presses the starter button. Only a disheartening groan results. The battery has been discharged, perhaps by a light left burning or by a bilge pump. Is the weekend cruise in limbo? Not necessarily; most marinas have "fast chargers."

The fast charger will push as many as 100 amperes into the battery, and within perhaps a quarter hour a push on the starter button brings the desired results. Fast charging is an acceptable practice for occasional use. But there are some cautions. The temperature of the electrolyte must be watched and kept below 125° F. The vents must be opened to permit free exit of the added gas. Gassing should not be so severe that liquid is sputtered out and lost. Of course, the fast charge will not bring the battery up to full specific gravity, but it will place it back in service where the regular charging means will take over. A photo of a representative fast charger or booster is shown in Figure 16-9.

Chargers that plug into house current are available from the very flimsy, dime-store variety to sophisticated, well-engineered units that shut themselves off when the battery is full. Chargers for use on a boat must meet more stringent safety standards because of the marine hazards. Cheap chargers are often built around "autotransformers" that have only one winding and therefore do not isolate the battery circuit from the high voltage. These may get by for use in a garage but could be a dangerous source of electric shock when used afloat. Good battery chargers are made with full transformers that provide isolation. A standard charger is shown in Figure 16-10.

It is detrimental to storage batteries to continue to charge them after they have reached full specific gravity. Years ago, it was common to use "trickle chargers," which continuously kept a small current going into the battery; this practice has been abandoned. Overcharging knocks active material from the plates and impairs battery life. A

Figure 16-9. A booster charger can bring a discharged battery up to working condition in one half hour or less. Close watch should be kept on electrolyte temperature and excessive rise avoided because it is detrimental to battery life.

battery in otherwise good condition that constantly needs the addition of water is trying to signal that it is being overcharged.

From an engineering standpoint, the two basic methods of charging storage batteries are the "constant voltage" and the "constant current." The names refer to the output of the charger and are self-explanatory. The constant current method is preferable provided the charger is shut off when the battery has reached full charge. The classic method of determining when full charge has been attained is to take hydrometer readings at one-hour intervals. If the battery is gassing and the gravity has not increased after three such readings, the battery is fully charged.

Two storage batteries of nominally equal terminal voltage may be connected in parallel (see Chapter 7) to supply extra heavy current for a particularly difficult starting situation. With this connection, the current-de-

livering abilities of the two batteries will be added together. But it is not good practice to leave the batteries connected in this manner permanently, and battery manufacturers advise against doing so.

Despite the nominal voltage rating, the actual terminal voltages of two batteries are seldom exactly equal. This inequality causes a potential difference between the two and leads to a current flow from the higher to the lower when they are connected in parallel. This current flow may seesaw back and forth as terminal voltages change and is not conducive to best battery service.

Batteries may be connected in series when higher voltages are desired, and this is a perfectly legitimate

Figure 16-10. The idea of a battery charger permanently installed at the batteries is excellent, but the sloppiness of this installation should not be duplicated. The batteries should have hold-downs and covers.

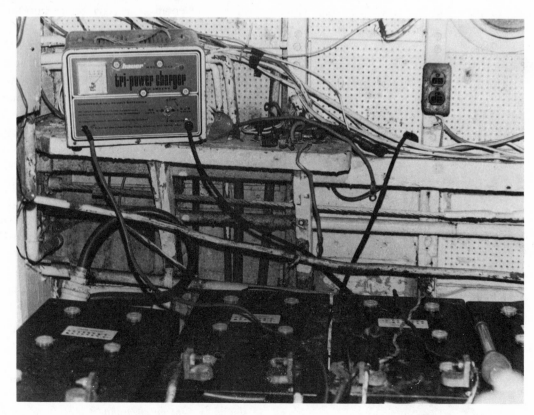

practice. They may also be connected in series for charging and this is done by many large service shops that wish to hold down the amperes of charging current. Thus two 12-volt batteries in series can be charged by a 24-volt charger with only the current requirements of one battery.

The standard battery voltage on the average boat is 12 volts, and electrical shock is impossible. However, there is another danger, perhaps even greater, in its potential.

A short circuit, for instance with a dropped tool, can easily discharge several hundred amperes. Such current can melt a heavy metal rod explosively and cause a fire.

Unfortunately, a comparison of the power consumed in charging a storage battery and the power the battery subsequently supplies leads to the conclusion that it is not a very efficient electrical device. But think of the muscle needed to crank an engine if the storage battery did not exist!

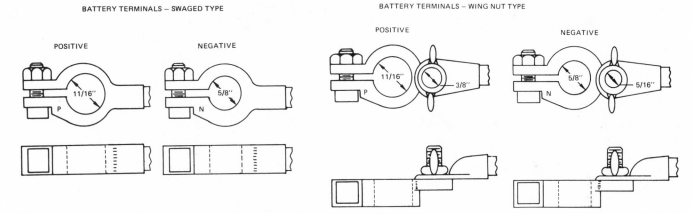

Figure 16-11. Positive and negative terminals of storage batteries usually are marked, but, in the absence of markings, identification may be made by the difference in size as shown above.

17. Air, Fuel and Oil Filters

The clearances between moving parts in the modern marine engine are so minute that any foreign particles entering with the air, the fuel or the lubricating oil can do great damage. Filters stand guard at each of these entrance possibilities and protect the engine. Some filters are so efficient that particles down to micron sizes are effectively excluded. (A micron is one-millionth of a meter, hundreds of times *less* than the thickness of this paper.)

A distinction is made between "filters" and "strainers." A strainer's ability involves only the removal of the larger particles, leaving it to the filter to stop the smaller ones. Broadly, strainers are merely fine mesh screens installed over the intakes to pumps and other mechanisms that handle fluids. A common example is the screen over the intake in the crankcase through which the lubricating pump draws its oil supply. This is shown in Figure 17-1.

The easiest to filter of the substances ingested by a marine engine is air. The air filter or cleaner atop the automobile engine is a familiar sight. It consists essen-

tially of treated paper with controlled porosity within a suitable container. But Coast Guard regulations prohibit this type of air filter on inboard marine engines because it is unable to smother the flame from a carburetor backfire. In its place, marine gasoline engines mount filters called flame arrestors whose elements are nonflammable yet able to perform the more limited filtering of air that a boat engine requries. A flame arrestor, sometimes also called a backfire trap, is shown in Figure 17-2. Flame arrestors are not required on outboard motors because location makes the danger from their backfire minimal.

Figure 17-2. Two types of flame arrestors found on the carburetors of marine engines. Flame arrestors are required by law on gasoline engines.

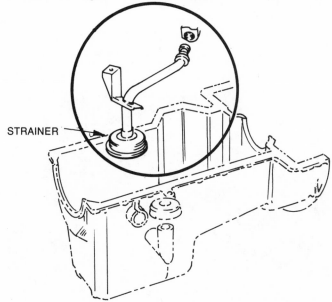

STRAINER

Figure 17-1. The first guardian in the pressure lubricating system of a marine engine is the strainer in the crankcase pickup leading to the oil pump. (Lehman Power Corporation)

In performing its function as a backfire trap, the flame arrestor still must not appreciably impede the inflow of air. Any resistance to the free passage of air to the carburetor has the same effect as partially closing the choke; the result is a richer mixture of fuel to the engine. "Richer," of course, means that the optimum ratio of gasoline to air has been increased with a proportionate decrease in operating economy and perhaps also with the addition of sluggish response to the throttle.

A portion of the effectiveness of a flame arrestor can be attributed to its adoption of the principle of the Davy miner's lamp. Sir Humphrey Davy, a nineteenth-century scientist, found that encasing the open flame of a miner's lamp in a metal screen made it safe to use in the explosive atmosphere of a coal mine. The flame will not penetrate the screen to ignite anything outside. The enclosing metal screen of the flame arrestor just as effectively tames the flame of a backfire. (See Figure 17-3.)

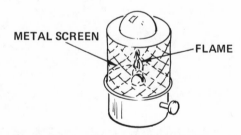

Figure 17-3. *The principle of the metal screen to prevent passage of flame originated in the Davy miner's lamp, and is used in the flame arrestor required on marine gasoline engines.*

Since carburetors are of two types, "down draft" and "up draft," flame arrestors necessarily also must be. The difference in the arrestors lies in the configuration of the housings and not in their function nor in the enclosed filter materials. The discussion and the illustrations in Chapter 31 will clarify the relationships between carburetors and flame arrestors.

The flame arrestor on a marine engine is not usually replaced under normal operating conditions, and in this it differs from most other engine filters which must be changed periodically as they become clogged with contaminants. Some filters, notably those that filter water, can be cleaned and put back in service. Most filters, and especially those elements that guard oil lines, are the throwaway type whose reward for faithful service is the garbage can.

The need for replacement automatically mandates an easy method of doing so, and this, of course, is reflected in filter design. A common form has the filter material packed into a metal housing threaded at one end. This housing screws into a receptacle on the engine and unscrews for replacement. A suitable gasket and a special wrench make this simple attachment oil-tight.

The provision for filter replacement on the larger diesel engines takes another form. Here the housing is permanent, and only the internal filter element is changed. A metal cylinder with a domed top fits on a mating, shelflike projection on the engine and is held in place against the operating pressure of the oil by a long through-bolt. The filter element is supplied as a canister that fits within the cylindrical housing. Gaskets keep everything free of leaks when the bolt is snugged down. Figure 17-4 shows an installation of this kind.

Figure 17-4. *This removable, cleanable element of a filter consists of a fine mesh brass screen. A gasket and a clamp ring prevent leaking when the element is in place.*

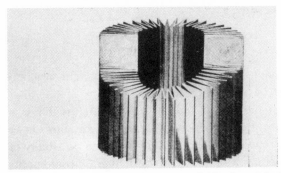

Figure 17-5. *Folding the filter material back and forth into an endless number of vees increases the area available for filtration and produces a longer lasting filter element.* (Facet Enterprises)

Figure 17-6. *The W folds in this filter element increase the area through which the fluid must flow, thus reducing back pressure.* (AC Delco)

The materials of which the filter elements are manufactured are varied and range from paper and cloth to metal wire woven into a mesh. Of all these, paper undergoes the greatest "rags to riches" transformation during its processing. What goes in as a low-cost paper sheet comes out as a filter component whose staid appearance seems at odds with its elevated price.

Cellulose, of which paper consists, is well adapted by nature to be a filter material. Its cell and tube structure has myriads of microscopic interstices which reject unwanted particles but let fluids pass. Thus paper starts off with the advantage of natural porosity. Filter users, from housewives to chemists, know this and employ paper to separate solids from liquids. Adding more layers of paper through which the fluid must pass automatically makes the filtering process finer and finer.

To adapt paper to its much harder role in the marine engine system, it is coated and saturated with chemical compounds. These substances resist fuels and oils, and the degree to which they are applied controls the porosity of the paper. The chemicals are generally resins, and many impart the ability to coalesce contaminating water droplets and prevent their passing through with the fuel or oil. This is a valuable service because the moist marine atmosphere often condenses water into the fuel or the lubricating oil, where its presence is harmful.

The secret of employing paper as an efficient filter element seems to be the method by which it is folded. The conventional method creases the paper into a great number of closely packed V's, as shown in Figure 17-5. A

claimed improvement folds a smaller W between each two V's, and this is shown in Figure 17-6.

The purpose behind all this folding and creasing is to provide a large area of paper through which the fluid to be filtered must pass, yet keep the element as compact as possible. Space must remain in the filter housing to hold the contaminants that the filter stops. The length of time the filter can render its full rated service depends on the combination of this space with the area available for filtering; clogging of either storage space or filter area makes the unit worthless.

Providing a large area of filtering surface has another important purpose. It reduces the loss in pressure that the fluid suffers in passing through. One technical specification for a filter enumerates the energy required to push a liquid through; this is measured as a loss in pressure. Many systems and pumps are critical in the amount of such loss they should be required to absorb.

Other cellulose products, such as cotton, also find their way into the realm of filter materials. They are impregnated with resins and chemicals to the desired level of porosity while in sheet form and then cut, slit, stamped or folded to the desired shapes. Filter elements may be tight stacks of disks or even cylinders of helically wound ribbon. All these manipulations have one thing in common: close control of the open spaces through which fluids can pass and, as a consequence, the ability to fix the minimum size of the particle that will be rejected.

The more durable filter materials are stainless steel, copper, inconel, nickel and nichrome. Metals are not

161

naturally porous in themselves; porosity is achieved by the manner in which they are used. The metals are taken in the form of fine-diameter wire that is woven or wound to the required shapes or thicknesses. The necessary porosity exists in the spaces between wires and between layers of wire mesh. In other words, the degree of compactness to which a metal filter element is compressed determines its effectiveness as a fine or coarse filter. Figure 17-7 illustrates the principles of filter element construction.

An obviously important caution in filter construction is that it be impossible for any portion of the filter material to slough off and get into the engine that it is installed to protect. This would refer to any threads or chips that could break loose. Although the possibility of this happening is remote in modern filters, it could occur when there is an extreme lack of maintenance.

Filters designed for use in high-pressure systems, such as lubricating lines, must be able to withstand much more than the actual pressures involved in order to establish a

Figure 17-7. Actual photographs, taken under high magnification, show the nature of the surface of six different filter materials and explain why undesired contaminants are prevented from getting through. (Fram Corporation)

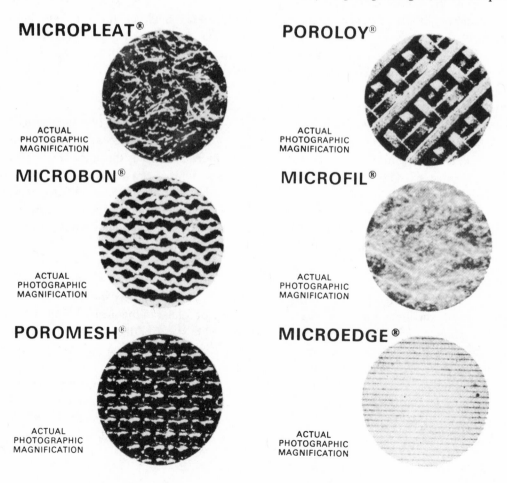

MICROPLEAT® ACTUAL PHOTOGRAPHIC MAGNIFICATION

POROLOY® ACTUAL PHOTOGRAPHIC MAGNIFICATION

MICROBON® ACTUAL PHOTOGRAPHIC MAGNIFICATION

MICROFIL® ACTUAL PHOTOGRAPHIC MAGNIFICATION

POROMESH® ACTUAL PHOTOGRAPHIC MAGNIFICATION

MICROEDGE® ACTUAL PHOTOGRAPHIC MAGNIFICATION

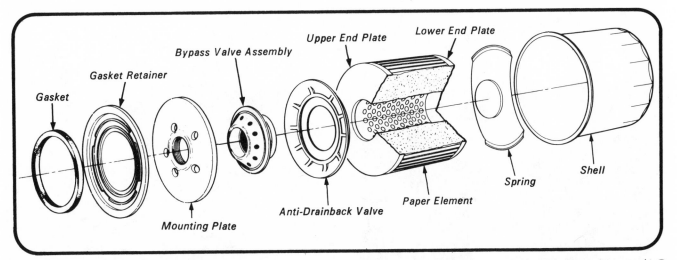

Figure 17-8. Note the bypass valve in this exploded view of a full flow oil filter. The valve allows lubricating oil to get to the engine despite a neglected and clogged filter element. (AC Delco).

safety factor. A common commercial parameter is a bursting strength five times greater than the working pressure. The lubricating oil in a running engine becomes very hot; consequently filters intended for this service must withstand high temperatures without loss in efficiency.

Filters for lubricating oil are either "full flow" or "bypass," and the names really tell how they function. The full-flow filter is in the direct line from oil pump to engine interior, and thus all oil must pass through it before it goes to work. The bypass, or partial-flow, filter is on a branch line from the pump, and only a fixed percentage of the lubricating oil passes through it. Often, especially on large diesel engines, both filters are used together for maximum protection.

An exploded view of a full-flow filter is shown in Figure 17-8. In essence, this again is a standard filter element in a standard housing with provision for input and outflow. However, one new item has been added: a bypass valve. This is a safety feature. If the filter were to become clogged in the absence of the bypass valve, all lubrication of the engine would cease—a disastrous situation. The bypass valve permits lubricating oil, albeit unfiltered, to reach the engine regardless. Thus failure to replace a clogged full-flow filter does not automatically condemn the engine.

Full-flow filters intended for mounting in nonstandard positions add another item called an anti-drain back valve. This valve goes into action when the engine is stopped and prevents the oil from draining out of the filter. It is also a barrier between filtered and unfiltered oil in the housing.

Whereas oil from the full-flow filter goes directly to the moving parts of the engine, the output of the bypass filter runs only into the crankcase sump. Calibrated orifices determine the percentage of the engine oil flow that is directed to the bypass filter; a common condition is 10 percent. The bypass filter provides continuous additional filtration of the lubricating oil and adds substantially to the purity of the lubricant and indirectly to the longevity of the engine.

Lubrication pumps in marine engines are capable of developing pressures much greater than required for normal engine operation. Relief valves in the engine control this excess pressure. Often a bulged filter housing will be a telltale that this valve is malfunctioning. A similar, but usually unseen, sign of trouble is a collapsed filter element.

Filters in the fuel line are important for gasoline engines and even more important for diesel engines. Despite careful handling, fuel can become contaminated while in the care of the supplier and again while in the boat tank. The contaminants are varied and include water, dirt, rust and other products of corrosion. The need for purity is accentuated by the minute passages in a carburetor and the microscopic clearances in a diesel injector. Some impurities, such as varnish, are the result of natural chemical action during long periods of storage. A good fuel filter must be able to remove all of these unwanted intruders.

Water is unique among the many contaminants that can find their way into the fuel drawn in by an engine. Whereas the others make their presence known by damage over a period of time, water stops the machine immediately. Often, even a few drops of water at the carburetor jet or at the injector nozzle can do this. Moreover, stoppage may be only part of the resulting trouble because water is incompressible and could break what-

(A)

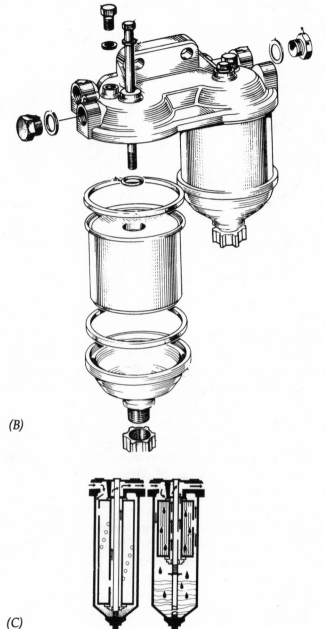

(B)

(C)

Figure 17-9. This double filter (A) cleanses the fuel of all contaminants and traps any contained water for later removal through a drain cock. The disastrous effects of water in the fuel line are avoided by these filters (B) that coalesce the drops of water, retain them so they may be drawn off at intervals and prevent their passage to the engine. The drawing (C) shows how this is done. (Fram Corporation)

ever is trying to compress it. The stringent need for a filter that is able to eliminate water from the fuel is thus apparent.

Many modern fuel filters are designed to remove water, and they perform their function admirably. Their action is one of coalescence. Generally, the water is not picked up from the tank as such but exists as microscopic "beads" suspended in the fuel. Normally, these would pass through an ordinary filter element. The special chemical coating on the fuel filter element coalesces these beads into droplets that fall to the bottom of the housing. The rejected water may be drawn off from the housing sump via a threaded plug included for that purpose. Incidentally, it is illegal to have a drain cock in the bottom

of a fuel filter; only the plug is permitted. (See Figure 17-9.)

It is customary to have a rudimentary filter at the outlet of the gasoline tank to remove the worst of the undesirables. This also protects the fuel pump. The next filter is installed in the tubing from the fuel pump to the carburetor, or else it may be in the carburetor itself; very often, both are used. The most common form of in-carburetor filter is a spool-like roll of treated paper, an inch or two long, which fits into the intake passage. An alternate to this is a spool of sintered bronze placed in the same location. Both are removable and are intended to be replaced as needed.

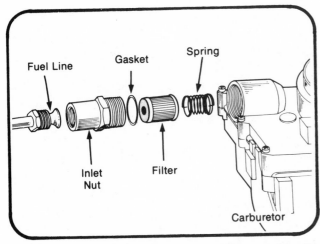

Figure 17-10. All the parts of an in-carburetor gasoline filter are shown in this exploded view. How the filter element may be replaced is self-explanatory. (AC Delco)

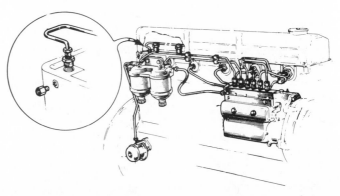

Figure 17-11. The vulnerability of diesel injectors to damage by foreign matter in the fuel makes primary and secondary filters necessary. The successive filtration removes debris down to the micro range in addition to removing water. (Lehman Power Corporation)

Fuel filtration for the diesel engine is super-critical if reliable operation is to be maintained. The standard method of doing this job is to employ two filters, a primary and a secondary. The primary filter is placed between the tank and the pump that brings the fuel to the engine; the secondary filter then takes over and adds its cleansing action before the fuel reaches the injectors. Both filters will have provision for trapping water, that archenemy of injectors.

There is a substantial difference in the fuel filtering requirements of a gasoline engine and those of a diesel engine of comparable size. Only the gasoline actually burned in the engine passes through its filtering system. The diesel filters, by contrast, continually supply more fuel than the engine requires—the excess is returned to the tank. This is a unique feature of injector operation. Thus the diesel engine filters and refilters a portion of its fuel at all times that the machine is in operation. (See Figure 17-11.)

Diesel fuel filters must often overcome an obstacle that is foreign to the gasoline engine. Bacteria! The interface between the water that collects in the fuel tank and the fuel is a snug home for certain bacteria that are

prevalent in the atmosphere. The by-product of these microorganisms is a scum that can completely block the fuel filter element and stall the engine. Many diesel fuels contain chemicals that destroy the bacteria, but the problem crops up nevertheless. (See Figure 17-12.)

Figure 17-12. This large unit is the secondary fuel filter on a diesel engine. A small plug at the bottom permits draining off any water that may find its way this far along the fuel path.

It is wise to install filters or strainers at the through-hull fittings which admit the cooling water for the engines and generators. This is especially important for boats that operate on small bodies of water that are subject to pollution. Heavy rains wash silt and grass into the water; these are harmful to the cooling pump and in addition can clog engine passages. In salt and brackish water areas the contaminants may include tiny mussels and barnacles.

Water-cooled air-conditioning units should also have filters in their intake lines. The condensers of such equipment are vulnerable to foreign matter, and even partial clogging reduces the efficiency of heat transfer.

Filters come in almost innumerable shapes, sizes, capacities and purposes. The filter manufacturers supply charts that relate available filters to commercial engines. The engine makers publish owner's manuals and shop manuals that list their own preferences of make and model of filter. Consequently, everything is spelled out, and there is no need of expertise in filter selection. Experience does enter the picture when determining the correct filter replacement routine for a particular type of engine usage.

One criterion of filter use is whether it operates under pressure or under suction. A filter in the intake line to a pump operates under suction; the pressure differential across it and on its housing is minimal. Contrarily, a filter in the output system of a pump must be able to withstand pressure differentials of considerable size; a malfunction could engender forces great enough to burst a housing or collapse an element. The technical specifications for filters generally state the maximum pressures to which the units may be subjected.

One peculiarity of a filter element is that its ability to remove particles of minimal size will improve after a short period of use. This can be explained easily. As contaminants begin to close the spaces through which the fluid flows, the passages become smaller and smaller, and the size of particles that can get through is reduced progressively. But this is a bonus of very short duration. Eventually, the clogging proceeds to the point where even the fluid cannot get through and the element becomes worthless.

Some filter elements designed for use in the intake lines of pumps used for cooling have the ability to soften water. Hard water, meaning water containing certain minerals, has the detrimental ability to form scale on the surfaces of heat exchangers and the passages in engines. This interferes with heat transfer and is undesirable. Chemicals in the filter element withdraw the offending minerals and make the water "soft" and better for cooling. Since the active chemicals eventually become satiated, the water-softening ability of the filter element is not permanent; its service life is determined by the degree of hardness of the water.

Hydraulic marine transmissions also make use of filters. While these filters may differ in shape, size and location, their functioning is exactly along the lines already described.

Filters and strainers on marine engines perform a service whose importance to the longevity of the machine is far greater than the simplicity of the elements would indicate.

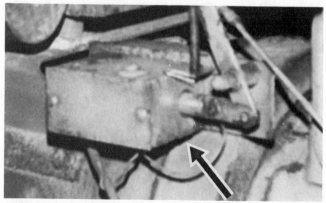

Figure 17-13. Generating plants are often left running unattended for long periods of time and therefore a safety device that monitors temperature and lubrication is essential. Shown above is the safety stop solenoid connected to the throttle of a diesel generating plant. A signal of abnormal conditons from the temperature sensor or the oil pressure sensor shuts the machine down.

18. *Corrosion and Galvanic Protection*

Corrosion is nature's way of reclaiming the metals that man mines from her earth. Oxides of iron (iron ores) are taken from the ground, smelted into iron and steel, manufactured into the many products modern man requires—but eventually corrosion steps in and reduces it all back to rust, an iron oxide. Inexorably, everything has gone full circle. It is nature's fantastic recycling process which has gone on for eons and will continue for eons more.

Corrosion is a lethal enemy of metals, and that makes corrosion an enemy of the skipper as well. The vulnerability of the marine engine is increased by the moist atmosphere in which, perforce, it must do its work; the usual engine space is forever damp. Luckily, many vital parts of the engine are bathed continuously in oil, and therefore they are reasonably safe from corrosion. But other parts, especially those exposed to water or air, require protective measures for survival. While all boating locales contain the seeds of metal destruction, saltwater areas compound the danger.

Rust is only one form of metal deterioration, and it is unique to iron and steel. The destructive process in all other metals is similar, but there is no single generic term, such as "rust," to describe the reaction. In all cases, the oxygen in the air and the additional oxygen and hydrogen available from the dissociation of water are the culprits. Counteracting the normal chemical actions of oxygen and hydrogen, therefore, becomes the name of the game in corrosion prevention.

Corrosion is an electrochemical process normally proceeding continuously at an almost imperceptively slow rate. Certain conditions must prevail before any destructive action can take place. Moisture or actual water must be present and in contact with the metal. Oxygen and hydrogen must be available, either directly or as a result of chemical action and the resultant dissociation of water into its two constituents. For meaningful corrosion, the moisture or water must be able to function as an electrolyte.

An electrolyte is any liquid able to transmit an electric current. Absolutely pure water will not do this. However, almost any pollutant brings with it some amount of current-carrying ability and transforms the water into a weak electrolyte. When the pollutant chemicals are acids or salts, the water becomes a strong electrolyte and poses a dire threat to metals immersed in it. This explains the faster deterioration of metals in a salt water bay than in a freshwater lake.

In the terminology of chemistry, corrosion is a reaction between metals and water that proceeds only to the right (is not reversible) and changes the metal to an oxide or a hydroxide with the evolution of a gas, hydrogen. An electric current is generated, actually is the prime mover, although this is not apparent except with precise laboratory control and measurement. The hydrogen is an ambivalent actor in this chemical drama whose role can change from villain who helps corrosion to hero who prevents its continuance.

The oxide or hydroxide of the metal, although itself a product of the corrosion, in some instances also becomes a protective shield. The formation of aluminum oxide on aluminum is one example of such action. When exposed to the atmosphere aluminum quickly becomes covered with a film of its oxide or hydroxide as a result of the corrosive influence of the oxygen in the air. This film is tightly adherent and impervious to the elements that caused it originally. Oxygen and moisture are denied further contact with the metal by the film, and the aluminum can be exposed to the air safely without paint or similar coating. Unfortunately, this protection does not extend to immersion in boating waters except for special alloys.

Rust occasionally adheres so tightly to iron and steel that it, too, becomes a barrier to further deterioration. In most cases, however, rust is flaky and loose and consequently not protective. Hence, either a protective coating or a galvanic means must be relied on to keep iron and steel safe from corrosive harm.

The degree of pollution of the atmosphere has a great bearing on the severity of corrosion that metals will suffer. Since water is needed for corrosion to take place, the amount of moisture in the air is a vital factor. Equally deleterious constituents of the air are salts, gases and sulfur, because these become acids with strong attacking power when they combine with moisture. Strangely, the oxygen content of the atmosphere, so necessary to life, is a principal agent of destruction for metals.

Technical descriptions of corrosion are never without mention of the parts played by hydrogen and oxygen. Every corrosion reaction releases hydrogen as a positive ion that may pick up a free electron and go off as hydrogen gas. Under certain conditions this hydrogen plates itself as a film onto the immersed surface of the cathode metal and becomes an insulating barrier. This effectively stops the flow of electricity and halts the corrosion until the film is broken either spontaneously or by mechanical abrasion. As noted earlier, electric current is the "flywheel" for the entire process.

The terms "anode" and "cathode" are in common use and should be understood. The anode is the metal from which the electric current enters the electrolyte; in doing so, the current takes with it minute amounts of metal; hence the anode wears away. The cathode is the re-entering metal for the current leaving the electrolyte, and thus the cathode may be added to but never diminished. In the average boat installation the anode is a purposely added protective zinc, and the various underwater appendages collectively are the cathode.

Oxygen operates under several guises in its role as corroder. It can combine with metal in a simple chemical reaction as, for instance, with iron to form iron oxide or rust. Oxygen can combine with and destroy the protective film of hydrogen that often forms on the cathode, thereby allowing corrosion to continue. Oxygen can abet corrosion in an entirely different manner by spreading itself unevenly over the surface of a metal to form areas of depletion. These depleted areas are anodic to their surroundings, and, as expected of anodes, they will sacrifice themselves to form unwanted pitting. Paradoxically, oxygen can corrode by its presence and by its absence as well.

The most intensive form of corrosion is that in which dissimilar metals are involved. This is the kind most likely to occur on boats, yet the very one against which protective measures can be taken. It is known by the generic term "galvanic corrosion."

For galvanic corrosion to ensue, two dissimilar metals must be connected by an electrically conductive path, and both must be immersed in the same electrolyte. The similarity with the primary battery cell discussed in Chapter 16 should be apparent immediately. The system is, in fact, an electric battery cell wherein one metal is eaten away with a coincident generation of electricity. The electrolyte, be it weaker or stronger, is the water in which the boat floats plus the ambient moist air.

What makes this all possible is the fact that metals "dissolve" in water. It may be hard to visualize any metal dissolving in water, but all metals possess this tendency. Of course, the dissolution is not like that of a lump of sugar dropped into a cup of tea; it proceeds at the submicroscopic level of ions and atoms. The normally balanced electric charges in the atoms become unbalanced as the ions slip into the water, and this is one source of the energy that keeps the process going.

Every metal has a known rate at which its ions will go into solution. The various rates have been arranged into a progressive table called the electrochemical series, and this is shown in Figure 18-1. At one end of the list is magnesium, which is the most soluble; at the other end is platinum, the least soluble. The tabulation has great value because it allows a prediction of the voltage that will be developed by metals in corrosive conjunction. For example, when a copper-bronze fitting is connected to a protective zinc anode, 1.103 volts will be generated. (From the table: zinc at .758 plus copper-bronze at .345 equals 1.103). With this knowledge and a determination

Galvanic Series of Metals in Sea Water

ANODIC OR LEAST NOBLE—ACTIVE

Magnesium and magnesium alloys
CB75 aluminum anode alloy
Zinc
B605 aluminum anode alloy
Galvanized steel or galvanized wrought iron
Aluminum 7072 (cladding alloy)
Aluminum 5456
Aluminum 5086
Aluminum 5052
Aluminum 3003, 1100, 6061, 356
Cadmium
2117 aluminum rivet alloy
Mild steel
Wrought iron
Cast Iron
Ni-Resist
13% chromium stainless steel, type 410 (active)
50-50 lead tin solder
18-8 stainless steel, type 304 (active)
18-8 3% NO stainless steel, type 316 (active)
Lead
Tin
Muntz metal
Manganese bronze
Naval brass (60% copper—39% zinc)
Nickel (active)
78% Ni.-13.5% Cr.-6% Fe. (Inconel) (Active)
Yellow brass (65% copper—35% zinc)
Admiralty brass
Aluminum bronze
Red brass (85% copper—15% zinc)
Copper
Silicon bronze
 5% Zn.—20% Ni—75% Cu.
90% Cu.—10% Ni.
70% Cu.—30% Ni.
88% Cu.— 2% Zn.—10% Sn. (Composition G-bronze)
88% Cu.— 3% Zn.—6.5% Sn.—1.5% Pb (composition M-bronze)
Nickel (passive)
78% Ni.—13.5% Cr.—6% Fe. (Inconel) (Passive)
70% Ni.—30% Cu.
18-8 stainless steel type 304 (passive)
18-8 3% Mo. stainless steel, type 316 (passive)
Hastelloy C
Titanium
Platinum

CATHODIC OR MOST NOBLE—PASSIVE

Figure 18-1. Whenever two metals must be in electrical contact with each other, and subject to sea water or moisture, the best guard against corrosion is to select identical kinds. The closer together the metals are in this listing, the safer; the further apart, the more rapid the corrosion. For instance, aluminum screws holding a copper plate will soon disintegrate. (American Boat and Yacht Council)

of the ohmic resistance of the electrolyte, the rate at which the zinc will disappear can be calculated.

The electrochemical series serves as a safety check by which the suitability for immersion of a proposed component can be judged in advance. Furthermore, the table proves the wisdom of having all underwater appendages made of the same metal. When dissimilar metals must be used, the listing identifies the one that will be sacrificed. (Often this sacrifice is intentional, as in the case of zinc anodes.)

The tabulated numbers represent voltages, which makes the information valuable in yet another way. Each voltage is a measure of that metal's "pressure" to send its ions into solution, a sort of "solution pressure index." It reveals that an opposing voltage of the same or greater amount, acting as a counterpressure, will neutralize the tendency of the metal's ions to leave and thus make it stable. This is the basis for "impressed current cathodic protection" systems such as the unit shown in Figure 18-2.

Although impressed current systems are not yet in wide use on pleasure boats, it is well to understand them just in case. The direct current needed by these installations is small and easily supplied from the boat battery or even from a separate source. An immersed reference electrode senses the voltage required to counteract galvanic action of the underwater metal. This voltage will vary with changes in salinity or pollution of the water and also with changes in the speed of the boat. The control panel uses this information to provide an output voltage of the correct value. An anode of noble metal that does not waste away then puts the output voltage to work to protect the metal appendages under the hull.

The standard zinc anodes placed under the hull or directly on metal hull appendages are effective deterrents, but their action is uncontrolled. Unless there is a careful balancing of the amount of exposed zinc area to the exposed area of the metal to be protected, action may be too fast or too slow. The zinc may be used up at a greater rate than necessary and thus at greater expense.

The more common form of galvanic protection for the

Figure 18-2. This impressed current system fights galvanic deterioration with current drawn from the boat battery. The load placed upon the battery is negligible. The monitor panel provides a test button to prove that everything is working. The immersed electrodes also are shown. (Mercury Maine)

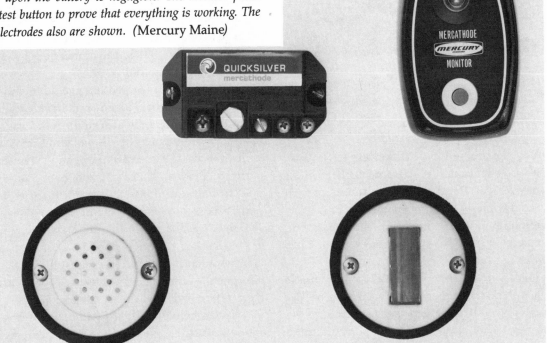

engine is with zinc anodes that sacrifice themselves as one would expect from reading the table. These are placed at various locations in the circulating cooling system; one location is shown in Figure 18-3. The entire engine becomes the cathode, and the cooling water is the electrolyte. The dissolution of the zinc versus the iron, exactly as in a primary battery, causes the protective current to flow as long as active zinc remains. Because of the complexity of their cooling water passages, most large marine engines have two or more anodes.

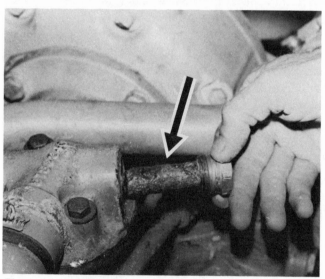

Figure 18-3. *One of the zinc anodes in the raw water cooling system of a marine engine is shown withdrawn from its fitting. By sacrificing itself, the zinc saves the engine metal from being wasted by corrosion.*

Zincs must be extremely pure if they are to function effectively as protective anodes. The acceptable level for any impurity averages 1 part in 100,000, and more than 99 percent of the anode must be chemically pure zinc. Even minuscule amounts of iron and lead deteriorate performance greatly. For this reason, junkyard zinc has little reason to be used.

The all-important point to remember about anodic protection is that the anode must be connected electrically with the metal objects it is to guard, and all must be in the same electrolyte. This means that a copper grounding strap, preferably inside the hull, should tie everything together with low-resistance connections. The voltages generated are low; hence electrical resistance must be negligible if sufficient current for protection is to flow.

Although galvanic corrosion requires two dissimilar metals, it is often possible for one metal to act as though it were two. A variation in heat treatment or in peaks of stress can make a localized area of a metal sufficiently different from the adjacent surface to cause it to behave like a less noble metal. Add moisture, and all the elements for galvanic corrosion are in place. Soon the area will be pitted and corroded.

Crevices in metal may be subject to corrosion because of a similar phenomenon. An enclosed pocket or crevice is generally lower in oxygen than its neighbors. This makes it equivalent to a less noble metal and therefore anodic. When moisture is added to form the electrolyte, the familiar anode-cathode reaction takes place to the detriment of the crevice.

Oxygen, a major culprit in all corrosion, must also be watched for its role in freshwater engine cooling systems. The freshwater entrains considerable free oxygen, but this is progressively reduced as the water is circulated and heated and cooled. After a period of time, the oxygen content becomes negligible. For this reason, it is good practice to retain the water instead of constantly changing it. Corrosion inhibitors recommended by the engine manufacturer are helpful.

Insulators are presumed to have infinite resistance to the passage of electric current, but they may fall from this perfection because they absorb moisture and salt in the marine environment. These weak points may allow electricity to leave the intended paths and escape as "leakage currents" that can cause galvanic action or electrolysis. Such troubles are almost impossible to trace, and prevention is the best policy. Tying all metal objects together electrically with a grounding strap and including anodes in the circuit is good prevention.

Aluminum is a vulnerable metal in the saltwater environment, although its ability to protect itself in the atmosphere has been noted. Its position next to zinc in the electrochemical series signifies it to be a powerful anode ready to sacrifice itself to many other metals. Since outboard motor housings are aluminum, this is a matter of great moment to the skipper whose power is hung on the transom.

Paint is the principal corrosion protector for aluminum outboard motor housings. In most cases, the paint is an epoxy formulation baked on to form an impervious coating of good effectiveness. Aluminum can also be treated and made passive by an electric process called anodizing, but the impervious paint coating is superior while it remains unbroken. Small, unintentional openings in the paint film, called holidays, localize galvanic action and become the scene of intense corrosion. Thus it is important to seek out and correct any imperfections or damages that negate the integrity of the protective coating.

Some authorities recommend that the power cord connecting the boat with shore current on the pier include a green, non-current-carrying grounding wire. This has its good points but, unfortunately, also a bad one as the sketch in Figure 18-4 illustrates. Assume that two boats

Figure 18-5. *This isolator maintains the protection afforded by the ground wire but prevents the galvanic problems, mentioned in the text, which could result from grounding. (Mercury Marine)*

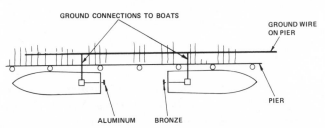

Figure 18-4. *This diagram shows what happens, circuitwise, when several boats are all connected to the pier ground wire through their shore power cables. In this instance, a galvanic cell has been established and the aluminum prop will eventually disappear. See Figure 18-5.*

are at the pier, each connected to shore with power cords that contain this grounding wire. The two boats are connected together electrically by a low-resistance path. Assume, further, that one boat has an aluminum propeller while the other boat's screw is bronze. The requirements for galvanic action mentioned earlier are now met: Two dissimilar metals, aluminum and bronze, are in contact, and both are immersed in the same saltwater electrolyte. It is obvious that the aluminum propeller will slowly disappear.

A remedy for the foregoing situation has appeared in the form of an "isolator," shown in Figure 18-5. This is an

electronic device featuring diodes, which may be thought of as one-way "electric valves." The isolator blocks the small direct current generated by the galvanic action of the dissimilar metals but nevertheless acts as a solid safety connection in the event of any malfunctions in the electric system. In effect, the green grounding wire remains as a preventive of accidental electric shock.

Zinc's ability to protect iron from corrosion is applied commercially on a large scale in the form of "galvanizing." Galvanized fasteners find considerable use aboard because they are less costly than stainless steel and bronze. The zinc is a thin coating applied either by hot dipping or by electroplating.

A glance at the electrochemical listing shows that magnesium is much more active than zinc. The question naturally arises, Why is not a magnesium anode preferable to zinc? In practice, magnesium is *much* too active! The voltage generated by a magnesium anode is higher than that of a zinc under similar conditions, and, therefore, the current flowing is greater to the point of "burning" surrounding paint.

The action of plain zinc anodes is uncontrolled—often they may be supplying more protective current than is absolutely needed and consequently may wear themselves away faster than necessary. The device illustrated in Figure 18-6 is claimed by its manufacturer to correct this situation. It interposes an automatically variable re-

sistance between the anode and the metal to be protected.

Zinc anodes are supplied commercially in various shapes that make them easy to install on shafts, rudders, struts, and other underwater metal parts (Figure 18-7.)

The validity of the discussion on electrolysis and galvanic deterioration is proved by the photo in Figure 18-8. Here aluminum was in contact with brass with strikingly disastrous results.

Figure 18-6. The system shown here controls the action and increases the life of sacrificial zinc anodes without reducing their effectiveness. (Krell Electric Co.)

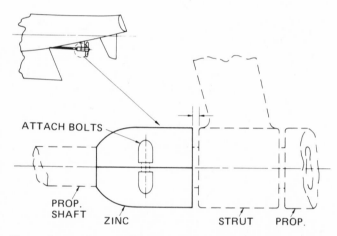

Figure 18-7. Zinc sacrificial anodes for the propeller shaft are designed to create minimal turbulence and as little interference with the prop stream as possible. (Martec Engineering Co.)

Figure 18-8. Galvanic corrosion on a boat is a real threat and must be guarded against. This ruined aluminum header plate was in contact with a brass screen on a diesel engine. The culprit was the copper in the brass—as reference to the table in Figure 18-1 will verify. (International Nickel Co.)

PART FOUR
ENGINE CARE

19. Engine Installation

P
roblems of engine installation are almost nil for the skipper who uses outboard power, although there are a few cautions that will be discussed. At the other end of the scale of difficulty is the installation of an inboard engine, and this often becomes almost an engineering feat. In between, and borrowing a little from both, is the stern-drive engine, which nestles in a box at the transom.

The outboard motor and the stern drive have one requirement in common: Each requires a strong, beefed-up transom. Both forms of propulsion exert the severe stresses of forward and aftward thrust, as well as the stresses of steering, against this part of the boat—although some designs of stern drive are less demanding. In the early days, when outboard motors were hung on any old rowboat, many a fisherman was surprised to see the transom part company with the hull when he gunned the engine.

The preferred installation for an outboard motor of more than minimum size is the double transom illustrated in Figure 19-1. The space between the two transoms is self-bailing. Thus a following sea that climbs aboard to poop the boat presents less danger, and the wake that overtakes the hull after a sudden stop can be tolerated. The double transom design also strengthens the stern of the craft, a very worthwhile bonus. Many skippers use this 'tween-transom space for batteries and portable gasoline tanks.

Small boat transoms are built in a variety of heights and inclinations, and the correct outboard installation adapts to this. The manufacturers take care of the height

Figure 19-1. Twin outboards on the transom mean the ultimate in maneuverability and security. Speed often is enhanced also. Note the double transom. (Johnson Outboards)

differences by supplying motors with a choice of long or short lower units. The matter of inclination is up to the skipper, but again the manufacurers supply the means in the form of an adjustable setting. The photo in Figure 19-2 shows how proper tilt is obtained by aligning the motor with any of several holes. The cavitation plate, the flat surface directly above the propeller, should be horizontal and slightly below the bottom line of the hull.

Figure 19-2. The cavitation plate of an outboard motor should be parallel to the surface of the water. The series of holes (arrow) allow this adjustment to be made easily. (Honda Motors)

Since outboard motors are tilted up out of the water when not in use, sufficient clearance must be provided. With the double transom installation, this clearance exists automatically; in other cases, care must be taken to see that the power head does not swing into conflict with a passenger seat or with cargo.

Many sailboats eschew the common practice of fastening the outboard motor to the stern with a retractable bracket; instead they carry their motor in a stern well. Motor thrust is affected only to a negligible degree, and the classic hull lines of a sailboat are not marred by the overhang. In addition, the hidden motor often saves the skipper from the supposed stigma of resorting to power

instead of using only pure wind. A well installation is shown in Figure 19-3.

Larger outboard motors invariably are remote-controlled from a forward steering position. This places the skipper's weight at a position that permits the hull to plane at a more comfortable angle. Small outboards are tiller-controlled, forcing the skipper to sit right at the stern where the combined weight of him and the motor

Figure 19-3. The covered well at the stern of a sailboat keeps the outboard motor hidden when it is not in use. (See Chapter 6 also.)

forces the bow up into an angle that is uncomfortable and often unsafe. Extension handles that fit over the tiller can correct this situation somewhat by allowing the operator to move bowward, but the forward-neutral-reverse lever must still be operated at the motor.

The more elaborate outboard installations include an instrument console with a temperature gauge that monitors the motor. In the absence of this telltale, the skipper has only his eyes to tell him whether or not cooling water is being pumped as required. He must watch a designated motor orifice to verify that water is being discharged at the correct rate. Thus an anomaly: Although the skipper preferably is forward of the motor, his ability to view the after end of the motor should remain unimpaired.

Despite the fact that its rotating parts are precisely balanced, a powerful outboard motor is nevertheless a source of strong vibrations because of its reciprocating components and the reaction of its propeller. Manufacturers make great effort to prevent these vibrations from reaching the hull. Rubber and other elastic mounts are interposed between outboard and transom; these transmit the thrust without (hopefully) also passing the vibrations.

Incidentally, this transmittal of vibration and noise is a problem definitely not unique to outboards. All power installations on all boats have it to some degree. In fact, the outboard motor is least culpable because of its advantageous position outside the stern, as far away from passengers as it is possible to be. Noise level is receiving increasing attention, not only because of its physiological effect but because of its legal aspect as well. Laws are zeroing in on the exact number of decibels (units that measure loudness) that will be permitted in every situation.

The stern-drive engine enjoys some of the advantages of the outboard when it comes to the matter of noise. It is situated at the stern, almost as far away from the boat's occupants as the outboard. (Noise is covered fully in Chapter 22.) While the stern-drive engine is larger and sometimes noisier, this is offset by the sound-absorbing cover that invariably is a part of the installation. The stern drive has one valuable and unique advantage over any other form of propulsion, although the engine room of a very large yacht might come close: Lift the cover and every component of the engine is readily at hand for maintenance and adjustment.

The stern-drive engine and the inboard engine are each installed on, and fastened to, so-called stringers. Stringers are lengthwise structural members that distribute the stresses and the weight of the engine over a large area of the hull. In the wooden boat, the stringers are long, thick planks set on edge and spaced a distance apart that exactly matches the spacing of the engine's own supports. In the fiber glass hull, the stringers may be similar planks but entirely encased in fiber glass and chemically bonded to the hull. Contrarily, the stringers in the fiber glass hull may also take the form of integrally molded box girders. Of course, in metal hulls, the stringers are simply I beams or U beams welded in place.

Rarely would all four engine mounts fit squarely on the stringers without some provision for minor adjustment. The small changes in height needed to make mount and stringer meet in solid, load-bearing contact are often achieved with shims or wedges. Another, simpler method is with threaded supports that can be screwed up or down. These adjustments also serve as a means of attaining the required alignment between the engine and its drive shaft.

The stringers make an excellent, but totally unwanted, transmitter of engine noise and vibration. This so-called telegraphing makes a sounding board of the entire hull and amplifies the annoyance. Good installation practice therefore places an absorbent between engine mount and stringer. In its simplest form this could be a slab of rubber, preferably synthetic rubber that would not be affected by oil. Commercial vibration dampeners would be a better choice, and such a device is illustrated in Figure 19-4.

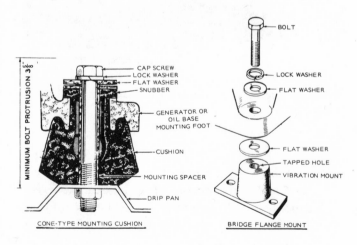

Figure 19-4. Insulating the vibration of the engine from the hull is an effective method of reducing noise aboard. The intermediate rubber cushion absorbs the sound. The mounts shown above are suitable for generator sets; mounts for propulsion engines must also be able to transmit thrust to the hull. (Onan Corp.)

Even the best-mannered engine will occasionally drip some oil, and a pan beneath it, between the stringers, will prevent a messy bilge. Unfortunately, most boat engine installations are shy on vertical clearance underneath them, and emptying such a drip pan may be possible only with a pump such as those made for use with electric drills. Extending the drip pan beyond the engine (where available space permits) will allow access and may make the pump unnecessary.

The same lack of clearance makes it impossible to drain the lubricating oil through the plug in the bottom of the crankcase, as is customary with automobiles. The electric drill with pump attachment again comes in handy. The usual scheme is to insert the pump pickup tube through the dipstick hole. This procedure works well if the draining is done after the engine has been run sufficiently long to heat the oil and thin it. Of course, the engine is stopped during the draining. (See Figure 19-5.)

The fact that an engine vibrates strongly while running must be taken into account when rigging the various lines

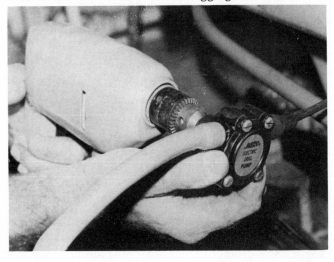

Figure 19-5. The easy draining of lubricating oil that characterizes automobiles is not possible on most boats because the crankcase plug of a marine engine is not accessible. An excellent method of draining a marine engine is shown above using a popular drill pump. A thin pickup tube is inserted through the dip stick hole. The oil should be warm from immediately previous engine running.

that connect to it. The fuel connection must be through approved flexible hose. Electric wires must have slack. The speedometer-type cables that lead to mechanical tachometers must allow motion. Controls preferably are actuated by Bowden wire devices unaffected by the lack of rigidity. (See Chapter 13.)

Engine installations should be planned to provide reasonably easy access to fuel filters, lubricating oil filters and air cleaners because these components should have frequent inspection and maintenance. The spark plugs on gasoline engines should also be handy to get at, although on most boats this is more a desire than a reality. Although strictly not a part of the engine, the reverse gear should be accessible, and the shaft too, all the way to the stuffing box.

An earlier chapter spoke of the tremendous volumes of air gulped by internal combusion engines and therefore the need for adequate ventilation to the engine space. It is well to repeat the caution. Restricted air supply can become a partial vacuum when the engines are gunned; the result is an immediate loss in power. With two propulsion engines and an engine-driven generator all cooped together in a small enclosure, the subject of air supply deserves serious thought.

Engine spaces become sauna baths when under way, and the heat can become a nuisance. The outboard motor is immune from this problem because the heat not carried off by the cooling water is lost to the surrounding atmosphere. The stern-drive engine is almost as fortunate. A great deal of its surplus heat can be contained in the insulated cover; what leaks out is at the stern of the boat and not much of a bother. But the problem becomes acute with decked-over, cabin-type craft whose engine rooms are totally enclosed.

Many cruisers carry their engine rooms directly below the salon. In many of these installations, the only insulation is the carpet on the salon sole. Quite understandably, a long cruise raises salon temperature above the comfort point. Good insulation on the under side of the sole and plenty of air circulation in the engine room can reduce the discomfort. Luckily, thermal insulation usually has the ability to absorb noise as well.

Often misunderstood is the exact role the engine plays in pushing the hull through the water. That the engine turns the propeller and that the prop transforms engine power into thrust is, of course, generally known. But that the "push" is transmitted to the boat by the engine through its fastenings is often overlooked. Hence the engine fastenings, whether they are the clamps of an outboard or the bolts in the stringers of an inboard, must be able to take forward and backward stresses in addition to those imposed by the engine itself. Small pressure plates on the stringers at the engine mounts help distribute the stresses over a wider area.

A new method of exhausting the engine has taken its place beside the standard choice of either wet or dry exhaust. This new system discharges the engine gases directly under the hull instead of out the transom for the wet type or through a stack for the dry type. Comparative

(A)

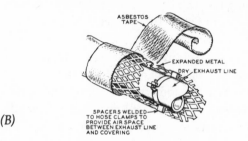

(B)

Figure 19-7. *Self-opening flaps covering the stack exhaust pipes prevent the entry of rain (A). As a fire prevention measure, the piping to the stack is insulated as shown at (B).*

freedom from noxious fumes and great reduction in noise are claimed for this innovation.

The diagram in Figure 19-6 explains the under-hull system. A large diameter U pipe leads up from the engine exhaust manifold to a height above the waterline and then straight down through the hull. To offset the considerable back pressure, which would affect engine idling, a valve permits exhausting directly into the atmosphere until cruising speed is reached. The high U makes it impossible for seawater to reach the manifold and damage the machine. As with all exhaust systems, this pipe, too, must be kept clear of everything that can be damaged or ignited by high temperatures.

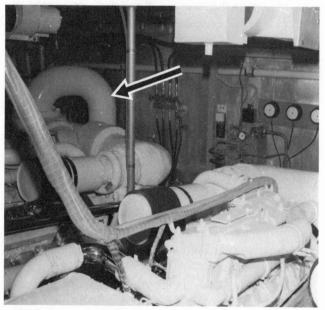

Figure 19-6. *The engines of this large yacht discharge their exhausts directly under the hull through large, U-shaped pipes (arrow). Advantages are noise reduction, fume elimination and a certain amount of hull cushioning. (Bradford Marine, Dieter Cosman)*

Simple common sense added to intelligent observation is an excellent guide to the details of right and wrong engine installation. For instance, it is obvious that the vertical pipes in the stack of a dry exhaust system need protection from entering rain. Certainly the skipper cannot be expected to climb up to place and remove caps in accordance with the weather. The practical solution takes the form of the uncomplicated flaps shown in Figure 19-7. These flaps swing easily on their hinge pins

Figure 19-8. Automatic flaps closing the outlet pipes of transom exhausts prevent the entry of seawater into the exhaust lines. The flow of exhaust gas opens the flaps; gravity and spring action close them. (Salisbury Rubber Prods.)

back pressure on the engine. Stops prevent the flaps from staying open and thus they close immediately when the engine is shut down. Some large, over-the-road diesel trucks use the same idea.

The same common sense will mandate transom exhaust ports to be placed sufficiently above the waterline to prevent seawater from entering. Where underwater exhaust is desired for its noise and fume-absorbing ability, fixtures on the transom placed over the pipe opening direct the gases downward. Some transom exhaust ports are covered by simple rubber flaps that keep waves out of the pipe when the vessel is not under way. (See Figure 19-8.)

Although each of the engine's life-support components and systems is covered individually in the various chapters of this book, an overall review of the details that have to do with powerplant installation will help bring everything into focus. Manufacturers of inboard engines supply recommendations that outline ideal installations and tell how far conditions may deviate from the ideal without serious power loss or actual damage; these edicts are the final arbiter in what may or may not be done with each individual machine.

Alignment of the engine and its transmission gear with the propeller shaft is undoubtedly the single most important item in the installation process. Misalignment will spawn many undesired results. The strain on engine, transmission and shaft bearings will lead to early failure, meanwhile contributing to noise and vibration. The friction caused by bearings operating out of line will raise temperatures and hasten failure; under certain conditions these temperatures could climb high enough to become a fire hazard.

Boat hulls purposely are made flexible to help them overcome the wavy environment in which they live. This flexibility must be taken into account when aligning shaft and powerplant. Hence, alignment is never made when the boat is hauled out on shore, nor should it be attempted until the hull has been back in the water long enough to resume its natural shape. The method of alignment is easy enough and merely requires careful work under the guidance of a dial indicator or a shim "feeler" gauge, or both.

A dial indicator is illustrated in Figure 19-9. Microscopic movement of the tip is amplified by the internal

Figure 19-9. The dial indicator magnifies infinitely small hull movements on its sensing prod and displays the amount on its dial. Movement as small as .00025 may be measured. Uses for the dial indicator in repair and maintenance are described in the text.

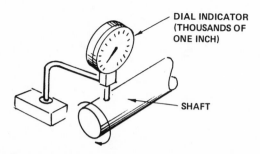

DIAL INDICATOR
(THOUSANDS OF
ONE INCH)

SHAFT

Figure 19-10. The propeller shaft is checked for straightness with the aid of a machinist's indicator as shown. The slightest bend is registered on the dial in thousandths of one inch.

mechanism so that it can be read clearly on the dial. The better instruments make it possible to read movements as small as one ten-thousandth of an inch, but for alignment work an indicator reading only in thousandths of an inch is adequate.

Making certain that the shaft itself is straight and not bent is a wise forerunner of the alignment procedure. This can be done handily with the indicator set up as in Figure 19-10. When a bent shaft is turned slowly by hand, the indicator pointer will swing wildly back and forth; a straight shaft will allow the pointer to remain at rest—at least in theory. Actually, no shaft installed on a boat will be so perfectly true that the indicator will notice no imperfection. This is overcome by taking a practical view and allowing a certain number of thousandths, say less than ten, to be considered serviceable. Some manufacturers may hold the threshold figure to less than five. Nor is it redundant to check the output flange of the powerplant in the same manner to make certain that it also runs true.

The misalignment between engine and shaft can be either lateral or angular and sometimes even both. The explanation for these terms is found in the drawings of Figure 19-11. Lateral misalignment is corrected by moving the engine either sideways or up and down; the remedy for angular misalignment is tilting the engine. The feeler gauge is the handy tool for detecting angularity problems, but a small straightedge will serve for lateral trouble. The shims and bolts mentioned earlier serve to hold the installation in the corrected position.

Air blowers are desirable for enclosed spaces housing diesel engines and become a necessity when the power is derived from gasoline. When ventilation to the engine room is not all that could be desired, a blower forcing air in from the outside will help if it has sufficient capacity. It may be hooked up to the intake and exhaust vents that Coast Guard regulations require for enclosed engine rooms. With gasoline engines, the blower assumes a

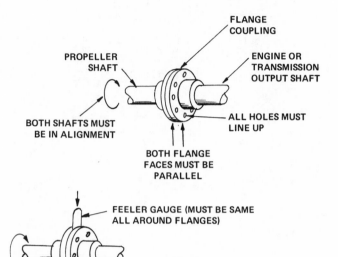

FLANGE COUPLING

PROPELLER SHAFT

ENGINE OR TRANSMISSION OUTPUT SHAFT

BOTH SHAFTS MUST BE IN ALIGNMENT

ALL HOLES MUST LINE UP

BOTH FLANGE FACES MUST BE PARALLEL

FEELER GAUGE (MUST BE SAME ALL AROUND FLANGES)

STRAIGHT EDGE (MUST BE SQUARE AND FLUSH ALL AROUND OUTSIDE SURFACE)

Figure 19-11. The importance of having propeller shaft and output shaft of engine or transmission absolutely in line cannot be overemphasized. Shown are several methods by which alignment may be checked with no more equipment than a straight edge and a feeler gauge.

safety function as well. Recommended practice calls for such a blower to be operated for five minutes before the engines are started; the purpose of this is to clear the space of flammable vapors.

(If the blower is to be mounted in the engine space of a gasoline installation, its motor should be of the sparkless, explosion-proof type. Standard electric motors with sparking commutators could set off the very explosion they are installed to prevent. Blowers with standard motors may be used if they can be mounted outside the engine space.)

The dipsticks of automobile engines are always clearly marked with "full," "fill" or similar admonitions, but marine engine dipsticks never are, at least not when they leave the factory. The reason is understandable. The manufacturer does not know at what angle his engine will be installed in a boat, and consequently he cannot know how the required quantity of lubricating oil will rest in the crankcase.

Dipstick calibration is performed by the engine installer. Once the machine is permanently in place, he fills the crankcase with the specified amount of oil. The level of oil on the dipstick then shows where the word "full" is to be placed.

Accessory devices, such for example as oversize alternators supplying 110-volt alternating current or emergency bilge pumps, are often installed to be driven by belt from the propulsion engine. Unless these devices can be mounted directly on the engine, a belt problem could result. The problem is brought about by the relative motion between engine and device when the latter is mounted separately. The minute changes in distance between drive pulley and driven pulley caused by engine vibration affect belt tension. A belt set up for proper tightness at standstill could be stressed to failure when running. Incidentally, the longer the drive belt, the longer its expected service life.

Some accessory devices constitute sharp intermittent loads of several horsepower on the propulsion engine. Air-conditioning compressors are an example. The sudden "on" and "off" may have an undesirable effect on smooth engine performance as well as on belt service life. Needless to say, where belts are run in locations that could be hazardous to personnel, they should be protected by suitable guards.

While not strictly a part of engine installation, electric wiring in the engine room is ancillary to it. Earlier it was stated that the wires from battery to starter motor should be short and of ample diameter. Undersize cable chokes back needed current and may make engine starting a marginal affair. Wiring on the engine itself, such as from alternator to voltage regulator, or from spark coil to distributor, should be secured from vibration and protected from oil. The engine block is grounded; abrasion that brings wire in metallic contact with it could cause a short circuit and a fire. The American Boat and Yacht Council standard of colors for wire insulation is given in Figure 19-12; compliance with this will make troubleshooting easier.

RECOMMENDED MARINE WIRING COLOR CODE
DIRECT CURRENT SYSTEMS — UNDER 50 VOLTS

COLOR	ITEM	USE
Yellow w/Red Stripe (YR)	Starting Circuit	Starting Switch to Solenoid
Yellow (Y)	Generator or Alternator Field	Generator or Alternator Field to Regulator Field Terminal
	Bilge Blowers	Fuse or Switch to Blowers
Dark Gray (Gy)	Navigation Lights	Fuse or Switch to Lights
	Tachometer	Tachometer Sender to Gauge
Brown (Br)	Generator Armature	Generator Armature to Regulator
	Alternator Charge Light	Generator Terminal/Alternator Auxiliary Terminal to Light Regulator
	Pumps	Fuse or Switch to Pumps
Orange (O)	Accessory Feed	Ammeter to Alternator or Generator Output and Accessory Fuses or Switches
	Accessory Common Feed	Distribution Panel to Accessory Switch
Purple (Pu)	Ignition	Ignition Switch to Coil and Electrical Instruments
	Instrument Feed	Distribution Panel to Electric Instruments
Dark Blue	Cabin and Instrument Lights	Fuse or Switch to Lights
Light Blue (Lt Bl)	Oil Pressure	Oil Pressure Sender to Gauge
Tan	Water Temperature	Water Temperature Sender to Gauge
Pink (Pk)	Fuel Gauge	Fuel Gauge Sender to Gauge

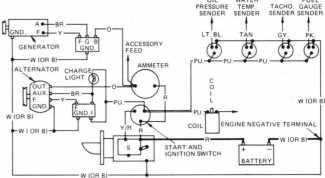

Figure 19-12. Maintaining a systematic code of colors for the insulation of the wires in the boat's electrical system pays off when a circuit must be traced. Above is the color code recommended by the American Boat & Yacht Council.

Small misalignments between transmission and drive shaft may be neutralized with the aid of flexible couplings. Many designs of such devices are commercially available, and one type is shown in Figure 19-13. The principle behind all of them is the same: A member intermediate between the driving and driven parts of the coupling is able to absorb the forces of misalignment, usually by being alternately compressed and tensioned. Synthetic rubber is a favorite intermediate.

Often the misalignment between transmission and drive shaft is deliberate. For instance, the designer desires

(A)

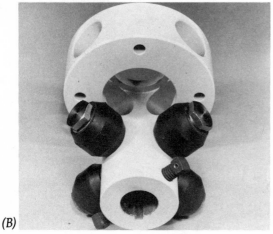

(B)

Figure 19-13. Flexible couplings between propeller shaft and engine transmission absorb the small misalignments caused by the "working" of the boat hull. In addition, the unit shown here electrically insulates the shaft from the engine, and this may reduce the tendency to electrolysis. The complete unit at (A); an exploded view showing the rubber load bearers at (B). (Federal Marine Motors)

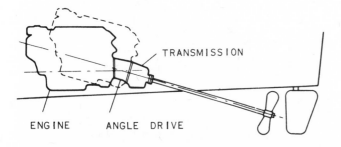

Figure 19-14. The headroom needed for a tilted engine often can be reduced by adding an angle drive and keeping the engine level.

Figure 19-15. Careful handling of a long-arm crane enables these engines to be removed and replaced through a door without cutting through an upper deck. (Eau Gallie Marine Basin)

the engine to be installed more level than the drive shaft normally would permit. The answer lies in the angle drive unit shown in Figure 19-14. Angle drives are manufactured for a wide spectrum of angular differences between input and output.

Removing an inboard engine for replacement or major overhaul can become a trauma even greater than the original installation. This is notably true on pleasure boats with full cabins where the engines are located under the sole of the salon. Removing carpets and furniture gives access, but very often removal can be accomplished only by cutting through the overhead deck and picking the machine out with a crane. Sometimes the cutting can be averted by the use of a lifter that can reach in horizontally through door or window. (See Figure 19-15.)

Even getting into the engine room is a struggle on most completely decked-over pleasure boats. Many large yachts provide only a rat hole behind a liftable ladder for access. Pity the skipper with a little excess avoirdupois!

The story is told of the owner, looking for a man to work on his engines, who turned down all applicants but zeroed in on a passing midget. He hired the little man despite his disclaimer of all expertise. The midget was the only one who could get through the rathole.

20. *Troubleshooting and Diagnosis*

Troubleshooting, to the uninitiated, may seem like mysterious wizardry. Actually, troubleshooting is merely a practical exercise in logical thinking, the mental ability to proceed from A to B to C and on. Say that the desired final result of a certain sequential operation is dependent upon a known series of individual events taking place. Suddenly the operation fails to yield that final result. It is evident that the chain of events has been broken, that a necessary event is missing. Logical thinking checks the events off, one by one in sequence, to pinpoint the absent one. Replacing the offender restores the chain and enables the operation again to produce the desired final result. Troubleshooting is as simple as that.

A primitive example of troubleshooting by logical thinking may be taken from a spring-wound clock that has stopped. The needed individual events that combine to make the clock operative are known: The spring must be wound with a key to supply power to the gears that drive the hands to indicate the time. It is also known that winding the clock brings the key to a position of resistance beyond which it cannot be turned. Troubleshooting therefore begins with a trial of the key.

If the key offers great resistance, the spring is fully wound, the power is available and the fault lies with the internal gearing or perhaps with hands that are stuck. If the key turns easily but with increasing resistance, the spring was not wound sufficiently to supply the needed power; most likely the clock will run when the winding is completed. If the key turns freely regardless of how often it is rotated, the connection between it and the spring has been broken or the spring has loosened from its anchor; no power is being supplied to the clock, and no amount of turning will make it run.

Troubleshooting a balky engine is no more difficult if the "events," the individual functions that are necessary to its operation, are firmly in mind and checked off in logical sequence. Each event in the chain that makes up the operating cycle of a gasoline engine or of a diesel engine is studied in a separate chapter of this book. Thus the path of logical thinking can be traced out chapter by chapter until memory takes over and makes it habitual. The various diagrams that will follow later are actually mental joggers.

The beauty of being able to troubleshoot lies in the versatility of this accomplishment. Once the sequence of troubleshooting a certain gasoline engine is learned, the knowledge is equally applicable to all other gasoline engines, large or small. Mastering a diesel leads to mastery of all other diesels, regardless of size. Logical thinking will overcome what small variations in functioning there may be.

It is, of course, well known that an internal combustion engine will not start spontaneously like an electric motor or a steam engine; it must be cranked over before it will run of its own accord. The cranking is performed by an electric starter, and this brings in a whole chain of additional components or "events" that must be examined when troubleshooting the powerplant that will not crank. There are the battery, the wiring, the switch, the solenoid and finally the starting motor itself, any one of which could be the cause of a failure to get the engine cranked. (See Figure 20-1.)

Logical thinking in this situation begins with the battery. It could be insufficiently charged or even dead. A hydrometer would be the technical means of determining this because such a reading is the most accurate gauge. If all the other items in the chain are functioning, even the operator's ear can assess the state of charge because a low battery will cause the starter to make merely a more or less pronounced grunt when the switch key is turned.

Sometimes a fully charged battery will give all the telltale effects of a dead one when the starting switch is actuated. The most common cause is corrosion between the battery posts and the cable terminals, which acts as a partial insulator. Visual inspection detects this. The correct remedy is removal and cleaning of the terminals plus cleaning of the battery posts before replacement. Some-

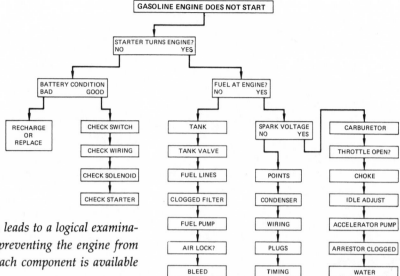

Figure 20-1. Following the arrows leads to a logical examination of the condition that may be preventing the engine from starting. More information about each component is available in the text.

times in an emergency, a temporary fix can be made by tapping the terminals with a hammer; this breaks through the corrosion and allows short-term current flow.

The wiring from the battery to the starting motor could be subject to two types of failure: open circuit or short circuit. An open circuit is a discontinuity, a break in the wire. A short circuit is caused when the positive wire is abraded and metallically touches the grounded engine block. Because of the vibratory and environmental conditions in the engine space, an open circuit is a fairly common complaint. A short circuit is rare, and, when it does occur, it announces itself immediately with a dangerous flash.

The next "event" to be examined in the logical sequence of troubleshooting the engine that fails to crank is the solenoid, which, as explained in Chapter 7, is the remotely controlled switch for the heavy starting current. Turning the switch key should evince a click in the solenoid, and the absence of this sound indicates either a defective solenoid or trouble in the circuit to the switch.

A normal click with nevertheless a failure to crank despite an adequate battery, points to either defective solenoid internal contacts or else a defective starting motor. To differentiate between these two possibilities, a heavy insulated screwdriver or a similar metal tool may be used. It is a procedure not recommended for unskilled hands because of the danger of sparks, although profes-

sionals exercising proper caution do this routinely. The screwdriver is placed to short the two main terminals on the solenoid and thus eliminate the internal contacts from the path to the starting motor. If this activates the starting motor, obviously the solenoid is defective; if it does not, the trouble is in the starter.

All of the foregoing troubleshooting actions are shown, shorthand form, in the diagrams that end this chapter. Similar additional diagrams depict the steps described in the explanations or the other troubleshooting routines that follow.

Suppose that the switch key triggers normal cranking but despite this the engine will not start. A different chain of events now must be examined in logical sequence.

It is known that an internal combustion engine must have fuel, air and ignition, and Chapter 4 discusses the required relationships between these necessities. Thus, troubleshooting the recalcitrant boat engine must verify the presence and check the condition of each of these basics. Fuel is the logical first choice.

Engines have been cussed out and even dismantled, only to discover that fuel was absent, at least absent from the critical point where it had to be present. It may seem childishly elementary to say this, but the first place to look is the fuel tank. Emptiness could be the result of forgetfulness or of a fuel gauge that does not tell the truth.

In the days of gravity feed, fuel in the tank meant fuel

at the engine—provided, of course, that the tank valve had been opened. In present-day installations, a pump interfaces between tank and engine; this introduces a possible point of failure.

Pumps are either mechanical or electrical. Mechanical pumps are actuated by a cam on a shaft of the larger gasoline engines, by gear drive on diesel engines and by vacuum or pressure on most outboards. The cam drive rarely fails, and difficulty with these pumps is traceable to internal parts such as springs and diaphragms. The construction of the outboard's vacuum fuel pump is exceedingly simple and consists of a diaphragm and rudimentary valves; these parts can and do wear out. The vacuum supply is usually through an engine port and thus quite permanent, but on occasion through a tube, which should be a point of suspicion. On some outboard motors, positive pressure pulsations instead of negative vacuum act upon the diaphragm, but the action is identical. A further variation sends the positive pressure to the outboard fuel tank to displace the fuel and send it to the engine.

Electrical fuel pumps used with gasoline powerplants are completely separate from the engine and depend upon battery power for their operation. A solenoid transmits reciprocating motion to a diaphragm, which moves the fuel through inlet and outlet check valves. These pumps are controlled by the ignition key so that they are activated in unison with the engine. If tests show that electric current is reaching the pump terminals, then the failure is internal. Often the failure is not complete; some fuel is being pumped, but not sufficient for full throttle operation of the engine, and perhaps even low speed is erratic.

If inspection proves that fuel is reaching the carburetor, the engine's determination to remain stationary may be traceable to the ignition system. Rereading Chapter 12 and fixing the electrical basics firmly in mind will prove helpful.

A quick, overall check of the ignition system, which is as applicable to large engines as to outboards, is made with a spark-plug wire. Any convenient wire is removed from its spark plug, and its terminal end is held about ¼

inch from the engine block while the engine is being cranked. Healthy sparks should be evident. If this is true, then the ignition system has qualified, and the trouble is elsewhere.

In the absence of sparks, logical thinking first determines whether electric current is reaching the ignition system. This is easy on larger engines whose ignition systems are identical with those on automobiles. Outboard engines with their magnetos and individual ignition coils do not make this procedure applicable.

The current not only must reach the ignition system but must be interrupted properly by the breaker points in the distributor. Whether or not this is happening can be determined with the aid of the little gadget shown in Figure 20-2. It consists of a miniature light bulb of the same voltage as the battery with two clip leads attached.

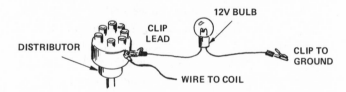

Figure 20-2. An ordinary 12-volt bulb, connected as shown, is a simple check for breaker point trouble. Cranking the engine should cause a rhythmic flicker. Continuously lit bulb means points are remaining open. Continuously dark bulb means points are remaining closed.

One clip goes to the terminal on the distributor that is connected to the spark coil, and the other clip is attached to the engine block. The bulb will be lighted when the points are not touching and will be dark when the points are closed. Naturally, during cranking the bulb will flash on and off.

The carburetor could be a source of trouble, and often is the first to be accused, but it is remarkable how seldom this component is at fault. A small burst of fuel can be seen in the throat of the correctly functioning carburetor when the throttle is opened quickly. The flame arrestor on the carburetor must be removed for this observation, and caution should be exercised when it is not in place.

The foregoing directives for troubleshooting, with their mention of ignition and carburetion, obviously apply to gasoline engines, although the discussion on cranking is universal. Since diesel engines have no spark plugs and carburetors, troubleshooting them is even simpler.

The diesel engine, just as its look-alike gasoline power-plant, cannot function without fuel, air and ignition—only in this case the ignition is the extremely high temperature reached by air when it is highly compressed. When these three necessities are adequately present, the diesel will run, barring, of course, a great internal mechanical difficulty. It is therefore reasonable to assume that failure to run indicates the absence of one or more of these three items and that logical troubleshooting should trace these down.

As in the earlier discussion of gasoline engine failure, here, too, lack of fuel at the engine should trigger first a look at the diesel fuel tank. Gauges are not infallible, and human memory certainly is not.

Filters are more common in diesel fuel lines than in gasoline supplies, and they can be a source of trouble. Filters could be clogged, and this could prevent the pump from moving the fuel. Filters also could be loaded with entrapped water. These conditions are found by inspection, although a test gauge at the pump will give finite readings that can be compared with the manufacturer's specifications of allowable vacuum and pressure.

Failure of the pump to deliver fuel to the injector pump or in some cases directly to the injectors could also be attributed to air in the fuel lines. Air will most likely be found if the fuel tank previously had been let run dry. The remedy for air is bleeding of the fuel lines at the highest point or at the end point, bleeding being accomplished by disconnecting the lines and allowing fuel to flow into a container until all air bubbles have disappeared. Many systems provide vent cocks in the fuel lines to facilitate bleeding.

Air is a most vital component because, as discussed earlier, the diesel engine functions in an excess of air, whereas the gasoline engine does its job with a slight shortage. A blocked air filter could prevent sufficient quantities of air from reaching the cylinders, and so could excessive exhaust back pressure. Even before these exigencies come into play, an engine space without large enough openings to the atmosphere could be the cause. The remedy for each of these ills is self-evident.

The injector system could be at fault for the diesel engine's failure to start when cranked. On engines with self-contained individual injectors, hardly ever would all injectors be at fault at the same time, and the engine would fire on some cyclinders. Where a single-unit injector pump feeds all injectors, trouble here could well be the stumbling block to starting. A short whiff of ether shot into the air cleaner may be used as a test—and as an answer if this starts the engine. (Spray cans of ether, so-called starting liquid, are available in marine stores.)

Most difficulties with internal combustion engines do not involve such catastrophic situations as failure to crank or failure to start when cranked. Usually the problem is subnormal operation once the machine has started running. Logically, this means that the required components or "events" are present but that one or more is deficient in quantity or quality or timeliness. The indicators that apprise the skipper that everything is not up to standard may be irregular operation, foreign noises, excessive vibration, lack of response to the throttle, large deviations from normal gauge readings, smoke in the exhaust, lack of power. Each of these signs has its special meaning.

A "missing" engine, one that is not firing sequentially in all its cylinders, is the most probable cause of excessive vibration. Checking this out in a gasoline engine is quite simple; in a diesel engine it is a bit more complicated. The spark plugs of the gasoline engine are "shorted out" one by one by using an insulated screwdriver to bridge each plug terminal to the engine block, thus preventing ignition in that cylinder. Shorting the plug of an active cylinder will cause the engine to slow down and vibrate. The same thing done to a cylinder already inactive will have no effect on engine operation.

An equivalent test may be made only on diesel engines with self-contained unit injectors. The valve cover is removed and the injectors are held down, one by one, with a tool or screwdriver so that the rocker arms cannot activate them. Again, performing the test on a functioning cylinder will cause the engine to lose speed and vibrate, whereas the same test on a dead cylinder will have no effect.

Spark plugs and injectors play somewhat similar roles because both determine when the combustion for the power stroke will be initiated. There the similarity ends. The spark plug is a simple item, easily replaced. The injector, in all its various forms, is highly complicated and beyond the average skipper's ability to adjust and repair. Thus failure to fire caused by a fouled or defective spark plug is quickly corrected with only a spare plug and a wrench. Replacing a defective injector is a more difficult task involving the disconnection and reconnection of tubing and sometimes the added complication of adjusting a throttle mechanism.

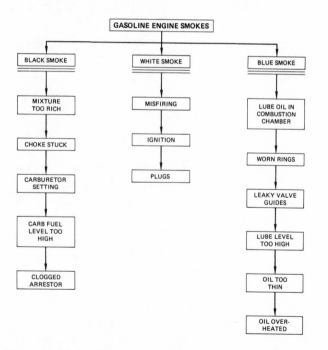

Figure 20-3. A smoking engine is not only a nuisance but also a waster of fuel and possibly lubricant as well. After determining the color of the smoke, the appropriate section of the chart should pinpoint logical causes.

The advent of transistorized capacitor discharge ignition (see Chapter 12) has reduced the fouled plug type of trouble because that system will fire plugs too dirty to function with standard ignition. No similar panacea has appeared for injectors, but then injectors are a hardy breed and stay out of trouble for unbelievably long periods of time.

"Smoky exhaust" is a common complaint around powerboats. The mere presence of the smoke and its color are clues to the probable cause. (See Figure 20-3.) Blue smoke is the universal sign of old age or decrepitude of piston rings, pistons, cylinder walls or valve guides. The smoke is caused by lubricating oil leaking past these components and then begin burned in the cylinder. The appearance of blue smoke is not necessarily the signal for immediate major overhaul. If the smoke is not excessive to the point of annoyance, and if the engine's oil consumption has not exceeded reasonable limits, considerable acceptable service life may still be in the machine.

Black smoke and gray smoke are indicators of improper combustion. The fuel is being burned incompletely, either because of insufficient air or because too much fuel is being supplied for the amount of air available. In the gasoline engine this could be traced to clogged flame arrestors or wrongly used chokes or incorrectly adjusted carburetors. The contributing causes of these symptoms in the diesel engine are clogged air filters, defective injectors and poor injector timing. A white smoke or haze from either engine is a sign that unburned fuel is going into the exhaust.

The exhaust system seems an unlikely place to look for causes of unsatisfactory operation of an internal combustion engine. Yet the exhaust system, strange as it may seem, can affect the intake system due to the pressure buildup mentioned earlier. Circuitous piping or pipes too small in diameter will result in high back pressure, and this in turn will prevent the cylinders from receiving their full charge of fuel and air. A poorly designed muffler, or one too small for the engine, will create back pressure. Early automobiles had "cutouts" that disconnected the exhaust system and allowed the manifold to discharge directly into the atmosphere.

Overheating is another persistent ill. (See Figure 20-4.) The first place to check is the through-hull fitting and its associated valve. Is the screen clogged, is the valve completely open, is enough raw water reaching the pump? Since all raw water is eventually returned to the sea, sufficient water coming out of the exhaust pipe absolves the system. Lack of water could be traceable to a faulty pump.

A raw-water-cooled engine with correct water flow should not overheat. If it does, the fault may lie with clogged passages in the block. A thick buildup of salt and scale on the water side of the cylinders reduces heat transfer and ultimately brings on overheating. Rust has the same effect. Various cleaners are effective in the early stages of scaling; advanced conditions are often beyond help.

The freshwater-cooled engine that overheats may have the same problem of insufficient raw-water flow because

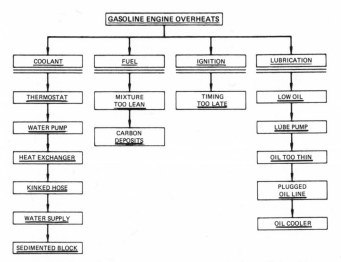

Figure 20-4. An overheating engine is trying to tell the skipper that something is wrong. The trouble should be found in one of the four categories shown. Continued overheating can destroy an engine.

the heat picked up by the freshwater must be transferred to the raw water. Here, again, the answer can be had by a look at the exhaust water. The freshwater pump on the engine may not be doing its job, allowing heat to accumulate because of lack of circulation. Contrariwise, a defective thermostat may be cutting off freshwater flow.

The most serious omen at the instrument console is a sudden drop of the needle on the oil pressure gauge, and the safe reaction to this is immediate engine shutdown. Several conditions could cause this, the most obvious being too little oil in the crankcase. The next probability is a defective oil pump or its associated pressure regulator valve. Less likely causes are oil tubing rupture and bearing failure. Where engines are set so low that their crankcases are often washed by bilge water, corrosion-caused leaks should be considered a possibility.

It is often said about automobiles that failure to start is sad but failure to stop is tragic. The reverse can be true on a boat, where an engine stoppage in a heavy sea can be tragic.

Engines can stop of their own accord suddenly or gradually. A gasoline engine that stops suddenly invariably does so because of ignition failure. When it gives up its ghost gradually and perhaps reluctantly, the problem will usually be found in the fuel system. The effect is the same as though the throttle were being slowly closed.

When a diesel engine stops unexpectedly, the trouble will most likely be traced to the fuel system. Fuel is not reaching the injectors, for whatever reason. The logical checking again begins at the fuel tank and progresses through every item on the route to the engine. (See Figure 20-5.) Fuel flow may be normal at the time of inspection, but previously flowing air bubbles may have been the reason for stoppage.

Pulling the spark plugs from an ailing marine gasoline engine often points the way to the trouble. The plug appearances for various engine conditions are shown in the series of photos in Figure 20-6. Oil fouling, for instance, should lead to an examination of piston rings, valve guides and other points at which undesired oil

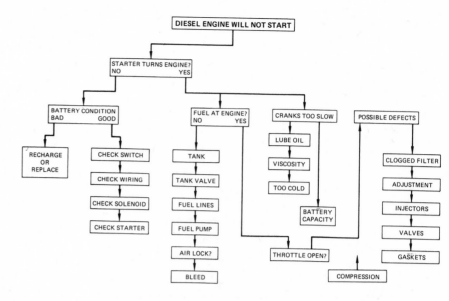

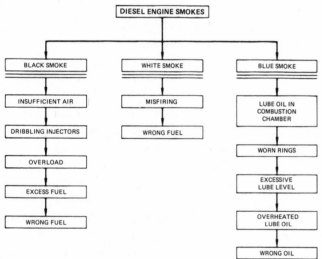

Figure 20-5A. *The diesel engine is generally inherently harder to start than a gasoline engine, so a slight increase in starting effort need not be a cause for alarm. However, if the diesel is determined not to start, following the arrows should uncover the trouble. Detailed information about the various components is found in the text.*

Figure 20-5B. *Even the best behaved diesel engine wafts a characteristic odor into the air. When the engine smokes, the odor is accentuated and may become a nuisance. Additionally, a smoking engine is wasting fuel or lubricant or both.*

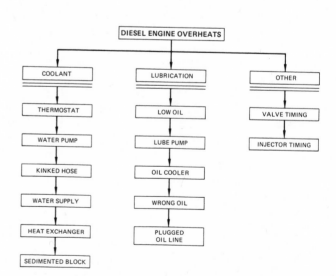

Figure 20-5C. *The diesel engine operates under greater stress than the gasoline engine, works at higher compression and puts out more power per unit. Its cooling system is more critical and overheating is more likely. Following the arrows should reveal the source of the problem.*

could reach the combustion chamber. Detonation could be a result of overadvanced ignition or a fuel too low in its octane rating. Spark plugs that are "too hot" for the engine could suffer from preignition damage. A plug fouled by soot is trying to tell a mechanic that the fuel mixture is too rich or that the engine is running too cold. A glazed insulator has been "roasted" in an engine because it is an incorrect type or even because the engine has a faulty cooling system and is operating far above its normal temperature. The ability to "read" spark plugs comes with experience.

The noises a running engine makes are a wonderful indicator of its state of health. The skipper who gets himself attuned to these sounds by constant attention

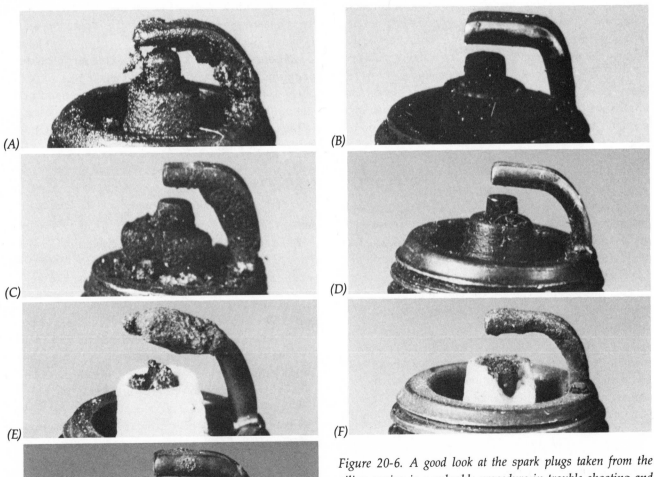

Figure 20-6. *A good look at the spark plugs taken from the ailing engine is a valuable procedure in trouble shooting and may point to the problem. A plug fouled by dirt is shown at (A), fouled by soot at (B), fouled by carbon at (C), and fouled by oil at (D). The effect of pre-ignition is shown at (E), the damage from detonation is seen at (F), a glazed insulator is depicted at (G). (Fram/Autolite)*

develops an automatic and reliable danger alarm. He will be alerted to trouble like the soundly sleeping mother, who, immune to other disturbances, wakens immediately upon the slightest cry from her baby.

Vibration, however slight, can also be an engine tell-tale. The experienced skipper is subconsciously attuned to the boat vibration felt from a correctly functioning powerplant. Any change flashes a mental red light and triggers an investigation.

As with all human endeavors, luck is an essential ingredient in powerboating also. Despite all the tender loving care, all the close attention to what the instruments are reporting, an occasional catastrophic breakdown will occur somewhere sometime and will put an engine irrevocably out of business. When that happens, the twin-engine boat will come home on its other powerplant without much ado. The skipper of the single-engine vessel will resort to good preventive seamanship and his radio.

Marine engines have such an outstanding record of faithful, continuous, unobtrusive service that the very rare breakdown must be excused—except, of course, by the skipper to whom it happens.

The charts that follow are based on the same logical troubleshooting procedure espoused in the text. They are arranged in order of major symptoms that become evident when an engine balks. Thus, for instance, when turning the key does not elicit the normal engine starting response, looking under the heading of "hard starting" gives the various possible causes of this problem. Other uncharacteristic symptoms of engine operation may be similarly checked out.

Of course, the charts assume that the technical details of marine engine internals, the subject of this book, have been assimilated at least to the point of general understanding. Such knowledge fleshes out the bare essentials in the troubleshooting charts and enables any skipper to proceed like a professional.

Step-by-Step Troubleshooting Procedures

The following troubleshooting diagnoses are arranged in groups under the headings of the major symptoms that would draw the attention of the skipper when his engine misbehaves. Thus, if inordinate smoke is noticed in the exhaust, the possible causes will be found in the paragraph headed SMOKE. Undue vibration would turn attention to VIBRATION, and so forth.

Each enumerated cause should be traced down and verified as to its presence or absence. This process of elimination will zero down to one final cause, which, if corrected, should restore normal operation. (See text for methods of checking causes.) An asterisk (*) indicates gasoline engine.

SWITCH ON, NOTHING HAPPENS

Defective switch. Broken wire. Defective starter solenoid. Starter motor brushes worn and not touching commutator. Corroded battery terminals. Dead battery. Defective starter motor. Safety interlock switch defective. Fuse.

SWITCH ON, STARTER ONLY GRUNTS

Dead or low battery. Corroded battery terminals. Starter pinion stuck in gear. Engine oil too heavy in cold weather. Water in cylinder. Defective transmission.

SWITCH ON, ENGINE SPINS, NO START

*No ignition. *No fuel in carburetor. Empty tank. Clogged fuel filter. Defective fuel pump. *No compression because of loose spark plugs. No compression because of valve or piston ring failure. Water in fuel or in fuel system. Air in fuel system. *Fouled spark plugs. *Breaker point/condenser problem. *Choke improperly set. *Cylinders flooded.

ENGINE STARTS, THEN STOPS

Fuel line valve closed. Fuel strainer clogged. *Choke improperly set. Water in fuel line or in fuel. Wrong throttle setting. Load applied to cold engine. *Loose ignition wire. *Clogged carburetor jet. *Stuck float valve in carburetor.

ENGINE MISFIRES

*Fouled spark plugs. *Wet spark-plug wires. *Carbon-tracked distributor. *Loose ignition wires. *Cold engine with improperly set choke. Defective fuel pump. Partially clogged fuel filter. *Incorrect carburetor mixture. Contaminated fuel. Leaky valves or piston rings. Excessive load.

GOOD LOW SPEED, BAD HIGH SPEED

Tank valve not fully open. *Ignition timing incorrect. Injector timing incorrect. Partially clogged fuel filter. *Weak spark coil. *Defective condenser. *Breaker point adjustment. Governor adjustment. *Leaky spark-plug wiring.

EXCESSIVE VIBRATION

Cylinders missing fire. *Faulty spark plug. Faulty injector. Loose engine mounts. Incorrect timing. Transmission and/or drive train trouble. Damaged propeller. Loose flywheel. Loose balancer. Uneven cylinder compression. Defective head gasket.

KNOCKING OR PINGING

Wrong fuel. Incorrect timing. Accumulated carbon in cylinders. Pre-ignition. Bearing trouble. Slapping pistons. Overheated engine. Cooling system trouble. Incorrect valve adjustment.

SQUEALING SOUNDS

Bearings about to seize. Insufficient lubrication. Low oil level. Defective oil pump. Defective oil pressure regulating valve. Overheating.

RATTLING SOUNDS

Valve tappet clearance excessive. Stuck valve guide. Stuck hydraulic valve lifters. Timing gear clearance adjustment. Loose fuel pump.

STARTER STALLS

Low battery. Corroded battery terminals. Damaged starter wiring. Water in cylinders. Defective starter. Starter pinion locked in flywheel.

ENGINE OVERHEATS

Clogged intake strainer. Collapsed water hose. Insufficient cooling water. Defective water pump. Defective thermostat. Water pump belt. Internal engine water leak. Lubrication failure. Heat exchanger clogged. Cooling system airbound.

RUNS BUT NO POWER

*Incorrect carburetor setting. Incorrect timing. *Stuck choke. Contaminated fuel. Partially clogged fuel filter. Obstructed fuel supply. Leaky valves. Leaky piston rings. Low compression. *Air leaking into intake manifold. Injector trouble.

TOO LOW OIL PRESSURE

Low oil level. Overheated oil. Oil grade too light. Defective gauge. Defective sensor. Defective oil pressure relief valve. Crankcase strainer partially clogged. Clogged oil filter. Defective oil pump. Oil leak.

TOO HIGH OIL PRESSURE

Cold engine. Oil too heavy. Stuck oil pressure relief valve. Defective gauge. Defective sensor. Oil circuit obstruction. Clogged oil filter.

RUNS, NO OIL PRESSURE

This is a dangerous symptom and could foreshadow total failure. No oil in crankcase. Defective gauge. Defective sensor. Defective oil pump. Defective oil pressure relief valve. Broken oil line. Strainer to pump line open. Oil pump drawing air.

OIL PRESSURE FLUCTUATES

Defective oil pressure relief valve. Low oil level. Oil pump drawing air. Defective oil pump. Lubricating oil badly sludged. Oil filter partially clogged.

BLUE SMOKE IN EXHAUST

Lubricating oil getting into combustion chamber. Worn valve guides. Worn piston rings. Too high oil level. Oil overheated and too thin. Defective oil scraper rings. Worn cylinders. Oil grade too light or wrong.

BLACK SMOKE IN EXHAUST

*Choke partially closed. *Incorrect carburetor setting. *Defective carburetor jet. *Carburetor float level too high. Partially clogged air intake. Wrong injector setting. Engine overload. Improper grade fuel.

WHITE SMOKE IN EXHAUST

Misfiring cylinders. *Fouled spark plugs. *Defective ignition system. Defective injectors. Defective injector pump. Low compression.

TOO HIGH OIL CONSUMPTION

Defective oil scraper piston rings. Worn cylinders. Crankcase oil level too high. Oil overheated. Oil viscosity too low. Engine too much off horizontal. Leaky oil filter. Leaky gaskets. Defective oil seals. Leaky oil cooler. Piping or crankcase leads. Worn valve guides. Too high oil pressure.

*PITTED BREAKER POINTS

*Defective condenser. *Shorted ballast resistor. *Oil contamination. *Incorrect gap. *Poor quality points.

*TOO HIGH CARBURETOR BOWL LEVEL

*Incorrect float adjustment. *Worn input needle valve. *Defective float. *Excessive fuel pump pressure. *Stuck input needle valve.

ROUGH IDLING

Idle adjustment too low. *Carburetor adjustment. Injector adjustment. *Incorrect ignition timing. Incorrect injector timing. *Fouled spark plugs. Fouled injector nozzles. *Leaky intake manifold gasket. Air in fuel system. (See Figure 20-7.)

TROUBLE CHART

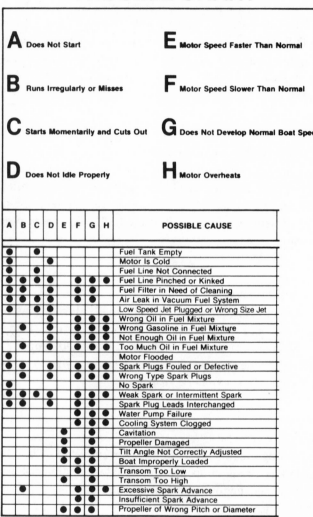

A Does Not Start
B Runs Irregularly or Misses
C Starts Momentarily and Cuts Out
D Does Not Idle Properly
E Motor Speed Faster Than Normal
F Motor Speed Slower Than Normal
G Does Not Develop Normal Boat Speed
H Motor Overheats

A	B	C	D	E	F	G	H	POSSIBLE CAUSE
•		•						Fuel Tank Empty
•			•					Motor Is Cold
•		•						Fuel Line Not Connected
•	•	•	•		•	•	•	Fuel Line Pinched or Kinked
•	•		•		•	•		Fuel Filter in Need of Cleaning
•	•		•		•	•		Air Leak in Vacuum Fuel System
•		•	•					Low Speed Jet Plugged or Wrong Size Jet
			•		•	•	•	Wrong Oil in Fuel Mixture
	•		•		•	•		Wrong Gasoline in Fuel Mixture
			•		•	•	•	Not Enough Oil in Fuel Mixture
	•		•		•	•		Too Much Oil in Fuel Mixture
•								Motor Flooded
•	•		•		•	•	•	Spark Plugs Fouled or Defective
	•		•		•	•		Wrong Type Spark Plugs
•								No Spark
•	•	•	•		•	•	•	Weak Spark or Intermittent Spark
•	•		•		•	•		Spark Plug Leads Interchanged
					•	•	•	Water Pump Failure
					•	•	•	Cooling System Clogged
				•		•		Cavitation
				•		•		Propeller Damaged
				•		•		Tilt Angle Not Correctly Adjusted
				•		•		Boat Improperly Loaded
				•		•		Transom Too Low
				•		•		Transom Too High
	•				•	•	•	Excessive Spark Advance
					•	•		Insufficient Spark Advance
					•	•		Propeller of Wrong Pitch or Diameter

Figure 20-7. The eight problems most likely to plague the outboard skipper are tabulated here with suggestions for solutions. Note that identical symptoms may be produced by different causes and that step-by-step elimination is the logical procedure. (Mercury Marine)

21. *Maintenance and Repair*

"A penny's worth of maintenance buys a dollar's worth of repair." The sage who said that surely must have been the owner of a powerboat, and doubtless he was referring to his own powerplant. No piece of seagoing equipment has greater need for tender loving care than does the marine engine, and none shows its gratitude more in the form of faithful service.

Many facets of engine maintenance are based on common sense and presuppose little or no mechanical expertise. If one component turns, slides or rubs on another, a friction surface is created. It does not take much thinking to decide that such a surface should be lubricated. Nor does one have to be an engineer to maintain oil at dipstick levels, to see that filters are not clogged and to inspect driving belts for tightness.

The combination of common sense and the owner's manual supplied with every engine is a surefire duo. The manuals contain illustrations that target the lubrication areas and tabulations that state the time intervals recommended between the necessary attentions. The little tricks of getting at things, peculiar to every engine, are detailed and save cussing. The manuals often warn the skipper away from those service routines that should be the province of experienced technicians. Thus there is no need of "getting in over one's head."

Spark plugs are the least complicated components of a gasoline engine, and yet they account for the greatest percentage of starting and running troubles. Therefore it behooves the cautious skipper to include a close examination of the engine's spark plugs with every maintenance routine. Fortunately, plug removal requires only a simple plug wrench. Only two cautions need apply to taking plugs out and putting them back: Make certain that the small ring gaskets (where used) are in good shape and that the plug starts into the cylinder finger-easy and is not cross-threaded. Final tightening should be to manufacturer's specifications, but in the absence of the required torque wrench a feeling of firmness should make a close approximation. (See Figure 21-1.)

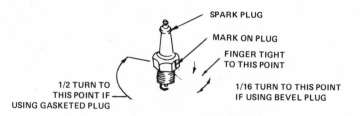

Figure 21-1. Correct spark plug tightening may be accomplished handily by following the simple procedure illustrated above. A beveled plug without gasket is wrenched 1/16 turn beyond finger tight. A plug with gasket is rotated 1/2 turn beyond finger tight.

The good or bad condition of a spark plug can be assessed by comparing its appearance with the illustrations in Figure 20-6. A fouled plug is the most frequent cause of failure to fire; oil, soot and carbon have given the ignition voltage such an easy path to ground that it no longer jumps the gap to cause a spark.

Many service centers have machines that clean spark plugs. These devices are actually miniature sand blasters in which compressed air forces abrasive particles into the inserted plug to carry off the fouling. See Figure 21-2. Spark plugs can also be cleaned by hand, although more laboriously. The tools for doing this are a piece of stiff wire, small strips of sandpaper, perhaps a penknife and a good amount of patience and ingenuity.

Figure 21-2. Machines are available that clean spark plugs by subjecting them to an air blast of fine abrasives. A small device that does this is shown; it operates off a 12-volt battery. (Elco Int.)

The correct gap setting of the spark plugs for a given engine is extremely important and should conform to the owner's manual. The length of the gap determines the ignition voltage required for operation, and this in turn governs the size and intensity of the spark and its adequacy for the job in hand. The gap should always be measured with a round wire of the specified diameter. This is shown in Figure 21-3 at (A), while at (B) is shown how a flat thickness gauge is used to make the same measurement.

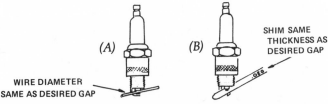

Figure 21-3. The gap of a spark plug may be set to manufacturer's specifications with either a wire gauge (A) or a shim gauge (B) of the desired diameter or thickness. Only the outer electrode is bent, never the inner one.

A newer, specialized type of spark plug, the surface gap plug (see Chapter 12), is found on some engines, usually outboards. These plugs should be compared to the chart in Figure 12-4 because their casual appearance is not a true indicator of their ability to function. No ad-

Figure 21-4. The surface gap spark plug omits the usual outer electrode. Sparks travel from the center electrode across the insulator to the outer shell. The surface gap plug is recommended especially for capacitor discharge ignition.

justment is made to these plugs. They are discarded when the gap is exceeded. Normally, this is the only reason for rejection. Surface gap spark plugs are not recommended for standard ignition systems. (See Figure 21-4.)

Modern practice places rubber boots over the projecting, ceramic ends of spark plugs. These form tight closures from high-tension wires to plugs, and prevent the accumulation of moisture and salt films on the insulators, a primary cause of trouble. So-called leaky leads, spark-plug wires with defective insulation, often rob the ignition system of the necessary zing. Spark-plug testers containing miniature neon bulbs will glow when these leaky spots in the cables are touched. The leaks make themselves self-evident at night because they emit a faint bluish discharge in the dark.

Figure 21-5. A volt-ohm-ampere meter such as this, popularly called a V-O-M, is indispensable in troubleshooting electrical problems aboard and in evaluating certain electrical and electronic components. (Eico Electronic Instrument Co.)

Carburetors provide very little need or opportunity for do-it-yourself servicing—and carburetor specialists generally believe that even this little is too much for unskilled hands. Translated into boat talk: If the carburetor is working satisfactorily, leave it alone; if it is not, ship it off to a properly equipped shop. The skipper competent to delve a bit deeper can try his hand cautiously at the idle adjusting screw. This governs the mixture of air and gasoline at idling speed with the throttle closed. (See Chapter 31.) Turning one way leans the mixture; the other way enriches it. The response is seen in the ease with which the engine idles.

The flame arrestor calls for a simple maintenance procedure, which nevertheless pays off in fuel savings. The idea is to keep the arresting material as clean as possible and thus cause as little impediment as possible to the entering air. Gasoline can be used if the cleaning is done away from the boat, but kerosene or a nonvolatile solvent is preferable. In either case, the flame arresting material should be thoroughly dry before the unit is replaced on the engine.

Service shops test the tightness of drive belts with special instruments, but the skipper can test with his thumb quite adequately. The upper part of the belt is pressed down firmly with the forefinger, as shown in Figure 21-6, halfway between the two driving pulleys.

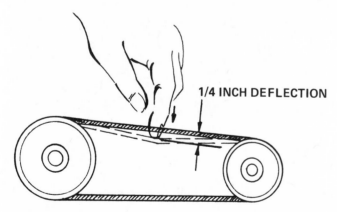

Figure 21-6. A properly tensioned belt will not deflect more than 1/4 inch at its center with moderate applied pressure. Obviously, this test is made with everything stationary.

The resulting deflection should not exceed approximately ¼ inch. Obviously, this is done with the engine stopped. A loose belt wears quickly and does not transmit full power. A belt set too tight places unnecessary strain on shaft bearings. All this is true whether the engine is gasoline or diesel.

A word on belt replacement. Driving belts develop ailments peculiar to themselves that arise out of both age and use. The outer covering hardens, and fine cracks are seen, or else the various layers of the belt begin to part company. Either of these signs should trigger immediate discard because otherwise the belt will surely fail at the least opportune moment.

Incidentally, installing a replacement belt improperly will start it off with two strikes against its probable life. Forcing the belt over the sheaves with a lever of some sort is the unforgivable method that causes damage before even the engine is run. The adjustment on one or both of the sheaves or pulleys in question should be loosened and the wheels brought closer together so that the belt goes into place easily. The sheaves are then brought back toward their original positions until the proper belt tension is reached.

A marine gasoline engine that has given many hours of hard service may have ignition points that should be inspected. The gap between the contacts when the points are wide open is checked with a thickness or shim gauge and should agree with manufacturer's specification. The fiber rubbing block that bears against the central cam would appreciate a minute dab of oil. The instant the contacts open bears an important relationship to the position of the piston in its travel and determines the "timing" of the engine. This adjustment is critical and is best left to a technician who has a timing light that enables him to "time" the engine while it is running.

Every fuel filter eventually becomes a collecting place for contaminating dirt and water; in fact, that is its purpose in life. The collection may be in the bottom of the housing or else in a bowl, usually glass. In addition to removing the contaminants, the filter element itself is either cleaned (where possible) or replaced. The signal for replacement may be either appearance or else the length of time considered adequate service in the owner's manual.

Day-to-day maintenance of the cooling system boils

down to making certain that sufficient water is being pumped through. With raw-water cooling, there is only one system, and its adequacy can be judged by observing the amount of water going overboard. With freshwater cooling, there are actually two systems, with the second one internal and not easily observable. The immediate check on this is the temperature gauge on the console. Other than keeping the internal system correctly filled with an approved mixture of water and antifreeze, nothing much remains to be done. The purpose of the antifreeze is mainly rust and oxidation prevention; pleasure boats are seldom in use during freezing weather.

Badly fouled internal engine water passages often respond to a homemade nostrum concocted with 1 ounce of oxalic acid to 1 gallon of water. This is used as a flush and is best handled with rubber gloves. After flushing, the acid is neutralized with a solution of trisodium phosphate, known to the trade as TSP. Luckily for skippers, the easily cloggable radiator of automobiles is absent from boats.

The storage battery recurs as the culprit in many cases of engine trouble and failure. Thus preventive maintenance directed at this component becomes easily obtainable insurance. A battery hydrometer is an essential maintenance tool and should be aboard. Two types of hydrometer are commercially available: one containing three little pellets supposedly signifying full, half and empty and intended for people who cannot read, and the other, the preferable kind, graduated in specific gravity.

Figure 21-7 shows the relationship between specific gravity and battery charge.

Oil changing always occupies an important place in the list of maintenance routines, and yet it is a moot point open to differences of opinion. Lubricating oil directives from the automobile manufacturers started with mandatory replacement at not more than a few hundred miles; today some specifications allow 10,000 miles. This wide gap cannot be explained merely by citing improvements in oils and engines. Many engineers and other knowledgeable drivers never actually change oil; they just add oil as needed to keep it up to the required level.

The claim is made that the additives in lubricating oil

SPECIFIC GRAVITY vs STATE OF CHARGE

APPROX	1.260	100%
''	1.230	75%
''	1.200	50%
''	1.700	25%
''	1.140 TO 1.110	NO LONGER USEFUL

Figure 21-7. The most accurate method of checking the state of charge of a storage battery is with a hydrometer. The relationship between hydrometer reading and charge is shown in the above table. A slight correction is made for the temperature of the electrolyte but, for the temperatures encountered in boating, the difference is negligible.

lose their effectiveness and therefore the oil must be discarded. No practical method exists whereby the skipper can check whether they have or have not done so. Consequently, caution may dictate adherence to the oil routine advocated in the owner's manual.

The subject of additives brings to mind the various magical and highly secret compounds sold for addition to the crankcase. High-pressure advertising touts these as valued bearers of widespread benefits to the engine. Both oil and engine companies are unanimous in advising against the use of *these* additives.

Maintenance of both generator or alternator and starting motor is minimal on gasoline and diesel engines. Besides adding a few drops of oil at the designated points, there is not much else that a skipper can do. Eventually both machines will need new brushes, but this is a dismantling job and best left to a mechanic. The pinion on the starter that engages the flywheel should be checked for ease of movement on its spline and lubricated.

Lubrication is also advised on the controls that govern engine and transmission. Where control is by Bowden wire devices, chances are that the factory lubrication is intended to last for life. Where control is by cables that pass over pulleys and cranks, the need and the points for lubrication are obvious.

The danger of destructive galvanic action is always present in marine engines, and this subject is discussed thoroughly in Chapter 18. The basic preventive maintenance procedures are to guard against having dissimilar metals in contact with each other and with seawater and to replace sacrificial zinc anodes promptly. The criterion here is mostly visual: If the zinc looks pretty well shot, the chances are it is.

Most maintenance directives, except those dealing with the fuel systems, are equally applicable to all marine engines regardless of the fuel they burn. Perhaps the only caution is that more care to do the job correctly must be taken with the diesel engine because it is stressed more highly.

Outboard motors need some special pampering when they are through with the day's work, especially if they operate in salt water. The entire engine should be flushed out with freshwater. The need to do this is intensified because most outboards are aluminum and subject to attack by salt.

Some outboard motors have provision for the attachment of a garden hose, and flushing them is no problem. For the others, owner's manuals give diverse instructions. One sample is to remove the propeller, set the outboard into a large pail of freshwater and run the engine until everything is clean. A scheme for flushing an outboard with freshwater while it is still attached to the boat is shown in Figure 21-8. The trick is accomplished with a

Figure 21-8. Manufacturers recommend fresh water flushing after the outboard motor has been used in salt or brackish water. The bag illustrated above makes the job easy; it also may be used while the boat is afloat. (Multipur Bag Co.)

large plastic garbage bag that separates the freshwater within it from the salt water around it. Of course, the transmission is set in neutral while the motor is running in the bag so that the propeller does not turn.

Many pleasure boats are dock sitters, floating platforms for lounging and entertaining, whose powerplants are rarely in use for serious cruising. These engines need maintenance of a slightly different kind. Obviously, there is no normal wear of bearings, no erosion of cylinder walls, no pressure against seals to make them leak. The problem with these machines is the gradual dissipation of the protective oil films on the many internal surfaces and the consequent opportunity for moist air to cause corrosion.

It is generally agreed that engines that spend most of their lives standing still should be "turned over" about once a week. The turning-over process consists in starting the engines and allowing them to run at idle speed until they warm up sufficiently for good lubricant distribution. Transmission controls are put momentarily in forward and in reverse for the same purpose of distributing the lubricant in these units. A bonus of the procedure is that moist air is expelled from the internals of the machinery.

Dock sitters also need to pay special attention to their storage batteries because the few minutes of warm-up running will not supply sufficient charge. In most cases, small battery chargers connected to pier power will supply this charge. In others it may be necessary to run an engine long enough for its generator or alternator to do the required charging. If all else fails, the battery may be taken ashore to a service station.

Maintenance of the engine should include periodic checks of the through-hull fittings that supply cooling water. While these plumbing fixtures may seem innocuous and able to last "forever," they have the potential of sinking the boat. Hoses should be discarded at the very first sign of age. Clamps on these hoses should always be doubled so that the possible failure of one can be tolerated. The shutoff valves or sea cocks should work freely, and a touch of lubricant will help them do so.

Whenever space permits, a drip pan under the engine is a good investment. It does more than just keep the bilge free of oil and fuel. A clean pan highlights any engine leak and pinpoints its general location to make repair easier. Stainless steel is excellent pan material but expensive. Galvanized steel will do with reasonable care. Aluminum and plain steel are not recommended.

Some maintenance routines may make the removal of a component necessary, and, if this concerns the fuel or the lubricating systems, spillage may result. All spills on a boat are messy, but spills of gasoline are dangerous in addition. The experienced mechanic will try to drain all lines before any units are removed, and he will have plenty of rags and cans ready at hand to catch what flow cannot be avoided. When the job is done, the oil rags should be disposed of off the boat; oily rags are a source of spontaneous combustion.

When engine parts must be cleaned, gasoline is an excellent solvent, but its advantages are not enough to warrant the dangers of its use. Diesel fuel is almost as good a cleaner, and it leaves a slight oily residue, which continues to act as a protective film. Carbon tetrachloride type cleaners are not recommended because of their harmful vapors.

The discussion so far has been about maintenance, with very little said about repair. Yet, sooner or later, the need for repair will loom into every skipper's boating life with more or less traumatic impact. Repairs can range from the minor replacing of a bolt to the major overhaul of an engine. How far along this path any individual boatman will go is determined by his expertise, his desires, his pocketbook and the leisure time at his disposal. Luckily, professionals stand ready to take over (for a fee, of course) whenever the amateur has had enough. (See Figure 21-9.)

It is wise to think every intended job out, down to the very last detail, before picking up a single tool. Go through the motions mentally. Do you understand the what and why and how? Have you the needed tools and measuring instruments plus the factory specifications to which the work should be done? Are the replacement parts available? Are the components so heavy that you will need help?

Some repair operations may well be within the skipper's ability to perform, but the equipment required could be too expensive to warrant its purchase for a single job. Cylinder reboring is an example. Modern, specialized cylinder rebore tooling almost guarantees a perfect result with minimal experience, but the cost of the

*Figure 21-9A. Repairing an engine out of the boat and in a sling in the shop is a boon to a mechanic because everything now is accessible. (*Indian River Marine Basin*)*

*Figure 21-9B. Returning an overhauled engine to a yacht without damaging the superstructure takes expert handling of the crane. (*Eau Gallie Yacht Basin*)*

Figure 21-10. A screwdriver permits the knowledgeable mechanic to listen to the internal workings of an engine. The handle of the screwdriver is placed on the bone behind the ear, the point at the desired listening location.

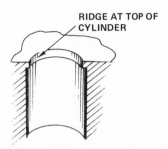

Figure 21-12. The wear on the cylinder wall caused by the piston in its travel often leaves a ridge at the top. Proper overhaul and reconditioning removes this ridge.

equipment takes it out of sensible consideration for onetime use. (See Figure 21-10.)

A so-called valve job on an overhead valve engine may be considered within the realm of the mechanically able boatowner. One reason is that the entire engine head with its valve mechanism and its valves is removable as a unit and can be taken to a convenient working place. Rocker arms, springs and their retainers, the valves themselves, all can be removed leisurely and comfortably. The photograph in Figure 21-11 shows the complete engine head in its assembled condition.

The condition of the cylinder walls can be examined

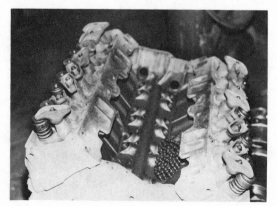

Figure 21-11. The two heads are in place on this vee-type overhead valve engine. The space between is called the "valley."

while the head is off. The first thing to check is whether or not an objectionable ridge has formed at the top of the piston travel. The sketch in Figure 21-12 explains this. This ridge need not be removed if the old piston rings are to stay. However, its removal is mandatory if piston rings are to be replaced because it will interfere with the new top ring. This is another example of a simple job being taken out of reach of the boatman because a ridge cutter is expensive.

The skipper's part in the repair of starting motors and generators or alternators is confined to removing them and reinstalling them after they have been fixed. One likely trouble with these components is a short-circuited turn in the winding. Repair shops have a "growler" that spots this trouble instantly; without the growler the search could be endless. Nor is winding the wire into the slots as easy as it looks.

The same restriction to taking it off and putting it back holds for carburetors. Although repair kits containing needed parts are sold for most standard carburetors, the cost of the kit is not a great deal less than a service shop would charge for putting the carburetor back in shape and, most important, checking it against factory specs.

One thing the do-it-yourselfer will need is plenty of gaskets because seldom is one in good enough condition for reuse once it has been taken off. A sheet of gasket material from which gaskets can be cut is a handy item aboard. The fine points of gaskets are discussed in Chapter 28.

Valve clearances (the "play" between valve stem end and rocker when the valve is closed; Figure 21-13) are specified by the manufacturer for each engine and must be followed for good engine performance. The clearance is stated in thousandths of an inch and is measured with a flat-thickness or shim gauge. Some directives call for the measurement to be made while the engine is running, some while the engine is hot, others with the engine cold and the concerned cylinder on its power stroke. Owner's manuals seldom give information to this depth, and the shop manual supplied by the manufacturer to its dealers must be in hand.

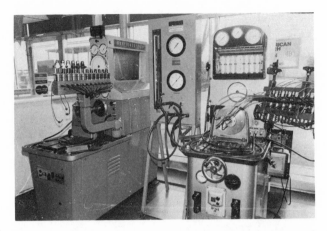

Figure 21-14. *This is some of the precision equipment required for optimum servicing of diesel engine injectors.* (RPM Diesel)

Seals (see Chapter 27) are tricky little items that must be assembled just so, and they are expensive enough to make it worthwhile to install them correctly the first time. One place where the skipper acting as fixer may come into contact with seals is in the water pump, for water pump repairs are not difficult and are needed often. Usually, the nub of these repairs is replacing a plastic or rubber impeller.

Diesel injectors rarely give trouble, and when they do they can be removed easily. However, any internal repair of an injector necessitates extremely close tolerance work with skill and instruments beyond the reach of the amateur. The photo in Figure 21-14 gives an idea of the equipment that a commercial shop finds required. It is routine for the dimensions of injector parts to be stated in ten-thousandths of an inch.

The spray from an active injector is so finely divided and under such extreme pressure that it will penetrate the skin without showing any visible marks of entry. This phenomenon is the basis of the latest medical hypodermic apparatus which gives "shots" on contact with the skin without the formerly used needle.

Discretion must govern economy when making engine repairs and deciding what parts may be reused and what parts are best thrown away. Certain broad rules can be given: Discard all cotter pins, most gaskets, all safety binding wires, all bolts that have been subject to high temperatures. On all questions of suitability it is best to err on the safe side even though it may add slightly to the cost.

It is said that surgeons left sponges in patients before operating rooms instituted an exact counting system of what went into the body and what came out. A similar

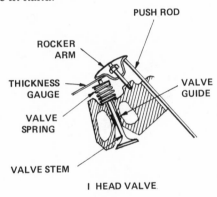

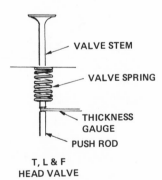

Figure 21-13. *A thickness gauge is used to measure valve clearance. On I head engines, the gauge is inserted between the valve end and the rocker arm. On T, L, and F head engines, the gauge is placed between valve end and push rod. The setting is correct when the gauge may be pulled out with slight resistance.*

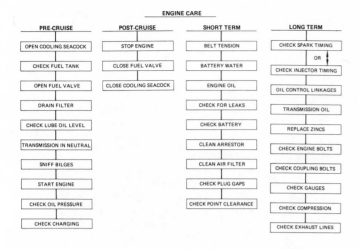

ENGINE CARE

PRE-CRUISE	POST-CRUISE	SHORT TERM	LONG TERM
OPEN COOLING SEACOCK	STOP ENGINE	BELT TENSION	CHECK SPARK TIMING
CHECK FUEL TANK	CLOSE FUEL VALVE	BATTERY WATER	OR
OPEN FUEL VALVE	CLOSE COOLING SEACOCK	ENGINE OIL	CHECK INJECTOR TIMING
DRAIN FILTER		CHECK FOR LEAKS	OIL CONTROL LINKAGES
CHECK LUBE OIL LEVEL		CHECK BATTERY	TRANSMISSION OIL
TRANSMISSION IN NEUTRAL		CLEAN ARRESTOR	REPLACE ZINCS
SNIFF BILGES		CLEAN AIR FILTER	CHECK ENGINE BOLTS
START ENGINE		CHECK PLUG GAPS	CHECK COUPLING BOLTS
CHECK OIL PRESSURE		CHECK POINT CLEARANCE	CHECK GAUGES
CHECK CHARGING			CHECK COMPRESSION
			CHECK EXHAUST LINES

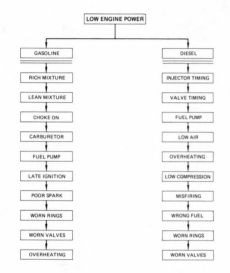

LOW ENGINE POWER

GASOLINE	DIESEL
RICH MIXTURE	INJECTOR TIMING
LEAN MIXTURE	VALVE TIMING
CHOKE ON	FUEL PUMP
CARBURETOR	LOW AIR
FUEL PUMP	OVERHEATING
LATE IGNITION	LOW COMPRESSION
POOR SPARK	MISFIRING
WORN RINGS	WRONG FUEL
WORN VALVES	WORN RINGS
OVERHEATING	WORN VALVES

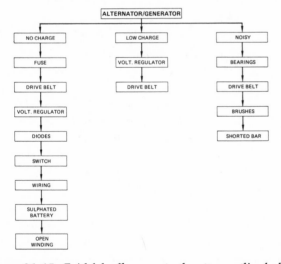

ALTERNATOR/GENERATOR

NO CHARGE	LOW CHARGE	NOISY
FUSE	VOLT. REGULATOR	BEARINGS
DRIVE BELT	DRIVE BELT	DRIVE BELT
VOLT. REGULATOR		BRUSHES
DIODES		SHORTED BAR
SWITCH		
WIRING		
SULPHATED BATTERY		
OPEN WINDING		

Figure 21-15. Faithful adherence to the steps outlined above assure happy, long-lived engines.

count will guard against parts left over after the engine job is finished or, what is worse, something left inside the engine to become a veritable time bomb.

The table in Figure 21-15 lists suggested maintenance procedures.

Water seems to be both benefit and plague for the seafaring man. If there is an insufficient quantity of it outside the boat, he runs aground; too much of it inside can cause engine failure and even sinking. Even a tiny amount of water can cause engine failure if it gets into the fuel system, and means to prevent this happening should have high priority. Filters that can separate fuel and water become excellent insurance against breakdown. The retained water is removed easily, as shown in Figure 21-16.

Figure 21-16. That ever-present bugaboo of water in the fuel, primarily because of condensation, must be guarded against constantly. A good filter separates the water which may then be drained as shown.

22.

Noise Reduction and Safety Measures

More and more, noise is being recognized as an actual instrument of damage to the human sensory system. Noise has other black marks against it: It causes fatigue, it lessens awareness of surrounding potential dangers, it slows reaction time and it impairs logical thinking. With all these demerits, noise is hardly a passenger of choice, but, nevertheless, it is an unwelcome stowaway on most powerboats.

Every mechanical operation generates *some* noise. The noise may be so slight that its detection requires an amplifier or so cataclysmic that it hurts the ear, but in either case the noise is there and cannot be eliminated. Only the transmission of noise to the hearer can be altered or cut off. Without a medium along which noise can travel, there would be no noise, just as there would be no electricity in the home without wires that bring it. Noise travels through air, water and solids in about that order of increasing speed.

Extremely loud noise approaches the realm of pain and can inflict physical damage. The ear can lose its ability to hear when affronted by extreme noise even as the eye can be made sightless when exposed to concentrated bright light. The tolerance of the ear to strong sounds is built up at the expense of its sensitivity to weak sounds. Thus a skipper subject all day to the roar of his engines may fail to be alerted by a weak sound that portends danger.

To understand noise, and to outwit its ability to be transmitted to distant points, the genesis of noise must be understood. Under the heading of "noise" we group random sounds, especially those that have no pattern and are displeasing. Sound is a wave phenomenon. If we could see sound coming through the air, it would look like the approach of a nonbreaking ocean wave. Low-pitched sounds would have fewer wave crests within a given distance; high-pitched sounds would have more. The waves themselves can be analyzed as a series of intermittent higher and lower pressures. It is these pressure differences that move the eardrum back and forth to pass the vibrations on to the aural bones and fluid and stimulate the auditory nerve to give us the sensation we know as sound.

The human ear is not a linear instrument. In other words, when the ear tells the brain that a certain sound is twice as loud as a previous one, it does not mean that the energy causing the louder sound was doubled; actually, the energy was quadrupled. Speaking mathematically, the response of the ear is logarithmic. This peculiarity of the ear makes sound-level measurements tricky and often incomprehensible to the layman.

Since the ear functions logarithmically, it is fitting and proper that the instruments measuring sound and the charts and graphs recording it also be logarithmic. The spacing on a logarithmic chart makes the distance between 1 and 2 equal to the distance between 2 and 4 and equal to the distance between 4 and 8 and so on. This scheme naturally requires a logarithmic unit of measurement, and the bel is such.

The bel was named after Alexander Graham Bell. The bel unit is too large for practical use; a unit one-tenth as great, the decibel (abbreviated dB), is employed in sound measurement. As an example of relative values, a sound just barely distinguishable by a person with perfect hearing is rated 0 dB. Normal conversation might register 60 dB, the buzz-buzz in a crowded restaurant could reach 90 dB and it would not be surprising to have the sound level meter swing up to 110 dB on a medium-size cruiser with both engines roaring wide open. (See Figure 22-1.)

Since sound is vibratory, it is to be expected that it will be transmitted through any medium capable of passing vibrations from one point to another. Air does this job well, water does it better and most metals do it even more efficiently. The rates of propagation through all these media are known; depth-sounders work because we know how fast sound travels through water. Incidentally, if a vacuum existed between the sound and yourself, you would not hear the sound because the vibrations would have no means of reaching you.

Obviously the main source of noise on a powerboat is the propulsion engine. An onboard alternating-current generator is a close second, rated lower only because its power output is lower. Far below these two in intensity are the noise of the wind blowing against the nonaerodynamic contours of the cabin structure and the sound of

(A)

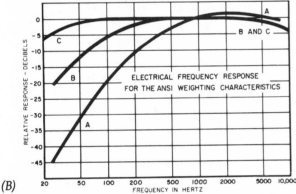

(B)

Figure 22-1. Excess engine noise can detract from the pleasure of boating. Sound level is measured by an instrument such as the one shown at (A) which reads in decibels or dB. The faintest sound a normal human can hear is pegged at O dB. An average twin-screw inboard may register 85 dB. A level of 140 dB is painful. The curves at (B) shown the three methods of measuring. (GenRad Corp.)

the bow wave and the water moving along the hull. From a practical standpoint, little can be done about these latter two.

The noise of the engines is transmitted through the air and through the materials of which the boat is made. The problem therefore becomes twofold: Reduce the transmission by blocking the air path and by isolating the engine from the hull. Some help can be obtained from the judicious use of certain substances that absorb sound and thus detract from the total volume that must be squelched.

When several noise sources combine to produce the unwelcome clamor, the solution becomes confusing mathematically and logarithmically. Forgetting the physics involved, if you had two simultaneous noise sources of equal intensity and you quieted one, you would expect

the noise level to drop to one-half. But not so by a long shot. Fact is, the noise level would drop only a few dB's, and the change would scarcely be noticeable. The lesson learned from this is that all contributing noise sources must each be reduced in order to achieve a practical overall reduction. For the cruising skipper who has two engines and a generator roaring along, the lesson states that each machine must be silenced before the sought-for drop in the din can be discerned.

The first step in noise reduction is to isolate the engines from the hull. The stringers on which the engines rest transmit the vibrations to most of the frames, and these in turn pass the sound on to the ship's shell, which acts as an effective sounding board. The action is somewhat similar to a loudspeaker in which the central magnetic system drives a large cone that in turn moves the surrounding air to produce the sound. Number-one step therefore becomes the installation of commercial isolators or of isolating material.

Isolating the generator is easier than isolating the engines. The reason is that propeller, shaft, transmission and engine function as one unit that applies the developed thrust to the hull through the engine mounts. Thus the mounts must be able to resist extreme fore and aft forces, and this reduces the flexibility permissible for any isolator. By contrast, the generator is a self-contained unit that can be mounted as softly as desired.

Generators may be supplied routinely with boxes that cover them completely and severely cut down the transmitted noise. (See Figure 22-2.) The boxes are constructed of materials that act as barriers to and absorbers of sound. But sound is almost as "leaky" as water and the covering box must be completely tight because even small holes will release a disproportionate amount of noise. The problem, of course, is to enable the entry of large volumes of air without impairing silencing efficiency; this is done with filter mufflers. Flammable fumes inside the box are another problem. Generators often run when the propulsion engines are stopped and things are relatively quiet.

Mufflers are an important factor in the quieting scheme of any engine, but it must be admitted that many marine

Figure 22-2. The generating plant is completely enclosed in this soundproof cabinet. Note the sound insulated air inlet. (Onan)

mufflers are not so effective as they might be. There has been a tendency to skimp, to depend too heavily for quieting on the effect of the cooling water passing through. The larger yachts with dry stack exhaust of course do not have this aid. The principle on which a muffler functions is either a labyrinthine path for the gases or a resonant chamber to dissipate sound, and Chapter 30 discusses these. Automotive mufflers must meet more stringent requirements and generally do a better job than a comparable marine unit.

Sound is a form of energy, and a basic physics law states that energy cannot be destroyed but only changed. An absorbent material that reduces the intensity of sound does so by changing the sound energy into heat. This does not mean that the absorber will eventually become dangerously hot because the energy in question is small and the heating effect minuscule. Furthermore, most absorbers dissipate only a portion of the sound energy with the remainder emanating as the same sound with lessened intensity.

Absorbers can be made so efficient that they will dissipate almost the entire energy content of a sound wave and thus act as almost complete barriers to the passage of the sound. To do this they must have mass, because it is the work done in vibrating the mass at the sound frequency that dissipates the energy. Lead is one material that fills this bill.

Lead is used as a sound barrier/insulator/isolator in various ways. The simplest method is to line the engine room with lead sheet. Preferably, the lead sheet would be backed by a soft material to prevent direct contact with the hull and bulkheads. Still more sophisticated, the lead would be only one layer of a sandwich whose other materials had complementary functions. The lead might

even be discontinuous and distributed as granules or powder in synthetic carriers. Bear in mind that the purpose of all this is to put as much absorbent mass into the path of the sound waves as economically possible. The name of the game is for the sound to kill itself by working.

An unfortunate peculiarity of sound, which increases the difficulty of silencing it, is its ability to generate secondary sound sources. It does this by resonance. Assume a certain sound of a given pitch and intensity impinging upon a loose item whose physical dimensions make it resonant. The item will become vibrant at the exciting pitch and will become a secondary sound source adding its annoyance to that of the original.

Secondary sound sources can also be set into vibration and noise production through direct mechanical contact. Under this heading are metal exhaust pipes not securely fastened, pillow blocks for propeller shafts not sufficiently dogged down, pipes and conduits susceptible to vibration.

The efficacy of any sound-reducing material is rated technically in decibels of loss between the impinging sound and the emanating sound. Most materials are selective in their ability to reduce intensity; the reduction for a high-pitched sound will be different from that for a low pitch. Even changes in temperature and humidity may affect the results. Specifications may be based both on transmission loss and on absorbing effectiveness, and these will be broken down for high and low pitch.

Earlier it was stated that sound travels at different velocity through various media. As examples, the speed through air is approximately 1,100 feet per second, through water approximately 4,700 feet per second and through aluminum approximately 16,000 feet per second. Thus the same sound could travel over different routes at different speeds and reach the hearer several times in succession as a garbled noise and become still more annoying.

The standard design of larger cruisers puts the engines directly under the salon sole, thereby making this premium space completely uninhabitable under way. Something can be done about this, though probably not enough. Assuming that the silencing measures already discussed have been put into effect in the engine space, additional acoustic improvements can be made in the salon itself. The underside of the sole can be lined with sound absorbers or sound barriers. Thick, soft carpet can be laid on the sole. Heavy drapes can be hung around the room's periphery. Sound absorbent material can be installed overhead. Any openings leading from the engine space to the salon must, of course, be plugged.

Much of what has been said so far has had an inboard engine in mind, but the principles apply to a stern-drive engine as well. In many ways, the stern drive presents fewer noise problems because the major noise source is tucked away in its own box at the transom. This box can be soundproofed with less trouble and at less expense because it is compact. The same materials and the same schemes are employed. The opening provided for the required air must be built correctly to avoid leaking sound. An excellent idea here is to make the passage labyrinthine and well lined with sound absorbers. (See Figure 22-3.)

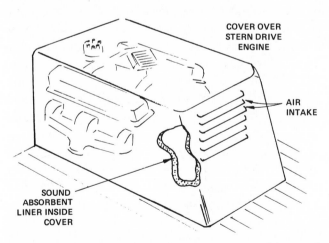

Figure 22-3. The cover for the engine of a stern drive can be made a factor in noise reduction. Sound absorbent material lines the inside of the box. Sufficient air intake must be provided and this should be baffled if possible.

Unfortunately, despite money and effort spent, the famous automobile advertisement stating that the loudest noise in the car was the ticking of the clock will hardly every apply to a powerboat under way. No attention has been paid to noise reduction of outboards because the

manufacturers already have done all that can be done in this regard.

And now, how do safety measures justify companionship in this same chapter with noise reduction? Safety implies protection of humans against harm; noise reduction also protects against harm. Furthermore, a high noise area contains many seeds of accidents because human protective senses are dulled.

The engine spaces of a powerboat under way can become the locale for two types of accidents and personal injuries: that resulting from contact with moving parts of machinery and that caused by contact with hot surfaces. Fire can become an overall danger to the boat as well as to personnel. The danger of electric shock is added on vessels wired for shore current and having switch boxes in the engine room.

Good housekeeping is at the very top of the list of safety measures. An engine room kept scrupulously clean will not have grease or oil on its sole in which personnel can slip and fall. Falls in an engine room are almost certain to inflict injury because of the cramped space and the surrounding hazards. Engine "rooms" whose overall height is sufficient only for crawling are extremely dangerous and should not be entered under way except for great emergency.

Gasoline is an incipient bomb, yet millions of gasoline-powered pleasure boats are in continued use, and news of a fire is a rarity. The answer lies in common sense and caution, both applied in liberal doses. The best fume detector, the one constantly available, is the human nose. The faintest trace of odor should be the signal to ventilate thoroughly before anything else is done, certainly before engines are started. Fuel lines should be under constant surveillance. Compared to gasoline, diesel fuel is relatively safe, yet even here a generous dosage of caution and common sense is not out of place.

The ultimate disaster to a boat is sinking. The engine room, with its through-hull fittings for the input of cooling water, is the area where accidents that can cause sinking are most likely to occur. Earlier it was stated that all hoses on these fittings should be double clamped. Despite this precaution, the hose itself could fail. The best safety measure is a warning device that alerts the skipper as soon as more than a few inches of water are in the hull; in other words, a bilge alarm.

Bilge alarms may be purchased off the shelf, ready to install, but they can be put together almost as easily on a do-it-yourself basis. The diagram in Figure 22-4 shows how it is done. Essentially, a standard float switch is connected to a bell or other signal, and the whole is powered by the boat battery.

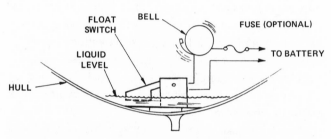

Figure 22-4. That ever-present problem of accidental flooding may be watched constantly and automatically with a simple bilge alarm. A standard float switch and a bell are connected to the battery as shown. The switch should be located at the lowest point of bilge water collection.

The fan, an integral part of all automobile engines, luckily is absent from the marine powerplant. In the confines of a pleasure boat's engine space, a whirring fan could be lethal unless caged in to an extent that would be impractical.

Storage batteries present three threats to safety; the corrosive acid, the destructive potential of a heavy mass getting loose from its moorings and the possibilities for short circuit.

Accidents involving machinery in motion are primarily those in which a part of the body is thrown against a moving belt or a rotating wheel or coupling. Belts, for instance those that drive the generator, alternator or water pump, can cause the greatest injury. A finger caught between belt and sheave may be amputated quicker than a surgeon could do it. Badly lacerated flesh would be the least to expect from an encounter with a swiftly turning wheel.

Earplugs should be worn for any lengthy stay in the engine room when everything is up to speed. As already

noted, continued exposure to extra-loud noise desensitizes the ear and may lead to permanent impairment. The "headphones" worn by flight attendants on an airfield give excellent protection.

A peculiar accident is an engine being worked on suddenly "catching" while being turned over and starting inadvertently. This can be avoided on a gasoline engine by grounding the wire that leads from the spark coil tower and normally goes to the distributor. The countermeasure for a diesel engine would be to block the air intake, although this form of accident is rare on these machines.

The nasty burns suffered from accidental contact with manifolds and other hot components can be guarded against only by being careful. Generally, there is not space available for installing screens around the dangerously hot parts.

To a large extent, the stern-drive engine is accident-proof because everything on it is easily reachable. Removing the enclosing box or swinging it out of the way eliminates the reaching and crawling that causes accidents in crowded engine spaces. Again, the outboard is in the clear because one must be really careless to have an accident with its engine.

The switch shown in Figure 22-5 attaches to a transmission and makes it impossible to start the engine

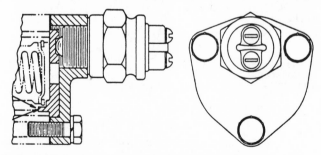

Figure 22-5. This switch, attached to a transmission, makes it impossible to start the engine unless the shift is in neutral. (Warner Gear)

unless the shift is in neutral. It is wired in series with the starting motor solenoid. This simple gadget is an important safety device for forgetful skippers.

Noise has a debilitating effect, and any effort to reduce

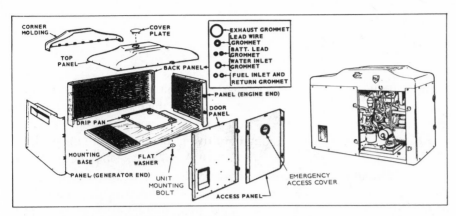

Figure 22-6. The details of construction of a sound absorbing enclosure are shown in this exploded view. (Onan Corp.)

it aboard is worthwhile and pays dividends in increased cruising pleasure. Sound-deadening enclosures are the basic procedure where offending onboard machinery is concerned. Some of these devices may be constructed on a do-it-yourself basis. The illustration in Figure 22-6 provides one suggestion. The materials must have the ability to dissipate the energy in the sound waves.

The galley and the engine room are the two most vulnerable places for the start of fire, and of these, the engine room is the one to guard more closely. Sensors that detect smoke and sensors responsive to unduly rapid increases in temperature may be connected to any of several available alarm systems. In Figure 22-7, a simple

thermal switch, overhead, is calibrated to make contact if engine-room temperature reaches a dangerous level. The device on the bulkhead closes a circuit (or opens it) immediately it finds any smoke in the air.

Detecting a fire is one thing, but immediate measures for quenching it are perhaps even more important. A tried-and-true method of fighting fire is to smother it with carbon dioxide, chemically known as CO_2. The gas is contained under great pressure in heavy cylinders such as pictured in Figure 22-8. Emergency release of the

Figure 22-7. The temperature sensor overhead and the smoke sensor on the bulkhead are recommended safety devices for the engine room. Both units are connected into a central alarm system. (Eico Electronics)

Figure 22-8. The heavy steel cylinders that contain the carbon dioxide for fire fighting could inflict great damage in a seaway if they are not anchored securely to a bulkhead.

215

carbon dioxide is accomplished either automatically in response to appropriate sensors, or manually. One form of manual activation is the "break glass in case of fire" box.

The standard bilge pumps universally found on pleasure boats are adequate for routine service but would prove totally ineffectual in a true emergency such as holing of the hull. That situation requires giant size pumping ability, and this can be had only in the multi-

horsepower range. One solution is a large centrifugal pump that will be driven by the propulsion engine in the event of trouble. Figure 22-9 pictures such an installation.

The method of driving this pump from the engine is shown in Figure 22-10. A power takeoff pulley or sheave is mounted permanently on the forward end of the crankshaft. A belt connects this with the pump when required. Of course, this same takeoff may be used to drive other accessories.

Figure 22-9. This emergency pump is positioned with its sheave in line with the pulley on the propulsion engine so that a belt may be run between them. This husky could take over in an emergency flooding and perhaps save the ship in a situation beyond the capability of the ordinary bilge pump.

Figure 22-10. The power take-off sheave on the forward end of the propulsion engine is a handy source of power. It may be used to drive the emergency pump shown in Figure 22-9 with a suitable belt.

23. Tools and Spare Parts

Tools should be aboard every powerboat, but the question is what kinds of tools? And how many? The pat answer calls for all the tools required to maintain the equipment on board. Yet that dictum, carried out literally, would have the vessel supplied like a manufacturer's official service station. Obviously, the correct answer must be worked out with compromise and good judgment.

A main factor in the selection of tools for the boat concerns the person who is going to use them. What is his level of skill? Putting tools in the wrong hands could very well *de*maintain an engine, to say nothing about the personal injury that the fumbling use of tools could cause. Thus the roster of tools carried aboard represents a practical correlation of man and machine.

The spare-parts list is another matter open to wide interpretation. Each individual situation must be evaluated carefully. Certainly it would be foolish to store a part whose technical difficulty of installation would make it impossible for any one normally aboard to perform. Nor does it make sense for a small pleasure boat, whose cruising range is from one nearby marina to another, to load itself down with routine spare parts available at every marine store. Yet common sense must never be omitted from these decisions. A truly worldwide cruiser would have good reason to disregard all of these warnings in order to be prepared for the unknown.

Increasingly, manufacturers have seen to it that certain manipulations around their engines can be performed only with special tools. Some foreign powerplants contain components whose dimensions are based on the metric system; obviously these require metric tools. Thus the tool kits in these situations must comprise additional items.

Tools are available on the market in various quality levels and consequently at various price levels. These gradations are most noticeable in power tools but exist in ordinary hand tools as well. The lowest level of quality, the "bargain" level, is no bargain at all and is usually attractively packaged to entice the amateurs. The highest level is directed at professionals and is too expensive to become a practical choice for the occasional do-it-yourselfer. In between is a level of quality and price suitable for the boatowner who performs average maintenance and limited repair.

Naturally, a poor quality tool will not bear a label that proclaims it to be only marginally useful and a bad buy. The discernment must be in the eye and judgment of the buyer. Unfortunately, the buyer has few signposts to guide him. Comparative price is one that is usually reliable. An inordinately low price should be looked at with suspicion because altruism exists only in storybooks, and purveyors must make a profit.

In hand tools, the higher price should buy better base material and finer craftsmanship. For example, a higher-priced chisel should be fashioned from special alloy steel, carefully hardened and tempered to hold its edge. It should show evidence of meticulous hand sharpening and have an ample hardwood or plastic handle. Good wrenches are drop-forged and not stamped out of sheet steel. Screwdrivers also must be made of hardened steel. A poor screwdriver will mutilate screwheads and make eventual removal of the screw impossible.

Power tools seem to have stabilized along two levels: light, intermittent duty models for the do-it-yourself market and sturdy, constant-duty units for the professionals. Each is readily recognized by the price, and the differential could be as much as three to one. Professional tools have stronger motors, better bearings, and are able to work uninterruptedly for long periods. The cheaper power tools soon become too hot to handle and must be given a rest if steady work is attempted. Work surface size is another difference between pros and amateurs; for instance, the pro sander exposes more abrasive to the work and thus completes the job in less time. Professional electric drills can make larger holes; pro electric saws can cut faster and deeper. Whatever the power tool, these same characteristics will differentiate between the two levels. Finally, the hardier tool will usually show more amperage on its label.

The possibility of electric shock is an important factor in evaluating a power tool for use on a boat. Until

Figure 23-1. This vibrating sander may be adjusted for either orbital or straight motion. The bag catches dust when working inside the boat. (Sears Roebuck Co.)

recently, the three-wire connecting cable with a grounding contact on its plug was considered the safest, but it did not live up to expectations. Certain conditions sometimes found onboard could negate the supposed protection of the operator against electric shock. Not only that, but very often the grounding plug was circumvented either for convenience or because the receptacle did not have a grounding connection. So the more modern double-insulated power tools have taken over.

As its name implies, the double-insulated power tool has a second, overall (double) insulation which makes it impossible for the operator to come in contact with any current-carrying portion of the device. Generally, this extra insulation consists of a complete plastic shell over the entire tool. Because of this safety feature, double-insulated tools are recommended over the older style. An added convenience of these power tools is that the connecting cable has a standard two-prong plug which fits all receptacles.

In accordance with the apparently universal spirit of giving less for more, some manufacturers of power tools are supplying them with power cables less than 1 foot long. These "shorties" replace the usual 6- or 8-foot cables of bygone times. Such short cables are a nuisance and a hazard because they bring the connecting receptacle inconveniently close to the working tool.

When extension cords are used around boats, a note of caution is indicated: A substandard extension can reduce the effective power of the tool. These, usually bargain, extensions are made with wire of less than optimum cross section and this impedes the flow of necessary current. Since most power tools require a relatively heavy current, the reduction of power may be considerable. Many owner's manuals that come packed with power tools state the minimum size of extension wire recommended.

Perhaps the sander is the most likely form of power tool to be found aboard. The sander can take any one of three forms: the vibrating sander, the disk sander and the belt sander. The well-equipped skipper may have all three.

The vibrating sander, Figure 23-1, moves the abrasive paper attached to its pad over a very short stroke, but it

does this at high speed. The stroke in lower-priced units is orbital; the more expensive devices allow a selection of either straight or orbital motion. It is claimed that the straight movement is better for fine work, such as that which will be varnished. The pad size on these sanders allows a standard sheet of abrasive paper to be cut into three pieces for proper fit. The vibrating sander is a forgiving machine; it cuts slowly enough to hide the effect of an amateur's occasional misstep.

The disk sander is a faster cutter and therefore must be handled with greater care. In unskilled hands, it may leave deep swirls that are difficult to hide. These machines are labeled by the size of the abrasive disk they are designed to use. Thus a 5-inch disk sander employs abrasive paper cut to a 5-inch diameter, and this is a common do-it-yourself size. Professional units will accommodate abrasive papers several inches larger. The photo in Figure 23-2 shows a representative disk sander

Figure 23-2. The electric disk sander is a fast-cutting tool that must be employed with care to avoid cutting undesired swirls into the work. The photo shows the correct angle of application. (Sears Roebuck Co.)

and the photo depicts the manner in which the spinning abrasive is applied to the work.

The belt sander is the fastest cutter and unexcelled for plane surface work. Its speed of action, its weight and its tendency to cut grooves if held stationary, all mitigate against the amateur, and he is wise to practice on scrap before attacking the boat. Belts can be made up by the user from a roll of abrasive, but the simpler course is to purchase them ready made to fit a particular machine.

Since sanding in any form reduces the work surface to tiny particles, all sanding creates unwelcome dust. Dust-catching attachments are available for most sanders; some utilize the tool's own motor to create the needed airflow.

The electric drill is another ubiquitous power tool. Drill quality varies more with price than does perhaps the quality of any other power tool. Electric drill design starts with two conflicting requirements: The motor must be extremely high speed in order to get the power into small space; the drill must rotate fairly slowly to avoid being "burned." The solution lies in reduction gearing, and this is where the difference between cheap and good stands out.

The cheap drills employ rudimentary bearings and cast gears whose teeth wear down with very little age. The worn bearings and the lost teeth combine to isolate the motor from the chuck holding the drill bit; the snap of the switch then engenders a loud whine from the motor without any result at the business end. Electric drills are described by the largest diameter drill bit the chuck will accommodate. The popular do-it-yourself sizes are ¼ inch and ⅜ inch. A representative unit is shown in Figure 23-3.

Electric saber saws, also called jigsaws, make the cutting of random shapes in wood and metal easy. Better units provide a selection of two speeds, the faster for wood and the slower for metal, of course with appropriate blades for each service. Most saber saws permit the blade action to be tilted, enabling bevel cuts to be made. (See Figure 23-4.)

Portable electric circular saws have made hand saws almost obsolete. These power tools have no equal when it comes to sawing off timbers or planks with ease and

Figure 23-3. The electric drill is a basic power tool and doubles for many other jobs such as the one shown in Figure 19-5. The largest drill accommodated determines the nominal size of the tool. (Sears Roebuck Co.)

Figure 23-4. The electric saber saw is a power jigsaw that is able to cut intricate patterns in wood, fiberglass and metal with appropriate blades. (Sears Roebuck Co.)

Figure 23-5. *The electric circular saw has pushed the old familiar carpenter's hand saw almost into limbo. Clever automatic guards protect the operator from what otherwise could be a dangerous device. (Sears Roebuck Co.)*

Figure 23-6. *The electric plane does a fast job of wood removal, but not necessarily with a cabinet grade finish.*

Figure 23-7. *The electric router is handy for creating or repairing mouldings and for cutting channels and fancy edges in boat trim. (Sears Roebuck Co.)*

Figure 23-8. *The ball peen is the only proper hammer to use around machinery.*

Figure 23-9. *A set of socket wrenches is a virtual necessity around a marine engine. The ratchet handle permits turning bolts in tight places.*

dispatch. Here, also, there are levels of quality and price, but the need for the tool is usually so infrequent and the duty cycle so short in boat work that almost any saw on the market will do for the skipper. (See Figure 23-5.)

Electric routers and electric planes find ready use by the boat builder, but these are marginal for the normal maintenance required on the average pleasure boat. The router is an extremely high-speed tool. A wide selection of available bits or cutters enables the router to do work as varied as cutting grooves and putting fancy edges on flatwork. The electric plane is intended as a substitute for the time-honored carpenter's hand plane, and it performs reasonably well on certain jobs. But the output of the electric plane is no match for what a skilled artisan can do with the hand plane. Figure 23-6 shows the plane, Figure 23-7, the router.

The all-purpose hammer, with which everyone is familiar, is the carpenter's claw hammer, but it is out of place in the engine room. Here the proper tool is the ball peen hammer, shown in Figure 23-8. This is the great persuader in the hands of a skilled mechanic. A few sharp raps on the head of a recalcitrant bolt persuades it to turn more readily than do numerous squirts of the many proprietary nostrums advertised for this purpose. Light taps in the right places makes components go together that otherwise refuse to. The ball end of the hammer can also flange tubing in the absence of the special tools.

Wrenches come in many styles for many purposes: open end, box end, combination end and socket, in addition to the variety of adjustable wrenches. Figure 23-9 shows a set of ratchet type socket wrenches.

The accessibility of the nut or bolt to be turned to a large extent determines the type of wrench to be used. Since bolt heads are hexagonal, with faces at 60°, the open-end wrench must be swung through that angle before it can take a new hold—although turning the wrench over reduces this necessary angle somewhat because of the angled handle. By contrast, the box wrench needs only a 30° swing due to its twelve holding points being only 30° apart.

Even better for tight spaces is the socket wrench with its ratchet handle. The sockets also have a twelve-point holding pattern, but, in addition, the handle need be

221

swung only one click at a time to seat or unscrew a bolt or nut. In general, these twelve-point holding designs are kinder to bolt heads than parallel jaws.

Actually, adjustable wrenches should be only stand-bys because of their tendency to cause damage if the jaws are not opened exactly to the bolt-head width. The bonus of the adjustable is that one tool can handle all sizes up to its capacity, thereby substituting for many fixed wrenches. A special form of the adjustable is the pipe wrench, or Stillson. It has serrated jaws that move with a cam action and thereby are able to grab smooth round pipe. It should never be used on bolts or nuts in place of standard wrenches.

The screwdriver is one of the most abused tools in the kit, doubling for everything from cold chisel to pry bar. Actually, there is more to using a screwdriver correctly than meets the casual eye. The two principal types of screwdrivers are the standard slot and the Phillips, and these are used with the equivalent type screwheads (see the Phillips in Figure 23-10 and the standard type in Figure 23-11). The simple rule for the proper use of screwdrivers is that the blade fit the slot exactly with no looseness that could allow play and consequent defor-mation of the tool and screw. Although not truly a screwdriver, and called an Allen wrench, this simple tool performs the same duty of setting and removing screws having this configuration of slot.

A special form of screwdriver that holds on to its screw is shown in Figure 23-11. This tool is extremely handy around engines. It allows screws to be placed into holes not accessible to the hands.

Pliers are sold in almost infinite types and sizes, and a reasonable assortment should be in every skipper's tool kit. The jaws of pliers may be either serrated or flat, and some tools have additional sharp meeting edges for cutting wire. Most serrated jaw pliers are made with adjustable slots that permit them to grab objects of vari-ous sizes. A newer development in this category is the vise-grip plier with a toggle action that causes its jaws to function like a vise. (See Figure 23-12.)

A set of drill bits should be aboard to accompany the electric drill. These may be purchased in sets that cover a range of hole sizes. Drills are a favorite item on bargain

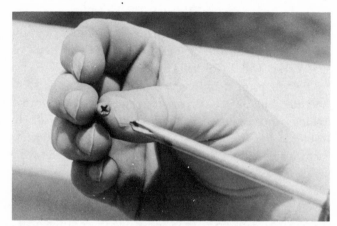

Figure 23-10. The so-called Phillips head screw requires a screwdriver blade shaped especially for it. Both are shown above.

Figure 23-11. This screwdriver is extremely useful for getting into tight places. Spring jaws hold the screw head while the screw is being put in place and driven.

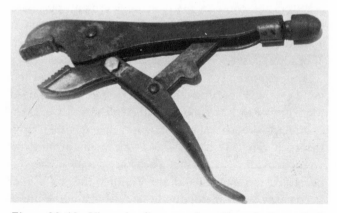

Figure 23-12. Vise-grip pliers are often able to do the work of a wrench or a vise or, of course, a pliers. The construction depends on toggle action to multiply the force applied greatly and transmit it to the jaws.

counters, and no admonition to avoid these so-called bargains can be too strong. Obviously, a drill must be harder and tougher than the metal it is about to cut; bargain drills are not, and consequently they are a waste of money. The best drill bits are manufactured from high-speed steel and are so marked. These cost a little more but easily are worth it. When space and pocketbook permit, an electric grinder is a worthwhile addition to the electric drill. With it, drill bits may be resharpened many times.

The electric drill is often asked to take over the work of the disk sander and the polisher, but its value at these jobs is marginal and useful only for very light operations. The drill performs this duty with an attachment that fits its chuck. Two reasons support the condemnation of "marginal": The chuck speed is too low to be effective either at sanding or at polishing; the power of the average drill is insufficient for meaningful stock removal. The attachment is shown in Figure 23-13.

Figure 23-13. An ordinary electric drill may be used as power sander with the gadget shown above. The sanding disks are held to the rubber platen with a central screw.

As said earlier, the list of tools aboard is a compromise between man and machine. Consequently every skipper will have some particular leaning or skill versus his engines, and this will make itself evident in the special tools he chooses as his shipmates.

The matter of spare parts is not so easily settled.

Naturally, the type of engine and auxiliary equipment carried by the vessel will determine what components must be at hand for routine maintenance and for safety. A few basic spare parts are applicable to all powerplants. Then the choice divides to suit either gasoline engines, diesel engines or outboards.

On the basic list are spare belts of the required lengths. An adjustable link belt that may be varied in size could be an emergency substitute for several exact-size rigid belts. In selecting belts, it should be borne in mind that the widths of the driving areas of sheaves vary in standard steps, such as A, B and C, and that belts must be chosen accordingly.

Fuses are a basic spare, but regardless of the number carried, the correct one never seems to be at hand. Normally, the fuses will be required only for the low-voltage direct-current battery system; the shore power circuits aboard will be protected by circuit breakers. The commonly used fuses are the glass tube type, which present a visual indication of failure. These are available in several lengths and many current ratings. Motors, such as those in bilge pumps and refrigerator compressors, require a starting current that is almost twice as large as the current consumed when they are running steadily. This must be taken into consideration when allocating fuses. The correct length of the fuse is determined by the fuse holder.

A small coil of insulated electric wire is handy to have around any engine when electrical trouble develops. Hose clamps and a length of hose could help with problems in the cooling system. Nor would a few spare gaskets be remiss. More specific spares must be tailored to individual powerplants.

Spark plugs seem to be the number-one spare for gasoline engines; an extra set should always be aboard. Breaker points and a condenser are equally important and are usually sold together as a repair kit. A spare in-line filter for the carburetor (see Chapter 31) will save the day, and possibly the ship, if contaminants get into the fuel line and block the flow of gasoline. Modern spark coils rarely go bad, but if the one on the engine packs up, a spare would prove a godsend.

Injectors are to the diesel engine what spark plugs are

Figure 23-15. A set of wrenches in graduated sizes is a worthwhile addition to the tool complement aboard. The wrenches shown are open at one end and closed box at the other.

to the gasoline engine, and spares should be aboard. Fuel filters assume added importance in the diesel installation because of the vulnerability of injectors to contaminants; the need for spares is thus apparent. Of course, the diesel skipper is divorced entirely from the need for spare ignition parts.

The spare-parts list for outboard motors includes spark plugs and adds shear pins and cotter pins for the propeller drive. An extra starting cord for motors that are manually started is a good idea. Adapters are available for some outboard motors to enable the attachment of a garden hose for flushing. These are worth having because they lessen the fuss of cleaning up after a cruise. In the absence of these attachments, the garbage bags mentioned in Chapter 21 should be kept handy for motor flushing.

One ingenious outboard motor manufacturer places the needed spare parts into a simulated end-panel of the fuel tank and even includes a bottle of oil. Everything is there, but nothing is loose. This excellent idea is shown in Figure 23-14.

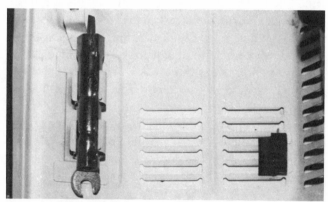

Figure 23-16. The back cover of the Honda portable generator contains a set of emergency tools consisting of screwdriver, plug wrench, and open-end wrench.

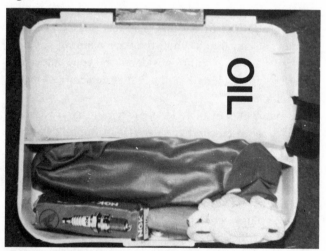

Figure 23-14. An ingenious addition to the Honda fuel tank is a metal side flap that folds down and contains a bottle of oil, tools, spare spark plug and a spare starting cord.

Figure 23-17. This large assortment of screws, nuts and other fasteners is a handy addition to a vessel's tool complement. The whole arrangement folds into a compact carrying case (see insert). (DRI Industries)

PART FIVE
ENGINE COMPONENTS

24. Engine Blocks and Heads

he block is the basic, massive unit of the marine engine. All other components are either built into it or else fastened to it. Large holes form the cylinders, integral passages provide the paths for lubricant and coolant to circulate. Appropriate pads accommodate engine supports that transmit engine reactions to the hull stringers to generate the propulsive forces that move the boat. All in all, a surprising accomplishment for what merely looks like a big hunk of metal! A typical marine engine block is shown in Figure 24-1.

Engine blocks may appear rough, but from a dimensional standpoint they are superbly accurate. All critical measurements are made to a few one-thousandths of an inch, and many reach the almost incredible precision of a few *ten*-thousandths of an inch. Not only that, but the internal construction of walls and webs is so carefully arranged that warpage and expansion are balanced out to reduce distortion during service to a negligible minimum.

Engine blocks are generally cast of iron, often alloyed with other metals to achieve desired mechanical properties. These castings are known technically as "cored" castings because a core forms the internal hollow cavities when the metal is poured. Cores are made of fine sand and a binder tightly compressed to the desired shape. Cores are fastened in place in a mold, and the liquid metal flows into the remaining spaces to form the complicated block. Of course, the sand must later be removed, and this is done with vigorous shaking by machine and with the help of compressed air.

The penalty of making cored castings is that holes must be left through which the sand core may be removed when the casting is finished. Some of these holes in an engine block are subsequently coverable with a gasket and, therefore, may be left as is. Other holes, especially those leading to the outside of the block, must be machined for tight-fitting plugs. Typically, these plugs are in the coolant passages and, in automobile parlance, are called freeze plugs. Properly installed, plugs seldom leak under the moderate coolant pressures, but if they do, a few taps with a hammer generally set them aright. (See Figure 24-3.)

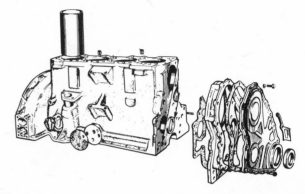

Figure 24-1. A cylinder block is shown together with a cylinder liner and a front end plate with gaskets. (Lehman Power Corporation)

Figure 24-2. The valves, valve springs, and valve retainers are in place on this head of an overhead valve engine. The rocker arms have not yet been added.

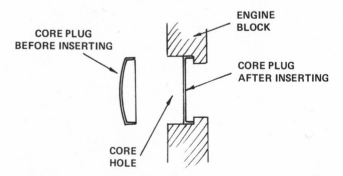

Figure 24-3. Core holes, necessary in the casting process that produces the engine block, are closed in service with core plugs that make water-tight seals.

The use of cast iron for blocks is common for marine engines but not for the engines in outboard motors, many of which are aluminum. Blocks for these small engines are not cast as above but are *die*-cast, a process in which molten aluminum is forced under pressure into machined cavities of desired shape instead of being poured into molds. Die-casting produces parts with very smooth surfaces that require no or at most minimum machining.

The cylinders of earlier die-cast aluminum blocks lacked the surface hardness needed to resist the wear of piston travel. It therefore was necessary to insert liners of iron or steel in which the pistons moved. Present-day die-casting has overcome this drawback by using an alloy of silicon and aluminum that hardens with a surface like steel and makes liners superfluous.

However, cylinder liners are much in use in large marine engines. These liners are of steel with an inner surface polished to mirror smoothness. Some liners are entirely in contact with the surface of the cylinder hole in the block and are called dry liners. Wet liners are exposed to the cooling water and are considered more desirable. Dry liners are fitted tightly to prevent their leaking. Flexible sealant rings and gaskets prevent leaks in wet liners. The sketch in Figure 24-4 shows the wet-liner assembly.

As the technique of casting has become more refined, the thickness of the walls within the engine block has been reduced. Thinner walls speed heat transfer and reduce engine weight. The reductions can be made with safety because foundries have learned to make homogeneous castings free from undesired blowholes and without detrimental sand inclusions.

The greater precision required of passages in the block for lubricating oil mandates that they be drilled, instead of being simply cored, as are the coolant paths. The drilling is ingenious and borrows from the practice of gun-barrel drilling. Long holes are bored with great accuracy. However, drills can cut only a straight line, and oil holes have changes in direction. The solution lies in the boring of intersecting holes at the desired angle. The unused ends of both holes are plugged, leaving an oil duct that connects critical areas. The diagram in Figure 24-5 explains this.

The configuration of the cylinder holes determines the style of the engine. The common 4-cylinder engine has its cylinders in a straight line. The 6-cylinder machine arranges its cylinders in the same straight line. At one time, 8-cylinder engines also were in line, but such practice has been discontinued for technical reasons and 8s are now built in vee shape, as also are 12s.

Crankshaft problems are a major factor in changing the common 8-cylinder engine from an in-line unit to a vee. The longer crankshaft of the in-line engine has a greater tendency to whip and twist under the stresses of

Figure 24-4. The "wet liner" is a polished steel tube that functions as the engine cylinder. It is set into the engine block with watertight gaskets as shown so that cooling water can circulate against it.

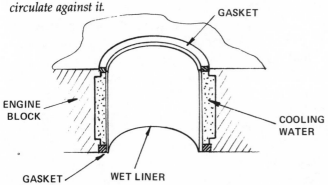

Figure 24-5. Drills can bore only straight holes. However, by combining two holes drilled in different directions and plugging the unused ends as shown, oil may be routed from A to B around an obstruction.

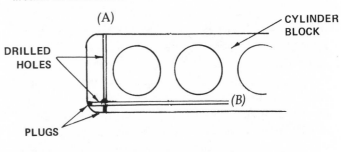

high speed and great torque. Furthermore, the longer the crankshaft, the more bearings the engine block must have to control it adequately. Gasoline engines also develop fuel distribution difficulties as the distance from the first to the last cylinder increases.

The 8-cylinder vee engine may be considered to be two 4-cylinder in-line engines set at an angle to each other and using the same crankshaft. Likewise, the 12 would be two 6s. However, there is no reason why 4- and 6-cylinder powerplants could not be built in the vee style, and truly some are. Even small 2-cylinder engines are being manufactured as vees. The overall height of a vee engine is generally lower than that of an equivalent in-line, and this is an advantage on a boat when the power-plant nestles below a deck. The area of the vee called the valley offers space for components that otherwise would occupy external space.

The aim of engine design is to achieve smooth power flow, and this requires combustion pulses spaced evenly around a revolution. In an 8-cylinder four-stroke-cycle engine (see Chapter 3) it takes two revolutions or 720° for all 8 cylinders to fire. The crankshaft, therefore, rotates $\frac{1}{8}$ of 720° (or 90°) between firings. Thus an 8-cylinder vee engine must have its two rows of cylinders inclined at 90° to each other if it is to have the evenly spaced power pulses required for smooth running. By the same reasoning, a 12-cylinder four-stroke-cycle vee engine would use a 60° inclination. The determining factor is whether each piston has its own crank throw or whether two pistons share one throw.

The lower ends of the internal ribs and walls of the engine blocks are generally used to carry the main crank-shaft bearings. Actually, these surfaces form the upper halves of the bearings, and bolted-on caps form the lower halves. These bearings are a critical component, and they must be on an absolutely straight line if the crankshaft is to turn freely without binding. Trueness is established during manufacture by installing all the rough bearings and boring them in one pass from end to end. Bearings are discussed in Chapter 27.

The upper surface of the cylinder block is machined smooth and flat to precise measurements. This is necessary to provide a fit for the cylinder head which will be both gastight and watertight. Studs rising from the block surface are a common method of fastening the head in place securely enough to resist the high pressures that will be encountered when the engine is running. It is customary to have a gasket between head and block.

The need to replace an engine block is rare. Only a major accident, extreme neglect or a crack caused by freezing of the coolant would normally be cause for replacement. Cylinder surfaces may wear and become oversize from long use, but these may be rebored to a slightly larger diameter and become as good as new. Studs and bolts may break off in the block casting, but these can be removed with special tools. Threads that have worn beyond the point of use can be replaced with inserts.

Cylinder heads for marine engines are either simple castings that form the upper ends of the combustion chambers of the cylinders, or else they will include all valves and the actuating rocker arms. Which of these two types is present is determined by the type of engine. The L-head engine (see Chapter 4) has the simple casting minus valves and valve gear because the valves are in the cylinder block. The overhead-valve engine has the more complicated cylinder head because the engine block contains no valves. See Figure 24-6.

Some cylinder heads for gasoline engines carry the spark plugs. Likewise, some cylinder heads for diesel engines mount injectors. Another function assigned to the overhead-valve cylinder head is the attachment of manifolds. In some designs, the cylinder head for the L-head engine has a smooth surface rather than the combustion-chamber contours. Instead, the contours are recessed into the heads of the pistons, in effect turning the combustion chamber upside down, although this is of no consequence. (The combustion chamber is formed by the variable volume bounded by the top of the piston, the cylinder walls and the cylinder head.)

The shape of the combustion chamber, when at its smallest volume, exerts great effect on the nature of fuel combustion in a gasoline engine. This is because the charge is a mixture of fuel and air, and the mix must be kept homogeneous for efficient burning. Many manufacturers have their own pet shapes, arrived at after much experimenting, to get the smoothest and strongest push out of the fuel. An engine runs smoothly only if its

(A)

(B)

Figure 24-6. A cylinder head with its gasket and its valve cover are shown (Lehman Power Corporation); also a head with valves in place.

combustions are smooth. The shape of the combustion chamber is also a factor in determining how high a compression ratio can be designed into the engine without predisposing it to detonation or "knocking."

Despite the many variations in detail of the combustion chambers of commercial marine gasoline engines, the principles behind the shapes may be discussed broadly. All fall under one or the other of two classifications: Either they are quasi-hemispherical or else they are irregularly tapered. Designers often see desirable features in each type and borrow from both to evolve an original concept.

The fuel charge in the hemispherical chamber remains relatively quiescent after its induction and burns rapidly outward from its central spark plug. A fast rise in pressure is created with a consequent hammerlike push against the piston. This is a good feature for high-speed engines but not necessarily acceptable for a powerplant that must be equally smooth at slow as well as at high revolution

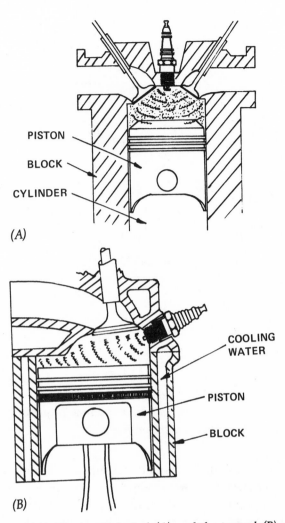

Figure 24-7. The hemispherical (A) and the tapered (B) are two configurations of combustion chambers of modern marine engines. The purpose of each is more efficient combustion.

The secret of the tapered combustion chamber is high turbulence. Turbulence is created by the piston as it closes in on the thin end of the taper and drives the fuel out toward the spark plug in the large end. The fuel charge remains well mixed and burns evenly without detonation. One of the problems of early, rudimentary combustion chambers was the irregular flame propagation and the rough-running engine that resulted. Figure 24-7 indicates the general shapes of the two basic combustion-chamber designs.

The combustion chamber for the diesel engine must be designed from a different viewpoint. The reason is that only air is compressed in the diesel cylinder (see Chapter 2) instead of a fuel mixture, as in the gasoline engine. Furthermore, diesel combustion takes place in an excess of air, quite the opposite of what happens in a gasoline chamber.

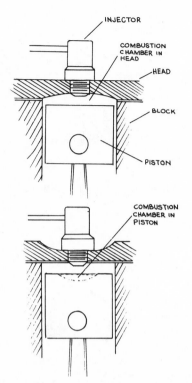

Figure 24-8. A common practice with diesel engines is to make the combustion chamber a part of the head or a part of the piston. Both methods are shown above.

Many manufacturers of diesel engines choose a simple combustion chamber similar to the hemispherical. The injector shoots its finely dispersed fuel into the entire area, and combustion is even and rapid. Other makers opt for combustion-chamber designs that accentuate some feature such as turbulence, or easier starting or more efficient fuel usage or smoother running. The claimed advantage then becomes a central factor in the sales talk. Figure 24-8 sketches some bases for some of the combustion-chamber innovations.

The marine engine cylinder head is a casting, generally of iron but sometimes of aluminum. The inner cavities and passages are made with sand cores exactly as is done with the cylinder block. Similarly, these inner spaces become paths for coolant and lubricant. Cooling the cylinder head is critically important because it bears the brunt of the high temperatures of combustion, especially if exhaust gases pass through it.

The cylinder head of the overhead-valve engine requires a considerable amount of machining, broaching and boring. Valve seats must be provided, either directly or with inserts. Valve guides and rocker arm supports are needed. Intake and exhaust manifolds must have suitable bosses or pads for their attachment.

Cylinder heads are held down to their blocks by many closely spaced fasteners. The fasteners may be either studs projecting from the cylinder block or bolts inserted from the head. The bolts must be of special alloy able to resist the stresses; ordinary hardware-store bolts will not do.

Tightening the cylinder head of a marine engine is an art, and random application of a wrench is taboo. Tightening is started at the center and proceeds alternately to each end. Figure 24-9 illustrates the general idea. The ultimate purpose is to lock two castings together with utmost tightness, yet in such manner that the severe stresses of heating, cooling and great pressures will not distort or harm them.

Occasionally cylinder heads will warp despite all care and simply out of perversity and a desire to plague the skipper. Mild cases can be overcome by remachining the mating surface, although the amount of metal that may be removed is minimal. More severe cases end as temporary anchors, and these heads must be replaced.

A pan fastened to the lower surface of the cylinder block functions as the sump for the lubricating oil needed by the engine. Automotive practice places a removable plug in the bottom of this pan to facilitate oil changing. However, in most marine applications the small clearance between pan and hull makes the use of such a plug impossible. As explained earlier, the usual manner of removing oil from marine engine crank pans is with a pump inserted through the dipstick hole.

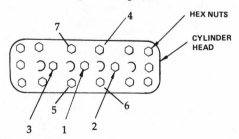

Figure 24-9. Cylinder heads or engines must be tightened down in a manner that avoids warping stresses. Starting at the center, bolts are tightened alternately in both directions until the end bolts are reached.

25. *Pistons and Connecting Rods*

The piston makes the first actual move in the chain of events that transform fuel into propulsive force for the boat. The piston reacts to the expanding gases of combustion and, with its partner, the connecting rod, transmits this power to the crankshaft and thus eventually to the propeller. The working life of the piston comprises an astronomical number of ups and downs with lightning-fast reversals from one to the other.

Pistons are cast either of aluminum or of iron. Modern high-speed gasoline engines generally make use of aluminum pistons, although iron pistons, which were quasi-standard a few years ago, are still preferred for the larger diesel engines. The main advantage of aluminum is that it weighs only about one-third as much as cast iron.

Keeping weight low is important in piston construction because of the nature of piston travel. The sudden stop and reversal of direction at the end of each piston movement generates tremendous inertial forces. Since inertia is a function of mass, the less the weight, the less the force that must be absorbed by bearings, connecting rods and wrist pins. It naturally follows, then, that these components need not be beefed up so heavily.

Smooth engine running also demands that the inertial forces be equal in all cylinders. Thus all pistons in an engine must be of the same weight within fairly close tolerances. To achieve this, pistons have special small areas in the castings from which weight may be removed as necessary to gain parity. The higher the speed of the engine, the more closely the weight of the pistons must be matched. (The weight removal is done at the time of manufacture.)

The preference for aluminum brought with it an expansion problem because an increase in temperature expands aluminum twice as fast as it does iron. An aluminum piston fitted closely in a cast-iron cylinder would bind when things got hot. The original solution to the problem was slots cut into the piston skirt, as shown in Figure 25-1. The heated piston expanded into the slots rather than jamming itself into the cylinder. But slots weakened the piston structure beyond the point that could be tolerated with the ever-increasing horsepower demanded of marine engines.

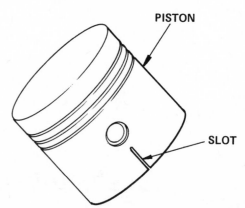

Figure 25-1. Piston expansion versus cylinder clearance is one of the engine designer's problems. A slot in the piston skirt is one of the common solutions.

The latest method of counteracting expansion alters the piston shape from perfectly cylindrical to slightly flattened opposite sides, or elliptical. This is shown diagrammatically in Figure 25-2 and is known in the trade as "cam-ground." The full diameter fits the cylinder closely; the reduced diameter fills out toward the cylinder wall

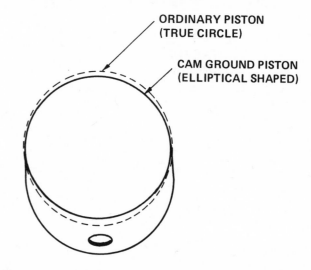

Figure 25-2. Cam grinding a piston brings its cross section into a slightly elliptical or oval shape and is one method of coping with expansion when the engine reaches running temperature.

when the piston heats up in operation. Often the lower part of the piston, the skirt, is allowed to remain cylindrical because it functions in a cooler zone and expands less.

The piston casting is subjected to machining by lathes, boring mills and grinders, but all these operations are performed automatically by mechanisms that pass the unfinished piston from one to another without the intervention of human hands. The casting emerges as a finished cam-ground piston with an accurately bored crosshole for the piston pin and grooves for the piston rings. The diagram in Figure 25-3 shows the relative locations of these features.

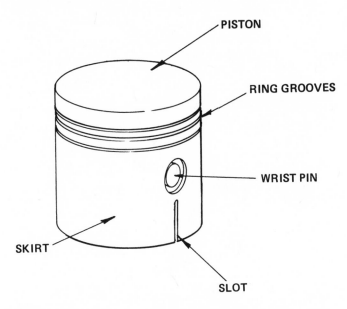

Figure 25-3. *The grooves for the piston rings are at the upper end of the piston. Some heavy duty diesel engines may have an additional groove lower down on the skirt.*

The rings are the real secret of the piston's ability to do its job of containing the expanding gases and controlling the lubrication of the cylinder walls. Two types of piston rings are provided for this purpose: One seals compression, the other removes excess oil and prevents it from getting into the combustion chamber. When these rings

stop functioning properly, the engine becomes a cripple. Many automobile owners are familiar with engines that "pump oil," make more smoke than mileage and need a "ring job."

Piston rings that control compression quite logically are called compression rings, and those that monitor oil are known as oil rings. The compression ring is a split circle of malleable iron or steel whose normal diameter is slightly larger than that of the cylinder and whose width slides easily in the piston grooves. The overage in diameter causes the ring to press tightly against the cylinder wall when in place.

The normal pressure of the ring is amplified with the aid of the expanding gases of combustion. These are allowed to get behind the ring and push it out against the cylinder wall to form an exceedingly efficient sliding seal. How this takes place is shown in the diagram of Figure 25-4.

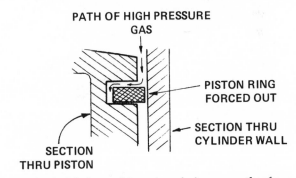

Figure 25-4. *Modern piston ring design uses the force of combustion to help seal the ring against the cylinder. The gases are allowed to get behind the ring to push it out.*

The cross-sectional shape of compression rings started out as simple rectangles, and the ends were square butts. The rectangles have been modified in the interest of better performance and with the ideas of various manufacturers. Corners were cut back; outer surfaces were tapered. Often the wear surfaces of the rings are plated with chromium or molybdenum to increase service life. Plain butt ends create a slight leakage path with the

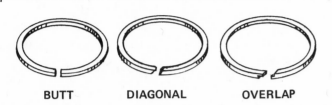

BUTT   DIAGONAL   OVERLAP

Figure 25-5. Piston rings must encircle the piston as completely as possible, yet must allow for expansion when the engine is hot. Three methods of treating the gap in the ring are shown.

clearance that must be allowed for expansion when the ring is in place. Differently shaped ring ends strive to eliminate this leakage and still permit the ring to expand without buckling. (See Figure 25-5.)

The oil control ring is a more complicated component, as the illustration in Figure 25-6 will show. This piston ring is relieved of compression-sealing duty by the rings above it and therefore is free to scrape excess oil from the cylinder wall and return it to the sump. Manufacturers have had wide latitude in expressing their concepts of what is best, and oil control rings on the market take many forms.

A typical oil control piston ring is shown in Figure 25-6. Unlike this solid compression ring, some are slotted all around the periphery so that two edges in place

The piston and the connecting rod are connected together by a piston pin, a short tube of hardened and polished steel. The connecting rod oscillates while the piston moves up and down, thereby creating relative motions which the piston pin must allow. The pin does this in one of three ways, all illustrated in Figure 25-7.

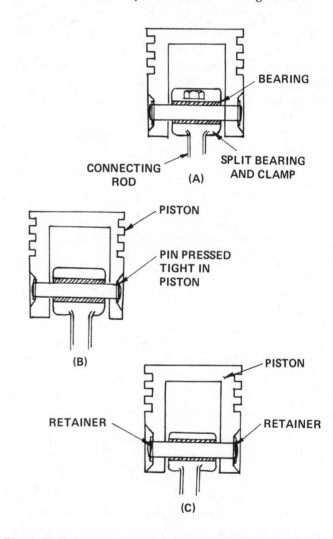

Figure 25-7. Three commercial methods of holding the piston pin in place are shown. At (A), the pin is gripped tightly by the connecting rod. At (B), the pin is a forced fit in the piston. At (C), the pin is loose in both connecting rod and piston and is prevented from wandering by the retainers.

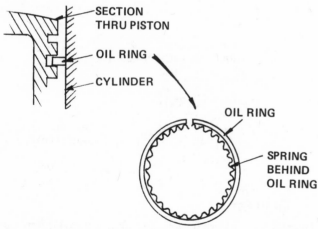

Figure 25-6. The purpose of the oil control ring in the piston is to scrape excess oil off the cylinder wall. Contact between ring and wall is increased by the spring as shown.

of one contact the cylinder wall. The oil collected in the slots passes through holes drilled in the piston wall and falls down into the crankcase sump. Springs called expanders are placed behind the oil control rings to increase the ring's pressure against the cylinder wall and improve the scraping action. Several flat steel rings stacked in the piston groove also have been used as oil control rings.

In one method of installation, the piston pin is held securely at its center in the connecting rod and loosely at its two ends in the piston. The pin thus oscillates with the connecting rod. Another design secures the pin tightly in the piston but loosely at the connecting rod. Here the piston pin is stationary during operation. The third style has looseness at both piston and connecting rod to produce a so-called free-floating piston pin. Retainers at each end of the pin maintain it in its assigned position.

The word "loose" in the foregoing descriptions is not to be confused with sloppy, because it designates a standard bearing fit that permits controlled motion without play. Actually, the meeting surfaces are antifriction bushings bored to close tolerances. Any sloppiness in these bushings would result in unacceptable noises when the engine is running.

Just as pistons must be as light in weight as possible because of inertia, so, too, must the weight of connecting rods be held down to minimize these same inertial forces. Engineering-wise, the connecting rod acts like a column receiving intermittent loads in compression. The crankshaft compresses the columnar connecting rod upward during the compression stroke of the cylinder, and the piston compresses it downward during the power stroke. The connecting rod therefore must be able to withstand great compressive forces without buckling. It derives this strength from an I cross section similar to the I beams and columns found in building construction. (See Figure 25-8.)

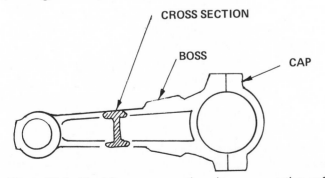

CROSS SECTION

BOSS

CAP

Figure 25-8. The I beam cross-section gives a connecting rod great strength and stiffness with minimum weight. The connecting rods of an engine are matched to each other in exact weight by grinding small amounts of metal from the bosses.

Like pistons, all connecting rods in an engine also must be equal in weight in order to achieve smooth running. Several small excesses of metal, called balancing bosses, are left on the connecting rod when it is forged in order to provide a means of delicate weight control. Connecting rods are brought to a specified weight during engine assembly by removing small amounts of metal from these bosses.

The upper end of the connecting rod may be split but is usually left solid and is bored for the already mentioned bushing. The lower end is always split. This is necessary to enable the rod to be assembled over the crankshaft throw. The split lower half, called the bearing cap, retains the bearing inserts when the connecting rod is in place in the engine.

Connecting rods are often drilled lengthwise to pass lubricating oil from the crankshaft to the piston pin. However, this drilling is an expensive operation and therefore not standard. Sometimes a small tube is attached to the side of the rod for oil passage. More common are "spit" holes which squirt streams of high-pressure oil at desired lubricating points. Ideally, the centers of the piston pin and of the lower bearing of the connecting rod lie in the same plane, but some designers offset them to gain other advantages.

The bolts that hold the lower caps of the connecting rod bearings in place are critical items because of the high stresses imposed on them. Consequently they are made of premium steel. The airplane practice of wiring bolts and nuts for safety is often resorted to. Holes in the bolt heads and castellations in the nuts accommodate wires that prevent turning. Connecting rods rarely get loose, but when they do, the damage is extreme.

The oppositely directed forces applied to the piston during compression and combustion tend to exert a cocking influence. On the compression stroke, one side of the piston bears more heavily on the cylinder wall; this is called the minor thrust. The power stroke of combustion causes the opposite side of the piston to bear unevenly; this is the major thrust. Both forces are crosswise of the engine. If wear or improper fitting permits appreciable movement between major and minor thrusts, then "piston slap" will result. Early engines routinely suffered from piston slap, and owners ignored it. Today, owners are more sophisticated, and piston slap is not acceptable. Fact is, the fine design of modern marine engines has made piston slap obsolete. The diagrams in Figure 25-9 exaggerate the basics of piston slap for purposes of explanation.

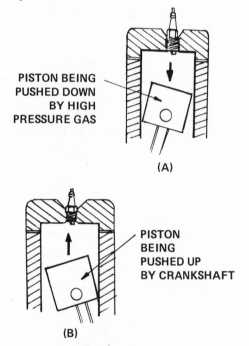

PISTON BEING
PUSHED DOWN
BY HIGH
PRESSURE GAS

(A)

PISTON
BEING
PUSHED UP
BY CRANKSHAFT

(B)

Figure 25-9. These exaggerated drawings show how major and minor thrusts tend to cock a piston in its cylinder. The power stroke tries to cock the piston in one direction, (A), the subsequent up stroke has the opposite effect, (B).

The wear on piston rings is determined largely by the character of the surface of the cylinder wall. Casual examination may find that the wall is smoothly polished. More careful viewing, especially with a magnifier, will show a pattern of microscopic crosshatches. These are the result of the planned motion the honing stones make when the cylinder is being manufactured. Although this has been found to be the ideal surface, it does cause slight wear of the piston rings when the engine is first run. This initial minute wear is needed to produce the tight seal the rings must make in service.

The surface left on the piston skirt by the machining process is also important for correct functioning and long service life. In effect, this surface is a series of concentric microscopic grooves invisible to the naked eye. The purpose of these contours is oil retention. Without an oil film between piston and cylinder, damaging scoring would result quickly.

Certain unique local problems affect most components of the marine engine, and the piston has its share, some of which have already been discussed. One acute hurdle for designers is the great differences in temperature that exist within the working piston. The piston head is exposed to the actual flame of combustion; the piston skirt is sprayed with relatively cool oil and contacts the cooler vapors from the crankcase. Obviously, such temperature gradients could father unequal expansion and severe distortion. Here the skill of the foundry comes to the aid of the engineer.

Critically located ribs inside the piston casting act as carriers of heat. They also introduce counterexpansive forces that fight to retain the piston's correct shape. One avenue of heat disposal is the contact between piston rings and cylinder wall that leads eventually to heat transfer to the liquid coolant.

Despite the rigors of their duty, pistons rarely fail in normal service. When they do give up the ghost, some accidental condition will almost always be found to have been the cause of their demise. Water in the cylinder is the most common. Water will have gotten into the cylinder of the stationary engine through some mishap. The starting motor whams the piston up into what should have been an empty space. The classic irresistible force meets the equally classic immovable object because water is not compressible. Something has to give, and often it is the piston.

Some difference of opinion exists among manufacturers as to whether the shape of the combustion chamber should be determined by the head of the piston or by the cylinder head. At one extreme, the piston head is flat, and contouring is accomplished in the cylinder head. At the other pole, the cylinder head is flat, and the piston head, either by cavity or by protuberance, forms the critical shape. Then, too, there are designs in which both cylinder head and piston head contribute to the combustion-chamber features. The combustion-chamber shape is a strong factor in the ability of a marine engine to run equally well at idle and at speed.

The universal use of the internal combustion engine on land, on water, and in the air has sponsored many innovations and minor improvements. One such is the plated piston. Electroplating the surface of the standard piston with tin reduces friction and lengthens service life. It is not surprising that tin should do this, because this metal has been an ingredient in alloys for bearings since the beginning. (See Chapter 27.)

Often a component, similarly employed in both gasoline and diesel engines, will have different effects on performance in the two types of powerplants when it fails. As an example, piston rings are more critical in the diesel engine. This is understandable because of the much greater pressures that must be maintained in the diesel cylinder in order to trigger combustion. Worn piston rings will make the diesel engine much harder to start. The same degree of wear of the rings in a gasoline engine will affect starting very little.

The very nature and material of piston rings makes them fragile, although it may seem strange to apply such a description to a part that is able to take so much punishment in service. Piston rings are springy but, at the same time, brittle. Their range of permissible deformation is slight. They must be expanded carefully just enough to pass over the piston head and no more when they are installed. They must be compressed with a special tool when the piston is pushed into the cylinder. Occasionally, piston rings will break in service to cause a compression leak and perhaps also to score the cylinder.

Forgings such as connecting rods may be susceptible to internal cracks or flaws not discernible by visual inspection. All manufacturers search this out carefully with a process known as magnetic inspection. A fine ferritic powder is dusted over the suspected connecting rod. The powder will adhere to the surface only where there exists an internal flaw, and it will mirror the configuration of that flaw. The scheme works because an internal crack will cause a discontinuity in the normal lines of magnetic flux, and divert their attraction to the surface.

Incidentally, the forgings are made by placing a white-hot billet of steel into the lower half of a die whose cavity is the shape of the connecting rod. A drop hammer then rams the upper half down to close the die and shape the billet. Quite naturally, components manufactured in this manner are called drop forgings. (See Figure 25-10.)

Figure 25-10. Hand gauging and inspection takes over at the end of the mechanized piston production line as a final assurance of product perfection. (GM Central Foundry Div.)

26. *Intake and Exhaust Valves*

The intake and exhaust valves of the marine engine function like automatic doors that open and close at precisely specified intervals. The valves control the fuel mixture throughout the combustion process and release the spent gases to the atmosphere only after the energy originally locked in the fuel has been converted to useful work. The opening and closing of the valves is critical, and even a slight change in the timing of this action can degrade engine performance seriously or perhaps stop it altogether.

Some early engines made use of sleeve valves, and some had rotary valves, but modern practice has settled exclusively on poppet valves, often called mushroom valves because of their shape. The drawing in Figure 26-1 shows a standard valve and names the parts. Intake and exhaust valves look alike but are often vastly different in their metallurgy. Some valves do not resemble valves at all; for example, the ports in the cylinder walls of two-cycle engines function as valves. (See Chapter 3.)

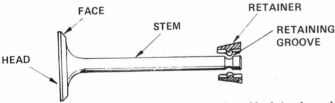

Figure 26-1. This drawing is representative of both intake and exhaust valves.

The dissimilarity of the steel alloys in intake and in exhaust valves stems from the contrast in the conditions under which each works. Although both intake and exhaust valves are exposed to the flames of combustion, the intake valve is cooled by the inrush of air and fuel. The exhaust valve has no such surcease. The hot, and perhaps still burning, gases rush by it to continue the heat torture. The only paths through which the exhaust valve can discharge its excess heat are the valve guide, which partially surrounds the valve stem, and the valve seat, on which the valve head rests.

Trying to keep valves relatively cool has always been,

and still is, a problem for designers. One solution for exhaust valves has the valve stem hollow and filled with sodium. The high temperature encountered during service melts the sodium into a liquid, which sloshes back and forth as the valve opens and closes. Each slosh picks up and carries with it a quantum of heat. Sodium was chosen because of its comparatively high specific heat, in other words, its high capacity for holding heat.

Intake valves are often slightly larger than neighboring exhaust valves. This is done to improve the engine's "breathing," its ability to accelerate the inrush of the fuel mixture. The intake valve and not the exhaust valve is made larger because this portion of the cycle functions under low pressure. The much higher pressure at the exhaust permits the exhaust valve to pass a greater volume of gas in equal time. Increased height of valve opening, which would also improve breathing, is restricted by the short interval of time allowed.

The normal manufacturing technique for valves is drop forging. The slightly oversize forged piece is then machined to desired dimension and shape. A valve for extreme heavy duty may be constructed of two different alloys, one for the stem, the other for the head. The two parts are then welded into a homogeneous unit. Heat treating the valves improves their service life. Heat treating is a process of holding the valves at various critical temperatures and then cooling them under controlled conditions. The procedure rearranges the molecular structure into a more favorable pattern.

The valve face and the valve seat meet to close at an angle that falls between 30° and 45°. (See Figure 26-2.) This angle is a compromise between the widest possible opening and the tightest seal. On lighter duty engines, the seal is machined directly into the cylinder block on L- and T-head designs and into the cylinder head on overhead valve machines. Heavy-duty marine engines reinforce this seat with a hard metal insert, as shown in Figure 26-3.

In earlier days, whenever engine valves began to leak because of pitting or other causes, grinding the valves

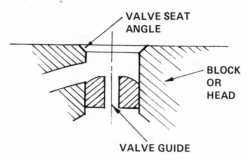

Figure 26-2. *The valve seat angle coincides with the angle of the face of the valve. The valve seat may be integral with the engine block or head or it may be a hard insert. See Figure 26-3.*

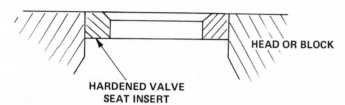

Figure 26-3. *The punishment a valve inflicts on its seat often is too severe to be borne by the metal comprising the block or the head. The insertion of a valve seat of hardened metal is the solution.*

back into a tight fit was a popular and not difficult do-it-yourself project. The valve was merely rubbed against its seat with an abrasive slurry until the two surfaces matched exactly. Today, with the hard seat inserts that hardly ever show wear, only the valve is machined. A special grinder is used by service shops to bring the valve face back to the required angle.

Theoretically, a valve in its closed position should be a perfect seal against the passages of gases, and, properly installed, new valves come close to this ideal. As service life progresses, the inferno in the cylinder takes its toll gradually, although total failure is rare, barring accidents. Pitting caused by heat and chemical action is the main destructive force. Warping of the valve head is more serious; this problem often arises from incorrect ignition and valve timing and from improper engine operation.

The valves themselves are part of a system commonly called the valve train. The system begins at the cam shaft and proceeds via valve lifters, push rods, rocker arms, valve springs, valve retainers, and valve stem seals; and the system ends at the valve. The camshaft is discussed in Chapter 29, but all the other items in the valve train will now be looked at more closely. The system is reasonably representative of all marine powerplants, although certain engine designs may omit one or more of the components. For example, the L and T head engines do not make use of rocker arms. A typical valve train is illustrated in Figure 26-4.

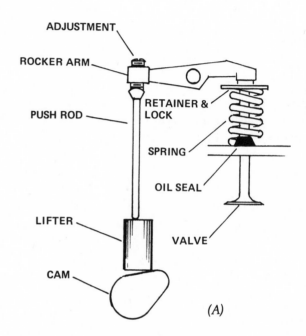

(A)

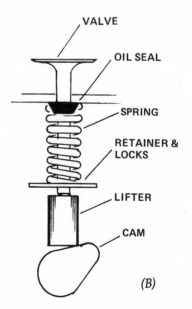

(B)

Figure 26-4. *The schematic diagrams here depict the two most common valve systems and name their components. At (A) is the valve train for an overhead valve engine; at (B) is the system found on L head and T head engines. The adjustment for (B) is in the lifter.*

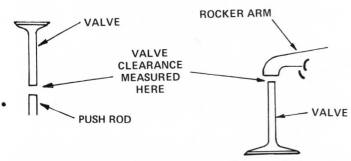

Figure 26-5. *Valve clearance is measured between valve stem and either push rod or rocker arm. Manufacturer's specifications set the exact value of clearance for each engine and state whether measurement is to be made with the engine hot or cold.*

Figure 26-6. *Valve lifters are either mechanical or hydraulic. The hydraulic lifter interposes an oil-operated piston between the cam and push rod. Hydraulic lifters do not need adjustment, operate with zero clearance at the push rod and are practically noiseless when running. A hydraulic valve lifter and a plain valve lifter are compared. Note the adjustment screw (arrow) on the plain lifter; hydraulic lifters require no adjustment means.*

The valve lifters are in direct contact with the cams of the camshaft, and they transform the rotary motion into an up-and-down reciprocation. Lifters are either mechanical or hydraulic, with the latter found in the better engines. The mechanical lifters are carefully machined small cylinders with one end flat to ride on the cam. Some include a threaded section for adjusting the overall length of the lifter. The adjustment is needed for setting the specified valve clearance when the engine is tuned up. How this clearance is measured is shown in Figure 26-5.

Valve clearance is necessary because of the expansion that the metal of the engine undergoes when it heats up. The clearance at the valve stem is a small amount, something like an average of 10 one-thousandths of an inch, but it is critical. If a valve train were set up without clearance on a cold engine, the valve would remain partially open when operating temperature is reached; that the valve would soon fail under these conditions is obvious.

Hydraulic valve lifters require no clearance. This may seem like a refutation of what has just been written, but it is not. The answer lies in the nature of this device. The hydraulic valve lifter continuously and automatically changes its length to suit the amount of expansion that has taken place. Thus, at no time is it too long, thereby holding the valve open, or too short and causing incomplete valve opening. The photo in Figure 26-6 shows hydraulic as well as mechanical valve lifters.

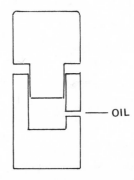

Figure 26-7. *This schematic drawing illustrates the principle of operation of the hydraulic valve lifter. Lubricating oil entering the body of the lifter under pressure extends the length of the unit to take up the space between pushrod and rocker, thereby eliminating the need for valve adjustment.*

The hydraulic lifter depends for its functioning on the pressurized lubricating oil of the engine. Oil enters the lifter and expands it to full length while the valve is closed and no force is being exerted by the valve train. This oil is contained within the lifter by a ball check and acts like a solid when the lifter must transmit a push to open the valve. The cutaway view of a hydraulic valve lifter in Figure 26-7 clarifies the action.

The push rod is the intermediary between lifter and valve stem in some engines and between lifter and rocker arm in overhead-valve engines. It is a hollow rod, and the hollow is often used to carry oil to the contact surface at its end. A popular design makes the lower end hemispherical to fit into a corresponding hollow in the upper cavity of the valve lifter. If there is one component of an engine that never needs replacing, it is probably the push rod, accidents excepted, of course.

The valves on an overhead-valve engine must move down when the push rod moves up. This complete reversal of motion is accomplished by the rocker arm illustrated in Figure 26-8. Rocker arms coupled with

Figure 26-9. *A valve assembly comprises the valve, a spring, a retainer and the locks—all shown above.*

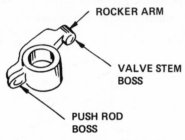

Figure 26-8. *The rocker arm reverses the direction of motion of the push rod and actuates the cylinder valve.*

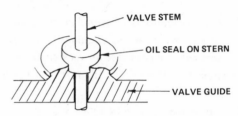

Figure 26-10. *Valve stems often provide a path for undesired oil leaks into the cylinder. A seal on the stem eliminates this leakage.*

nonadjustable valve lifters have an adjusting screw at one end. Rocker arms with hydraulic lifters usually omit this screw because, as noted earlier, the necessary adjustment is continuous and automatic. Since the rocker arm is a lever, the ratio of arm lengths to central fulcrum point can be varied by the designer to achieve desired valve opening within a given push-rod movement.

In addition to the valve itself, the valve assembly comprises an oil seal, a spring, a spring retainer and a valve lock. These parts are shown in exploded form in Figure 26-9. Valve springs must be husky to be able to keep the valve tightly closed during the extremely short periods of time that a running engine permits. Special tools are needed to compress the springs during installation and even during removal; they are far too strong for simple hand manipulation. An incorrectly chosen spring may resonate at certain engine speeds and cause erratic operation.

In a new installation, the valve stem slides closely in its guide. As wear ensues, the close fit loosens, and a space

develops through which lubricating oil could be sucked into the cylinder to cause fouling. Oil seals prevent this unwanted contamination. The seal fits tightly over the end of the guide and hugs the valve stem, as shown in Figure 26-10. The seals may be installed on engines that do not have them.

The valve assembly is held together by two small semicircular pieces called locks that fit into grooves in the valve stem and also into the spring retainer. These simple little pieces do the job; the greater the spring pressure, the harder they grip. The detail sketch in Figure 26-11 gives a close-up view of the locks. As with many parts of the marine engine, valve locks have achieved their present simplicity through evolution from less efficient ideas.

VALVE STEM KEEPERS

Figure 26-11. *Valve stem keepers or locks are a common method of locking valves into their assemblies. The ridges fit into grooves in the valve stem.*

Valves will usually move up and down without any tendency to rotate. Carbon and other hindrances to smooth valve operation thus can accumulate at critical points and eventually cause sticking. Valve rotators reduce the possibility of this happening. They give the valve a slight twist at every opening. They form part of the valve assembly as shown in Figure 26-12.

Valve problems often announce themselves to the skipper as a clattering noise. Failure of a hydraulic valve lifter, for instance, introduces excessive clearance into the

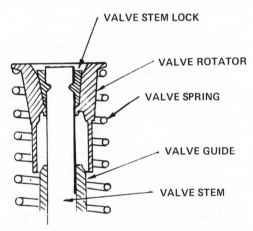

VALVE STEM LOCK

VALVE ROTATOR

VALVE SPRING

VALVE GUIDE

VALVE STEM

Figure 26-12. The valve rotator gives the valve a slight twist at each stroke and evens the wear between valve lip and valve seat.

valve train and marks each valve opening with a sharp clack. An adjustment screw that loosens will have the same result.

Improper valve clearance adjustment will also announce itself in the form of worsened engine performance. Too little clearance causes loss of compression and consequent power loss in addition to eventual burned valves. Misfiring is another probability.

Valve clearance on some engines is adjusted with the machine stationary, on others while it is running. The overhead-valve engine, whether gasoline or diesel, usually falls into the latter classification. While this sounds difficult to do, it really is not because the overhead valves are completely accessible with the valve cover removed. The clearance is measured with shim-thickness gauges

that are inserted between valve stem and rocker while the adjustment screw is being turned. The mechanic in Figure 26-13 is performing this operation.

Figure 26-13. The clearance of overhead valves is adjusted with the aid of a shim gauge of the correct thickness. Note how gauge is being used by the mechanic.

Some engine manufacturers are not content with merely drilling a hole in the block or head casting to form a valve guide. They insert a hard metal sleeve. This is akin to the insertion of a hard metal valve seat mentioned earlier.

Even rocker arms are undergoing changes. Forged rocker arms are the best, but they require expensive machining. One development stamps the rocker arm shape out of sheet steel and welds several stampings together to obtain desired thickness and contours.

Removable side cover plates on L-head engines are the equivalent of the valve cover on overhead-valve

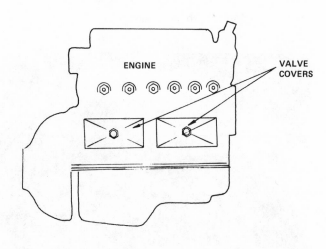

ENGINE   VALVE
                          COVERS

Figure 26-14. Valve covers on an L head or T head engine are removed for access to the valve clearance adjustments.

powerplants. These plates allow access to the valve adjustments. They are shown in Figure 26-14.

Theoretically, it would seem that the intake valve should not open until after the exhaust stroke has been completed and the exhaust valve has closed. In actual practice, these valves overlap their openings in most engine designs. Several factors make up the reason for this seeming peculiarity. Among them are the inertia of the fuel mixture mass and the manner in which the opening increases as the valve is lifted. It takes finite time to accelerate gases into motion, and the valve must hinder them as little as possible.

The intake valve begins to open slightly before the piston starts down on its suction stroke. It does not close again until just after the piston has begun its compression stroke. The exhaust valve opens just before completion of the power stroke. It closes when the intake stroke has already commenced. Thus, at the instant the piston is at top center between exhaust and intake, both intake and exhaust valves are open and overlap.

Inertia was mentioned earlier as an abiding force to be considered in the design of pistons and connecting rods because of their reciprocating motion and the almost instant stops and starts. The valve train is subject to the same problem. Although the components in the valve train do not travel the same distance as do the pistons, their need for instant stops and starts is the same. Consequently, valves, push rods, rocker arms and valve lifters—all must be designed to be sufficiently strong with minimum weight.

The physician takes the blood pressure of his patient and from the readings deduces a great deal about body condition. You might say the expert mechanic follows the same pattern with his patient, the marine engine. He hooks a compression gauge to a cylinder and cranks the engine. What he sees on the dial tells him what is wrong and how badly. In one case the heart is the telltale; in the other it is the intake and the exhaust valves, and perhaps even the piston rings.

27. Bearings and Seals

Nature has some unique laws governing friction, and one of them decrees that a material rubbing on the surface of an identical material is not a good working combination. Thus a steel shaft, for instance, rotating at high speed in a bearing support made of steel, becomes a self-destructing mechanism due to the heat created by excessive friction. Only a few special alloys possess the ability to allow other metals to rub or slide on their surfaces with minimal friction; in other words, only these few alloys can act as practical bearings for machinery.

Friction between moving parts exists because what we visually consider to be smooth, polished surfaces turn out, under the microscope, to be a perspective of mountains and valleys. These irregularities tend to interlock when one is moved over the other, much as two files would balk at an attempt to slide them together. Thus, the nature of the mating surfaces, the heights of the mountains, is the primary consideration in the degree of friction that will be developed. Lubrication becomes an important factor because filling the valleys with oil reduces the severity of interlocking and hence the amount of friction. Curiously, neither the speed of sliding or rubbing nor the size of the area of contact involved influences the friction equation.

The friction in any given circumstance is rated by a dimensionless number called the coefficient of friction. This apparently awesome term in reality is quite simple, and, indeed, one form of the coefficient can be measured with no more equipment than a fish-weighing scale. This is the coefficient of sliding friction, and the drawing in Figure 27-1 shows how it can be determined easily for any combination of materials. (There is also a "coefficient of rolling friction.")

A block of the material in question is placed upon the chosen surface, and the fish scale is hooked to it. In the illustration, the block is chosen arbitrarily at 10 pounds, but any weight may be used. The block is now pulled with the fish scale and a reading is taken, in this case 4 pounds. The scale reading divided by the weight of the block equals the coefficient of sliding friction, and performing this simple arithmetic produces an answer of 0.4. This value might be representative of a steel block sliding on a steel surface without lubrication. Lubricating the surface would make the block easier to pull, the scale reading would be less and therefore the coefficient would be smaller.

As already stated, the coefficient of sliding friction of any combination of materials is independent of the area of contact between them. The block in the example could slide on its narrow side or on its wide side without changing the final result. The weight pressing the surfaces together is the all-important factor in the equation. A little thought will make this understandable because, since the weight is the same, the total pressure must remain the same.

Rolling friction is always less than sliding friction for the same materials. This becomes obvious when one considers that it surely takes less effort to roll a wheel along than to slide it. Rolling friction and its coefficient are the critical parameters in the design of a marine engine because of the many bearings and shafts. Here again, complete lubrication results in smaller numbers. The chief exponents of rolling friction are ball bearings and roller bearings.

A proper concept of friction is vital to understanding machinery because friction is such a huge devourer of energy. Despite the finest engineering, a large percentage of the energy purchased in fuel is lost to friction. This is true of the marine engine as it is true of all engines. The ultimate aim of all good bearings is to reduce that loss.

The bearings in a marine engine are of several types (Figure 27-2). The simplest form of bearing is a bronze sleeve or bushing within which a shaft rotates. The larger

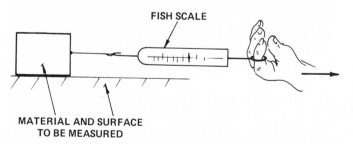

FISH SCALE

MATERIAL AND SURFACE TO BE MEASURED

Figure 27-1. The coefficient of sliding friction may be measured by means as simple as this shown.

Figure 27-2. Seals such as these are often placed close to bearings to prevent the loss of lubricant.

plain bearings, such as for crankshaft and connecting rod, for instance, are made in equal semicircles to facilitate placement. The outer face is generally steel for strength; the inner face is the low friction bearing material. All of these plain bearings are subject to the laws of sliding friction, although, under optimum conditions of speed and lubrication, the friction may exist totally within the film of oil.

The more sophisticated bearings divorce themselves from the stringent laws of sliding friction and depend upon the much greater efficiency allowed by the coefficient of rolling friction. This gives an advantage that may be as much as a hundredfold. These are roller bearings and ball bearings in their various forms.

Ball bearings are familiar to almost everyone from childhood on because they distinguished the better roller skates. The balls are held tightly between two grooved rings, the inner and outer races. The outer race is held firmly. The inner race is tight on the shaft. As the shaft turns, the balls roll around the races. The friction is almost negligible, even though the popular designation of these bearings as "antifriction" is a bit optimistic.

The apparent simplicity of plain bearings belies the many difficult problems that must be solved in designing them. The bearing must be able to sustain the load the engine will put on it, and yet the service life must be long enough to be economically acceptable. Once the total load in pounds is known, it is divided by the projected area of the bearing to get a value of pounds per square inch. The bearing material is then chosen for at least that much or preferably more pounds per square inch capability. (The "projected area" of a bearing is its length multiplied by its diameter.)

When metals are fused together into an alloy, the final properties that evolve may be decidedly different from those of the constituents. This is proved by one of the best known bearing materials, Babbitt metal, so named after its inventor, Isaac Babbitt. Babbitt is an alloy of copper, antimony, lead and tin. Yet none of these ingredients, by itself, would serve satisfactorily as a bearing.

Babbitt is relatively soft, and while it can serve in many engine applications, some heavy-duty areas require hardier stuff. Strangely, even minor variations in the percentages of the same ingredients in the alloy make surprising differences in the final properties. Thus, allowing copper and lead to be the major constituents with minute amounts of tin results in a stronger, tougher and generally superior bearing material. The construction of a bearing shell is shown in Figure 27-3.

Aluminum is a recent newcomer to the bearing material field. A common use alloys aluminum with lead to achieve a bearing that is superior to its predecessors. It is much better able to handle high-speed service conditions.

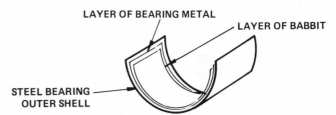

Figure 27-3. Most plain bearing shells are constructed in layers with a steel backing. Choosing the metals in the layers allows the bearing to be tailored for specific uses.

As everyone knows, new engines must be "broken in." This is the initial running of the engine during which microscopic changes in form take place in a bearing and its journal to fit them closely to each other. Some bearings facilitate this procedure with a plating of Babbitt less than a hair thick on the inner surface. The Babbitt becomes a sacrificial layer that protects while it wears away during the conforming process to reveal the final bearing surface.

Microscopic bits of contaminant, too small to be stopped by the oil filter, often get into engine bearings. A good bearing will permit these to become embedded in the bearing material and thereby be held out of harm's way. The oil film in the bearings is incomplete when the engine is started after a long period of inaction, and this makes metal-to-metal contact possible. A good bearing material forgives these momentary lapses from complete lubrication. Regardless of the precision of manufacture, a certain amount of pounding takes place against the bear-

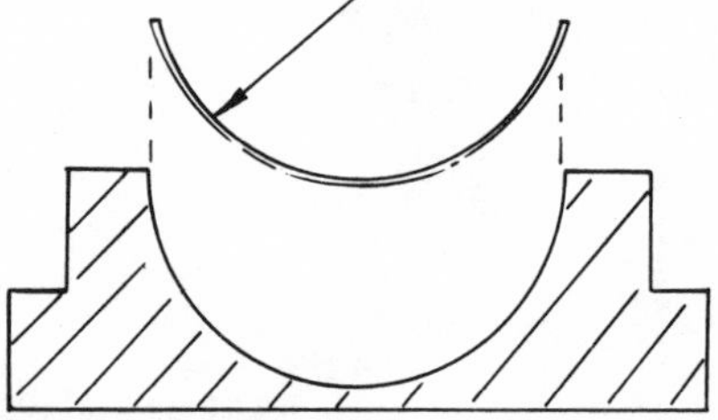

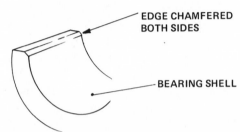

Figure 27-4. *A bearing shell very slightly larger than the opening in the bearing block is forced into place. This provides "bearing crush" and keeps everything in position.*

Figure 27-5. *A slight chamfer or bevel on the ends of bearing shell halves prevents lubricant being wiped off by sharp edges.*

ing in all reciprocating engines. Such pounding could induce failure through fatigue; a good bearing material stands up against this punishment.

The bearings for early engines were actually poured in place. The Babbitt metal, easily caused to flow at moderate temperatures, was ladled into prepared spaces and then precision-bored to size. Bearings in modern engines are steel-backed inserts. They are already machined to specification, and replacing worn bearings thus becomes a matter of taking out the old and putting in the new. Rarely is additional machining required. Oversize bearings are available to compensate for journal wear.

The manufacture of bearings has come a long way from the early-century pouring process. Molten bearing metal is applied to the hot steel backing and bonds solidly to it. This is done in large sections, which are later cut to size and formed to correct curvature. Oil holes are drilled, and often oil grooves are cut in addition in those areas that interfere least with load-carrying ability. Some bearings are made to allow continuous oil flow through them, with the discharge going to some vital part of the engine.

Bearings must also be able to resist the several lightly corrosive acids that are often present in a hardworking engine. These acids are the breakdown products of the chemical changes that affect fuel and oil in the searing internals of a powerplant. The acids etch the highly polished bearing surface into one of increased friction that eventually fails. Leading lubricating oils claim that their additives mitigate this problem.

Designers have learned many tricks over the years, and one of them is to make the bearing insert slightly larger than the housing that is to receive it. This is best explained by a look at Figure 27-4, and the idea is called bearing crush. The purpose is to anchor the insert immovably and prevent it from trying to follow the turning shaft. When the bearing is assembled, the crush of the extra size, although amounting to only a few thousandths of an inch, sets the insert firmly.

Another trick is to chamfer the parting line between the upper and lower insert halves. This is illustrated in Figure 27-5. Without the chamfer, the sharp edges could wipe off the oil film and defeat the purpose of lubri-

cation. Again, the dimensions under discussion are in thousandths of an inch and barely noticeable, but they do the required job.

The two great enemies of plain bearings are dirt and high temperature. The dirt may come through defective oil filters or from a generally dirty condition of the engine. Although the bearings will take up a minimal amount of intruding dirt, as already mentioned, there comes a time when they are overwhelmed. The destructive temperature is the frictional result of faulty lubrication or, rarely, the outcome of coolant failure.

The main bearings of the crankshaft and the connecting rod bearings are in the main line of the high-pressure lubricating oil flow that is indicated on the console pressure gauge. This gauge can therefore become a warning of imminent trouble. Increased clearance in the bearings resulting from wear will allow added oil leakage and consequently a drop in the gauge reading. But the gauge must be read with some discretion because the lowered viscosity of the oil as it becomes hot will also drop the readings.

Ball bearings, roller bearings and needle bearings constitute the family of so-called antifriction bearings. The difference between them, other than internal construction, is the amount of load each can carry for a given size. A ball contacts the surface upon which it rolls only at a point, and therefore the stress concentration is highest

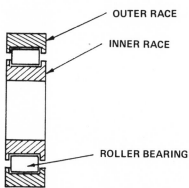

Figure 27-6. *The diagram of a roller bearing shows how the rollers are placed between the inner and outer races. The lubricant is kept in place by a retainer (not shown).*

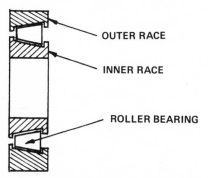

Figure 27-7. *A roller bearing that makes use of truncated cones instead of cylindrical rollers is able to resist side thrust. The lubricant is held by a retainer (not shown). The cones are exaggerated.*

and the load ability least. A roll or cylinder rests on a line, thereby lowering stress concentration and increasing loading ability because both are spread over a greater area. The cutaway view of Figure 27-6 shows this.

Some bearings must resist an axial thrust in addition to their work of supporting a revolving shaft. The tapered roller bearing is ideally suited to do this. As the drawing in Figure 27-7 shows, the tapered rollers act as wedges that prevent axial movement of the inner race. One point of thrust in a marine engine and its transmission is at the propeller shaft. The total thrust generated by the propeller is transmitted by the shaft to a thrust bearing, which passes it on to the engine and thence through the engine mounts to the engine stringers of the hull.

Theoretically, the coefficient of rolling friction being so small, ball and roller bearings could be run without lubrication. Of course they never are in commercial practice. The spaces between balls and rollers are commonly filled with heavy grease at the factory. Tight-fitting shields keep this grease from escaping, and the bearings are considered to be "lubricated for life."

The balls and rollers of these bearings are made to incredible precision. Their greatest deviation from being perfectly round is measured in *millionths* of an inch. The steel used is the hardest and toughest alloy with sprinklings of the exotic metals chromium, vanadium and tungsten. The shaped pieces undergo a process of heating, cooling and tempering in furnaces from which air is excluded. They emerge almost as hard as a diamond and receive a final grinding and polishing that leaves them glass-smooth. The bearing races are coddled with equal care and exactitude. The casual appearance of a finished bearing certainly does not suggest all the expertise that went into producing it.

The makers of ball and roller bearings supply life-expectancy figures for their products, something not available with plain bearings. Unlike the simple numbers published by insurance companies for the life expectancy of humans, the bearing specifications are formulas. Into these formulas are plugged such factors as speed of rotation, lubrication, temperature, load and others. Just like humans, a few (very few) bearings die before their expected time, but most live enough longer to make the prognostications plausible.

Much has been written thus far about bearings and their lubrication, and, in fact, the two are inseparable. However, no special attention has been paid to excess oil oozing from bearings because the oil simply drained back into the engine sump as part of the general circulation. But what about bearings located at the ends of the engine whose excess oil would drain outside? Surely such oil spillage cannot be tolerated either from a safety or from an economics point of view. Luckily, a device called a seal can take care of the problem nicely—and does so in all engines.

Seals progress in complication from the very simple rope seal shown in Figure 27-8. As pictured, an extra groove is cut in the end bearing support on the side toward the exterior of the engine. This groove is forcibly packed with rope or similar synthetic material to a height slightly beyond the diameter of the shaft. The seal thus rubs closely on the shaft and prevents oil from getting by. Often a knurl is cut on the shaft where it rubs the seal. The purpose of the cuts is to force the oil stopped by the seal back into the engine. Since the rope seal is installed in

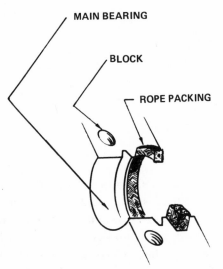

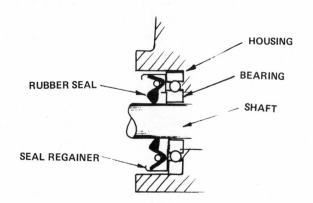

Figure 27-8. A rope seal, inserted in the bearing block as shown, prevents loss of lubricating oil around the main shaft.

halves, it can be put in place without disassembling nearby components.

Next in complication is the lip seal illustrated in Figure 27-9. This is a synthetic ring curved back on itself with a final lip that rubs the shaft or bearing it protects. An endless coil spring inside the lip ensures tight contact with the rotating shaft. The lip is oriented in a direction that

Figure 27-9. Lubricating oil is prevented from escaping around rotating shafts by seals that fit tightly.

will intercept the escaping oil. Often this seal contains two rings, each with its lip, and has the lips facing in opposite directions. This type of seal is used where oil seepage from two directions is to be prevented from meeting, for example, at the junction between the marine engine and its transmission unit.

Knurling the shaft, as mentioned earlier, is one scheme used in the constant vigilance needed to keep lubricating oil where it belongs. Another scheme makes use of what

are called slingers placed at shaft ends. Slingers are nothing more than disks, fastened to the shaft, that literally sling the oil back into the engine by centrifugal force. They are usually placed ahead of the seal to reduce the seal's work.

The most complicated seal on the marine engine is probably found on the water pump, In this case, the seal is concerned with preventing water leakage when the pump is operating. This type of seal consists of an assembly of many parts, as shown in the exploded view of Figure 27-10. Of course, the problem is the same: cutting off the fluid's escape route consisting of the clearance between a shaft and its bearing.

The more or less standard practice in these assembled seals is to have two low-friction surfaces rubbing on each other, one stationary and the other rotating, pressed closely together by a spring. The surfaces chosen are usually carbon and ceramic. These seals are delicate and expensive, and great care is necessary during installation; misalign the thing and it won't work.

The whole subject of bearings and seals may be capsulized into one sentence: Keep the oil captive in the bearings to do its work of reducing friction, and don't let it escape.

Figure 27-10. The individual components that make up a small seal for an engine water pump are shown. The rubbing surfaces are carbon.

28. *Gaskets and Mating Surfaces*

Several areas in the marine engine require that two metal surfaces mate in a joint that is both gastight and watertight. This could be accomplished by grinding the two surfaces to perfect smoothness and flatness; modern machine-shop practice makes this possible. In fact, Johansson blocks, used in super-accurate measurements, are so microscopically flat that two blocks will adhere to each other by basic molecular force when brought together. But such finishing is much too expensive for routine engine manufacture. Instead, gaskets are placed between the two normally machined surfaces.

Gaskets are relatively soft and conform themselves to minor irregularities in the surfaces to achieve tight joints. Gasket materials range from paper to metal, and from single sheets to built-up assemblies of many layers. The material and the style of the gasket are determined by the job it must do and by the location at which it is placed. The illustration in Figure 28-1 shows gaskets of several kinds.

Perhaps the most critical gasket in the marine engine is the one between engine block and cylinder head. Its primary function is to retain the high-pressure products of combustion. Additionally, it must segregate the various water passages that cool the head and the block and strictly prevent any coolant from getting into the cylinder. This means that the gasket is, at one and the same time, subjected to the temperature of hot water and the vastly hotter temperature of flame. Good head gaskets, as they are called, are able to do this well and for long periods of service. A typical head gasket with its water passages and cylinder holes, is shown in Figure 28-2.

The head gasket illustrates two attributes that satisfactory gasket material must have: (1) sufficient softness and pliability to adapt itself to the surface on which it is used and (2) the ability to resist penetration and deterioration by the liquids or gases it will encounter during service. Often, one material alone is able to meet only part of the requirements, so other materials are added in the form of a sandwich.

The head gasket is such a sandwich. One form has a center of asbestos and outer surfaces of thin sheet copper. When the cylinder holes are cut into this layered gasket, the asbestos center is exposed edgewise and the flames in the combustion chamber would make short shrift of it. The remedy is a fire ring crimped to the edge of the hole, as shown in the cutaway view of Figure 28-3. The crimping, performed in a press under great pressure, maintains the level surface of the gasket.

Cork is a favorite material for gaskets that are in contact with water or fuel. Cork, originally the bark of a tree, is ground into small granules. These are mixed with an adhesive binder, and the paste is rolled out into desired thicknesses that dry as homogeneous sheets. The gaskets with their various shapes and holes are die-cut from these sheets. Cork gaskets are somewhat brittle and must be handled carefully. (See Figure 28-4.)

Many components are sealed to the engine with paper gaskets. The paper is tough and heavy rag stock, treated to be impervious to whatever must be kept in or kept out

Figure 28-1. Some of the many gaskets required in the assembly of a marine engine are pictured above. The materials range from metal to synthetic fiber.

Figure 28-2. The head gasket of an internal combustion engine is a composite of two copper outer surfaces enclosing an asbestos filler. Shown is the head gasket for a six-cylinder engine.

at its service position. Some mechanics soak paper gaskets in oil before installing them. By their nature, paper gaskets are restricted to being used only between very smoothly finished surfaces.

A popular gasket material is available in sheets from which the mechanic may cut his own shapes as needed. It is a proprietary mix probably containing asbestos and synthetics. It is less brittle than cork and as pliable as thin cardboard in its usual thickness. Gaskets cut from these sheets are usable at many points of the marine engine but, of course, not as head gaskets.

A small roll of this gasket material is well worth the space it takes in the boat toolbox. The following tricks of the trade in making gaskets from this material could bail a skipper out of an emergency. The area to be gasketed is coated with oil or grease, and a flat sheet of gasket

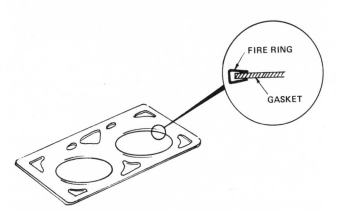

Figure 28-3. A fire ring protects the exposed edge of a head gasket from the flames in the combustion chamber. The fire ring is shown before it has been crimped flat.

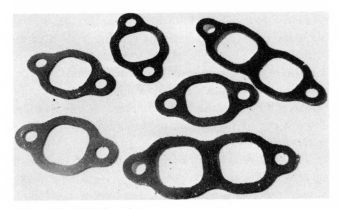

Figure 28-4. Cork gaskets.

material is pressed firmly against it. An imprint will result which clearly shows the outline and details of all holes. The outline is then cut with ordinary scissors or small tin snips. It is difficult to cut small holes, and the scheme shown in Figure 28-5 is a do-it-yourself form of stamping. A socket of the correct size is selected from a wrench set and placed on the designated hole imprint. A sharp blow with a hammer produces a clean-cut hole.

Thin sheet steel is also used as a gasket material, but, since it is much less malleable than copper, it is more restricted in its applications. A slightly raised ridge, or embossing, sometimes surrounds important passage holes on steel gaskets. The ridges are crushed to form tight seals when the encircling bolts are snugged down during installation. The steel gives better service than copper under modern high-pressure engine conditions.

Some earlier shops made a practice of shellacking both sides of a gasket as it was put in place. This surely made a tight joint and prevented customer comebacks, but woe to the unfortunate mechanic who, at some future date, had to disassemble the engine. When he finally got the parts separated, he spent time scraping pieces of the old gasket off the mating surfaces. A better scheme, which leaves no bad aftereffects, is to coat the gasket with grease.

Gasket failure often results from insufficient tightening, or uneven tightening, of the surrounding bolts. However, the corollary, that leaks always may be stopped by tightening bolts, is not true. In most instances, a gasket that has been leaking for any appreciable length of time has had it and must be replaced. In fact, gasket replace-

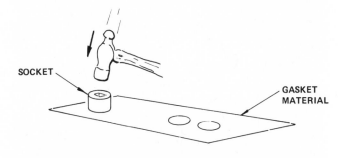

Figure 28-5. A quick method of cutting holes in a sheet of gasket material is shown. The outside diameter of the socket determines the size of the hole. The job is done on a hard surface.

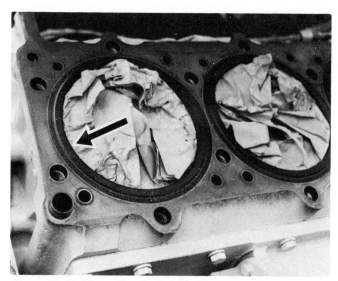

Figure 28-7. The gasket that maintains water tightness where the cylinder liner meets the cylinder wall is identified by the arrow. (The paper protects the newly-refurbished pistons until assembly.)

ment looms large in a good mechanic's routine; rarely will he reuse a gasket, even one that looks all right.

Although they are not gaskets in the full sense of the word, O rings often serve the same purpose of sealing and acting as a barrier. O rings are toroids of synthetic rubber that are manufactured to close tolerances in myriad sizes. O rings are generally fitted into grooves made exactly for them. They seal by being compressed into an oval cross section from their normal roundness. O rings are illustrated in Figure 28-6.

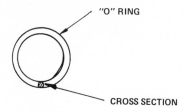

Figure 28-6. The O ring is a widely used form of gasket. The material of the O ring is synthetic rubber and the cross-section is circular.

What might be called instant gaskets are available in tubes and cans. These are viscous liquids that set into a firm consistency without ever becoming hard or brittle. These compounds are applied to the mating engine surfaces and develop enough body to act as reasonably good gaskets at points where high pressures are not encountered. Manufacturers supply these liquid gasket materials in fast-setting and slow-setting mixtures.

Sometimes, what might have become a designer's headache is solved with an ingenious, special gasket. Sealing the top of the cylinder liner of a marine diesel engine is a case in point, as Figure 28-7 shows. In this case, the gasket is a cleverly formed ring containing a compressible member. It flattens into a tight seal for the combustion chamber when the cylinder head is fastened down.

The gaskets of a running marine engine are subjected to more forces than simply the pressures of the passages they surround. The amount of compression applied to them varies with the temperature because of the expansion and contraction of the metal and of the bolts. The

gasket material must have enough resilience or elasticity to take up the slack that results, and it must be able to do this many times. Laminated gaskets, those with sheet metal on both sides of a central, comparatively soft material, derive this elasticity from this central core.

The galvanic corrosion discussed in Chapter 18 could become a factor in a marine engine whose cylinder head, block and gasket are all of different metals. It is not uncommon for a high-speed gasoline engine to have an aluminum cylinder head, and a corrosive galvanic situation could exist in such an engine. However, manufacturers are well aware of this possibility, and their manuals leave no excuse for error in the choice of the correct gasket.

Gaskets seldom cause serious engine problems; when they fail, they do so gradually, and the usual result of their slow demise is a leak that increases as time goes on but permits the engine to be run a reasonable length of time until repairs can be made. An exception to this kindly rule is the head gasket, and its fatal illness is notorious as a "blown gasket."

Blown gaskets are known to motorists as well as skippers. Exactly what happens is a breakdown of the narrow strip of head gasket that separates two cylinders, and this removes the normal isolation between them. The firing of one cylinder may now interrupt the suction stroke of the other, and both cylinders lose effectiveness. From a power standpoint, the engine becomes almost useless.

The only remedy for a blown gasket is complete replacement. On an L-head engine, this is a comparatively simple procedure because the removal of bolts alone allows the head to be taken off. For the overhead-valve engine, the job is more involved. Valves and rocker arms are integral with the cylinder head, and removal leaves the push rods free even though some will have been under compression because of valve positions. Most mechanics loosen the rocker arm assemblies to make reinstallation easier, and they make a final valve adjustment when everything has been reinstalled. Some try to avoid this readjustment by leaving the valve assemblies intact, but usually find they must readjust anyway.

Skippers with gasoline engines find that a very small gasket, approximately only 1 inch in diameter, wields an importance entirely disproportionate to its size. This is the copper spark-plug gasket. Cylinder compression is subject to this midget. When this gasket is not in good

shape and properly compressed, power loss ensues. Manufacturers recommended that new gaskets be installed every time spark plugs are taken out for adjustment and replaced. Admittedly, this is the perfectionist's view. But certainly these important little gaskets should be inspected carefully before they are reused. (See Figure 28-8.)

"Your engine blew a head gasket." Many a skipper has heard that sad report from his mechanic after an ailing powerplant has been examined. What that actually means is shown in Figure 28-9. The integrity of the gasket separating two combustion chambers has been destroyed and hence neither can operate properly. Depending upon the severity of the gasket break, the engine reaction will range from misfiring to complete refusal to function.

Figure 28-8. The spark plug gasket seals against leakage of the high pressure gases generated in the cylinder. Note that spark plugs with tapered seats do not require gaskets.

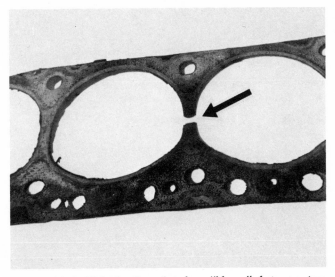

Figure 28-9. This head gasket has "blown" between two cylinders, thus making both cylinders inoperative. This gasket must be replaced.

29. Crankshafts, Flywheels and Camshafts

The movements of the pistons in response to combustion pressures in the cylinders are combined by the crankshaft and transformed into rotary motion. The flywheel smooths these intermittent impulses into a continuous flow of power. The camshaft, by actuating the valves in proper sequence, controls the gases from which the energy is derived. Crankshaft, flywheel and camshaft function as a finely coordinated team to accomplish one phase in the complicated process of converting fuel into propulsion.

The crankshaft is the sturdiest and huskiest single member of the marine engine. It must resist fantastic stresses of twisting and bending without losing even one degree of its designed shape. Despite its convoluted construction, it must be able to rotate at high speed without causing vibrations born of imbalance. Usually, it is drilled with oil passages and takes on the additional chore of acting as one of the avenues of lubrication. A crankshaft is shown in Figure 29-1.

The crankshaft has one offset, or "throw," for each cylinder, and the connecting rod is attached there. The point of attachment, called a journal, is cylindrical in form and is ground and polished for an exact fit to the lower bearing of the connecting rod. The journal is drilled for lubrication, and it often also passes oil on up to the piston via the connecting rod. Large journals at the ends and at the center of the crankshaft support it in the main bearings of the engine.

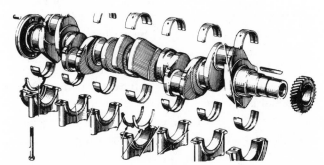

Figure 29-1. A crankshaft with its bearings is shown. The gear drives the camshaft gear which is twice its diameter. (Lehman Power Corporation)

The throws of the crankshaft are spaced around the 360° of a circle in a manner to make the motion of the pistons evenly distributed over one revolution. To accomplish this for a V-8 engine, the throws must be 90° apart. For a 6-cylinder marine engine the spacing of the throws must be 120°. The sequence in which the throws are set at these angles determines the firing order of any particular engine. The firing order of a typical 6-cylinder powerplant, for example, is 1,5,3,6,2,4; the numbers refer to the cylinder positions.

From the firing order (which should not be confused with timing) it is evident that the cylinders do not fire in a row, from one end of the engine to the other, and this has a purpose. The purpose is to stagger the power thrusts in the interest of smooth running and to distribute the stresses more evenly. Obviously, the firing order is set at manufacture and cannot be changed subsequently—nor would there be any reason for changing it.

Crankshafts can be forged or cast, but forging is best and almost universally selected for heavy-duty engines. Crankshaft forging presses are gigantic machines of tremendous power. The forging process makes use of a series of dies whose cavities range from a beginning approximation of the crankshaft to its final form. A white-hot billet of selected steel is placed in one half of the first die and pounded with gargantuan blows by the other half until it completely fills the cavity. As the piece proceeds through the series, it becomes the crankshaft except for the final machining.

Forging also gives a metallurgical advantage: The internal grain of the steel follows the crankshaft shape and lends extra strength. Although grain is commonly known to exist in wood, its existence in steel may be surprising. Yet, just as in wood, grain in steel affects the amount of stress and strain that can be absorbed without failure. Certain sections of the crankshaft are points of stress concentration, and there grain plays an important role.

It is difficult to forge a crankshaft with all the throws in their correct positions. Consequently, one method of manufacture leaves the throws flat in one plane when the crankshaft leaves the forging press. A machine then twists the heated forging about its own axis until all cranks are at their designed angular position. It staggers the imagination to think that steel, several inches in diameter, can be twisted at will like warm taffy.

The crankshaft must be balanced dynamically as part of the constant effort to eliminate vibration in high-speed marine engines. Balancing is a factory operation and never required in the field. One method is to drill small amounts of metal from designated places on the throws. Another scheme for attaining balance drills holes concentrically with the journal at the end of each throw. Holes so placed do not weaken the construction to any noticeable extent because the metal at the center of any round column bears a negligible amount of the total stress.

Stress concentration is the watchword for any metal structure as full of holes and sudden changes of direction as a crankshaft. A sharp corner, for instance, is a point of extreme stress concentration. Fortunately, modern technology has found that rounding this corner to a smooth transition is a simple solution. Accordingly, all sharp corners of the crankshaft are rounded to form what are known as fillets. The sharp edge where a hole meets a surface is an equal point of danger and, therefore, is always rounded off, too.

Cast crankshafts are adequate for many services, and since they are also cheaper to manufacture, they are found in many engines. Casting produces surfaces that are closer to the finished product than forging does, and this means less final machining. Furthermore, the casting technique permits the various throws to be produced in their final positions without the twisting operation needed for forged crankshafts. The grain in a cast crankshaft is randomly distributed, in contrast to the lineal grain of a forged unit. Strangely, this is not an entire deficit because it provides strength to resist stresses from all directions.

One end of the crankshaft is flanged to receive the flywheel. The other end is treated in various ways to suit different engines, but a common termination is a sheave or pulley suitable for a belt. Auxiliary equipment aboard, such as a pump or a generator, may be driven by this belt, often with the interposition of a clutch to allow "on" and "off" conditions. When an installation requires driving the propeller shaft from the end of the engine opposite the flywheel, the sheave, of course, is omitted.

The flywheel is attached to the crankshaft flange with a ring of bolts. Carefully located and machined hub and bolt holes maintain the flywheel in absolute concentricity with the crankshaft, a necessary precaution against vibration.

The flywheel does for the mechanical system what the storage battery does for the electrical system, although on an instantaneous basis. It takes in and gives out energy in a manner to smooth the output of the engine. Its energy-storing capability is dependent upon its mass; hence flywheels are heavy. The further this mass is located from the center of rotation, the greater is its effectiveness. This explains why flywheels have a central section as light as possible and a heavy rim. It is also the reason why flywheels are as large in diameter as the engine design will permit.

Engine power is basically made up of a series of pulses resulting from the almost instantaneous combustion of fuel. The pulses would tend to make the engine speed increase with each firing stroke and slow down in between. This is where the flywheel does its job. It absorbs the excess energy at a pulse and puts it back again at an intervening lull to achieve an averaging effect which translates into smooth engine running.

The rim of the flywheel carries gear teeth with which the starting motor meshes. This so-called ring gear is a separate, closely fitted part and may be replaced in the event the teeth are damaged by starting motor mishap. The comparatively large radius of the ring gear gives the starting motor an effective lever arm and aids it in turning the engine over for starting. A flywheel with a vibrator dampener is shown in Figure 29-2.

Most engine flywheels carry so-called timing marks. These are parallel lines on the rim in juxtaposition to an arrow or other aligning device, as shown in Figure 29-3. The marks bear this name because they are used in

Figure 29-2. *The components of a typical flywheel assembly are shown above. The arrow points to the vibration dampener unit. The ring gear teeth are not shown.*

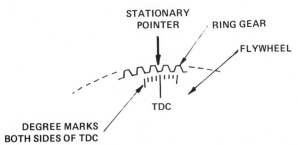

Figure 29-3. *Degree marks on the flywheel indicate the position of the piston in a given cylinder and are used in "timing" the engine.*

setting the exact point during a revolution at which ignition is to occur (the timing). A central, often heavier, line is marked "TDC" and stands for "top dead center." When the flywheel is brought to this point, the piston in the number-one cylinder is at its highest position. Other marks to right and left of TDC are calibrated in degrees of rotation and indicate the relative positions of the piston before and after its top dead center. Some engines may have a line marked "BDC" halfway around the rim from TDC; this signifies "bottom dead center."

The marks that show the piston to be before its top dead center position are especially important, because these are the ones actually used to time the engine. The fuel requires a finite amount of time to burn completely after its ignition (see Chapters 4 and 12), and the calibrated marks allow this to be set to the number of degrees recommended by the manufacturer. Timing guns for gasoline engines function stroboscopically and allow

Figure 29-4. *A timing gun provides the most accurate method of timing the ignition of a gasoline engine. The gun makes use of a stroboscopic effect to "stop" a mark on a rotating flywheel.*

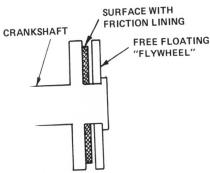

Figure 29-5. *A vibration damper is one method of absorbing the vibration emitted by an internal combustion engine. The free floating "flywheel" alternately is driven and slips and evens out the undesired pulses. Springs also are used in place of the friction drive.*

these marks to be seen clearly with the engine running because the strobe effect makes them appear to stand still. A timing gun is shown in Figure 29-4.

The sharp pulses of power from the cylinders exerted along the crankshaft, coupled with the restraining actions of the flywheel at one end and the propeller shaft at the other, tend to cause torsional distortion and vibration. This is counteracted by a device called a damper, and many engines have one. The damper often takes the form of a mini-flywheel within the actual flywheel, as illustrated in Figure 29-5. This smaller "flywheel" is not mounted fixedly to the crankshaft; instead, it is driven by a friction lining and can run free. The damper slips back and forth and neutralizes the undesired vibrations.

The journals of the crankshaft are ground on special machines with high-speed grinding wheels. This leaves hanging lips which are too small to be seen or to be felt by touch, but which are clearly evident under a microscope. Consequently, the journals run more efficiently in one direction than in the other, and the grinding operation must take into account the subsequent direction of rotation of the finished crankshaft. Little refinements like this are the result of the many years of internal combustion engine development.

The counterweights on the crankshaft are another refinement, albeit one of long standing. Each counterweight extends opposite to its throw and balances it. The combination of throws and counterweights adds an appreciable flywheel effect because of the masses involved.

The third member of the team, the camshaft, is shown in Figure 29-6. The concentric journals support the camshaft in bearings; the eccentric lobes or cams operate the valves through valve lifters. The drive gear at one end is

Figure 29-6. *A camshaft with its driving gear and some of its bearings is shown. (Lehman Power Corporation)*

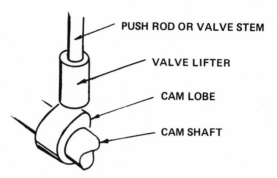

PUSH ROD OR VALVE STEM

VALVE LIFTER

CAM LOBE

CAM SHAFT

Figure 29-7. *The valve lifter rides the cam lobe and transmits the reciprocating motion to the valve push rod. Lifters may be mechanical or hydraulic.*

sized to run the camshaft at exactly one-half the speed of the crankshaft; why this is necessary is explained fully in Chapter 4.

The connection between crankshaft and camshaft may be by gear, by timing chain or by toothed belt, but the speed relationship must always be two to one. This means that the crankshaft gear, of whatever type, must be one-half the diameter of the camshaft gear. Several schemes are in vogue to reduce the noise of the crankshaft to camshaft drive. One makes use of a so-called silent chain. Another does the driving through a soft belt. Still another provides a nonmetallic gear on the camshaft to mesh with the steel gear on the crankshaft.

The camshaft functions as a master mind, and its geometry is a major factor in the performance of an engine. Stock marine engines can be given racing characteristics merely by changing camshafts. The changes would comprise differences in the shapes of the eccentric lobes. In effect, the special camshaft alters the relations between the opening of the valves and the positions of the pistons. However, the lobe changes are the result of careful engineering and beyond the scope of random do-it-yourselfing.

The best camshafts are made of steel. The lobes must have special metallurgical treatment to enable them to resist the extreme stresses caused by the valve lifters that slide over them. Case hardening is one such treatment. This is a chemical transformation that takes place when the camshaft is heated to a high temperature, and excess carbon is added to the desired surface. The result is a thin, hard outer skin able to withstand valve-lifter wear.

The simple appearance of an eccentric lobe on the camshaft does not give a clue to the engineering difficulty of designing it. The manner in which the off-center portion of the cam reaches its peak determines whether

the valve opens quickly or slowly, and how it closes—features that are strong determinants of engine performance. These same features also affect the torsional load on the camshaft resulting from the powerful valve springs that must be overcome during valve opening. Not least, lobe shape has a bearing on wear.

Figure 29-7 details the action that takes place as a camshaft lobe raises and lowers a valve lifter. Obviously, the sliding of lifter upon cam is not the most efficient mechanical motion nor one that would cause the least wear. The minimal leverages, operating first in one direction as the valve lifts and then in the other as the valve closes, have a deforming tendency on the camshaft that must be overcome by structural strength. An improvement on this system is to place a roller at the bottom of the lifter to contact the cam, and thus roll instead of slide. Some engines have this.

A close look at the camshaft will disclose that the journals for the bearings are greater in diameter than the highest points of the lobes. This feature makes it possible to remove the camshaft and reinstall it by sliding it through its bearings without dismantling the engine. Although this aspect may be of minimal benefit to the skipper, because it presupposes a major overhaul, it is valuable to the original assembler of the engine and, occasionally, even to the repairing mechanic.

Camshafts, like crankshafts, are also usually drilled for oil passage. This lubricates the camshaft bearings and in addition carries oil to parts of the valve train. Overflow goes to various oil galleries whence it drips back to the oil sump in the crankcase, doing odd lubricating jobs on the way.

The camshaft on gasoline engines has the additional duty of driving the ignition distributor (see Chapter 12), the fuel pump, and the oil pump. The drive to the dis-

Figure 29-8. Spiral gears on the camshaft drive a cross shaft that terminates in the distributor at one end and often in the lubricating oil pump at the other.

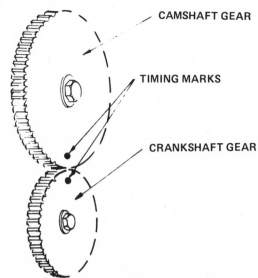

Figure 29-9. The camshaft gear and the crankshaft gear of an engine are "timed" to each other by lining up the timing marks as shown.

tributor and the oil pump is at right angles to the camshaft and accomplished with the gearing shown in Figure 29-8. The upper end of this cross-shaft is at the distributor, the lower end at the oil pump. The drive is at the ratio of one to one because, as noted earlier, the distributor also must rotate at one-half crankshaft speed like the camshaft.

The common practice on gasoline engines is to use a diaphragm-type fuel pump and to drive it from the camshaft. (By contrast, diesel engines favor gear-type, positive-pressure pumps for their fuel.) An extra eccentric on the camshaft, similar to the ones actuating the valves, moves a lever extending from the fuel pump. The lever, with an intermediate spring to regulate pressure, moves the diaphragm up and down to create the pumping action.

The camshaft is unique in that it must suffer forces from all directions: radial, axial and torsional. The radial and torsional problems have already been discussed. The axial forces tend to move the crankshaft fore and aft in the engine, a displacement that would destroy the correct relationships between driving and driven gears and between cams and lifters. Stability is designed into the system in two ways: by balancing opposing forces and by providing end plates that prevent movement axially.

The angular relation between crankshaft and camshaft is critical because it affects the timing of all the valves. Therefore, means must be provided to assure that reinstallation of a camshaft that has been removed for a service operation puts it back into absolutely correct relationship. Marks on the crankshaft gear and on the camshaft gear accomplish this. When both shafts are turned so that these marks are in strict alignment, the camshaft timing is correct. Figure 29-9 illustrates this.

Although gear-drive of the camshaft is preferred, the geometry of some engines makes chain-drive more suitable. The difference is negligible in a well-engineered powerplant. It may be nitpicking to state that chains may break and chains may stretch; over a normal life cycle of a marine engine, neither of these conditions is very probable. Chances are that most skippers of loyal, behaving engines will never know whether gears or chains are driving their camshafts.

Figure 29-10. A crankshaft being forged from a white hot billet of steel. The giant press can exert a pressure of 6,000 tons. (Detroit Diesel)

30. *Manifolds, Mufflers and Exhaust Lines*

P erhaps mufflers are the greatest invention of all because, without them, this internal combustion age would be intolerable. The true value of a muffler is best appreciated after being in proximity to an engine running without one. Considering the simplicity of its internal construction—without any moving parts—it is amazing that a muffler can subdue exhaust noise as much as it does.

In a certain sense the exhaust manifold works in conjunction with the muffler. It collects the exhausts of the various cylinders and presents them to the muffler as a continuous flow of gases. The homogeneity of the flow helps the muffler function according to the acoustic principles in its design.

The intake manifold of the gasoline engine takes the output of the carburetor and distributes it to the various cylinders. The smooth operation of the engine depends to a large extent on how evenly the intake manifold divides this fuel into exactly equal amounts for each cylinder. (The intake manifold of a diesel engine has an easier job because it carries only air.)

The necessity for providing all cylinders with exactly equal charges of the fuel mixture is basic. Assuming an engine in good order, equal charges assure that the pressures developed upon ignition are the same in all cylinders. This, in turn, means that the forces exerted on the crankshaft by the various pistons are equal, and therefore the turning effort is continuous and smooth.

A problem inherent in the fuel-air mixture affects intake manifold design. Although the carburetor mixes gasoline and air, these two fluids are not truly miscible, and suffer an uneasy companionship at best. At the high velocity of their passage through the carburetor, the gasoline remains suspended in the air; reduce this velocity and the gasoline droplets begin to fall out, causing the mixture reaching the cylinders to be starved of fuel. Intake manifold design, therefore, must strive to keep the mixture flowing faster than a critical minimum rate. But this presents a two-sided dilemma.

If the cross section of the manifold passages is small enough to create a high velocity at idle speed, when the engine's fuel requirements are low, it will be too small to handle the torrent demanded at high speed. Conversely, if the cross section is large enough for optimum high speed, troubles arise from consequent low fuel velocity at idling, making engine performance unacceptably rough. A workable compromise is reached by selecting an intermediate size that calls upon the carburetor for help and also by applying heat.

The heat is applied to the intake manifold by placing it in close proximity to the exhaust manifold. The hot manifold surfaces vaporize the gasoline and help keep it suspended in the fuel stream. (See Figure 30-2.)

Figure 30-2. The proximity of intake and exhaust manifolds (see arrow) heats the intake manifold and aids in keeping the fuel mixture properly vaporized. (Lehman Power Corporation)

Figure 30-1. This gasoline engine intake manifold has four ports to accommodate a four-barrel carburetor.

The automatic valve is used because reasonably good monitoring of the applied heat is essential. Too much heat can undo the desired beneficial results. Heat expands the fuel mixture, making it less dense, and a given volume thus contains less energy. A cylinder filled with this expanded charge has less actual fuel, and its combustion produces less power. A greatly overheated fuel charge can even trigger knocking and its coincident troubles. Thus, the valve regulating the heat applied to the intake manifold may assume greater importance than the average skipper assigns to it.

An intake manifold may take a serpentine shape, as borne out by the illustration; it all depends on the configuration of the engine and the possible paths from carburetor to cylinders. Preferably, the intake manifold contains a separate passage for each cylinder. Sometimes, when the intake ports of two cylinders are adjacent, one passage may serve both. Since both cylinders never take fuel at the same time, but do so sequentially, the single passage does not become a significant drawback. However, the ideal is separate passages for all cylinders, each identical in length and cross section, and this achieves the ultimate in accurately divided fuel.

Inboard engines on powerboats are never level, with the possible exception of powerplants hooked up to vee drives (see Chapter 14). This tilting from the horizontal can affect the fuel distribution in the intake manifold, especially if some gasoline has dropped out of the stream and has gone back to liquid form. Gravity would concentrate this fuel at one end in a tilted intake manifold and thus favor some cylinder to the detriment of the desired fuel balance. Angling the intake manifold slightly, so that it remains horizontal even when the engine is not, is one form of counteraction. The hot manifold that vaporizes this errant gasoline is another form.

A tube containing a column of air or gas that is periodically accelerated and slowed takes on the properties of an organ pipe and develops resonant waves with pressure areas. An intake manifold takes on some of these qualities, and the waves of pressure vary with the speed of the engine. Theoretically, these pressures could be used to help pack the fuel charge into the cylinder to obtain an increased energy efficiency. Some engines attempt this, and their manufacturers claim measurable benefits from this so-called tuning.

Of course, the complexity of intake manifold design is affected by the number of cylinders in the engine, and by whether it is a vee or a straight block. For a V-8, the intake manifold is actually two manifolds in one piece. The central portion is the base for a two-barrel carburetor, each barrel feeding one half of the manifold, and each in turn serving four cylinders on one side of the vee. In effect, two separate carburetors are supplying two separate 4-cylinder engines. The 6-cylinder engine, being usually in-line, requires a longer intake manifold with the attendant problems of long and short fuel paths from a central carburetor.

All marine engines, whether gasoline or diesel, are equipped with exhaust manifolds. This manifold collects the exhausts from each cylinder and combines them into a single stream suitable for the final muffler and tail pipe. Occasionally, on so-called racing installations, the exhaust muffler is absent and each cylinder has a short pipe leading from its exhaust port to the atmosphere. The results, in action, are deafening noise and dancing flame, which, while dear to the heart of an exhibitionist, are not really of that much engineering benefit.

The problems of the intake manifold are not carried over into the exhaust manifold. Here there is no need to coddle a mixture that may divide into its components because of velocity changes, nor any necessity to make the passages from all cylinders equal. The exhaust manifold simply must have all passages of large enough cross section to handle the maximum stream of gases at high speed without undue friction. The only problem for the designer is how to fit the unit into the available space. (See Figure 30-3.)

The tuning mentioned earlier for the intake manifold is applied more often to the exhaust manifold. As before, the organ-pipe effect is utilized, only this time the pressure waves help carry the gas away. This helps clear the cylinders of burned gases more rapidly and thoroughly so that the incoming charge is not hindered. The drawback of tuning is that it depends on resonance and,

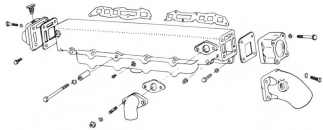

Figure 30-3. This exploded view of an exhaust manifold assembly shows gaskets, elbows and other parts. (Lehman Power Corporation)

therefore, is effective only at certain speeds of the engine.

The high temperature of the exhaust manifold is put to work in several ways on gasoline engines. It operates the valve that controls the heating of the intake manifold. It influences the thermostatic spring that automatically closes and opens the choke on the carburetor. It may warm the air taken in by the engine through the medium of a "stove" surrounding the exhaust manifold. None of these peripheral duties is imposed on the exhaust manifold of a diesel engine; here the only job is to get rid of the exhaust with as little back pressure as possible.

Exhaust gases are of extremely high temperature, and some means must be provided for cooling the exhaust manifold to keep it within safety limits. Automotive exhaust manifolds are cooled by the air flow from the radiator fan. Marine engine exhaust manifolds are cooled by water. Raw water, pumped up from a through-hull inlet, for engine cooling, is passed through a jacket surrounding the exhaust manifold before it is returned to the sea. Even with freshwater cooling (see Chapter 11) sea water is deflected into the exhaust manifold jacket. Obviously, exhaust manifold temperature assumes much greater safety importance on a boat than it does in an automobile. Figure 30-4 shows how one diesel engine solves the problem.

Manifolds, both intake and exhaust, are made of cast iron because this material is inexpensive and reasonably able to take the stresses of heating and cooling. The complicated configurations pose acute difficulties for the foundry that must cast the many devious passages leading in all directions. Cores of baked sand maintain the

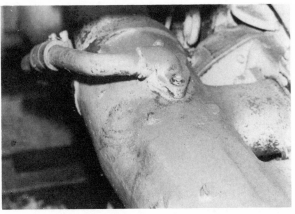

Figure 30-4. The water connection to a diesel engine's exhaust manifold is shown above.

necessary open runs; these are shaken and poked out of the finished casting. Minimal machining then prepares the surfaces, which must make accurate contact with other components, usually with the aid of gaskets.

Cast iron does have a certain brittleness, and so care and a knowing touch are required when bolting manifolds to engines. Uneven tightening with a heavy hand may snap off a connecting lug—as some skippers have discovered to their sorrow.

Internal combustion engines on land must have mufflers, and lucky that this is so; but the boat builder has a choice in the disposition of exhaust. He may dispense with the conventional muffler and decide that the cooling water going out with the exhaust gases quiets them sufficiently. However, mufflers are mandatory with the drystack exhaust systems found on some of the larger yachts because here the quieting action of water is absent.

The sudden release of high-pressure gases when the exhaust valve opens forms a steep sonic wave that assaults the ear like the crack of a gun. At high engine speed these impacts follow each other so closely that the effect is a loud roar. The muffler softens the impact of the exhaust gases on the atmosphere by causing them to expand freely in cavities designed for this purpose. Additionally, some mufflers contain resonant chambers and sound traps that rob the original explosive sound waves of their energy and hence of their capacity to make a loud

(A)

(B)

Figure 30-5. A silencer type muffler for an onboard generating plant is shown at (A), and at (B) is a muffler constructed of synthetic rubber.

Figure 30-6. This exhaust attachment leads the exhaust gases below the waterline before they are discharged. The result is a reduction in noise and a dissipation of noxious odors.

noise. The principle is exemplified in the Maxim silencer for guns. (See Figure 30-5.)

The surrounding water is often used as a means of silencing the exhaust. This is accomplished with the so-called underwater exhaust system shown in Figure 30-6. A right-angle extension to the transom exhaust pipe discharges the exhaust gases below the surface of the water. Not only does this quiet the exhaust, it effectively traps noxious odors and prevents them from coming back into the cockpit as so often happens with plain transom exhaust. Outboard motors routinely use this form of exhaust. Some large vessels do not bother to run the exhaust lines to the transom but instead point them straight down through openings in the bilge. In these installations, the forward movement of the boat creates a helpful slight suction. (See Figure 19-6.)

The important determinant with underwater exhaust is back pressure. Any back pressure created by the exhaust system seriously reduces the performance and the power of the engine. However, a well-designed underwater installation adds negligible back pressure and has no appreciable effect on the operation of the marine powerplant.

Most inboard engine installations, and practically all on powerboats, place the engine above the waterline. Furthermore, a down-slanting exhaust pipe, plus usually a section bent into an inverted U shape, make it impossible for seawater to reach the engine, even from a following waves.

But many sailboats carry their engines below the waterline, and precautions must be taken. The sketch in Figure 30-7 shows the relation between engine and waterline in a typical sailboat, with special emphasis on the location of the exhaust line. Since water seeks its own level, the exhaust line in sailboats such as that shown must have a section placed higher than the waterline. The usual section is an inverted U. Cooling water intended for discharge through the exhaust outlet must be introduced downstream of the U.

Mufflers, often called silencers in the marine trade, may be installed at any place in the exhaust line but generally are found near the exhaust outlet. The flow of cooling water keeps marine mufflers from becoming as

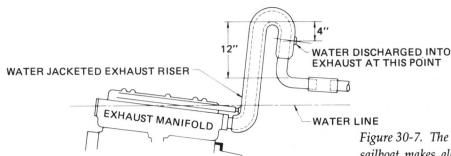

Figure 30-7. The correct installation of the engine exhaust on a sailboat makes allowance for heeling and assures that water cannot back up into the manifold.

hot as, for instance, the mufflers on automobiles, an important safety factor. Mufflers made of certain types of rubber are popular and have the advantage of not rusting. Mufflers for dry-stack systems, devoid of cooling water, are manufactured of metals such as hard aluminum alloys and stainless steel.

Water is a normal product of combustion and may collect in the mufflers of dry-stack exhausts. Drain plugs are provided for periodic inspection and emptying. Figure 30-8 shows a typical dry-stack installation.

Where dry-stack exhaust pipes terminate in such a manner that rain could enter, protection is necessary and usually takes the form of flapper valves. These normally closed flappers are counterbalanced to open by the exhaust stream without creating undue back pressure. Wise skippers of dry-stack diesel systems always make sure that the flappers are actually closed before they consider the vessel secure after a voyage.

Some transom exhausts that terminate near the waterline are often protected by rubber flappers. These close down over the exhaust pipe when the engine is not running; their purpose is to prevent a wave from pushing its way into the exhaust line. (See Figure 30-9.)

Figure 30-8. Mufflers for dry stack exhaust systems are larger because they must dissipate heat without the aid of cooling water.

Figure 30-9. The flaps on the end of the exhaust pipe prevent the entry of water when the engine is shut down. The added back pressure caused by the flap is minimal.

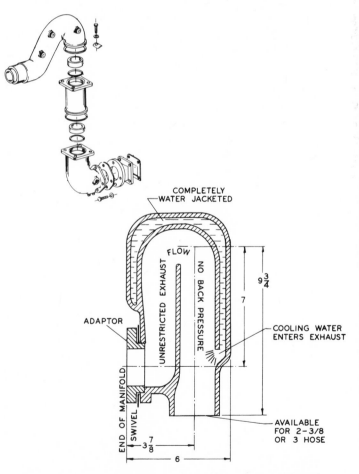

Figure 30-10. Two methods of raising the exhaust when the engine is installed below the waterline are shown. Standard parts are used. (Lehman Power Corporation)

31. *Carburetors and Injectors*

Carburetors blend fuel and air into an explosive combination and deliver this mixture in the form of a vapor to gasoline engines as their source of power. Injectors take raw fuel and atomize it into the cylinders of diesel engines for transformation into power. Both are the hearts of their respective powerplants. The basic difference between them is that carburetors depend upon negative pressure or vacuum, whereas injectors make use of extremely high pressure.

The downward movement of the piston in the cylinder on the intake stroke of the engine creates the vacuum that makes the operation of the carburetor possible. The air to fill this vacuum rushes in through the throat of the carburetor, where a restriction increases the velocity. It is the high velocity that enables actual carburetion to take place. What happens follows the dictates of a law of physics laid down by Bernoulli many years ago.

Bernoulli's law states, in essence, that the higher the velocity, the lower the pressure. This may seem arcane, but, luckily, a simple experiment with a sheet of paper will make the workings of the law clearer than words can. The drawing in Figure 31-1 shows how holding a sheet of paper and blowing parallel with it on one side creates the lower pressure that Bernoulli postulates.

Blowing causes a movement of air at high velocity on one side of the paper while the air on the other side is relatively motionless. Therefore, in accordance with the law, the pressure should be less—a partial vacuum—on the high-velocity side. That this is actually so is proved when the paper is drawn to this side.

The application of the experiment to the principle of a carburetor is straightforward and is shown by the drawing in Figure 31-2. The large vertical tube with the restriction symbolizes the throat of a standard carburetor, and the protruding central nozzle is connected to a source of liquid. Air rushing down through the tube increases its velocity at the restriction and creates a region of lowered pressure or partial vacuum at the nozzle in accordance with the Bernoulli theorem. Atmospheric pressure, being higher, forces liquid out of the nozzle and into the air stream. (Incidentally, the restriction is called a venturi, and it is the secret of the action.)

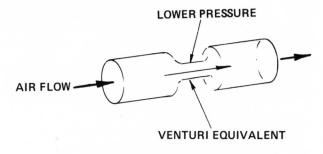

LOWER PRESSURE

AIR FLOW

VENTURI EQUIVALENT

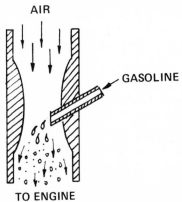

AIR

GASOLINE

TO ENGINE

Figure 31-2. The Bernoulli theorem is that "the higher the velocity, the lower the pressure." The illustration shows how a venturi makes use of this. The airflow attains a higher velocity in the constricted portion of the tube and thus the pressure in that area is lower. In a carburetor this lower pressure sucks in fuel.

PAPER MOVES
TOWARD AIR STREAM

Figure 31-1. Blowing past a sheet of paper illustrates Bernoulli's theorem dramatically. The paper always will move toward the air stream.

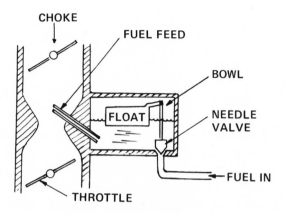

Figure 31-3. The basic manner in which all carburetors employ the Bernoulli principle is shown. A very primitive functioning carburetor could be constructed from this by the addition of throttle and choke valves plus a float and its needle valve to control the fuel level in the bowl.

Of course, a modern carburetor for a marine engine is considerably more complicated, although its principle of operation is the same as that just demonstrated. The fact is that a primitive carburetor could be constructed from the experimental setup of Figure 31-2 by adding a fuel reservoir, or bowl, plus a method for keeping it filled; this is shown in Figure 31-3. The engine's fuel pump (see Chapter 9) maintains the fuel at the proper level in the bowl by means of the float and its needle valve. The so-called butterfly at the lower end of the throat is similar to the damper in a stovepipe and controls the flow of the air-fuel mixture and therefore the speed of the engine.

The level of fuel in the bowl takes on great importance. It must be kept slightly below the height of the nozzle. Too high a level would cause the nozzle to dribble whether or not the engine is running. Too low a level would make it difficult for the partial vacuum at the nozzle to induce fuel flow.

Truly, the foregoing device is a carburetor but surely not a good one. Its simplicity breeds many shortcomings. First of all, the engine would be very difficult to start. Assuming that it could be started, the engine would run very raggedly with little or no thought for fuel economy. Any attempt at sudden acceleration would stall the engine without a doubt. The demands made on modern marine engines require carburetors of much greater intricacy, able to overcome the problems highlighted by this primitive forerunner.

Skippers today demand powerplants that start in a wink at the turn of a switch, whether the weather is hot or cold. The ability to do this lies mainly within the province of the carburetor. Stalling in response to a demand for acceleration is certainly not acceptable. The capacity of an engine to speed up suddenly without hesitation or stall also depends on the carburetor. In addition, a good carburetor blends gasoline and air in the optimum ratio for all conditions of load, and this results in smooth and economical engine performance.

Commercial carburetors are either "updraft" or "downdraft," with the latter predominantly popular. The distinction reflects the manner in which the carburetor is attached to the intake manifold and the direction of airflow through it. The updraft carburetor is attached below the manifold, and the intake air is drawn upward through it. The downdraft carburetor sits on top of the intake manifold, and the air travels downward. Of course, both types must be equipped with flame arrestors in service and with some means of catching dripped fuel. A downdraft carburetor is shown in Figure 31-4.

Figure 31-4. This is a typical downdraft carburetor. The edge of the choke valve may be seen at the top. The control arm of the throttle valve is at the lower left. The flame arrestor fits on the shoulder around the throat opening.

272

Carburetors, especially those of the downdraft type, are further classified by the number of throats or "barrels" in their construction. Common commercial models are single-barrel, two-barrel and four-barrel. In effect, the latter two would be the equivalent of two carburetors working from a single bowl and four carburetors being fed from a single bowl. A typical use of a two-barrel carb would be on a V-8 engine, each barrel feeding four cylinders.

Carburetors on outboard motors, especially on those of one cylinder and low horsepower, are considerably simplified. They may be described more correctly as mixing-valves with a minimum of adjustments. Nevertheless, they adequately meet the demands of these little engines with small-diameter cylinders, short strokes and consequent very low cubic-inch displacement. Like all carburetors, these, too, control engine speed by means of a butterfly throttle valve.

Modern carburetors are marvels of small, intricate passages; yet their manufacture has been standardized to the point of allowing a reasonable price level. Die-casting is a favorite construction technique. The material most often used is zinc or a similar alloy of relatively low melting temperature. Large carburetors are divided into two or three sections to meet the exigencies of die-making, and these sections subsequently are assembled with intervening gaskets into the finished unit. An unassembled section is shown in Figure 31-5.

The passages and valves of the marine carburetor are isolated into separate fuel supply systems, each supplying the needs of the engine under certain operating conditions. Thus there is the idling fuel system from which the engine draws when running at very low speed. The cruising system takes care of the engine during midrange speed operation, while the high-speed system becomes the fuel supply during the upper limit of the revolutions per minute. In addition, the accelerating system prevents stalling or stumbling of the engine when the throttle is shifted suddenly upward, and the choke system sees the engine through its original cold-starting phase.

The reason for these distinctions in fuel feed is the changing appetites of the engine in response to the various loads it must assume. The ideal mixture of air and fuel for an internal combustion engine is approximately 14 pounds of air to 1 pound of gasoline. However, this holds true in the average commercial engine only for normal midrange operation. For easy, quick cold-starting, the amount of air may be reduced to about 9 pounds, while for high speed, lightly loaded running, the air may be increased to more than 15 pounds. The carburetor handles these continuously varying requests by means of its several fuel systems, and it does this automatically. Although gasoline, admittedly, is a highly volatile, highly flammable fluid, it will not ignite in the engine cylinder unless its mix with air is in the correct ratio for the immediate condition.

Understanding the various phases of carburetor action is easiest if the normal running system is examined first, and the diagrammatic representation in Figure 31-6 is

Figure 31-5. This throttle plate of a 4-barrel carburetor shows the four butterfly valves that control engine speed. All four would be open only at high speed.

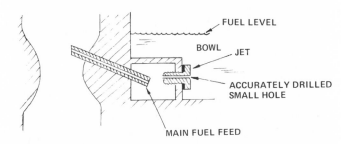

Figure 31-6. The main running system of the carburetor gets its fuel through a metering jet. The accurately drilled small hole in the jet is matched to the fuel requirements of a particular engine.

drawn accordingly. One complaint against the primitive carburetor discussed earlier is that there is no control over the amount of gasoline delivered into the airstream by the nozzle. This is remedied by the jet shown in the drawing. The hole in the jet is drilled accurately to within a few thousandths of an inch. Jets with holes of different diameters are available, and the choice of a correctly sized jet is critical for any given engine. The gasoline drawn into the well that feeds the nozzle must pass through the restriction of the jet, and the quantity is thus controlled.

A further refinement is the tiny bleed hole that allows air to enter the well. The pressure drop in a venturi does not decrease linearly with the increase of air velocity but, rather, takes a disproportionate drop. This would draw an increased amount of gasoline and would make the mixture richer, were it not for the bleed hole. The bleed air has a counteracting effect and to some extent also mixes with the gasoline in the well to reduce the volume at the nozzle. The net effect is that the fuel mixture remains reasonably constant throughout the midrange of engine speeds.

The diagram in Figure 31-7 shows the idling system of the carburetor that comes into play when the engine is running at its slowest speed. Here, too, a metering effect has been introduced, but, unlike the jet, the idling restriction is adjustable with the so-called idling screw. The throttle plate is almost closed at idling, open only a crack, and this puts the venturi out of business. However, there is great suction below the throttle plate, and this is utilized through the medium of the small idling hole that opens into the throat. Turning the idling screw increases or decreases the size of the available passage and thereby regulates the quantity of gasoline going into the airstream. Again, the bleed hole admits compensating air.

Since the idling screw controls the quantity of fuel reaching the cylinders, it naturally becomes a secondary control of engine speed as well. It is customary to set the idling speed of the engine by a combined adjustment of the throttle plate and the idling screw. After the throttle is set to its lowest stop, the idling screw is turned carefully in either direction until the performance of the engine at this low speed is optimum. (Early models of carburetors had idling screws that controlled air instead of fuel.)

Starting a cold engine confronts the carburetor with yet another problem: The fuel mixture must be enriched considerably. Present-day choke mechanisms accomplish this automatically, although mechanical and electrical choke appliers that depend on the skipper are still in use. The cold surfaces of the intake manifold condense some of the gasoline and rob the airstream of its flammable constituent, and this is counteracted by reducing air and increasing fuel. The choke system that does this is shown in Figure 31-8.

The choke is the equivalent of a second throttle plate placed at the air intake end of the carburetor throat. When this plate is in its closed position, it greatly impedes the flow of air to the engine. The suction below the choke plate is increased and serves to induce additional flow of

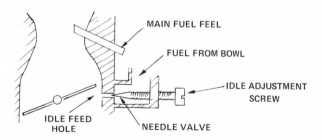

Figure 31-7. The idle feed hole in the carburetor throat remains uncovered when the throttle is closed. A needle valve adjustment determines how much fuel the engine receives at idling speed.

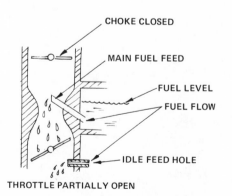

Figure 31-8. When the choke valve is closed during cranking, extremely high vacuum in the intake manifold draws fuel from both main and idle feeds, resulting in a rich mixture for starting cold engines.

gasoline from the nozzle and from the idle hole. The result is a fuel mixture high enough in gasoline to overcome the forces that wish to dilute it and one that can be ignited by the spark plugs in a cold engine.

The automatic feature of the choke depends upon temperature. A bimetallic spring, which coils when it is heated, pulls the choke open from its initially closed position. Since the heat is supplied by the exhaust manifold (see Chapter 30), the choke is opened automatically when the engine reaches its proper temperature. Some models of carburetors add a vacuum plunger that is responsive to the intake manifold to improve the automatic action.

If the throttle were opened abruptly, as in a sudden demand for greatly increased speed, the marine engine would stall without the accelerating pump that is built into modern marine carburetors. This accelerating system is diagrammed in Figure 31-9. The reason for the stall is that air can speed up more quickly than gasoline, which has far greater inertia. Thus the gasoline lags behind the air that suddenly rushes through the throat when a throttle is opened suddenly, and a leaner mixture results at the very moment when a richer one is needed. The accelerating system corrects this.

Sudden, wide opening of the throttle pushes the tiny piston down into its accelerating well in the carburetor by means of a linkage. This squirts raw gasoline into the throat through a separate nozzle and causes immediate enrichment of the final mixture. (Incidentally, a trick that mechanics use to determine whether an engine is getting fuel is to push the throttle open and look to see if fuel is spurting out of the accelerator nozzle.)

The final refinement demanded of a modern marine carburetor is to economize on fuel whenever the load and speed of the engine permit this, and yet instantly to enrich the fuel mixture when heavy going requires it. A simple little valve inside the carburetor is the key to such actions. Depending on its internal hookup, this device is called either an economizer or a power valve; in either case, the purpose is to make the operation of a marine engine more economical and responsive. A basic economizer is shown in the drawing of Figure 31-10.

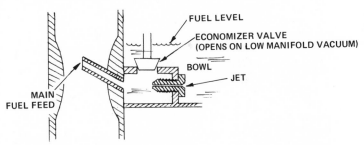

Figure 31-10. The economizer valve is controlled by manifold vacuum and passes fuel to the main feed in addition to that passed by the carburetor jet.

The economizer takes its cue from the degree of vacuum in the intake manifold. This is valid because intake manifold vacuum is an accurate indicator of how hard the engine is working and, in fact, many consoles include a vacuum gauge to keep the skipper apprised of what is happening in his powerplant. At moderate speeds and light loads the vacuum is high; as the load increases, the vacuum lessens. The economizer valve is sensitive to these changes.

The economizer valve illustrated is normally held closed by high-intake vacuum and has no effect on the operation of the carburetor. When a heavy load on the engine drops manifold vacuum, the valve is opened by its spring and permits additional gasoline to flow into the

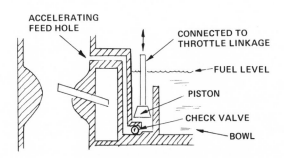

Figure 31-9. Sudden acceleration requires a rich mixture and the accelerating pump provides the necessary squirt of fuel when the throttle is opened. The accelerating piston is connected to the throttle linkage and functions with the aid of a check valve.

nozzle. The result is an immediate enrichment of the fuel mixture, and this is maintained until rising vacuum shows it to be no longer necessary. With automobile engines and their varying loads, this intermittent opening and closing could be taking place constantly; marine engines, with their more constant loads, may make less use of the economizer action.

The "metering rod" is another, perhaps simpler, method of obtaining metering action synchronized with throttle requirements. It is shown in Figure 31-11. A thin, pinlike rod is suspended in such a manner from the throttle linkages that it hangs in the center of the metering jet. When the throttle is opened wide, this rod is withdrawn. Therefore, at all positions of the throttle except wide open, the effective area of the jet is reduced; at full throttle, the rod is pulled up and the jet passes maximum fuel.

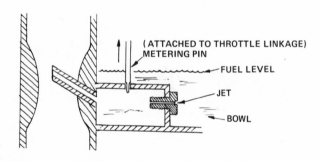

Figure 31-11. The metering pin also is a form of economizer. When the throttle linkage lifts the metering pin clear of its hole, the fuel passage is enlarged.

The marine carburetor has a problem that is unknown to its automotive counterpart: It is rarely on an even keel when at sea. This sloshes the gasoline in the bowl forward, backward and to the sides, and makes it difficult for the float to maintain the technically correct fuel level. It has already been stated that fuel level in the bowl is an important carburetor parameter. Ingenious solutions have been proposed from time to time, but all were complicated and expensive. Commercial carburetors make do with a compromise in float and needle valve geometry and bowl size and shape.

The bleed holes mentioned earlier usually have an additional function. They act as an escape for the vapors generated in the carburetor bowl by heat when a hot engine is shut down. Without the air escape, the vapor pressure would force unwanted fuel into the manifold and cause flooding.

Four-barrel carburetors have two main working barrels and two auxiliary barrels. Under normal loads and speeds the auxiliaries remain closed, and the main throats supply the engine. At high speed or heavy load, the auxiliary barrels open to add two more throats to the fuel system with consequent greatly added capacity. The opening action may be either mechanical with a linkage to the throttle system or in response to intake manifold vacuum.

Normally, the auxiliary barrels do not have choke plates as the main barrels do. Actually, choke mechanisms in the auxiliary throats would be redundant because these barrels come into use only at high loads and speeds and are never used for starting. The secondary barrels begin to open approximately when the primary barrels are about two-thirds open, but all four barrels reach the wide-open position at the same time.

Carburetor wear is especially critical at the bearing holes that support the throttle plate shaft. Enlargement of this bore, beyond that needed for good bearing, permits air that is not coordinated with the regular airstream to enter. This upsets the carburetor's mixing of fuel and air and may result in rough engine performance, particularly at idle speed.

Carburetors may be rebuilt without too great difficulty, although it takes a fairly skilled hand to do the work correctly. Kits are widely available that contain the parts and gaskets that must be replaced, plus more or less complete how-to instructions. Exchange service on carburetors is also available.

Diesel engine injectors are manufactured to a degree of precision higher than that required for most other engine components. Measurements of internal injector parts commonly are to tenths of one-thousandths of an inch, and surfaces are mirror-smooth. Injectors are beyond the scope of do-it-yourself service and repair except

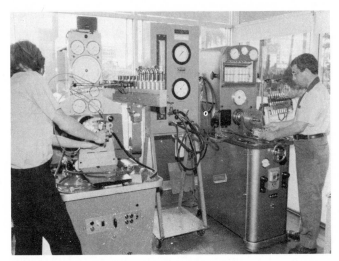

Figure 31-12. *Servicing injectors and injector pumps requires that skill be buttressed by considerable highly accurate special equipment, as proved by this corner of a commercial shop. (RPM Diesel, Ft. Lauderdale)*

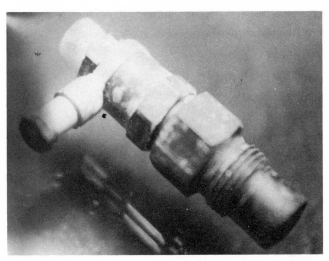

Figure 31-13. *The Bosch injector pictured above is, in essence, an extremely accurate nozzle backed by calibrated check valves. The two tubing attachment fittings are for input and return flow respectively.*

in the hands of a truly skilled skipper. The photograph in Figure 31-12 shows some of the equipment that a commercial service shop finds necessary for the repair of injectors.

Injectors are of two types: those that receive fuel at extremely high pressure and act merely as atomizers, and those that pressurize and measure their own fuel before atomizing it. The first type is under the command of a central injector pump. This pump raises the fuel to the required high pressure and divides it into equal gulps whose quantities are regulated by the position of the throttle. These gulps of fuel are sent to the injectors in the cylinders in correct rotation and at the proper instant by a distributor mechanism, much in the manner of the distributor on a gasoline engine directing sparks. A separate tube to each injector leads from the pump's distributor. The high pressure overcomes a spring in the injector, and the nozzle atomizes the fuel into the cylinder. This system's injector is illustrated in Figure 31-13.

As has already been stressed several times, one of the requirements for the smooth running of an engine is that the fuel charges to all cylinders be exactly equal. This is as true of diesel motive power as it is of gasoline. Consequently, the tubes leading from the distributor to the injectors in the aforementioned system must all be equal in length. Not only quantity but also the finite times it takes the fuel gulps to reach the injectors must also be equal. Diesel engines utilizing this fuel method are quickly distinguished from gasoline units because of the similarity of the pump and its tubes to the latter's distributor and its wires.

The second form of injector is a self-contained pump, metering and timing device. It is shown in cross-sectional

Figure 31-14. *The complexity of an injector of the self-contained type is vividly demonstrated by this cutaway view. The rack and pinion mechanism (center) controls the amount of fuel delivered at each stroke. (Detroit Diesel)*

view in Figure 31-14. It is operated by a rocker arm and push rod that take their impetus from a cam on a camshaft, an action similar to that of a valve. These injectors also serve as a throttle because the metering action is controlled simultaneously in the injectors in all cylinders. The fuel is supplied to these injectors at moderate pressure by a primary pump that draws on the tank.

The necessary timing of the injection from this form of injector is determined by the shape of the cam on the camshaft, as is the case with valves. Fine tuning of this timing is accomplished by adjusting the clearance between the head of the injector and the rocker arm, again as is done with valves.

One manner in which injectors can offend is by dribbling fuel after the fuel injection period has ended. The unwanted fuel may cause smoking and, of course, a rough-running engine. Malfunctioning check valves in the injector are the principal reasons for the nuisance of dribbling.

The shape of the nozzle at the lower end of the injector is the determinant of the nature and the completeness of atomization. This nozzle may consist of a single orifice ejecting a single spray, or of a multi-orifice better able to distribute the spray around the combustion chamber. The fineness of the orifice holes often leads to clogging either by carbon or by an impurity that has gotten by the various filters. A type of nozzle in which a pin on the check valve enters the hole is an aid in keeping the passage clear. (See Figure 31-15.)

Governors are common on diesel marine engines, and they carry out their function by controlling the amount of fuel delivered each time the injector is actuated. In the first described injector system, this control is exerted on the central injector pump. In the second system, the control is applied simultaneously to all the injectors, usually by a continuous rack and pinion arrangement.

When a comparison is made of the ease of adjustment for optimum running, of carburetors and injectors, the carburetor wins easily. But for overall satisfaction of operation, the injector is ahead. (See Figure 31-16.)

Figure 31-15. The tiny opening and pin in the nozzle end of this diesel injector atomizes the fuel delivered to it under high pressure.

Figure 31-16. One of the commercial injector pumps found on marine engines.

PART SIX
ENGINE HUSBANDRY

32. Tune-up and Lay-up

S ooner or later, and regardless of the waters in which he does his cruising, every powerboat skipper must decide on the desirability of a tune-up to bring his engine back to its pristine performance. Lay-up, in contrast, affects only boatmen in colder climates where freezing is a danger; and for them, lay-up is best followed by tune-up. Power, be it wind or fuel, must be used efficiently if the boat is to achieve its maximum performance. In this quest, the sailor tunes his rigging, the powerboat skipper tunes his engines. Both are seeking that last elusive bit of propulsive force. But the sailor must rely on his intuition and on his secret tricks because his procedure is more art than science. In contrast, the skipper has it easier; he can tune to exact manufacturer's specifications, which may be measured precisely.

Tuning up an engine should be considered as a process of restoring all the small changes in adjustments and alignments that have taken place as a result of prolonged use. For instance, on a gasoline engine the small block of fiber that contacts the distributor cam is subject to almost imperceptible wear. Yet the cumulative effect of this wear is to lessen the specified gap between the breaker points in the ignition system. A tune-up restores the correct gap. A similar example on a diesel engine is the change in valve clearance caused by wear that inhibits performance and must be rectified by a tune-up.

Mechanics about to perform a tune-up on a gasoline engine invariably zero in on the ignition system. "It needs points and a condenser and most likely spark plugs" is a dictum heard by almost every motorist. It must be admitted that often the points are not that bad, and could be rehabilitated with a little touching up, but nevertheless replacement is recommended as inexpensive insurance. The same thinking is applicable to the spark plugs. There is no simple test for condensers that simulates the electrostatic stresses they undergo in service; hence this replacement also becomes insurance.

Proper tune-up of a modern marine engine requires more instrumentation than that of the human eye and ear, although an experienced mechanic can perform great improvements with no more than that. A vacuum gauge, a compression gauge, a dwell meter and a volt-ohm-ampere meter are necessary to ferret out the small changes that make the difference between ordinary and optimum performance of an engine. The mechanically inclined boatowner may have this equipment, although it is questionable whether the cost of acquisition is warranted for occasional private use. Even oscilloscopes are now found in service shops.

So-called eyeballing, or visual inspection, is an important preliminary to tune-up. Many leaks can be found simply by looking. Hoses can be checked manually by pulling on them to determine the tightness of their clamps and by squeezing them to detect the condition of their material. Belt tightness can be verified. Spark-plug wires and rubber spark-plug boots exhibit a close relationship between their appearance and their serviceability, with cracks a reason for condemnation. Looseness in the control linkages is surely a sign that attention is needed to ward off future trouble.

Tune-up starts with the battery, although nothing much can be done, other than replacement, if the battery is on the way out. Routine testing with a hydrometer indicates the state of charge but does not tell whether the necessary current-delivering ability exists. Special meters that check the battery under load are needed for this. By rule of thumb, if the battery can spin the engine at good cranking speed, it is probably adequate. Charging the battery to bring it up to a full reading is always a logical first step in the tune-up procedure, preceded, of course, by restoring electrolyte levels with water.

Tune-up attention is directed next at the ignition system, with the spark coil as the first candidate for a close look. A good coil can easily throw a spark ½ inch long. A tried-and-true method of determining whether or not the coil in question is able to do this is to take the central wire out of the distributor cap, remove the cap itself and turn the ignition switch to "on" but *not* to "start." Now, holding the free end of the wire ½ inch from the engine block, open and close the breaker points manu-

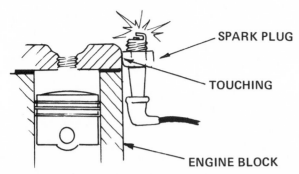

Figure 32-1. Touching the shell of a spark plug to the engine block while the engine is being cranked (and ignition switch is on) is a quick way to determine whether sparking ability is present.

ally several times. Each opening should produce the required spark. This test may also be made with one of the spark plugs as shown in Figure 32-1.

The gap between the opened breaker points should be adjusted to the specification given in the owner's manual before the distributor cap is replaced. Inexpensive gauges are available everywhere for measuring this gap, and usually also for checking the spark plugs. The screws or nuts inside the distributor for making the adjustment are easily recognizable. The engine is inched over, always in the running direction and never backward, until the top of the cam is directly under the rubbing block of the breaker point arm. This is the only position at which the gap is to be measured. Figure 32-2 shows this.

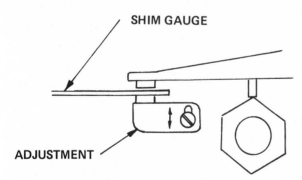

Figure 32-2. The gap between breaker points is adjusted with the aid of a shim gauge of the desired thickness. When the shim withdraws with a slight drag, the adjustment is correct.

The distributor cap should be checked carefully for cracks and carbon tracks, either of which will condemn it. Carbon tracks are formed by misguided sparks that follow the surface of the cap and carbonize it by burning. These carbon tracks then become an undesired alternate path for the sparking voltage to the detriment of the spark plug, and misfiring results.

It is possible to time an engine with fair accuracy by bringing the proper flywheel mark to the fixed pointer and turning the distributor housing so the points open at just that instant. But this does not take into account the vagaries of the centrifugal advance or of the vacuum advance. (See Chapter 12.) The only reliable manner in which to time the ignition of a modern marine engine is with a timing light and by following the directions that come with it.

A good tune-up includes an inspection of the spark plugs. Only a socket wrench designed for this purpose should be used to remove them; makeshift attempts with other wrenches usually end with broken insulators and ruined plugs. Spark plugs are usually placed in deep cavities that are excellent dirt catchers, and great care must be taken to remove this dirt and prevent its entrance into the cylinder before the plugs are unscrewed. The plug gap is adjusted to owner's manual specification by tapping or bending the outside electrode. The central electrode is never touched. With care and any needlelike tool, the internal space between the insulator and the metal housing can be cleaned. Most spark plugs will give good service much longer than the period after which the manufacturers suggest they be discarded. The illustration in Figure 32-3 shows the simplicity of spark-plug corrective action.

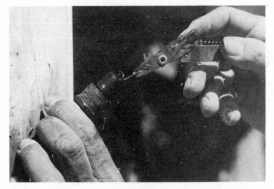

Figure 32-3. The correct gap for a spark plug is set with a gauge, preferably the wire-type gauge shown. Only the outer electrode is bent for setting, never the center electrode.

A good mechanic "reads" spark plugs and learns whether any major difficulties exist within the combustion process, and what they most likely are. A skipper may practice this same art for himself by comparing the removed spark plug with the photos in Figure 32-4. The plug taken from a marine engine in good shape and operating properly, for instance, would have the lower end of its insulator dry and slightly tanned in color.

Once the ignition system is in order, the next tune-up attention is directed at the carburetor. The carburetor

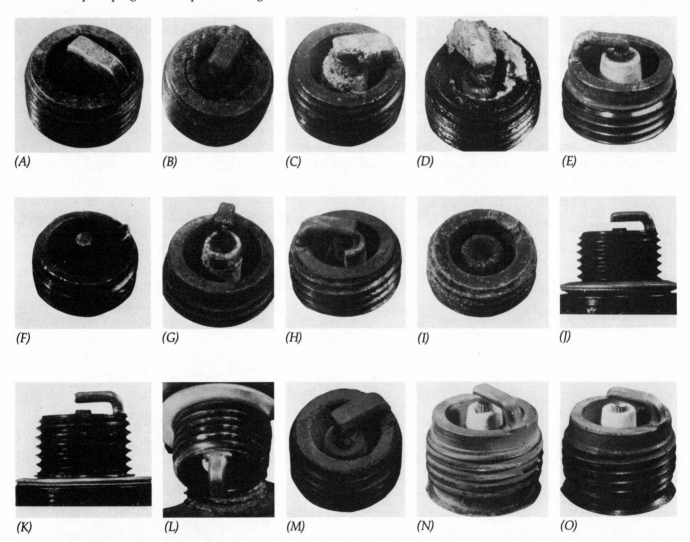

Figure 32-4. *Close examination of a withdrawn spark plug can tell a great deal about the internal happenings of an engine. (A) Carbon fouling, (B) oil fouling, (C), (D), and (E) several forms of deposit fouling, (F) detonation, (G) pre-ignition, (H) heat* shock, *(I) insufficient torque, (J) correct gasket compression, (K) no gasket compression, (L) thread seizure, (M) manganese deposit, (N) improper cleaning, (O) correct cleaning.* (AC Spark Plug Division)

cannot do its job without an unobstructed supply of air. To assure this, the flame arrestor must be clean and the choke valve must be open fully as soon as operating temperature is reached by the engine. Whether or not the choke is open to its fullest extent may be checked visually by stopping the engine as soon as it is warm and removing the flame arrestor. The choke-operating mechanism, be it manual, automatic or solenoid-controlled, should be lubricated at all linkages.

Usually, the idle adjusting screw is the only variable on the carburetor available to the skipper doing his own tune-up. With the throttle set at the desired minimum engine speed, the idle adjusting screw is turned slowly and carefully in either direction until the smoothest running results. This point will also be the greatest speed for any given idle throttle setting, and the highest vacuum gauge reading.

The final fuel filter often becomes clogged and thereafter is a cause of gasoline restriction to the carburetor. This can make the engine falter and even stop when asked to carry its load. This filter may be a separate unit just preceding the carburetor, or it may be entirely within the carburetor. The mesh of this filter is extremely fine and easily susceptible to serious clogging. In most instances, the screen may be cleaned with gasoline; heavy encroachment with varnish or gum necessitates replacement.

Valve clearance adjustment is an important phase of the tune-up job, although engines with hydraulic valve lifters do not require this operation since adjustment is maintained automatically. Whether or not the adjustments are to be made with the engine running or at a standstill is determined from the owner's manual or the service bulletins. The adjusting screws on an overhead-valve engine are exposed by removing the valve cover. Other engines expose their valve adjusters by means of removable side plates.

Once there is assurance that valves are in acceptable condition, a compression check is in order. The compression gauge, clearly understood and properly used, can be the arbiter on several internal conditions that affect the running of the engine. It can verify that everything is all right within the cylinder, and it can differentiate between piston rings and valves as the cause of a deficiency.

All spark plugs are removed for the compression check, and one cylinder is tested at a time. One of the two thin wires leading to the spark coil is disconnected to disable the coil and protect it. The compression gauge is inserted into a spark-plug hole, and the engine is turned over for several revolutions with the starter. If the pounds-per-square-inch pressure reading is reasonably near the specification set by the manufacturer, all is well. Should the reading be considerably lower, it becomes necessary to target either the rings or the valves as the offenders, and this can be done with a tablespoonful of heavy engine oil. Figure 32-5 shows a compression gauge in use.

The oil is poured into the spark-plug hole prior to the next test with the compression gauge. If the same number of engine revolutions now raises the indicated pressure, the rings are at fault; if it does not, blame the valves. All procedures are repeated for each cylinder. A smooth-running engine requires that the readings of all cylinders be approximately equal. Of course, judgment is required with consideration for the age of the engine. An old horse cannot show the briskness of a colt, regardless of how it is fed.

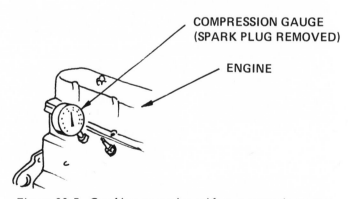

COMPRESSION GAUGE
(SPARK PLUG REMOVED)

ENGINE

Figure 32-5. Cranking an engine with a compression gauge inserted into a spark plug hole produces a reading of the maximum pressure in that cylinder.

The tune-up should include the usual routine check of coolant and lubrication. The thermostat in the cooling system plays an important part in the performance of the engine because it sets the temperature at which the machine runs. A suspected thermostat may be checked, as shown in Figure 32-6, by placing it in a container of water together with a thermometer. The temperature at which the thermostat opens when the water is heated is read on the thermometer and checked against specifications. Failure to perform is remedied by replacement. An antifreeze containing a rust inhibitor is well worth adding to a freshwater cooling system. (See Chapter 11.)

Figure 32-6. An engine thermostat is easily checked and calibrated with a thermometer. The temperature at which the thermostat opens as the water is heated is noted.

Not much can be done relative to the lubricating system other than maintaining the proper level on the dipstick and checking to see that the oil is in good condition. Owner's manuals state how often the lubricating oil should be changed, but the figures are notably conservative. American users of internal combustion engines have been educated to be profligate in the use of lubricant, and changing oil has become almost a religion.

Much lubricating oil still capable of rendering good service is discarded.

The transmission should be included in the tune-up effort, although there are no adjustments that truly fall within the ken of the average skipper. Visual inspection for leaks, a check on fluid level, and an oiling and freeing-up of all control linkages will do the job here. The tightening of bolts in shaft couplings is mandatory.

What has been said so far applies equally to outboard motors. Slight variations in procedure allow for the differences in size and location of components. The points for lubrication and the inlets and check holes for lower unit grease are clearly shown in the applicable owner's manual. Testing for play and sturdiness in the steering system should be included.

The tune-up for stern drives is a combination of the procedure for engines and that for outboards. The engine is a standard version; the transom-mounted portion of the installation has similarities to the lower units of outboard motors. One point of difference is the inspection for leakproof integrity of the seal between the engine inside and the drive unit outside.

The tune-up of a diesel engine is often much simpler than the corresponding operation on a gasoline engine because of the omission of an ignition system and of a carburetor. A corollary is that if the diesel is performing satisfactorily, it is best to leave it alone except for routine cleaning of filters and air cleaners and checking and oiling of all control linkages. As mentioned earlier (see Chapter 31), injectors and injector pumps, by their very nature, are better off in the more skilled hands of a specialized service shop. The average skipper will do the situation the most good by acute visual inspection for leaks and other untoward signs and by tightening all belts to the correct tension. Adjustment of the throttle stop screw in order to maintain a desired idling speed is made without difficulty.

For the skilled skipper, or the skipper who turns to professional tune-up service, several adjustments should be checked and corrected if need be. One of these is valve clearance. On some diesels, notably the two-cycle type, only exhaust valves are there for attention. Other diesel engines present the normal complement of intake and exhaust valves for adjustment. Injector timing is critical, and a good tune-up requires that it be brought to manufacturer's specifications.

Many marine diesel engines are under the automatic control of governors that limit their top speed. These governors take various forms, mechanical and hydraulic. Careful adjustment is required because governors are important safety mechanisms.

Two cautions are pertinent for everyone working on diesel engines: Never, under any circumstances, should the output of an injector be allowed to hit the human skin at close range. The output pressure is so great that the fluid will be forced through the skin and into the system. The "guns" used by medics in mass immunization shots work on this same principle and dispense with the usual hypodermic needle. The second caution is that, under certain conditions, diesel engines can "run away" and gain destructive speed, even after fuel is shut off, by consuming their own lubricating oil. Only complete shut-off of the air intake will stop them in such an emergency.

Lay–up

As mentioned earlier, only those skippers who do their boating in freezing climes are concerned with lay-up procedures. The basic reason for the actions taken during lay-up is that water expands when it freezes and develops sufficient force to split its container. When that "container" is an engine water jacket, the skipper's concern is real.

The essential purpose in conducting a lay-up is to remove water from every possible place where its presence could cause trouble during freezing temperatures. A further purpose is to protect metallic components from the rust and corrosion so prevalent in cold, wet weather. In addition, the lay-up plan removes from the boat all nonfixed parts and instruments that would be better off and safer spending the winter in a nice warm home.

A can of machine grease and a squirt can of lubricating oil are two essentials for the lay-up job. The grease is smeared on all exposed metal surfaces. This eliminates

the condensation that cannot be avoided in changeable weather and that is a prime cause of corrosion and pitting. The oil is squirted where the grease cannot be applied, plus a good dose into the spark-plug holes in each cylinder. Turning the engine over slowly once or twice distributes this oil along the cylinder walls.

Although a storage battery will not freeze in its charged condition, most manuals agree that it is best to remove the batteries unless they are too heavy and bulky and too inconveniently placed. A small inexpensive charger will keep batteries topped up in the comparative warmth of the home garage. Batteries left in the boat may be kept charged with pier power, but the charger should be one safe to use in the marine environment. (See Chapter 16.)

Some mechanics recommend that alternators, or generators, be removed from the engine at lay-up, but there does not seem much technical reason for doing this. However, it is a good idea to loosen all drive belts, perhaps even removing them, because corrosion forms on the sheave where the belt is in tight contact for long periods of time. Recommendations that carburetors and similar components also be removed for the winter are too drastic and generally unnecessary.

Spraying the ignition system with a water-repellent spray pays dividends in the spring in the form of wires that do not leak their high voltage. This spray is equally useful on switches and similar gear.

Engines have several drain cocks for allowing water to run out of pocketed enclosures in the cooling system. The location of the drains is given in the owner's manual. With freshwater cooling systems (see Chapter 13) the skipper has a choice of procedures: He may drain the freshwater completely, or he may add sufficient antifreeze to eliminate the danger of freezing in the lowest temperature normally encountered locally. The latter is the better way to go because the antifreeze will remain to act as a boiling point raiser and rust inhibitor during the following summer.

Maintaining air circulation about the laid-up engine is both good and bad, but fortunately, the good predominates. The bad part is that the moisture that condenses on

Figure 32-7. Catastrophic accidents are rare—but they happen. In this case a failed valve retainer allowed the valve to drop into the combustion chamber. Result: The valve head (arrow) embedded in a smashed piston plus possible cylinder wall damage.

the cold metal parts is brought in by the air. The redeeming feature is that much of this moisture will be evaporated and taken away by subsequent air circulation when the atmosphere becomes less humid. However, entrances to the engine's internals such as the intake and exhaust should be sealed off after they have received a generous squirt of corrosion-inhibiting oil.

The complete removal of all lubricating oil from the crankcase at lay-up time is often recommended. Many times, this means discarding perfectly good oil, a move that benefits only the oil suppliers. So a mature judgment should be made as to true oil condition. Oil that warrants rejection is generally a sign that the oil filter also needs inspection and possible replacement.

Whether the job is done by the skipper himself or by a boatyard, the main ingredient in an effective lay-up procedure is common sense. It does not require much technical knowledge to equate the machine with the type of weather it is to withstand, and to devise the needed countermeasures. It follows logically that the individual lay-up actions become more and more stringent as one proceeds northward into more drastic winter climates.

Life being what it is, misfortune may strike despite the most meticulous maintenance. An engine is purring along beautifully and a happy skipper is on the bridge. A valve retainer fails for some unknown reason. The valve falls into the combustion chamber and collides with a piston moving at projectile speed. The result is pictured in Figure 32-7. The valve head is deeply embedded in a totally fractured piston. Hopefully, cylinder wall and crankshaft have not been damaged.

Outboard Winter Storage Tips

1. Add fuel conditioner to fuel supply. Operate engine at part throttle with shift lever in neutral. Rapidly inject rust preventive (with pump type oil can) into carburetor air intake, or intakes until engine is smoking profusely. Stop engine immediately to prevent burning rust preventive out of cylinders. This will lubricate and protect internal parts of powerhead while outboard is in storage.

2. Place outboard on a stand in normal upright position. Remove motor cover.

3. Retard throttle all the way and disconnect spark plug leads. Manually rotate motor flywheel several times to drain the water from the water pump. Electric start (only) models use electric starter to rotate engine.

4. Clean and lubricate electric starter drive mechanism. Do not use oil on shaft, since it may run down into motor brushes.

5. Drain carburetor float chamber. Remove fuel filter bowl—drain, clean and replace filter element and gasket.

6. There are fuel preservatives on the market that eliminate the need to drain the fuel from your outboard and tank. They help keep spark plugs clean and prevent fuel line freeze up, too. When storing fuel you should use a strong, vapor-proof, air-tight container. Most tanks supplied with outboard engines are adequate for storing fuel *if* you disconnect the fuel line and make sure all vent screws are closed. The idea is to prevent any fumes from escaping and, certainly, the fuel should be kept away from pilot lights or sparking devices of any kind. Disconnect fuel line connector at the tank.

7. Remove propeller and check for condition and pitch. Inspect for burr at drive pin hole if propeller is difficult to remove. Inspect for propeller shaft seal damage from monofilament fishing line. Clean and liberally lubricate propeller shaft with anti-corrosion lube. Replace propeller drive pin if bent or worn. Apply gasket sealing compound to spline shaft model outboards.

8. Drain and refill gearcase, using recommended gearcase lubricant.

9. Wipe over entire external outboard surface with a clean cloth and then apply a good quality automotive wax.

10. Store in an upright position in a dry, well ventilated room. To prevent accidental starting, leave spark plug leads disconnected.

11. Remove battery from boat, check fluid level and keep it charged while in storage. Store in a cool, well-ventilated area.

Courtesy Johnson Outboards

33. Related Equipment

Several pieces of related equipment share the engine room on many yachts. This location is ideal for all such units because it concentrates in one accessible space those devices that need periodic maintenance or attention, and it isolates boat personnel from possible hazards.

In the category of "related equipment" are such products as fire-warning and fire-fighting devices, water heaters, air compressors, duplicate engine instrument panels, bilge pumps and remote compressors for refrigerators and air-conditioners. The engine room location conveniently provides through-hull fittings, electric power and connection to the boat's water system as these are needed.

Fire-fighting equipment is of prime importance on a gasoline-powered boat and greatly desirable even when the fuel is diesel. Automatic installations, of course, are best because they do not rely on human intervention at a time when human response could be slow or confused. Wide choice has centered on carbon dioxide (CO_2) as the extinguishing medium, although more recently developed gases claim greater effectiveness. The CO_2 is contained under high pressure in steel cylinders from which piping leads to strategically placed discharge nozzles. Hand held extinguishers are also placed strategically. (See Figure 33-1.)

In the automatic system, the valves on the CO_2 cylinders are controlled by sensors sensitive either to temperature or to smoke. These sensors, illustrated in Figure 33-2, are placed around the engine room at spots that, presumably, would show the first effects of fire. The one drawback of the automatic system is that it lacks judgment and could be triggered into operation in a situation that a human might consider not sufficiently drastic.

A standard form of control for the manual system of permanently installed carbon dioxide extinguishing systems is a small box with a glass window located just outside the engine room. The box bears the well-known instructions to "break the glass in case of fire" and has a small steel hammer attached for accomplishing this. Breaking the glass releases an actuating button, which in

Figure 33-1. Note that this CO_2 fire extinguisher is mounted outside the engine room door and not within the engine space. This permits escape and fire fighting from a safer vantage point.

Figure 33-2. Removal of the cover exposes the electronic internals of a typical smoke detector. The miniature bulb (upper right corner) shines on the photocell (lower right corner) causing a steady current to flow. Intervening particles of smoke cause this current to vary and activate the relay (upper left) to sound an alarm. (Eico Electronic Instruments)

turn opens the valves on the cylinder. (See Figure 33-3.)

Carbon dioxide extinguishes fires by withholding the oxygen necessary for combustion and thereby smothering them. The gas is noncorrosive and nondestructive. However, it can cause suffocation to humans engulfed in it because of this same ability to withhold oxygen.

Boats equipped with running hot water need a water heater or boiler, and the best location for this is the engine room. A common form of boiler makes use of engine-cooling water as its source of heat. A coil inside the boiler is in series with the engine-cooling system and utilizes heat that otherwise would be wasted. Since engine operating temperatures are in the 160° to 180° range and boiler temperatures are hardly ever set higher than 130°, there is ample leeway for satisfactory operation.

Of course, the foregoing arrangement yields hot water at the spigot only when the engines are running. To overcome this, the preferred type of water heater contains an additional electric heating coil powered either from shore or from an onboard generator. The average current draw of the electric coils is 1,500 watts, which, at a line voltage of 120, amounts to approximately 13 amperes. The photo in Figure 33-4 shows an onboard water heater.

Larger boats find an air compressor a valuable addition to the ship's equipment. The output of compressed air operates the whistle or horn and often also the windshield wipers. In addition, compressed air is available for general cleaning purposes. The compressor usually comprises a motor, pump and tank mounted together as a unit; it is located in a corner of the engine room. Copper tubing leads to an on-off valve at the helmsman's station and thence to horn or wiper. The machine automatically holds pressure at the previously set point and has a safety valve to protect the tank. An installation is shown in Figure 33-5.

An excellent addition at each propulsion engine is a small panel of instruments that duplicate the readings at the remote console. This close-up readout of what the

Figure 33-3. This glass front box, found on a large yacht, controls the valves on the carbon dioxide cylinders of the fire extinguishing system. Breaking the glass with the attached hammer and pulling the handle inside releases the gas into the engine room.

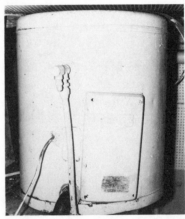

Figure 33-4. This 20-gallon water heater derives its power from shore current when the engines are stopped. An internal coil in series with the engine cooling system heats the water when the engines are running.

Figure 33-5. An air compressor is an excellent addition to an engine room that has space available for it. This self-contained unit has its own tank and is motor driven. Compressed air may be used to blow the horns, run the windshield wipers and, with the addition of spray gun and hose, permit spray painting for maintenance.

Figure 33-6A. Duplicate gauges mounted directly at the engine are a great convenience for tune-ups and adjustments. Shown are engine oil pressure gauge, transmission oil pressure gauge, ammeter and voltage regulator. The addition of temperature gauges is recommended.

engine is doing is a great help in any maintenance or tune-up procedure. Where the console pressure gauges are of the Bourdon type, the local panel must also use this form of gauge, connected via a tee in the line to the console. Electric-type gauges (see Chapter 15) are easier to connect, although the sensor may have to be changed for one that can accommodate two gauges. Typical installations are shown in Figure 33-6; this panel also mounts the voltage regulator for the generator or alternator.

The heat that an electric refrigerator throws into the galley may be eliminated by removing its compressor-condenser unit and relocating it in the engine room. The connection between the remote compressor and the refrigerator cabinet then becomes two copper tubes and an electric wire. One tube is at low pressure and carries the heat from the food; the other tube is at high pressure and supplies the refrigerant to the cabinet evaporator. The electric wire is from the thermostat and determines "on" and "off." The photo in Figure 33-7 shows an engine-room-located compressor and the insulated duct that contains the tubes and the wire.

Figure 33-6B. The two meters shown, one for frequency and one for voltage, are a recommended addition if an onboard generating plant is installed. The readings illustrated portray a perfect running generator: The frequency is 60 cycles per second and the voltage is 120 volts—ideal.

Figure 33-7. Recommended practice for galley refrigeration is to have only the cabinet itself in the food preparation area and the "works" in the engine room. Greater efficiency and a cooler galley are the result. A combination condenser/compressor remote unit is shown.

The illustration shows a standard air-cooled compressor for the refrigerator. Considerable economy of electric current may be achieved by substituting a water-cooled condenser. The water is picked up by a through-hull fitting, pumped through the condenser by a flea-powered pump, and discharged overboard. The pump is in parallel with the compressor and runs concurrently. With such an arrangement, the fan shown in the photo is eliminated.

The same system of remotely located compressors and condensers is even more valuable for air-conditioning installations because here current draw is greater and the economy more important. The engine room compressor-condenser makes it possible to replace the individual state-room self-contained air-conditioning units with simpler evaporators with fans. Or else a ducted central unit could entirely eliminate noisemaking mechanisms at each cooling point.

Perhaps the most ubiquitous piece of equipment in the engine room is the bilge pump. An approved installation always has this pump controlled automatically by a float switch, although an additional manual override switch may be included. Commercial float switch mechanisms function either mechanically, magnetically or with mercury. The mercury switch element is hermetically sealed and thus may be more reliable under adverse conditions. All of the switches have one drawback: The bilge water must reach a level of several inches before they can operate.

Despite what landlubbers think, it is not always cool "out on the water" and an air-conditioned boat is a great comfort. The installations run the gamut from shoreside window units to especially designed marine systems, but all have one thing in common—they gobble a great deal of power. This is not a great problem at the pier, but if cooled air is desired under way, the electric generating plant must be ample in capacity.

Standard window units are known as "air to air" because they discharge their heat into the surrounding atmosphere. A more efficient system is "water to air" in which circulating water removes the heat. How such a system functions is shown in the diagram of Figure 33-8B.

Figure 33-8A. Heat in the cabin air is absorbed by the refrigerant and discharged into the cooling water to bring cool comfort into the interior of the boat. For heating, the cycle is reversed and heat is extracted from the water and discharged into the cabin. The pump that circulates the seawater is shown here. (Climate Master)

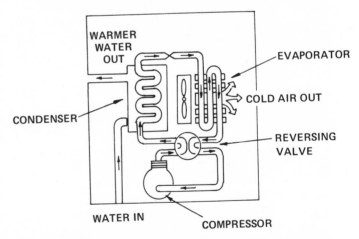

Figure 33-8B. The heart of the modern air conditioning system is the "heat pump" shown here in its cooling position. Refrigerant under low pressure expands in the evaporator and picks up heat from the cabin air. The refrigerant then is pumped through the condenser where it gives up its heat to the circulating raw water. The reversing valve reverses the cycle and the unit becomes a cabin heater. A pump runs in unison with the air conditioner and circulates the seawater that cools the condenser. (Climate Master)

Most air-conditioners of this type are "reverse cycle," meaning that they can heat as well as cool, and are called heat pumps.

The lack of thermal insulation on boats greatly increases the load placed upon heat pumps. Some of the tremendous heat generated by the propulsion engines often finds its way into the living spaces, adding further to the load.

It is often said that the best fume detector is the human nose, but, more often than not, the nose is not put to this task. To overcome this laxity, an automatic fume detector should be installed on every vessel that uses gasoline for fuel. A typical device is shown in Figure 33-9. Some detectors derive their current from the boat battery; others are self-sufficient with their own internal battery. Most units give visual and audible alarms.

An automatic bilge alarm makes for restful sleeping aboard. Every underwater through-hull fitting carries the potential of flooding if something goes wrong, and an automatic bilge alarm, in effect, is a watchdog over all of them, and over a failed bilge pump as well. If bilge water level rises higher than the normal point for bilge pump activation, the alarm alerts the skipper.

Figure 33-9. Gasoline vapors can become as explosively lethal as a bomb, and this device sounds an alarm as soon as they are present and before a dangerous concentration is reached. A fail safe circuit pilot light assures the skipper that the instrument is functioning. The solid state sensor element is replaceable. (Aqua Meter Instruments)

34.
The Practical Side

The many preceding pages have been read, hopefully, with pleasure as well as profit, and now this wealth of theoretical knowledge must be transformed into a practical familiarity with actual engines. This transformation takes place automatically over a period of time as the skipper correlates what he has learned with his control of his powerplant while cruising. Little noises, minute reactions, changes in the exhaust, heretofore ignored, suddenly take on meaning and perhaps warning.

Although the control console may be festooned with meters and gauges, the moving pointers achieve no result until a human mind is present to evaluate what is happening. The evaluation becomes possible when a good theoretical background turns every quiver of a pointer into a meaningful message.

The ideal relationship between skipper and powerplant develops with experience and eventually becomes almost subconscious. Something out of the ordinary happens. The skipper reacts immediately. His mental "computer" draws on the technical information stocked in his memory and triggers a correct response.

Choosing an engine is one of the early decisions that must be made by many newcomers to the realm of boat owning. The scope of this choice is widest for an outboard boat because of the variety of powerplants that could be suitable. The choice narrows down as the size of the boat increases because the power options are fewer. Finally, for the purchaser of a used boat the choice may be nonexistent because it is rare that engines already in place are changed.

The choice of an engine also involves the selection of a propeller since these two units are so interrelated. The load the propeller places on the engine is the determining factor in the powerplant's speed, and this load is the joint result of diameter and pitch. The correct propeller allows the engine to reach its rated rpm but prevents it from going beyond. By juggling propeller pitch and diameter, the correct load may be tailored for any given boat and power.

Very roughly, prop diameter is more closely related to engine horsepower, while pitch bears more relevance to boat speed. Consider that equal thrust (but not equal boat speed) can be generated by a propeller throwing a large volume of water back slowly or a smaller volume faster. The type of hull, whether a light planing type or a heavy displacement design, would determine the combination. As mentioned earlier in the text, propeller selection is an arcane art and often depends on experience.

Just as there exists the heavy-footed motorist, so too we find the heavy-handed skipper. The latter makes use of only two speeds: off and full bore—and he switches from one to the other instantly. He exacts a toll from engine lifespan while keeping his passengers' stomachs where their hearts should be. And engine warm-up is foreign to his thoughts.

Unlike automobiles, boat engines should be idled and warmed up before being asked to do their job because the load, once applied, is steady and heavy with no chance to coast. At the end of a cruise the engine again should be idled long enough for everything to equalize before it is shut down. This simple routine should become a habit, just as is sniffing the bilge for dangerous fumes.

A caution is in order when speaking of idling the engine. Idling beyond that necessary for warm-up should be avoided because it is detrimental. Excess idling of a gasoline engine tends to foul the spark plugs and causes missing and rough running. This condition is most acute with standard ignition but is alleviated somewhat with capacitor discharge ignition's ability to fire dirty spark plugs.

Few boatmen realize the total function of the propeller shaft and consider it merely the means through which the engine turns the prop. Actually, the thrust developed by the propeller is imparted to the hull through the shaft. In the forward mode, the prop pushes the shaft and the shaft in turn pushes the hull through the engine mountings. On reverse, the action is the opposite and the prop pulls the shaft and the boat back. Obviously, a shaft must be stiff enough and must be supported by enough struts to be able to turn this trick.

Transmissions on a boat also work much harder than do their counterparts on an automobile. Most marine transmissions serve as engine speed reducers in addition to their function of affording neutral, forward and reverse. Thus their gearing is constantly under load whereas the car's transmission, at highway speed, is in direct drive, its gears free. Lubrication and even cooling of the marine gearbox consequently becomes doubly important.

The type of hull, whether planing or displacement, determines not only the correct amount of horsepower but also how that power is best used. A displacement hull has a theoretical limit to its speed through the water and horsepower beyond that needed to achieve this is wasted. Contrarily, a planing hull goes faster and faster as power is piled on and the limits are common sense and the pocketbook.

The boat with a displacement hull becomes the more economical of fuel the slower it is run. Not so with the planing type. At slow speed such boats have the tendency to "push the river ahead of them" with great waste of power. They develop decent appetites for fuel only after enough power is applied to get them up on plane so they can skim the water. Hence their economy phase begins at the lowest planing speed.

This brings to mind the plethora of "slow speed, no wake" signs that line the Intracoastal Waterway. A planing hull traveling at slow speed throws a monstrous wake and forcing it to do this achieves a result opposite to the one desired.

The outboarder and the sterndriver have a control feature that is denied the boatman with standard inboard power. This is the ability to control boat trim by altering the angle of thrust of the propeller. Trim control on these boats usually is done from a console switch although it is accomplished manually on the smaller power units. Changing the angle of the propeller's push can raise or lower the bow or compensate for uneven distribution of weight aboard.

Despite all the tender loving care, there comes a time into the lives of most boatmen when professional repair is inevitable. Then it is a trip to the boatyard or marina with a mind wondering whether the bankbook will be able to survive.

"The trouble with owning a boat is the boatyard!" History has lost the name of the harried boatowner who made that historic statement, as true today as it was then. Boatowners and boat service people always have been at loggerheads and rising prices assure that the confrontation will continue. But there are some things owners can do to ease matters.

Going into a boatyard or marina with a vague allusion to the trouble and saying "Just go ahead and fix it" is an invitation to a big bill. Mechanics do not have second sight. While they are searching widely for the problem, the time clock marches on with per-hour rates going into the stratosphere. How much better to hand over an exact, terse, written description of what is wrong.

When the repair requires the clearing of an area for access, it saves money for the owner to do this. Paying someone to pick up belongings, move furniture and roll up carpets at today's hourly rates makes little sense. There is a bonus to doing this: Mechanics like it and work better.

Warranties, where applicable, can offset some of the repair costs. But the wording of warranties is becoming more and more restricted and the so-called limited warranty draws the noose even tighter. In many cases, proof is required that the manufacturer's service instructions have been followed to the letter before a warranty claim is honored.

Common sense goes a long way toward keeping an engine in good running shape. It does not require much knowledge to keep moving parts lubricated. Or to see to it that filters are not clogged and that the water in them is removed periodically. Or to maintain lubricating oil at its designated level. Or to eyeball electrical connections frequently to spot the green covering that heralds a poor contact.

As a skipper becomes truly familiar with his engine, he automatically becomes a gauge watcher. His eyes and mind are guiding the boat, of course, but the outer rim of his vision includes the pointers on the console. Meanwhile, his ears are on the alert for sounds of malfunction.

Power boating revolves around fuel, more so today than ever before because of the frenetic hikes in the prices of gasoline and diesel fuel. For the first time prospective buyers are making serious inquiries about "miles per gallon." The largest outboard motors are lagging in sales because their smaller kin have more fuel appeal. The big numbers on engine horsepower plates are not as enticing as they were until recently. Owning super-powerful boats for the sake of status and unreasonable speed has lost its allure.

All of this boils down to the fact that serious consideration of a boat's fuel appetite is very much in order. Fuel flow meters are a simple means for continuous checking of what goes into the engine, and they now are available at moderate prices for gasoline and for diesel fuel. Since diesel engines reject unused some of the fuel fed to them, the diesel flow meter must take this into account and consequently is a bit more complicated.

A great deal of vital information may be generated by combining the readings of the fuel flow meter and the tachometer. The ensuing figures will show at what rpm the engine does its work most economically and this can become a valuable cruise guide. The torrential rush of fuel indicated by the flow meter at top engine rpm may even psych the skipper into cutting the throttle back.

Fuel consumption may also be checked without instruments by a simple rule of thumb. Fill the tank to the top. Keep track of the miles run until the tank is refilled to the top. The number of miles divided by the number of gallons purchased the second time gives the miles per gallon. Of course, this primitive method requires a constant speed, and errors from wind and current may creep in.

Checking fuel consumption makes sense, from the standpoint of economy as well as the monitoring of engine functioning. Sudden increase over the normal fuel flow for a given engine speed is a danger signal, an early warning. With a gasoline engine it may announce fouled spark plugs or carburetor trouble; with a diesel, an injector may be out of whack. With either engine, increased fuel at a given rpm could also mean frictional or other problems in the drive line.

A common question among boatmen is whether single-engine or twin-engine power is preferable. There is no one correct answer. The only positive points are that a single-engine installation is lower in initial cost and more economical in operation, while twin engines offer more maneuverability and the ability to get home if one engine fails. Beyond that, it's boatman's choice.

Outboarders often choose a variation of the twin-engine idea by installing a large motor for propulsion and a little kicker as get-home insurance. The theory of this is better than the practice. Except under ideal conditions, the very small outboard motor cannot provide reliable propulsion for the boat. If adverse wind, wave and current are encountered while the small engine is working alone, the boat would be dangerously underpowered.

Little drops of water/Allowed to coalesce/Quickly stop the engine/And cause an awful mess. This adaptation of a children's jingle refers to the fuel filters that intercept the drops of condensate water coming from the tank. Condensation in the fuel tank cannot be prevented unless the tank is kept constantly full to the very brim. But filters can be drained regularly and that solves the problem. Another solution, adding a small quantity of straight alcohol, scotches the trouble right at the tank. The alky takes up the water and eventually burns with the fuel.

The traditional method of zeroing in on a missing cylinder in a gasoline engine is to short the spark plugs sequentially. This is done at idle speed, preferably at idle with a light load. Shorting the plug in the offending cylinder makes no difference in the rhythm, but doing this to a working cylinder does change the rhythm. A similar procedure may be used on diesel engines that have individually acting injectors. In this case, the injectors are inactivated sequentially.

Fire is still the one greatest hazard to powerboats afloat—and yet the easiest to prevent. Specific instructions and cautions seem almost superfluous because the words "common sense" should cover all contingencies. The two usual fire sources are the galley and the gasoline engine, with electrical wiring a possible third. Carelessness is the cause because no sane person purposely starts a dangerous fire. Constant vigilance is aided by an adequate number of fire extinguishers and wiring that meets safety codes.

Taking gasoline aboard calls for extreme caution because the heavier-than-air fumes can collect in hull cavities and bilges. Standard precautions are engines stopped, galley fires out and no smoking. (The danger with diesel fuel is minimal.)

How often should lubricating oil be changed? The oil companies say "often," the engine manufacturers extend the periods a bit and many experienced engineers never change oil but simply add to it as required. The oil companies have gotten rich on the American habit of throwing away perfectly good lube oil, whether from cars or boats.

Good lubricating oil does not "wear out." Small amounts of it may leak from bearings and some will get by piston rings and be burned in the combustion chamber, hence the need for occasional additions to maintain the desired level. However, the oil in the engine may need constant cleaning and that is where good filters come in. Filters should be changed as often as needed to purge the oil of contaminants.

One side of the oil change question is that the boatman whose engine is still under warranty does not have much choice. To keep the warranty in effect, he must follow manufacturer's instructions—and these usually mandate frequent oil changes. He becomes free to use his own judgment only after the expiration of the warranty period.

Speaking of oil inevitably brings up the question of additives. High power advertising would have the boatman believe that an engine running without these magic potions in its lubricating oil is doomed. Actually, most of the additives on sale do no good and the best that may be said for them is that they do no harm. Oil companies already place in their oils those chemicals that the latest technology finds useful.

Air is often overlooked as a vital ingredient in ignition. Both gasoline and diesel engines gulp tremendous quantities of it when running at full bore and the engine space must not restrict adequate air entry. This obviously is no problem for the outboard motor but becomes a factor for a boxed inboard engine and may prove acute for a large vessel with an enclosed engine room. A slight restriction will cause the fuel mixture to be enriched; increased hindrance will affect engine performance.

Drive belts on the engine tend to stretch during the first quarter hour of service. New belts therefore should be retightened after this period of running. Incidentally, belts never should be forced onto their sheaves by using screwdrivers as levers.

Finally, into each boatman's life comes tune-up time. The powerplant is beginning to show its age. It no longer leaps to the job when the throttle is advanced, even protests with various knocks and noises. How serious is the situation? Does it need professional help? The knowledge gained from the text should enable a boatman to make a decision and to do at least some of the work himself. It is a great feeling to know that you have become the master of the iron giant that pushes the boat.

Glossary

ADDITIVE a chemical added to fuel or to lubricating oil to accentuate certain desired properties such, for instance, as clean burning or prevention of corrosion

ADVANCE the degree to which a spark or a fuel injection anticipates the piston's rise to top dead center

ALLOY a homogeneous fusion of two or more metallic elements

ALTERNATER a rotating generator of alternating current

ALTERNATING CURRENT a current of electricity that reverses its polarity at a continuous rate

AMMETER a meter graduated in amperes for measuring the current flowing in a circuit

AMPERE the unit for measuring the flow of electric current

AMPERE HOUR the product of a current in amperes and the time in hours during which it flows

ANNEAL the process of reducing the temper of a metal by applying controlled heat to a certain temperature

ANODE the positive pole of an electrical device

ARMATURE the rotating element of an electric motor or generator

ARRESTOR, FLAME a device attached to the air intake of a carburetor to stifle the flame of a backfire

BALANCER a weight or wheel on the end of a crankshaft to neutralize vibration

BATTERY an electric current source composed of a combination of electrolytic cells

BATTERY, PRIMARY an electrolytic cell generating an electric current by the irreversible chemical deterioration of its constituents

BATTERY, STORAGE a secondary battery capable of being recharged after being discharged

BEARING an enclosure in which a shaft rotates

BELT a flexible, endless material with a round, flat or vee cross section connecting two or more sheaves or pulleys

BLOWER a rotary pump, usually of centrifugal design, for delivering quantities of air under pressure

BOOSTER usually referred to a battery temporarily connected in parallel to another battery in order to increase current delivery

BRAKE, PRONY a simple device for measuring the horsepower capability of an engine or a motor

BTU British thermal unit, a unit of energy

BUS the large conductor, usually a copper bar, in an electric supply panel to which outputs are connected

CAPACITANCE the ability of a capacitor or condenser to hold an electric charge

CAPACITOR another name for electric condenser

CARBURETOR the device on a gasoline engine that mixes air and fuel in proper proportion for combustion

CASE HARDEN a process for hardening only the outer skin of a steel piece

CATHODE the negative pole of an electric device

CAVITATION a condition in which a propeller loses complete contact with the surrounding water because of intervening vapor

CELL a single unit consisting of anode, cathode and electrolyte

CENTRIFUGAL the force tending to send into space any mass that is spun about an axis

CENTRIPETAL a force opposite to centrifugal

CETANE NUMBER a parameter that expresses the combustion ability of a diesel fuel

CHOKE a valve on a carburetor that enriches the fuel mixture to aid in starting a gasoline engine

CIRCUIT BREAKER a safety device that opens the circuit to prevent an excessive current drain

CLEARANCE the adjusted space between the valve end and the rod or rocker that is opening it

CLUTCH a mechanical device on a machine to take on or release a load

CONDENSER, ELECTRIC a device capable of holding and storing an electric charge consisting of two conductors separated by a dielectric.

CONDENSER, THERMODYNAMIC a device, usually consisting of tubing, for exchanging heat from one fluid to another

CORE a part within a mold that enables the making of hollow castings

CORROSION the chemical or electrochemical deterioration of a metal

DECIBEL a unit for measuring and rating sound intensity

DEW POINT the temperature at which vapor will condense from the air

DIELECTRIC any material that is an electric insulator

DIESEL an internal combustion process that ignites fuel by the heat of compression instead of by a spark

DIRECT CURRENT an electric current that maintains a set polarity

DISPLACEMENT the total cubic content of the volume traversed by the pistons of an engine in one revolution

DRY BATTERY a combination of primary cells whose electrolyte is an almost dry paste

DYNAMOMETER a machine for measuring the horsepower output of engines

ECONOMIZER a device within a carburetor for reducing fuel consumption under certain load conditions

ELECTROLYSIS a condition in which two different metals, electrically connected, deteriorate because of the flow of electric current

EXCITER a small direct-current generator on a larger alternator that supplies field (exciting) current for the larger machine

FARAD a unit for measuring capacitance

FATIQUE the failure of a metal after repeated stresses

FEELER GAUGE a measuring device consisting of shims of various thicknesses

FLASH POINT the temperature at which the vapor of a substance will burst into flame if ignited

FREQUENCY the rate at which an alternating current changes polarity

FRICTION a natural force that impedes motion

FUSE a link in an electric circuit that melts to prevent excessive current flow

GALVANIZE a zinc coating on steel to prevent corrosion

GASKET a soft material between two mating surfaces to prevent leaking

GOVERNOR a device on an engine that automatically holds the machine to a set speed or that prevents overspeeding

GROUND a common point to which one wire from each circuit is connected, usually negative

HEAT EXCHANGER a device for transferring heat from one fluid to another

HYDROMETER a device for measuring the specific gravity of electrolyte

IMPEDANCE a force in an alternating-current circuit that resists the flow of current

INDUCTANCE a condition acquired in an electric circuit by reason of the magnetic field about a current-carrying wire

INERTIA a natural force that tends to keep a moving body moving and a stationary body stationary

INJECTOR the device that supplies fuel to the combustion chamber of a diesel engine

INSULATOR any material that prevents the flow of electric current or heat

INVERTER a device for changing direct current to alternating current, the opposite of converter

JACKET the hollow spaces for cooling water that surround the combustion chamber of a cylinder

JET, CARBURETOR an orifice of closely controlled size in the carburetor that limits fuel flow

JET DRIVE a propulsion method for a boat utilizing the reaction from a high-velocity jet of water thrown aft

JOURNAL the bearing that encloses a shaft

KEYWAY a slot in a shaft or hub into which a key fits tightly for the purpose of solid connection to another member

KNOT a speed of one nautical mile in one hour

LAPPING a slow wearing down with an abrasive slurry for the purpose of creating a close fit

MAGNETO a form of self-contained generator usually found on outboard motors to supply the voltage for ignition

NICHROME the trade name for a metal, usually in the form of a wire, that has a high electrical resistance

OCTANE NUMBER a measure of the combustion characteristic of gasoline

PIN, WRIST the connection between the piston and the upper end of the connecting rod

PITCH the theoretical distance that a propeller should move forward in one revolution, expressed in inches

POTENTIAL same as voltate

PROPELLER a fanlike device that transforms rotative power into thrust

PYROMETER an instrument for measuring high temperatures

RECTIFIER an electrical device for changing alternating current to direct current

RELAY a magnetic device that permits one electrical circuit to control another circuit

RHEOSTAT a variable resistance to the passage of electric current

SHEAVE a pulley

SOLENOID a magnetic switch or actuator

STATIC ELECTRICITY voltage generated by friction

STUFFING BOX a tight enclosure of the shaft to prevent leakage where it passes through the hull at the stern

SUPERCHARGING forcing air or a mixture of air and fuel into a combustion chamber of an engine under pressure

SYNCHRONIZE to cause two engines to run in absolute unison

TACHOMETER a device for measuring speed of revolution

THERMOSTAT in an engine cooling system, a device that controls temperature by regulating coolant flow

TIMING adjusting the exact instant at which ignition or fuel injection occurs in an engine

TRANSFORMER an electromagnetic device for transferring electrical energy from one circuit to another

TORQUE a twisting force

TURBINE a mechanical device that generates power by simple rotation

TURBOCHARGING forcing air or a mixture of air and fuel into the combustion chamber of an engine by means of the energy in the exhaust

VAPOR LOCK stoppage of fuel flow caused by vaporization of the fuel

VENTURI a necked section in a tube that lowers pressure by increasing the velocity; the heart of a carburetor

VISCOSITY the ability of a liquid to flow

VOLT the unit of electrical tension

WATT the product of volts multiplied by amperes

WELD the homogeneous joining of two metals by applying sufficient heat to cause melting and fusion

Index

A

B

C